SINCLAIR LEWIS

Edward Agran has once again written a book showcasing what he does so well: revealing how much we gain from substantially rethinking a major figure in our cultural and political history. Sinclair Lewis becomes, in Agran's skillful scholarly hands, a way to rethink so much about the United States, including such momentous issues of our day as the fate of the middle class—and even the fate of our republic under the shadow of fascism.

—Robert D. Johnston, professor of History and director of the Teaching of History Program, University of Illinois Chicago; and author of *The Radical Middle Class*

In this winsomely written book Edward Agran repeatedly and brilliantly rescues Sinclair Lewis from the clutches of scholars who have (sadly) missed Lewis's import as a "photographer" and interpreter of 1920s America. This book matters, and it is a great pleasure to read.

—William Vance Trollinger, Jr., professor of History, University of Dayton; and author of *God's Empire: William Bell Riley and the Making of American Fundamentalism*

Edward Agran makes an enthusiastic case for reading Sinclair Lewis's major novels of the 1920s as a way of understanding that exciting and important decade in American history. By providing in-depth analyses of *Main Street, Babbitt, Arrowsmith, Elmer Gantry,* and *Dodsworth*, he shows how Lewis's writing captures the changing nature of the United States. The five novels critique and encapsulate our national identity, providing readers with a window into such aspects as rural versus urban living, business, medicine, and religion. Although Lewis offers no definitive prescription on how to improve the society he's critiquing, *Dodsworth*, his "capstone achievement" of the decade, provides some suggestions. Agran's presentation of the five novels shows the interconnectedness on Lewis's thoughts about his country, with *Dodsworth* becoming both a summing up and a summons to progress. Lewis's work is still so very relevant.

—Sally E. Parry, professor emerita, Illinois State University; executive director, Sinclair Lewis Society; and author, with Robert L. McLaughlin, of *Broadway Goes to War: American Theater during World War II*

Edward Agran views Sinclair Lewis through the generous eye of a historian. He pushes readers to acknowledge the novelist's contributions to literary studies and history. He defends Lewis against dismissive literary critics; he finds not only artistic but historical merit in his substantive 1920s works. Agran rightly sees Lewis's depiction of the hapless, but not hopeless, middle class as a touchstone in understanding the nation. The novelist could help us in our current predicament, as we stare collectively at our phones and fight meaninglessly with one another on social media as oligarchic despotism takes over. Agran argues Lewis's take on the 1920s adds to our understanding of the twentieth century. He believes Lewis's biting critique of the middle class reveals our collective problems and promise. Agran and Lewis want more for the United States than most of its citizens settle for: Snap out of our collective fog and build the democratic society of our political dreams.

—Ursula McTaggart, professor of English and area coordinator of Prison Education, Wilmington College; and author of *Guerrillas in the Industrial Jungle: Radicalism's Primitive and Industrial Rhetoric*

SINCLAIR LEWIS

The 1920s and the Shaping of American Identity

EDWARD GALE AGRAN

MERCER UNIVERSITY PRESS
Macon, Georgia

MUP/ P730

Published by Mercer University Press
1501 Mercer University Drive
Macon, Georgia 31207

29 28 27 26 25 5 4 3 2 1

Books published by Mercer University Press are printed on acid-free paper that meets the requirements of the American National Standard for Information Sciences—Permanence of Paper for Printed Library Materials.

Printed and bound in the United States.

This book is set in Adobe Caslon; title in Century Gothic.

Cover/jacket design by Burt&Burt.

ISBN 978-0-88146-996-7 (Print)
978-0-88146-997-4 (eBook)

Cataloging-in-Publication Data is available from the Library of Congress

Contents

To Charlotte, Hannah, and Thomas

Acknowledgments

I am a cultural historian, specializing in United States History, principally focused on the first four decades of the twentieth century. By luck, pluck too, across decades I have benefitted from my upbringing, family, friends, my education at UCLA, the University of Colorado at Boulder, and the University of Wisconsin at Madison. Colleagues in graduate school and in the institutions I worked at were by my side and often fast friends. All inspired me to take interest, to ask questions, to plumb deeper: to rethink with an open mind my teaching and my scholarship. Students I worked with as a teaching assistant and then in my own courses at Centre College and Wilmington College energized me. I was fortunate at both small, liberal arts institutions to teach to my strengths, often through seminars. And both institutions supported my research and writing. All these influences together made for a good education, sharpened my perspectives; and enhanced my take on who we are as a people, what makes us tick, where does individualism take us, and where does community in its variegated forms come to play in the national story. I have been privileged...and have learned, and continue to do so: how have those opportunities enhanced my viewpoints, skewed them as well; what new questions arise?

I am pleased to acknowledge those who most influenced me to be a teacher, a scholar, and to be in some fashion like them. Early on Howard Burge in the fourth grade and Isabel Rivera through five high school Spanish semesters modelled their gifts as educators. At UCLA teaching assistant Daniel Francois and freshly minted Assistant Professor John Timmons sparked confidence in my ability to succeed. Thomas Kincaid opened me up to teaching history from a cultural perspective—*a novel as a reading assignment in Civil War and Reconstruction*? I was flabbergasted and immediately won over. At Boulder Robert Pois, a German History specialist, sealed the deal with rich readings and seminar discussions; a deeply gifted teacher and dedicated scholar, Pois has stood throughout the years as a model to try to emulate. John Graham in Labor and Literature highlighted the power of cross-disciplinary study. Robert Athearn placed his trust in me to conduct research for his latest study of Colorado history. Ralph Mann was an enthusiastic teacher with whom I worked as a teaching assistant. Same, too, Stanley Schultz at Madison; and he asked me to help in research cultural history—the field was increasingly attractive to take on. As a teaching assistant for Barbara Melosh, my interests in culture, pedagogy, and research were further stimulated; and she became a fast friend.

Conference papers sharpen one's perspective; fellow panelists and audience participants encourage and push one ahead. Editors and anonymous readers invest time critiquing scholarship. Colleagues, old and new, critique manuscripts. My interest in cultural history was exponentially furthered by John Sharpless, a Wisconsin quantitative historian who suggested my dissertation topic and set me on the road to specializing in middle-class history. Walter Rideout at Madison encouraged me to further pursue literature. Stanley Kutler, Daniel Rogers, and Paul Boyer taught me a lot about pedagogy, scholarship, and integrity. All along Larry Friedman has been a pillar of support. Robert D. Johnston at the University of Illinois, Chicago, gave me an exceptionally rewarding chunk of his time refining my scholarship. Thomas Wells at the University of Tennessee Press was persistent in his support and generous in his advice; ultimately it was he who recommended I turn to Mercer University Press. Thank you to Marc Jolley, Marsha Luttrell, Mary Beth Kosowski, Jenny Toole, and Kelley Land for their spirited support as well as the entire staff in Macon, Georgia. And thank you to the copyeditor for valuable help.

There were, of course, fellow graduate students who made a difference in my schooling and my life. In particular, thanks to Elizabeth Jameson, Robert Tank, and Daniel Bradford at Colorado; Lisa Fine, Mary Neth, Donald Rodgers, David Blight, Elizabeth Keeney, Charlotte Borst, Robert Burk, JoAnne Brown, and Richard Pifer at Wisconsin. William Trollinger has been a tight friend, stimulating colleague, and close reader of my scholarship since we met in Madison. Colleagues and friends at Centre and Wilmington long have been supportive. Special thanks to Charles Vahlkamp, Ursula McTaggart, and Paul Moke. And thank you to University of Iowa Press's Holly Carver for advice and enthusiasm. Finally, I thank those students in all those courses, especially those enrolled at Wilmington in Special Topics: Sinclair Lewis and the 1920s, for your engagement; the give-and-take around the table was fun, the insights provocative. Significantly, thanks to some ninety students who enrolled in the University of Iowa Senior College course "Sinclair Lewis and the 1920s"; fully engaged and engaging, they provided insightful perspectives from their own histories to the novels Lewis wrote. And they fortified me in my belief that strong interest remains in the novelist.

I am grateful to the librarians working away plumbing the resources, giving direction and input for their patrons in their immediate and broader communities. For assistance in this project I owe a lot to Joni Streiber, Patti Kinsinger, and Lee Bowman at Wilmington College; Elizabeth Agramonte for swiftly procuring photographs at the Port Washington Public Library in New York; and Tom Stamen for similarly quick attention for my requests for photographs from the Lewis Collection at Saint Cloud State University in Minnesota. The librarians at the University of Iowa and the Iowa City Public Library always were eager to assist me in my work.

Finally, I appreciate all Lewis specialist Sally Parry has built into the Sinclair Lewis Society based at Illinois State University. Sally's commitment to the novelist, to scholarship, and to the greater public is exemplary. And thanks, too, to Sally for reading my manuscript.

If I have left any individual or institution out, it is not intentional. I am fully responsible for any shortcomings in *Sinclair Lewis: The 1920s and the Shaping of American Identity.*

INTRODUCTION

Sinclair Lewis was one of the most acclaimed American writers of the 1920s. Critiqued by the literati, celebrated (and demonized) by the general public, he was one of the more controversial figures in a celebrity-laden decade. The novelist recognized in the United States' transition from a nineteenth-century "pioneer" society to a twentieth-century "urban-industrial colossus" that an intense change in the manner of living, manners themselves, and identity was gripping the nation. This was no great revelation, but his ability as an artist to address a multitude of emergent concerns mesmerized the country at large. Plenty had no clue who was this Red Lewis; some mixed him up with Socialist Upton Sinclair; the majority of the citizenry naturally did not read him, but a significant number picked up his novels. In one hugely selling title after another (many produced as plays and films), Lewis queried and critiqued the temper of his times. His sights swept across roiling demographics, scoped in on skyrocketing consumerism, rising standardization, the emergence of the middle class as the American Standard of how life is to be lived, what characterized that life. Religion, politics, business, reform, mores, values, ethics—the identities of individuals and the country were up for grabs, and Sinclair Lewis was an artist of acute sensitivities in the third decade of the twentieth century. He endeavored to have his say.

The twenties roared, it was the New Era, and Lewis, insecure in his own identity, unsure of the America he envisioned fulfilling its "destiny," was attempting to find mooring and a course of action for the United States and himself. Sensitive to the pulse of the nation, he embodied with it a host of contradictions. Historians for scores of years have assigned Lewis in their courses, especially drawing upon the author's five primary twenties works: *Main Street*, *Babbitt*, *Arrowsmith*, *Elmer Gantry*, and *Dodsworth*. The novels work in the classroom just as they have resonated with millions, running now over a hundred years. For historians who specialize in twentieth-century culture, Lewis makes sense—in the same sense he was celebrated as a keen observer in his own time. This is why he is rich to teach; the novelist catches the historian's fancy and grabs the student's attention. He is an artist, funny, and deeply persuasive that we have to take a good look at ourselves as individuals, communities, a nation, a people. He exhibits a unique brand of common sense. While he was vociferously attacked (but read, just the same), he continues to add up, because in the 1920s America took on its essential twentieth-century identity: A land of promise, goods, security, and insecurity; a country and people increasingly commodified, seemingly more stable, and discouragingly more distant from rock-solid virtues of hard work, belief in God, commitment to family, and to community—those values we like to think the pioneers of a more halcyon period represented. Americans in the twenties appeared to be in search of an identity in which they could place their faith; a people somehow satisfied but dissatisfied just as Sinclair Lewis himself. Just as Americans well into the twenty-first century struggle to discern "who are we as a people," Lewis found the quandary stimulating and discomforting.

My aim is not to argue with literary scholars who discount the author's standing; rather, I encourage them and all students of American culture to recognize that Lewis's reception in the twenties was formidable because of his sensitivity to the nation's history, its promise, and at points troubling trajectory. I argue broaden the perspective, credit Lewis today for what in his day was considered a striking, lasting take on the American Experiment. Lewis's major biographers take account of the place of history in his work, but nowhere do they engage the breadth and depth of this aspect of his work. *Sinclair Lewis: The 1920s and the Shaping of American Identity* demonstrates why the novelist still resonates strongly a century on and why his books still sell—he speaks to identity in the United States with a style all his own. Historians have long taken Lewis to be a formidable primary resource. Students respond with considerable interest, seek additional readings, and appreciate the strength of interdisciplinary studies. I aim to make available to those interested in Lewis's work and place in American culture a deeper, accessible examination of the intersection of history and literature.

What a complex fellow, Harry Sinclair Lewis; his dissatisfaction with society and himself ran deep. At base he searched for resolution. Literary scholar Norman Grebstein in 1962 prefaced *Sinclair Lewis*:

> He was the conscience of his generation and he could well serve as the conscience of our own. His analysis of the America of the 1920s holds true for the America of today. His prophecies have become our truths and his fears our most crucial problems. [H]eadlines remind us bitterly of Lewis's repeated warning that if we have created only a high material culture without an equally high sense of beauty and decency and tolerance for individual differences, we have failed utterly.[1]

Grebstein read the novelist well; half-a-century on his take that the scholar still stands prophetic rings true. Along with contemporaries as Ernest Hemingway, Willa Cather, F. Scott Fitzgerald, and William Faulkner, Lewis would run the gauntlet, dipping out of fashion with the critics and academics. All ultimately would generate renewed recognition—not Lewis. Still, as a few critics in the twenties predicted, Lewis's work—the literary world might dismiss it—always would maintain the interest of historians.[2]

Among the critics, the last significant weigh-in on Lewis occurred in 1992 and 1993 as a celebratory re-issue of a combined volume of

---

[1]Sheldon Norman Grebstein, *Sinclair Lewis* (New Haven: Twayne Publishers, 1962), "Preface." Grebstein's fine, succinct literary critique was overshadowed by Mark Schorer's *Sinclair Lewis: An American Life* (New York: McGraw-Hill Book Company), 1961. Literary scholar Schorer has been credited (and damned) for launching the age of the mammoth biography; his work reigns as the Lewis standard. Richard Lingeman, *Sinclair Lewis: Rebel from Main Street* (New York: Random House, 2002), lengthy as Schorer is just as rich in biography and critique; the journalist and cultural historian offers significant counterpoints to Schorer's perspectives.

[2] Historian and journalist William L. Shirer observed, "Lewis lacked style, yet his impact on modern American life…was greater than Fitzgerald, Hemingway, Faulkner, and John Dos Passos combined. Quoted in Larry Parnass, "Why Writer Sinclair Lewis Keeps Paying Dividends from Pittsfield and Will Forever," *Sinclair Lewis Society Newsletter* 27 (Spring 2019), 11, 18–19, quoted 19.

Main Street and *Babbitt* hit the market. The author always presented an indecipherable conundrum and alluring target. In the *New York Review of Books* social commentator Gore Vidal pronounced Lewis dead as ever while in the *New Yorker* John Updike assayed, "[W]e are left to conclude that Lewis is a dwarf classic."[3] Some backdrop: Amongst the literary set starting in the thirties Lewis rarely is mentioned beyond snide dismissal. Again, for historians his relevance was never in doubt, nor was he confounding—quite the contrary, and the reasoning is explicit. Critic and cultural historian Louis Menand in 2014 eulogized Updike in the *New Yorker*; ironically, given Updike's dismissal of Lewis, Menand in offering tribute to the novelist and critic indirectly makes the case for Lewis sharing his greatest attribute:

> Updike wanted to do with the world of mid-century middle-class American Wasps what Proust had done with Belle Époque Paris and Joyce had done with a single day in 1904 Dublin—and, for that matter, Jane Austen had done with the landed gentry in the Home Counties at the time of the Napoleonic Wars and James had done with idle Americans living abroad at the turn of the nineteenth [twentieth] century. He wanted to biopsy a minute sample of the social tissue and reproduce the results in the form of a permanent verbal artifact.[4]

Indirect and to the point, Menand puts Lewis in appropriate company.

This passage in "Imitation of Life: John Updike's cultural project"

---

[3] Gore Vidal, "The Romance of Sinclair Lewis," New York Review of Books, October 8, 1992, http://www.nybooks.com. Vidal was vicious in references to Lewis's flawed personal attributes. John Updike, "Exile on Main Street," *New Yorker*, May 17, 1993, http://archives.newyorker.com. Updike believes Lewis's work, never stellar, makes a difficult read; significantly he and Vidal recognize his importance in the 1920s. A decade later, reviewing Lingeman, Updike briefly credits the value of Lewis for the classroom while the brunt of his criticism focuses on his surfeit of human failings. See "No Brakes: A New Biography of Sinclair Lewis," *New Yorker*, February 4, 2002, http://archives.newyorker.com.

[4] Louis Menand, "Imitation of Life: John Updike's cultural project," *New Yorker*, April 28, 2014, 76.

could just as well have been profiling Lewis back in the 1920s; it regularly was said he captured the essence of America's emergent middle-class society, that at his best he was literally a sociologist, an anthropologist, and a historian. Oddly, Updike contrary to his discounting of Lewis in *The New Yorker*, in an interview acknowledged his large debt to the novelist for his classic *Rabbit* series. Lewis flummoxed the critics. The novelist knew the American middle class; at base, Menand by inference and Updike with authority grasped how important that knowledge proved to be.[5]

Menand makes a strong case for the intellectual riches of interdisciplinary studies. And herein lies the erstwhile confusion of the literary set who place Lewis aside. Menand taps into the power of cultural history which has come into its own in the past fifty years. One of its most innovative seers, Lawrence W. Levine, warns it is mistaken

> to divide the world up too easily into reality and representations of reality. The latter—the representations—when they become embodied in theater, tales, radio, movies, become forms of reality themselves. I don't mean by this that audiences necessarily "confuse" them with reality. Indeed, I think the opposite is more often true. Rather, the entire setting constitutes an important form of reality in which many essential things are realized: lessons are learned, values enunciated and repeated, modes of behavior scrutinized, social institutions and their effects explored, fantasies indulged.[6]

Lewis's writing, ideas, even language became part of the passing scene, the currency of his day. Vidal, while arguing no one anymore speaks of Lewis, concedes "more of his inventions [coinages] have gone into the language than those of any other writer except Dickens." Even as an aside, that is a pronounced literary and historical tribute.[7]

---

[5] Interview referenced in James M. Hutchisson, *The Rise of Sinclair Lewis, 1920–1930* (University Park: Pennsylvania State University Press, 1996), 201 n. 17.

[6] Lawrence W. Levine, *The Unpredictable Past: Explorations in American Cultural History* (New York: Oxford University Press, 1993), 312–13.

[7] Vidal, "The Romance of Sinclair Lewis."

Proust, Joyce, Austen, James—so, too Crane, Norris, Dreiser, Wharton, Howells, et. al.— chroniclers of class in fiction long made real sense to readers. And if that "imitation of life" made sense then, historians wisely give weight to what commanded the attention of a wide as well as an influential readership privy to the cultural rhythms of its day. Menand argues, "Literature pulls the real up out of the realm of temporality and insignificance and remakes it into a form that will never decay and never die.... It is at the heart of modernism. 'It is art that *makes* life, makes interest, makes importance,' Henry James wrote to H. G. Wells." For Menand, "That's what Updike believed." So, too, Lewis; so, too, cultural historians.[8]

Lewis and his contemporaries became entangled in modernist debates, all part of a contest best left to literary scholars. Suffice it to say he had his defenders in his day and since; and he spoke up for himself. His sights, however, were focused on what he determined throughout his career a more worthy target than intellectual dustups. As Updike and other social observers, Lewis engaged middle-class readers because their lives mattered greatly to him. Just as Menand contends Updike wrote "deliberate responses to writers who he thought had given up" on the middle class, who "saw the world heading toward a brutal future," Lewis worked at salvation.[9] Among the twenties and thirties literati bending toward modernism (not all but most), Lewis was berated as irrelevant, a dated romanticist cum realist blind to the rhythms of modernity. That argument against him has long carried weight. He, on the other hand, precisely saw in what elites deigned the *nouveau* hoi polloi a robust, expanding middling class, troubled yes, troubling too. He respected it; he was compelled to address these denizens of the Republic. The emergent middle-class cultural norm, as Menand reminds readers, needed to be "chewed" over by the likes of Updike; as Updike, Lewis was "unusually" smart and gifted. He placed his faith in a middle-class Republic. Millions took him seriously. Menand praises Updike; in writing realistic fiction, "You can dismiss this conception of the literary vocation as pious or old-fashioned," but the public long had a

---

[8] Menand, 76.

[9] Ibid.

different read than elite critics. And as Updike acknowledges, they gobbled up Lewis. They, too, looked to a more promising future.[10]

The debates over Lewis's relevancy rarely if ever crop up in history or other interdisciplinary studies—the quality of his literature is never at issue. He is prized by those who share his sense of priorities. To his great credit, running against the tide of criticism, Lewis scholar Grebstein similarly caught the drift. He takes the author's measure against what he deems less-weighty disciplinary disputes: "He was at his best in denunciation, and at his best he created an image of twentieth-century American society which continues to haunt us in its essential truth."[11] It is not that everyone across the century agreed with Lewis's indictment—far from it; but the country has long relished the debate, fisticuffs flying. Grebstein recognizes those who teach literature have a lot to learn from Lewis—and history. He urges a half-century ago a fresh look remains in order. Literary specialists all along have acknowledged Sinclair Lewis reflected then current concerns but have

[10] Ibid. See David E. Shi, *Facing Facts: Realism in American Thought and Culture, 1850–1920* (New York: Oxford University Press, 1995). For a tight synopsis of the movement's trajectory and its continuing influence on twentieth and twenty-first century literature, see cultural historian Shi's Epilogue, 303–07; he succinctly treats modernism's relationship to the movement (and anti-modernism). "The extraordinary resilience of realism as a mode of cultural expressionism attests to its inherent appeal. In reflecting upon the redemptive ardor of the realist enterprise, novelist John Updike recently declared, 'Howells's agenda remains our agenda: for the American writer to live in America and to mirror it in writing, with 'everything brought out.'" See 307. For more on modernism, see Shi's take "An Epoch of Confusion," 273–302. He often addresses Lewis. See too, Peter Conn, *The American 1930s: A Literary History* (Cambridge: Cambridge University Press, 2009) and Ichiro Takayoshi, ed., *American Literature in Transition, 1920–1930* (Cambridge: Cambridge University Press, 2017) as well classic Frederick J. Hoffman, *The Twenties: American Writing in the Postwar Decade* (New York: Viking Press, 1955). Shi recognizes, "Since the end of World War II, realism and its accompanying ideology of liberal humanism have become objects of ferocious contempt." Earlier, too.

[11] Grebstein, Preface.

habitually discounted how powerful his observations were not only to Americans of the time but to later generations.

Grebstein gets the rub. Lewis was a satirist and a realist: "It implies his strengths and his weaknesses.... He wrote the novel as *history*; we prefer the novel as poetry...." Listen up, he admonishes: the novelist "helped to make Americans known to themselves and to the world." He was in "the line of Cooper, Emerson, Thoreau, Whitman, and Twain. Like them, he railed against the insidious effects of mass culture and the standardization of manners and ideas. Like his more immediate forebears, Bellamy and Henry George, he dreamed of a better America...." No revolutionary—in fact with his paeans to the pioneers perchance at points he might be charged a reactionary—Lewis at base was a reformer. He was a twentieth-century Dickens: "Lewis will last as long in America and in the English language as has Dickens, although he will probably never command the respect paid to Dickens."[12]

Possibly there is room for only one Dickens. The problem for Lewis, argues Grebstein, why he remains out of favor with literary critics and scholars, is his "angle of vision." How errant they are; this is his strength: "Indeed, at his best he fulfilled a basic American need for a bold and passionate writer who would assist us toward self-recognition." A satirist, a realist, and yes a romanticist, he hit the mark just as Dickens whom he greatly admired. Maybe for the literati the middle class as subject cannot support such a tribune; maybe those elites cannot grant historical relevance to the hoi polloi. Those dwindling number of literary scholars who read, study, teach, and critique Lewis agree with Grebstein: "He was too rarely a *novelist*, in the fullest sense. The novelist seeks to exhibit men and women and to search for a common emotion or basis of understanding. The satirist, on the other hand, pursues and scourges a common failing in men and women. His characters are most effective when they are 'types of their failures.'" Lewis at times succeeded in combining satire and realism into strong novelistic form, but classic style was not his forte: "In Lewis's books the reader gets a far stronger impression of the milieu in which things happen than he

---

[12] Ibid., 164, 19, and 36. Edward Bellamy and George were widely read turn-of-the-century social critics considered radical visionaries.

does, with a few exceptions, of the people to whom they happen." It makes sense; it is the milieu that challenges them, the angle of vision by which they measure their lives.[13]

What is the difficulty, why the continuous confusion amongst the literati? One of Lewis's fiercest judges, literary scholar Bernard DeVoto (and historian, but one who misread the breadth of the author's relevance), in 1944 charged Lewis was far too harsh in his critique of the U.S.A, and yet he still considered him the best novelist of "his decade."[14] He who was so vital in the twenties, so incisive, a satirist, perhaps for DeVoto could not be borne in war-torn America. Possibly

---

[13] Grebstein, 162–63.

[14] Ibid., 166; Section V, 161–66, "The Significance of Sinclair Lewis." Grebstein understands twenties history and its transitional importance. As he released his work, he granted the forthcoming Schorer opus would offer a more erudite treatment of Lewis's life; he was focused on his career. Complementary angles are essential. Schorer includes criticism and knows his history, but his biases against Lewis weaken his analysis. Grebstein offers more balanced if not always persuasive criticisms, and while not touting historical chops, he is sensitive to the study. Naturally within a narrower focus, he falls short of Schorer's excellent ability and later Lingeman's to interweave Lewis's expansive life with his works. Lingeman is strong in establishing the historical context, although it could use expansion. Schorer is disturbingly harsh toward Lewis while Lingeman too forgiving, too willing to accept a sugar-coating of his life and shortcomings and too ready to engage psycho-history. He respects Lewis in a way Schorer cannot; compare each one's treatment of Lewis's boyhood. Lingeman, too, is more respectful critiquing Lewis's writing; Schorer can be vile—but his treatment of Lewis and his work remains seminal; so much so, that to this day, as Vidal concedes, Schorer "killed him off." See Vidal, "Romance." Historian, biographer, and novelist Irving Howe scolded: "[A] reader looking back upon the shambles of Sinclair Lewis's years and reflecting that such tragic waste is far from unique to him, may feel for this brilliant and stricken man a more open sympathy…." "The World He Mimicked Was His Own," *New York Times Book Review* (October 1, 1961), 196 quoted in Gary Scharnhorst and Matthew Hofer, eds., *Sinclair Lewis Remembered* (Tuscaloosa: University of Alabama Press, 2012), 9. I have depended heavily on Grebstein, Schorer, Lingeman, and Hutchisson as strongly complementary Lewis scholars.

those in the twenties grasped what was at stake in a land of changing identity in a fashion those having survived the depression-wracked thirties and defended an "American Way of Life" on battlefields in the forties were at a loss to measure—or too traumatized to consider such an analysis. Maybe the modernist swell overwhelmed the critic. It may well be from that angle of vision an entrenched middle-class society, always in identity crisis, simply will not be taken seriously. Still, in DeVoto's critical eye, Lewis, dated at mid-century, had nailed *his decade*. This says everything. DeVoto the 1940s literary critic could no longer consider the twenties celebrity worthy of serious consideration; meanwhile historian DeVoto hastened to give him his due as a chronicler of the 1920s. There is a lesson to be learned here—a reconsideration of the relevance of literature in the light of history.

Lewis's decade ultimately proved pivotal as the country evolved further into the twentieth century; hence the argument for his lasting relevance. He was not a great novelist by the measure of many. But what does great signify? This is a perennial debate for those who study literature; history, too. For historians, from whom credibly Lewis valued approval more than his literary fellows, art is not the issue. For decades the twenties *is* an issue, a crucial era in the transition of twentieth-century society and culture. Lewis, reviewing another writer in 1940, took measure: "The superior survival value of novelists to historians may not be altogether in the eloquence with which fictioneers communicate Mildred's agonies over the virile high diving of Peter, or the glories of Kansas City by moonlight." The author relishes mocking antiquated fictioneers and their pretenses. But he makes his point: "It may be that the permanence of such institutions as Dickens is due to their recording not the dreary magnificences of coronations and battles, but instead the dear diminutive excitements in commonplace characters which make us identify ourselves with them...."[15] Lewis keenly fuses literature and history. Grebstein, a literary man, as others regret the author could not be more, a Tolstoy or a Flaubert roundly developing individual character (a great issue for literary critics) instead of establishing the generic substitute. But he argues Lewis was very much his

[15] Grebstein, 163.

own man. The novelist in his fashion sacrificed what might have been his more refined literary skills not only to record history, but because he was driven by his own gnawing character deficiencies. In the end, beyond his tongue-in-cheek aside about dated literary genres, Lewis considered both history and literature of equal value to society, a means for individuals to come to terms with themselves, not to mention the culture as a whole.

Lewis was a troubled soul. He worried he sold himself professionally short for trying to make money (pots of lucre he sneered), but he clearly liked the stuff; he suffered through childhood, an easy target for mockery; an adult he unceasingly conflicted with those close (and not so) to him; he pronounced patently hypocritical contradictions; he had a fiery impatience and a basketful of insecurities; and with grace and a degree of obnoxiousness—both characteristics not so ironically attributed to his country and its American Experiment—he carried on. Lewis was writing not just to establish a national identity; he wanted to find within that profile himself. He was at fisticuffs with the world; the unhappy fellow he was could find no peace. In the final analysis, Grebstein to his credit, not investigating at length his personal life grasps the professional: Lewis was an accessible writer, a fictionist of great insight because he understood from whence he came.

At his peak in the twenties, the novelist fulfilled Progressive-Era ideologue Herbert Croly's 1909 call for citizens to take a good, close look at their middling shortcomings within an emerging materialistic culture and reach for "The Promise of American Life." Lewis gravitated toward progressivism, not its baseline politics but its lofty aims. He carried that banner within war and past wartime disillusionment as few in the reform community could muster the energy. Their misplaced faith in U.S. entry into World War One, "a war to end all wars," the Great War as it was coined, had proved a bust. They conceived a revitalized United States, taking the grand progressive reform movement overseas, would achieve the establishment of that "city upon a hill" for all the world to emulate. The purported *entirely selfless* movement, amongst postwar despair, fast gave way to crass materialism. Progressivism, in its broadest sense, runs proudly through the history of the United States. It waxes and wanes. Provocation, the reformist's north star, is key to the American Experiment; the Founding Fathers with declarations and documents and war made the case—the tinkering never stops, it will swell and it will subside. Lewis, like any successful activist, provoked; that was his forte. Through the frothy twenties he relentlessly wrote what, in effect, were reform novels, a hallmark of the Progressive Era. Grebstein proclaims: "His powers to agitate the reader have not been equaled in America except by Paine, Twain, and Mencken." Sounds like good writing—and good history.[16]

Grebstein sees Lewis as a wordsmith who along with his colleague Sherwood Anderson opened "the way for the kind of realism which has prevailed in much American fiction of the twentieth century: the concentration on the domestic scene, on common life, on familiar types, on what might be called middle tragedy. In his art he hit a perfect average; had he been more profound he would have been less successful; had he been less skillful, he would not have been so influential." As historians value literature, literary scholars ought to grant more heft to other liberal-arts disciplines. The long, multi-faceted perspective of Interdisciplinary Studies makes sense. Whether or not Grebstein is correct regarding the roots and pervasiveness of realism through the twentieth century, whether Lewis's focus on the middle tragedy has continued to prevail in literature, the scholar demonstrates the author was no lightweight. The fact that he resonated so strongly in the 1920s, that seminal decade by which the U.S. identified itself as consequentially middle class, spoke to Grebstein at mid-century; he argues Lewis's observations four decades past "talk to us." Despite reformist despair, millions of Americans in the New Era did not give up on the attraction of advocacy; progressivism no longer was a fevered crusade, but the spirit had not totally succumbed amidst all the new decade's hoopla. Lewis represents that. That "perfect average" Grebstein attributes to Lewis still into the twenty-first century speaks to us; and progressivism still carries weight. At the end of his most fruitful decade, beyond the country's shores, a formidable group of social observers

[16] Ibid., 165. Herbert David Croly, *The Promise of American Life*, ed. Arthur M. Schlessinger, Jr. (Cambridge: Harvard University Press: Belknap Press, 1965).

hailed the author: "If Lewis's foes permit him nothing else, they must at least concede his historical importance, an importance fixed by the Nobel Prize." Grebstein concedes in all matters raging around the author, the 1930 award was controversial (and always there are those who do not place stock in the honor). Still, the Swedish Academy perceived merit: "He was the conscience of his generation." Grebstein regrets his discipline's lapse: "He is a more important writer than we now admit."[17]

Historians have long identified progressivism as a running constant in the country's history, an ideology always in flux and demanding re-evaluation. Social and cultural critics often overlook, miss the resilience, the lasting strength of the powerfully-driven reform movement. Cultural historians along with other humanists mean to rectify the lapse: sedulously search to fill out the nation's story; take pride in revision. Literary scholars re-evaluate resources, schools of thought, and "players" high and low. More enlightened every year, inspired as to how much more we must plumb, humanists revisit "who we are as a people." The American Experiment's success rests upon that inquiry. Those working in literature increasingly recognize as do historians, as all students of culture, the United States is always evolving; a society ever enriched by diversity; all purportedly are invested; and they as scholars have to play their role.

All along a vast array of players, *Americans* all, including those who narrate the country's sojourn, who studied the world about them *from their vantage points*, have attempted to have their say about this American Experiment, whether as female—and male—suffragists, union organizers, civil rights advocates, Whigs and Bull Moosers, of course the list goes on and on. Historians left out hosts of "others" as they studied *our past*; so also did the literary elite. A wealth of poetry and prose was ignored for the sole reason it was written by people of color, by immigrants, women, non-Christians, and by those of "doubtful" sexual identities—*others*. Indeed, the literature, the history...exclusivity runs deep; and we, today, humanists of all specializations, must take our own current measure. And we progress.

[17] Grebstein, 165–66; Preface.

Everyman and everywoman played a role in making a way, a life, shaping community, *and* this includes those elite cultural contributors who were short-sighted, prejudiced, ignorant, did not see the bigger picture as we now *envision* "who we are." What are we to make of them? Yes, those story-tellers spoke for only a slice of the world within which they lived; still, they represent a contribution which must be given its due if we are to be true to our story. Canons (and it is debatable if we need totems) can always expand; in the process scholars in all disciplines must not toss aside, discount what earlier spokespeople contributed. We may give them less overwhelming representation, but do we, in our current lexicon, need to cancel them all? To retain currency canons must take stock of all who contributed to our heritage; and to sustain the search, those who "fell short" in assessing "who we are" should not be short-changed; in doing so we short-change ourselves. "Novelists of old" made valuable contributions from their particular perspectives; they leave for later periods reminders of what they saw *and* what and why they neglected to look further out from their advantaged perches.

Sinclair Lewis in his day hardly represented in his work all the complex crosscurrents of race, gender, sexuality, ethnicity, class, religion, etc.—every day we learn how much we still leave out. None doubted in his day or since that he picked up on the rushing flow of the body politic. And he articulated (if he did not always headline) a wide array of wrongs done to Americans of all backgrounds. Who belongs in the literary canon is not a cause a historian should take up; but a weigh-in is not inappropriate. Sinclair Lewis a century ago touched on an array of social and cultural challenges that held and continue to hold great historical relevance. A century of literary scholarship and criticism misreads in part the overarching importance of what he was after. Historians value Lewis. He was taking on his society, his culture, the shortcomings of American life in light of the American Promise. Reconsidering Lewis, taking into account historians' appreciation of his contribution to our understanding of who made the United States, those who study, teach, and critique American Literature ought to recognize this author, a writer of profound note in his time, deserves a more catholic embrace. And as literary specialists revisit Lewis, historians, all students of culture, are richer for the endeavor.

Of interest to students, scholars, critics, to curious readers of all backgrounds seeking to flesh out our individual and broader identities, the work of a novelist who called out for higher aims than material well-being is relevant. *Sinclair Lewis: The 1920s and the Shaping of American Identity* offers another read of the writer's literary import, informed by his historical contribution. Lewis stands as one twenties critic acknowledged a harbinger of the ever-current demand for a reconsideration of perspective. British novelist E. M. Forster stood amongst the few who signaled caution as his literary compatriots piled on Lewis. Quit fussing about art, he advised. Broaden the measure: "[T]he historian of the future will cease to worry" over the question of art, he will not dismiss Lewis as the critics of his day had done as "superficial." The historian "will pick up the earlier and brighter volumes" within which the author's "genius is enshrined, and will find there not only that genius, but a recording of our age." Forster prophesied Lewis was something new, a "cameraman." In the twenties he produced a fresh art form. The novelist, he asserted, must be "classed with writers termed 'advanced,' with people who prefer truth to comfort, passion to stability, prevention to cure.... His commentary on society is constant, coherent, sincere...." He had lodged "a piece of a continent in our imaginations" as none before; and he had stored it away for generations to ponder, assess, measure how far they had come. His works "are done, safe, mankind's forever." E. M. Forster had it right about Sinclair Lewis. This remarkable observer of the American scene still has a lot to say.[18]

As students of culture, let us draw upon one another's studies, capitalize on our strengths as scholars, join forces to get at the full story. It is interesting, challenging, provocative, and simply fun to read Lewis

[18] E. M. Forster, "A Camera Man," *Life and Letters* 2, May 1929: 336–43; reprint, *New York Herald Tribune Books*, "Our Photography: Sinclair Lewis," April 28, 1929, 1 and 6, quoted 6. Forster sees in Lewis a savvy, modernist use of the camera in his writing. See Shi, *Facing Facts* for the huge impact of photography on realism: "The Media of Realism," 93–99.

and the considerations of those drawn to his work (a host of contemporary reviewers wrote with stunning finesse). Lewis was a formidable novelist, an insightful social commentator, a real character. What a tough nut to crack. Plenty took a crack at him throughout his career which stretched across the first half of the twentieth century. All agreed his work provoked conversation...all agreed it was necessary. As an historian, I have set out to re-air that dialogue, see what more we can learn from it. I have tried to give voice, a say again to reviewers, literary critics, yes readers, too, and scholars in literature and in history across one hundred years...in a sense resurrect the on-going conversations. Lewis, who most of the literary elite in the twenties took as a serious commentator on the scene, or as they would have it "the passing parade," still weighs in heavily on the American Experiment.

ONE

"CALL ME RED"

A difficult man, Sinclair Lewis, for those around him; and a challenge to bear himself. Despite careless disregard for his physical and mental well-being throughout adulthood, he was resilient. For an individual desperately in search of the company of others, he remained excruciatingly lonely. Possibly it was his boyish innocence that drew others to him—especially the nurturing women to whom he expressed his loneliness. Then there was the anger—possibly emanating from the bevy of self-doubts—which destroyed relationships. Whatever the psychological roots, Lewis drove practically every friend, colleague, and lover away, and two wives and two sons. A case can be made that insecurities account for his rich work as well as a life poorly led. The novelist was driven, in good part, in quest of stability.

Lewis literally could not sit still; jittery in the moment, he never established a permanent abode; John J. Koblas dedicated a book to the countless uprootings, some fifty. Over five decades he rented, leased, and purchased far-flung homes from Duluth, Minnesota to Carmel on the Pacific, Washington D.C. to Florence, Italy. He inhabited cottages in New England towns and down the East Coast; he lived on farms and in art colonies; he lodged near colleges and universities. Lewis sought refuge in hotel apartments and mansions; he found escape on lengthy day-trips, drives across the country, and sailings to Europe. The novelist seldom found sanctuary from the storm. In the turbulent wake he left behind spouses, short and long-term dalliances, and an impressive array of "best" friends and "irreplaceable" colleagues.[1]

[1] John J. Koblas, *Sinclair Lewis: Home at Last* (Bloomington, MN: Voyeuger Press), 1981. See Gary Schornhorst and Mathew Hofer, eds. *Sinclair Lewis Remembered* (Tuscaloosa: University of Alabama Press, 2012) a "collaborative biography published incrementally over a period of eighty years, with many of the entries recorded by friends, former friends, enemies, and

James M. Hutchisson, specializing in Lewis's twenties heyday, sums up: "Lewis was a restless man who never stayed in any one place for long. His creativity depended on contact with different people and places, and he forever feared being trapped in the type of conventional life that his characters lived."[2] He should not have feared. He never came close to settling anywhere long enough to appear now permanently rooted; none ever considered the author conventional. Harry Sinclair Lewis as a boy went by Harry; later to friends he was Hal; to most he favored Red.[3] Hutchisson attributes creativity to his

---

acquaintances after his death." "The list of people Lewis alienated during his life reads like a Who's Who of Anglo-American writers and publishers. With his prickly temperament, he may well have lost more friends than he made were it not a mathematical impossibility." See 7–9.

[2] James M. Hutchisson, *The Rise of Sinclair Lewis, 1920–1930* (University Park: Pennsylvania State University Press, 1996) assesses the twenties novels, drafts, and critical reviews: "Lewis selected usable materials and shaped them, through his unique vision, into novels that reached and remained part of the American imagination." See 4. The scholar works his material hard; assessing *Babbitt*, he parses multiple drafts. As with *Main Street* he spots many changes are stylistic: "[W]ith his characteristic meticulousness, Lewis tightened sentences, cut out prolixity, and paid great attention to diction, once again writing lists of three or four words and then circling his final choice." See 75–76. Hutchisson as Sheldon Norman Grebstein, *Sinclair Lewis* (New Haven: Twayne Publishers, Inc.) is an excellent source; neither is writing biography; the foremost biographers are Mark Schorer, *Sinclair Lewis: An American Life* (New York: McGraw-Hill Book Company, 1961) and Richard Lingeman, *Sinclair Lewis: Rebel From Main Street* (New York: Random House, Inc., 2002).

[3] Lewis's choice of names throughout his life is a mixed bag. Schornhorst and Hofer work to recall who called him Hal, who Red, and who the seldom-used Sinclair and why. Lewis sought to identity as "an ordinary guy." Biographers, reviewers, critics, and scholars for over a century have tried to suss this out. They familiarize themselves with their subject, sprinkle the various monikers into their observations, highlight his quest to be a "pal." They sense in this fashion a means to legitimize, convey one's perspective on the "real Lewis." He implored any new acquaintance, literary giant or hobo, "call me Red." Novelist Edna Ferber recollected of her old companion, "The cuckoo

unanchored temperament. What exactly was the purported trap and how did it affect his work? While he avoided convention, he craved it, too. Biographers Mark Schorer and Richard Lingeman expand on his life in their authoritative works. He discounted middle-class conventionality, and he wished in his own fashion to salvage it as a national institution. He was constantly in a punching match with the world and himself. He could be fleetingly enchanted with people and locales and then violently repulsed. He prided himself as an exceptionally well-dressed man-about-town meanwhile searching out pals amongst the hoi-polloi. What heartache was at the source of this creative dynamo

---

young man's name was Sinclair Lewis, but everyone called him Red." See 43. He took up Red in college; plenty affectionately called him Hal. Editor and critic Burton Rascoe recalled meeting him as both worked for publisher George H. Doran: "Soon afterwards I was calling him 'Red' whereas Miss Butcher stuck to 'Hal.'" Rascoe, a rare lasting friend, remembered, "I had never met anyone more agreeable or more entertaining as a person." See 65. Fellow-editor Fanny Butcher observed, "His oldest friends called him Hal, his later ones Red, inevitably because he had red hair, a red face, and a fiery disposition." She also remained a long-term friend. Butcher claimed she never quarreled with Lewis. She noted first wife Gracie Heger Lewis "was the only person who really knew him that I ever heard call him Sinclair." See 72, 62, and 22. Grace parenthetically recalled after his death she "called him 'Hal' because he had been christened 'Harry," which he had dropped at Yale, 'Sinclair' was too formal, and I did not like the 'Red' which, because of his red hair, came so easily to an acquaintance of even five minutes…." See 66. Eager to befriend, to discard elitism (never wholly successful), the novelist regularly pressed "Red." Journalist Frazier Hunt remembered their first meeting—"A little later he thundered: 'Say! what in hell is your real name anyway? You've surely got some other name besides Frazier. My name is Red.'" Frazier laughed when Red was introduced to writers Sir Philip Gibbs and A.S.M. Hutchisson at his London house—"At once Gibbs was 'Phil' to him while Hutchisson bowed to, 'I'll just call you "Hutch"'…." See 93 and 98. Editor and publisher George Jean Nathan reminisced of London days: "I would call on him in whatever hotel room he was occupying that week." With him there was a crowd, all "Christian names." See 131. Novelist and friend James Branch Cabell, compelled to address the issue, remarked, "I never called him 'Red'…." See 84.

who would collapse, defeated, onto and into himself, and then rise again across seven decades?

Schorer opens his opus with an early line out of Lewis's 1915 novel *The Trail of the Hawk*: "I guess imagination is partly wanting to be places where you aren't—well, I go when I want to, and I like that better." "Of course I do notice sunsets and so on a good deal but that is not imagination." What then did he want to imagine? Why was observing sunsets—which he admired along with all landscapes and of which he constructed glowing "fictions"—unnecessary; what was he after? Harry...Hal...Red always strived to get a handle on the world and its denizens, and he wanted "in." Schorer finds that "the real enigma of his novels" arose out of a "persistent conflict of values that clashed no less within him" as a child and adult. Lewis reacted to the fact he was cast out by those about him who vigorously participated "in the world"; he was left out, brutally "expelled from rather than repelled by his environment, ejected rather than rejecting." Again *Trail of the Hawk*: "I do like to go different places; possibly I take the imagination out that way...well, I go when I want to, and I like that better." Hence from youth he was "driven into an inner world even more bleak and barren than the exterior world that expelled him, who would gladly have chosen that world." That inner-world was no cakewalk. The subtitle of *The Trail of the Hawk*, completed just on the cusp of his rise to fame, is *A Comedy on the Seriousness of Life.*[4]

It is far from certain he'd gladly have chosen that world from which he stood askance; more to the point, the author wanted in so that he could reform it. For as much as Sinclair Lewis sought entree, he was not about to compromise, to discount his "superlative" values. What a dilemma. Red was a live-wire short-circuiting within and fuming without, engaged in thrusts at happiness often cloaked as satire. He burst with ideas fed by unquenchable curiosity and then summarily cast them off; he concocted glorious plans, followed through on some, never

[4] Schorer, Frontispiece and 4. Sinclair Lewis, *The Trail of the Hawk: A Comedy of the Seriousness of Life*, New York: Harper & Brothers, 1915). David Allen Simpkins, *Becoming Sinclair Lewis* (Independent Publishing, 2017) studies Lewis's teenage and young adult diaries.

again said a word about others; he pursued and fled loving and hate-filled relationships. Often he did all he could to make up again with wounded colleagues, friends, lovers; he forever sought companionship which imploded into painful solitude. Trapped indeed, forever in search of escape, he always carried his baggage. He trailed from town to country, art enclave to urban retreat; he sailed back and forth across the Atlantic in search of fresh stake holds. He wrote furiously in intensely productive spurts followed by lengthy professional and personal collapses. He led a life of too much alcohol and short-lived health cures. Lewis was crawling out of his skin. For that matter, he was tortured by terrible skin maladies which he treated with painful, scarring treatments to his face; many found Red ugly, and increasingly they said so in private and in public.[5]

Schorer asserts "the literary account derives immediately from the biographical...." He embarks, "He was a queer boy...." And he was an odd-duck adult. Schorer observes Lewis could be the center of attention, generally was, but the total misfit at the same time. Growing up in small-town, horse-drawn Sauk Centre, Minnesota in the late 1800s, he was the son of a doctor, privileged and unpopular. He had one real friend, and he was laughed at by the girls. Sauk Centre was a frontier environ on the make: "Thirty years before, there was nothing here but native earth, rolling prairie, roving Indians, a crossing of stagecoach trails." Seven years before Harry's birth in 1885, the railroad arrived—and with it "modern America." Harry would grow up to travel far, fast, in a fever; the trains would lay tracks down main street and across the emergent urban-industrial landscape, a key bridge to modernity. By

[5] Ernest Hemingway, once a purported friend, about the time of Lewis's death broadcast his disgust. In *Across the River and into the Trees*, Scharnhorst and Hofer write, "Hemingway caricatured him as a 'mediocre writer' who had 'outlived his talents,' a fellow with 'a strange face like an over-enlarged, disappointed weasel or ferret. It looked as pock-marked and blemished as the mountains of the moon seen through a cheap telescope and...it looked like Goebbels' face, if Herr Goebbels had ever been in a plane that burned, and not been able to bail out before the fire reached him.'" See 8. For more see Robert L. McLaughlin, "'only kind thing is silence': Ernest Hemingway vs. Sinclair Lewis," *Hemingway Review* 6 (1987): 46–53.

1882 there were three trunk-lines connecting the North Woods outpost with the main tracks crisscrossing the transforming nation. Sauk Centre strived to keep up to date—in 1884 "a system of waterworks was laid, and in 1889 a system of public sewerage, at first limited to the business district but extended to the whole village in 1903. In 1905 the Lewis residence achieved a bathroom."[6] It is hard to reckon with how important the bathroom was in that day…consider how important it remains. In 1922 Lewis famously opened the door to *Babbitt* with a meticulous description "imagining" in his role as "fictionist" what his audience needed to see, what it already sensed. He took readers into the businessman's bathroom. The *au currant* bathroom was a great achievement…but his readers needed to ask just how important did it really need to be? Where was their imagination? This becomes Babbitt's mid-life crisis as he surveys his own dreams gone to rot—George Babbitt remained the novelist's most famous protagonist.

Back in the late 1800s no modernity crisis was on Harry's mind. He was a kid—by early-twentieth century norms the recently perceived adolescent: smart, clever, and an outsider.

> He was nearly six feet tall before he was sixteen, with a short torso set on very long and spindly legs, and weighed only a hundred and twenty pounds; lank and lean, but with a puffy, acne-ridden face ("pimples," they said), big feet and hands, badly co-ordinated in his movements, everything about his body hanging and dangling and swinging and lunging and stumbling, and ice-blue eyes (astigmatic) rather protruding, all of this thatched with a carrot-colored wig. Or perhaps his own phrase, from an early story, is more exact: "hair like a new copper cent." Nicknames pursued him: Harry to his family and Hal to his few friends, he was first Doodle, then Mink or Minnie, then Ginger, then Bonfire, finally Red. He was the original reuben of the joke books and the itinerant vaudeville troupe of that time, and the butt of every crude piece of horseplay…. He was lonely.

Having had his fill of solitude, the young man set off to make a new

---

[6] Schorer, 3–5. Harry Sinclair Lewis—February 7, 1885, died January 10, 1951.

start at Yale in 1902.[7]

That first year "on his own" he missed out, Schorer observes, on "a few close friends, one or two of the kind of deep personal associations without which most of us would find life unsupportable—this he did not have at all...." Nor did the following years fill that void: "When Harry Lewis left Yale his was still a scattered self, as really it was always to remain." Instead of reaching an "easy maturity," college "left him the nervous tramp who aspired to elegance, the radical who really wished to conform, the puritan from the hinterland who yearned to be the man of the world.... All the sadness...." It reads heartbreakingly. He was emotive, counter to the opinion most readers, critics, and academics have held that "Sinclair Lewis was 'one of the least sentimental of men....'" It is an ill-founded reading of his torment; unemotive? Too facile—misleading as would be his humor. Novelist Vincent Sheean reminisced "at his best he was one of the funniest people in the world." At his best—just what was that? And what exactly was so funny, about him, about his work—what was it all about? All the sadness, yes, but all the drive, too.[8]

While for many such alienation would be insupportable, Hal Lewis found a way to sustain himself with the concomitant side-effect he was insufferable. He matured into a nasty alcoholic, an inveterate performer who drummed endlessly on with mimicry and humor, clever recitations and monologues, searing indictments and inflated pontificating before any available audience, be it one entrapped soul or an assortment of a hundred. Mary Heaton Vorse, labor and feminist activist, recalled the summer of 1912 where Lewis played and worked at his craft in Provincetown with other artists and activists of that prewar, reform-minded, excitable Progressive Era: "He was never still, his hair flamed, his blue eyes blazed, his long sensitive hand gesticulated. He got himself sunburned to dull plum color over and over again and peeled. He galloped over the dunes barefoot. He shook sand into the picnic basket. He came in shouting he had an idea, and a flood of nonsense to float Noah's Ark would resound...." But she was kind to him;

[7] Ibid., 67, 128–29, 7.

[8] Scharnhorst and Hofer, 174.

he was entertaining, possibly pathetic, to be pitied. Reformer Frances Perkins wondered: "He was queer, he was funny, he was also amusing. He was also appealing. That is, he appealed to one's parental sense, and one felt like protecting him and not letting him be hurt by other young men whom one knew, and who tended to make fun of him...."[9]

Cruelty, sometimes in his face, sometimes behind his back, haunted Lewis. Schorer cites Harry Kemp who in *More Miles* in 1926 transparently skewered his fellow bohemian in Greenwich Village, the pre-World War One New York haunt of the youthful *avant garde*:

> "'Red' Flatman, though he has his qualities...if you're looking for my opinion—just DOESN'T BELONG!—'Life of the Party'—have any of you ever traveled on shipboard?—well, on every ship a moron is sure to pop up, early during the voyage, known as 'Life of the Party'—nuf said."
>
> "That's what 'Red' has tried to be ever since he hit the Village...."
>
> "Right! He doesn't get us at all—"
>
> "You bet he doesn't—strives so hard to be 'Bohemian'...feels it incumbent on himself to try to kiss all the women."

Some women did like it. Lewis could be charming. Men, too, sought his companionship. But most could not stand the duration. Schorer notes, "Lewis could rage and sulk, plot and scheme, and on occasion hold a cunning silence, but to ask that he develop restraint and a true discretion was to ask for more than he could ever give or wish to." But

[9] Schorer, 191–92. Magazine editor Herbert R. Mayes took his measure: "Now and then he could be amusing—more than now and then—and he was a grand mimic. I got along with him, found him generally kind, but suffered when he gave vent to rage, which also was more than now and then." "His conduct could be irascible and irrational." After an embarrassing scene in the early 1940s Mayes remarked Lewis was a "rat," to which his tablemate added "bastard"—he knew him longer. See Scharnhorst and Hofer, 106 and 285–86.

in the moment, he was interesting, hilarious, thoughtful, and brilliant.[10]

Lewis commanded attention and insisted he be allowed the freedom to sink into stultifying silence and isolation. Schorer recollects novelist Carl Van Vechten's assessment. "It was difficult to see him alone, he says, because there could be no real conversation: the show-off always tried to take over. It was equally difficult to see him in the company of other people because of his unpredictability: either he would sit morosely in a corner and make everyone uneasy, or he would begin one of his interminable imitations and bore everyone to death." On one occasion, Lewis cast himself a dog nuzzling at one's feet: "I'm just like this dog. All I want is affection." But how could one offer it? Plenty tried and failed. An admiring—and tolerant—British journalist observed he possessed "an extraordinary energy of speech, a very great diversity of ideas, a certain air of frenzy in his look, speech and gait, a frenzy half comic, half melancholy." Melancholy, manic, hard to say, but hard to wait out: "He might have been poet or actor, so novel, so wild, so rhetorical were his sudden enthusiasms, his genial affectations, his native power of invention, mimicry and gesture."[11]

In later life Lewis did take up acting and directing theater productions—he was not very good. Off-stage, the quality of production was better but off-putting. Company at restaurants, bars, chic dining rooms, visits on rustic verandas were amused, vexed, and on the lookout to duck out. At a public dinner honored by his hosts in London, he thanked them by parodying a caricature of a U.S. Senator—for no apparent reason and to no good end. In New York, at a similar occasion

---

[10] Schorer, 184–85, deciphers his attraction for women. Second wife "Dorothy Thompson, enjoyed him. Like many other women, she soon forgot his ugliness and was made to feel that charm which arose in part from his clowning, in part from the incandescence of his mind, in largest part from the sense that he could give a woman of his own utter helplessness without her, the sense that only she could save him from despair and give his life direction." See 489. Historian and novelist, ultimately alienated friend William E. Woodward reminisced he was "homely as a rail fence, but he had a winning smile and a cordial handshake." See Scharnhorst and Hofer, 44.

[11] Schorer., 322, 329, and 378.

he was mute; then he set off on an interminable harangue—in German. In France, another dinner, he staged a Midwestern salesman meeting a royal aide-de-camp in a London pub. No one questioned he was one of the great mimics, catching every intonation, exacting gesture, never slipping up on idiom, accent. But in recalling such episodes, few harbored pleasant memories and certainly not lasting affection.[12]

Lewis was a master at observation. He poured all he absorbed and himself as far as he wanted to go (which was limited) into his writing. Here he was genius, appreciated as an impeccable wordsmith. Hutchisson relates:

---

[12] George Jean Nathan writes Lewis would drop in on him in London for a cocktail "sometimes so moody that he didn't speak five words and at other times so excited and voluble that he would stand up and, apropos of nothing at all, make speeches at me for an hour on end. These speeches, generally couched in dialect of one species or another, were invariably on one of two subjects: himself—in terms of a facetious self-appraisal predicated upon critics who did not sufficiently appreciate him, and myself" (whence he facetiously called Nathan to task on his shortcomings)." "At other times I would call on him in whatever hotel room he was occupying that week." Others would be present, crowds Lewis invited in off the street, none of whom Nathan had or ever again would know. He "called them all by diminutives of their Christian names...." Red had to be everyman, everybody's man. Nathan recalls a gathering of English men of letters: "[H]e had—after as is his custom, promptly addressing everyone by contradictions of their given names—wound his arms around two of the sedate valetudinarians present and insisted that he be allowed to teach them the American jazz dances." Nathan came to understand: "One can always tell a new novel coming on when the oratorical mood in any one, single thematic direction assails our friend." He remembers Lewis writing *The Man Who Knew Coolidge* in the mid-twenties: "They had been delivered in a variety of places and at a variety of times, including the corner of Fifth Avenue and Fifty-sixth Street at high noon, a beer-house in Hoboken at eleven o'clock at night...the bathroom of my apartment, the men's lavatory at the Rennert Hotel in Baltimore, a publisher's tea at the Sherry-Netherland, several taxicabs, two New York theatre lobbies on opening nights, and the steps of St. Ignatius Church." Nathan's "Smart Set" and "American Mercury" colleague H. L. Mencken after one such harangue singularly barked: "Bughouse!" See Scharnhorst and Hofer, 131 and 158.

> Lewis's ear for a language was only one part of his mimetic gift. As he sat in Pullman cars on train trips, took his meals in the dining rooms of athletic clubs, and in general insinuated himself into the world of the middle-class businessman, he was able to "absorb" or "memorize" people to such an astonishing degree that, like Dickens, to whom he has often been compared, he could virtually become them—speak as they spoke, walk the way they walked, anticipate their responses to certain statements, and render with eerie accuracy their facial expressions, hand gestures, even eye movements.[13]

That was the perfection he projected in the magazine stories and novels; there Lewis found an appreciative audience. Novelist Thomas Wolfe, a hard drinking companion who established with the writer a "roistering rapport that ended as abruptly as it began," carved up Lewis in a thinly veiled hundred-page caricature in his monumental *You Can't Go Home Again*. He had had his fill. Still Schorer admires: "The physical portrait of Lewis is perfect and no less is the representation of his behavior. His restlessness, his drinking, his compulsive informality, his generosity, his sweetness and his willfulness, his suffering, his dissatisfaction, his fits of exhaustion and sudden recovery, his imitations, his meaningless companionships—they are all here." Schorer, no Lewis

[13] Hutchisson, 62. "Lewis's writing gift was largely mimetic. One of his most impressive skills was his ability to reproduce the idiom and slang of American speech. Heywood Broun commented in his review of *Main Street* that Lewis was 'so unerringly right in reproducing talk' that his written dialogue possessed 'deeper than phonographic exactness.'" See 201. Schorer, too, cites Broun: "He hears even better than he sees. I can't think of anybody who has been so unerringly right in reproducing talk. See 285; and Heywood Broun, "Books," *New York Tribune*, October 20, 1920, https://www.newspapers.com. Broun extensively runs by passages demonstrating Lewis's command. Two days later he lengthily took on *Main Street*. See Heywood Broun, "Books," *New York Tribune*, October 22, 1920, https://www.newspapers.com. Drawing upon key scholars I have cross-checked most reviews and added my takes as well as scholars' critiques.

fan, savored the passage. And he recognized all concurred Lewis indeed mastered the idiom.[14]

Lingeman writing forty years beyond Schorer is more tolerant and assuredly patient with his subject. He does not shy, however, from laying it all out. His depiction of Lewis's descent into alcoholism is harrowing: endless drunks, tedious scenes, next-day apologies, weeks-long binges, lingering DTs. And there were the manic mood swings, extemporaneous drives across town, countryside, not to mention sodden voyages across the Atlantic; internment in sanitariums, lengthy drying-out spells, and to an astonishing extent an ability not only to don blinders to it all, but to fasten them to the eyes of others. Dorothy Thompson wrote her husband: "*And no one is permitted to mention it.*" The dipsomania took a toll in the twenties; by the thirties and forties Lewis was worn down, slowly, increasingly debilitated in body and mind. He married his second wife in the late twenties; they stayed together long into the thirties, his career on the decline, hers rising. Thompson was a remarkably talented journalist, a strong-minded woman breaking through the toughest professional barricades. Lewis taxed and silenced her—although she repeatedly broke quarantine and spoke up. She was in love and stood by him. No easy presence herself, Thompson in the end had to leave to protect herself and their son's well-being. "His cruelty when drunk was becoming too much to bear. He was ordinarily not physically violent, Dorothy said, but verbally so, spewing cruel, profane, sarcastic words that lacerated her. Like first wife Gracie before her (who once noted the pattern: 'Too much to drink [—]a resented remark [—]loud retaliation'), Dorothy said his outbursts were often 'occasioned by a wound to his amour proper. He was terribly vulnerable, very thin-skinned.'" There were brief and indeterminate separations, but it could not work. Dorothy admonished: "More and more your life becomes nothing at all except work and drinking and—recovering from drinking." Interestingly, Lingeman notes, for his work it worked: "His bibulous routine between books seemed to parody his work routine—bursts of inspiration (alcoholic elation), long hours of continuous work (steady drinking—and interruption of sleep patterns),

[14] Schorer, 558.

broken up by recuperative naps at all hours (drinking until he fell asleep). In either case, the twenty-four-hour day was vanquished."[15]

It was all part of a package which formidably influenced Lewis's work; it decimated days and months and a life he desperately wanted to work. What a conundrum: there is no separating the novelist as a troubled soul from his work. The end-product consisted of acute observations of those around him, around the country, and of the country itself. From it all he drew out and projected what seemed to make an awful lot of sense—he understood in some fashion the changing human condition, but he had no comprehensive answers to ease it. There he was, somewhere, lost in America. But along the way, Harry Sinclair Lewis prominently located what ailed so many and the nation. Conflation, too, is part of the national saga.

---

[15] Lingeman, 415 and 418. Gracie Heger Lewis's and Sinclair Lewis's son Wells died in World War II. Dorothy and Lewis's son Michael, like Wells, did not have an easy relationship with a father who could be distant emotionally as well as geographically. Eminent medical figure Morris Fishbein who worked with the novelist and became close in the twenties recollected: "Probably Lewis will be remembered also," beyond his twenties body of work, "for his extraordinary attachment to hard liquor. He was a hearty drinker. I have seen him tip up a pint of scotch and drink it down in a continuous swallow. Then he would stand and talk almost like one inspired until suddenly he would collapse and go to sleep." See Sharnhorst and Hofer, 133–34.

TWO

LEWIS AND THE UNITED STATES

The enormous hours Lewis worked, however scattershot, produced results; for forty years the novelist held a large readership. Drunk, dry, hinged or unhinged, once committed to writing he was purposeful, seeking something in himself, out to fill some void, reach some resolution—in tandem with a close examination of his society. While his work drew on his experiences, tastes, family, his friendships, acquaintances, and professional relationships, all his traveling and diverse habitations, it is a long stretch to consider the novels autobiographical. His writing aimed at the people and the country as a whole; and specifically the compromised middle-class world he curiously sought out but despaired to be too closely identified with. His personal dissatisfactions drove his work but did not compose the core of it. Novelists pour plenty of themselves into their writing, purposefully or less so; Lewis's prose offers a remarkable demonstration of it; but he could not face the whole story about himself, nor was he about to open the books on his troubled soul. Critics charged by not digging deeper he undercut his own ambitions by his facile caricatures of American "types." Some suggested he needed to dig deeper into himself. On the other hand, when it came to the "truths" about the United States, he was exacting, some charged brutal. By design he sought to expiate the nation's "sins." Because he was such a public sinner himself, because his behavior was so egregious, it was easy for detractors to fold the man into his work, to use his personal weaknesses to attack his art. Lewis, they charged, was not so much a craftsman—simply crafty. He *was* a craftsman; and his forte at caricature had a novel purpose for him, for the times, for his era's art. He was less determined to write the Great American Novel than he was to decipher what made the U.S.A. tick...or not. The work was not about him, read what you wish into it—it was about *us*, about the American Promise falling short. Within that saga, he yearned to track the trajectory of the American Experiment...and just possibly to better figure himself out.

Lewis, while not an aggressive Progressive Era activist, at base always was working within that moderate turn-of-the-century reform tradition. He was Middle American—middle class in upbringing, middlewestern in root values, forever trying to untangle the conundrum of his country, wrest a mid-course resolution toward securing the nation's destiny. H. L. Mencken, that other infamous critic of the first half of the twentieth century, that other 1920s scourge, for a long period a close friend who treasured Lewis as a compatriot, understood him particularly well. Mencken, too, in cunning fashion was a middle-of-the-road sort, cranky, in his case at points reactionary, but at base simply a committed citizen trying to make the U.S. rise to its promise. And Lewis prized Mencken. Richard Lingeman pegs the two of them: "[Lewis] always believed, defensively or not, that chronic scolds were the true patriots. As he once told George Seldes [another scold], 'Mencken and I are...accused of running down America, writing about nothing but her faults. We both criticize America, true, but it is because we want perfection....If Mencken and I didn't love America so much, we would not criticize what is wrong with her.'"[1]

If not an artist of the ordained high order, Lewis must be given due as a masterful craftsman of national identity. Historian and journalist William L. Shirer noted he did not share the common perception that Lewis was notches below Hemingway, Fitzgerald, Dos Passos, and Faulkner: "Lewis lacked style, yet his impact on modern American life...was greater than all of the other four writers together."[2] America,

[1] Richard Lingeman, *Sinclair Lewis: Rebel from Main Street* (New York: Random House, 2002), 474–75. See Stephen A. Young, "The Mencken-Lewis Connection," *Menckeniana* 94 (Summer 1985), 10–16. https://www.jstor.org/stable/26483767#metadata-info-tab-contents. "H. L. Mencken and Sinclair Lewis dominated a decade—the Twenties—in a way that we have not seen since. It is unlikely that we will ever see anything comparable again." Quoted, 10.

[2] Shirer quoted in Larry Parnass, "Why Writer Sinclair Lewis Keeps Paying Dividends from Pittsfield, and Will Forever," *Sinclair Lewis Society Newsletter* 27 (Spring 2019), 11 and 18–20.

identity, promise—this was what his art was all about. Not incidental to the task, if he could motivate the nation to rise to its greater promise he might, again, find some resolution for himself, a safer harbor from his demons.

Sinclair Lewis was not political in the sense he cared about policies, parties, positioning and posturing. His love for his country and his focus on its weaknesses and strengths were in the broad sense political in intent. He had his principles and occasionally would enter the political arena: World War One; the Women's Movement in the teens and twenties; two twenties cause célèbres, the Patterson textile strike and the Sacco and Vanzetti trial; fascism in the twenties and thirties; race in the forties—all would draw his attention, but it was rarely fevered. Mark Schorer observes he had "serious convictions if no real commitments, convictions perhaps no less tiresome than his imitations, but capable of being acted upon." Progressive reformer Frances Perkins "tolerated him": "She, like many another, was actively engaged in the causes of uplift—settlement houses, civic reform, the Consumer's League, and so on—but to that general atmosphere she now feels that Lewis did not 'react at all.'" The biographer contends Lewis was more about himself; for example he was attracted to the liberated sexuality of women more so than the expansion of their rights—to the opportunity to have an educated, outspoken companion (companionate marriage was in vogue) was an ideal he embraced. Floyd Dell, novelist and poet, recalled, "We were content with what was happening to woman because what we wanted was something for ourselves—a Glorious Playfellow." It was a gay as well as politicized era, *bohemian* as some activists picturesquely fancied themselves.[3]

---

[3] Mark Schorer, *Sinclair Lewis: An American Life* (New York: McGraw-Hill Book Company, 1961), 196, 813, 180, and 183. Schorer never disguises his disdain for Lewis which becomes tiresome itself—and confusing. At the end of his opus, he concludes the novelist is overrated and should for the most part be forgotten. "He was one of the worst writers in modern American literature, but without his writing one cannot imagine modern American literature. That is because, without his writing, we can hardly imagine ourselves."

Schorer does credit Lewis's sincere interest in Socialism in the prewar years. The aspiring writer wrote an essay in 1914 addressing the relationship of the novelist to the social unrest of the time: "[I]t may be contended that practically every thoughtful writer of today sees behind the individual dramas of his characters a background of coming struggle which shall threaten the very existence of this status called capitalism." Schorer amends as to what was to replace capitalism "he was not so clear that he could be certain, or not so certain that he could be quite clear." The construct of the coming struggle was hardly paramount to Lewis; he was most interested in the enfolding drama; and he most wanted to engage it.[4]

Lewis's uncertainty had to be rooted in the conflict between the inequities challenged by socialism and his upbringing: from the beginning of his career as a scion of the middle class to his dying days as the acclaimed, wealthy novelist, he was a bona-fide capitalist. Floyd Dell may have crowed in *The Masses*, an influential leftwing journal, "We can have any kind of bloody world we bloody want," and his colleague Lewis would have drunk to it, but the vast majority of progressive reformers, including a good number who called themselves radical, were middle-road in their philosophy.[5] Dell was, and certainly Lewis. Schorer points out Lewis bore a likeness to William Dean Howells, acknowledged overseer of the turn-of-the-century literary world. Howells in his fiction and literary and social criticism was imbued with "middle-class liberal optimism." He and Lewis "steering a clear line between a surly proletariat and a stuffed plutocracy, wished to assure the

---

Lingeman notes Perkins' observation: "He was at that time tasting of everything that came along, but he was always an outsider." See 44.

[4] Schorer, 217. "The Passing of Capitalism," *Bookman*, December, 1914, 280–86. Note Schorer's comprehensive "Check-List" of Lewis's prodigious output, 815–26. The biographer of record had done his research. The compilation of novels, short stories, poems, reviews, and editorials runs from 1902 to 1955, four years past the author's death. See too, Sinclair Lewis Society, https://english.illinoisstate.edu/sinclairlewis; and Robert E. Fleming, *Sinclair Lewis, A Reference Guide* (Boston: G.K. Hall, 1980).

[5] Lingeman, 40.

middle class that the promise of American life lay in its best values."[6] And this is key. Progressive reform was in the broadest sense premised upon American destiny. Ultimately, for the movement's most powerful constituency it was a rush to the middle, a means—practical at its core—to secure their strong, and they expected expanding, middle-class order. And they would succeed; fundamental changes in the established order were embedded in law in the first two decades of the new century; by the early 1920s, as the nation turned away from reform and heartily moved back to its mainstay making money, much of the impending prosperity was made in the name of the triumphant middle class. This is exactly where Sinclair Lewis landed in the twenties, where he stood, ill at ease, all along—besotted by creature comforts yet anxious about an ever-expansive rot in the works. The middle class had indeed expanded, although far distant from majority status; most essential, their middle-class standard of life had come to be the American Standard, the Good Life.

Before U.S. entry April, 1917 into the Great War and through to the Armistice in November, 1918, Lewis was working—as was his wont—hard at his craft. After graduating from Yale in 1908 he churned out short stories for popular magazines as well as promotions and ads for New York publishing agencies; he edited novels, and he wrote his own promising if not widely purchased novels. He was trying to make ends meet, and he was trying to break through.[7] The break, and it was

---

[6] Schorer, 231.

[7] Lewis was a persistent go-getter. Editor Fanny Butcher at George H. Doran Company, co-worker '14 to late fall '15, recalled their correspondence. This would be his last stint at grub work: "I've been writing newspaper ads, magazine ads, circulars, book jackets, descriptions of books for next spring's catalogues, all most breathless-like." He was good at hustling work, doing it well, all the while tending to his ambitions. Poet and editor William Rose Benét recalled he was living a frantic life: "The simile one instructively thinks of first for Sinclair Lewis is 'dynamo'…. He has that absorbing curiosity about life without which no great writer was ever born." Benét in 1934 in *Saturday Review of Literature* recollected "The Earlier Lewis." Red was "the critic of his country…a badly needed satirist of its institutions…the flame of his rage against our national stupidities has been a splendid cauterization…." See

spectacular, came directly after the war with his publication of *Main Street*. It is hard to project what this novel meant to the literary world, to the country, and to Lewis. He had become close friends with Alfred Harcourt who worked for the publisher Henry Holt; both young men saw the world from the same perspective. A lot of change was in the making, and they were going to make the most of it in professional, personal, and monetary currency. The Progressive Era, as Lingeman notes, had been "a time of optimism, romantic utopianism, free love, and youth." Of course, he knows it was much more. Still, Lewis had had fun, he had kept his head above water, but now along with Harcourt he was ready to get to business, stake their claim in the New Era.[8]

The upstart publisher was self-assured. "Harcourt had an ear for the zeitgeist," writes Lingeman. Harcourt recollected: "The war seemed to provoke an intellectual ferment, a questioning of standards…a thirst for a background of general knowledge." This was Lewis's balliwick. There had been an intense scrutiny of standards occurring long before and now following the war. Social activist Anna Louise Strong remembered a 1916 visit by Lewis: "He knew he intended to be a great American writer, depicting the life of Americans of his day and age. He worked toward it always." She recalled nothing missed his inspection. Lingeman: "He had collected reams of material—both in his notebook and in his 'phonographic' memory. He was a natural recorder of American speech.… He also made a regular practice of visiting cemeteries and listing names on tombstones—to be used for characters in future stories."[9] The characters were the means to the end—standards had to be uplifted; from his aspiring perch, deeply enmeshed within the incipient Roaring Twenties, Lewis, a moderate reformer, heard his siren call. And he had a friend, a kindred spirit, and subsequent partner in Alfred Harcourt.

Scharnhorst and Hofer,106, 141, and 57. For a strong consideration of early work see "Sheldon Norman Grebstein, *Sinclair Lewis* (New Haven: Twayne Publishers, 1962), 37–60.

[8] Lingeman, 44.

[9] Ibid., 126 and 91; Strong quoted Schorer, 236.

Two chums on the make, Lewis and Harcourt struck a bargain in Manhattan which would hurl them aloft, huge cultural figures in the rapidly changing literary milieu. Harcourt, scrambling to rise in publishing, "foresaw that nonfiction on urgent current topics would have bestseller potential, along with iconoclastic, realistic fiction." He was, writes Lingeman, "ambitious and creative," and he knew what would be of value and what would sell: works "showing the real America."[10] The United States was the young novelist's seminal interest. Back in 1916, he and Gracie on a cross-country trek by train, boat, and auto stayed with Anna Louise Strong in Seattle. The reformer surely found his politics vapid; indisputably he was a chronicler: "[H]e showed me notebooks full of descriptions. He went, for instance, to the docks in Seattle and wrote down lists of what he saw…the size of packages, what was in them, how they were loaded or unloaded, where they came from, what everything looked like on those docks….He did this everywhere he went, across the country…."[11] What exactly was he after? On the docks, labor and capital battled; it was not radical politics that drew his attention. He wanted to investigate the underpinnings of a new era. He was sympathetic to the labor movement; but for his country he would strive to ensure it was middle class at its core, prosperous, fair, good with deeds, up to fulfilling the nation's destiny; *that* would work for the workers. Here was the future, the "real America."

And he wanted to make money. He and Harcourt were a pair of New Era poster-boys. The bookman was eager to start out on his own; he thought Lewis's work contemporary. Lewis encouraged his new friend to strike out, set up his own publishing house right away; he invested two thousand dollars in Harcourt, Brace, and Howe in what Lingeman terms "an act of faith and friendship." He advised Harcourt not to "be such a damn fool as ever again to work for someone else. Start your own business. I'm going to write important books. You can publish these." He was as savvy a businessman as his hungry pal. The Armistice had been signed; Harcourt wanted to publish books taking

[10] Lingeman, 125–26.

[11] Schorer, 236.

on "the new ideas with which the world was seething."[12] He knew literature and the industry; Lewis was a promising writer of consequence, and he was extremely interested in and knowledgeable of the business-end of the game. Lewis would long worry over his bourgeois bents and readily admit to them. But at this moment he and Harcourt were on to something he valued even more. He wanted to say something about the country. These two Greenwich Village "radicals" were about to rise to the top in the intensely bourgeois twenties and tap not only into ideas, the zeitgeist, but buckets of greenbacks to boot—smells like America.

Harcourt, Brace, and Howe (soon, Harcourt, Brace & Company) caught fire. The house quickly signed up eleven books. On the list was John Maynard Keynes's *Economic Consequences of the Peace*, a best-seller and consequential indictment of the recently signed Versailles Treaty. W. E. B. Du Bois published *Darkwater*, a collection of incendiary essays addressing the race crisis. Best-selling novelist Dorothy Canfield Fisher signed on; *avant garde* British writers gravitated to the press; Harcourt sought more of that "iconoclastic, realistic" fiction. First, he pressed Lewis to publish his latest effort, *Free Air*; it hardly was iconoclastic, but it might sell; it had received much notice as a series in *The Saturday Evening Post*, and that spelled profits. He urged him to complete *Main Street*. Lewis was keen, took the prompt and finished *Free Air* and wrapped up *Main Street* with which he had been struggling. *Main Street*, publisher and novelist contended, was fresh, a harbinger of the *zeitgeist*.[13]

---

[12] Lingeman, 125–27.

[13] Sinclair, Lewis, *Free Air* (New York: Harcourt, Brace, and Howe), 1919. For the book Lewis expanded on the pieces he published in the summer of 1918 (the additional material as well was serialized). *Post* was one of the foremost popular magazines of the first half of the twentieth century, a great era for weeklies and monthlies. Hollywood joined in further to stoke the burst of media consumption (radio as well). Lewis, ever attentive to his interests, secured the sale of movie rights for *Free Air*. *Main Street: The Story of Carol Kennicott* (New York: Harcourt, Brace & Company), 1920 would be made into the 1923 film "I Married a Doctor." The most applauded of the many screenplays of Lewis novels remains "Dodsworth," 1936. Schorer checklists the author's plays and films, including those pursued but not produced. See

Harcourt and Lewis were waging on a huge hit with *Main Street: The Story of Carol Kennicott*. Its October, 1920 coming-out was a smash of historic proportions in the publishing industry. It made Lewis famous and rich, his name definitively a household word. The novel was considered sensational; marketing and sales heightened the excitement. *Main Street* was a literary and commercial marvel in an era soon to be consumed by ballyhooed firsts. Ernest Brace (brother of Donald, the Brace in the house name) remarked the book "was at the time, scandal, and scandal is always exhilarating."[14] Copies sold by the tens, scores, and rapidly hundreds of thousands. Stories abounded around its success. Malcolm Cowley, mainstay critic of the literary scene of the first half of the century, calculated: "Our normal book-buying public consists, perhaps, of two or three hundred thousand people. When a novel passes the latter figure, it is being purchased by families in the remoter villages, families which acquire no more than ten books in a generation. In the year 1921, if you visited the parlor of almost any boarding house, you would see a copy of 'Main Street' standing between the Bible and 'Ben Hur.'"[15] *Publisher's Weekly* declared the novel in 1925 the best-seller for the first quarter of the century. The first year's sales were just under 300,000.[16] The novel swamped the country; a literary tidal wave swept back and forth across the continent. *Main Street* inundated the nation's cultural well-water. John Farrar, who did not favor the book, worked a different angle on the mammoth public embrace. Two years on he penned in *The Bookman*: "His friends all bought the book, then the cognoscenti, then the literati, then the literate, a paltry thousand or so. Then the sleeping beast turned over, rubbed its eyes, and woke up.

Wheeler Dixon, "Cinematic Adaptations of the Works of Sinclair Lewis," in *Sinclair Lewis at 100: Papers Presented at a Centennial Conference*, comp. Michael Connaughton (St. Cloud, MN: St. Cloud State University, 1985), 191–200.

[14] Lingeman, 158

[15] Ibid. The Bible remains the all-time best-seller. Ben Wallace, *Ben-Hur: A Tale of the Christ* (New York: Harper & Brothers, 1880) held its own for decades.

[16] James M. Hutchisson, *The Rise of Sinclair Lewis, 1920–1930* (University Park: Pennsylvania State University Press, 1996), 42.

Fifty thousand. It howled in an ecstasy of self-torture. One hundred thousand. His publishers estimate it has beyond doubt reached two million readers. And people are still buying it and reading it for the first time...."[17]

A monumental shock to all: Harcourt and Lewis—hardly prepared for the explosive impact—recognized they were about to make more than their mark. They did all in their power to bust all records and make news—and more money. Initially, they had no idea what a cataract they had unleashed. Schorer points out the two were smart business-types, hardly naive bohemians, but neither had conceived just how successfully bourgeois they might be. Of course, all along, "Neither socially nor intellectually did Sinclair Lewis share very intimately in the life of Greenwich Village." As many in his milieu, he was a "skeptic," but never a "desperate, alienated pessimist."[18] Lewis and Harcourt were decidedly mainstream, okay with business, and while they got it, they had not reckoned on just how titanic "it" was. The "It Girl" and a host of other vague *its* caught the decade's frenzy: something electric was in the air. And making money definitely amounted to *it* during the Roaring Twenties. The novelist immediately got the reputation as a devastating critic of American norms and front-and-center stood as one of the most infamous: he loved the money and the celebrity culture within which he whirled. He and Harcourt had done the job; they pressed one another to push further sales, publicity, marketing angles; they, too, were *it*—consummate promoters, masterful pitchmen of the New Era. They had become "the news."

Harcourt recalled "a mad scramble" that first spring to keep books on the shelves: "If the book had suddenly stopped selling the consequences would have been very serious for so young a firm as ours. But it didn't stop.... We were never out of stock for more than a few hours."[19] The United States was embarking on a business-obsessed decade; at the outset these two young entrepreneurs dug in—"you gotta' know the territory" as Broadway's "The Music Man" would

---

[17] Schorer, 268–69.

[18] Ibid., 184.

[19] Lingeman, 155.

humor mid-century Americans. The country was changing, and *Main Street* addressed the growing recognition something was in the air. A culturally rich tale emerged: Increasingly backwater, forlorn small-town denizens who did not get the changes in America, most of whom did not want to (in part owing to they were not close enough to the consumer mania which evolved, the excitement); who were in the lexicon of the day parochial and ignorant, biased and conceited, and most importantly short-sighted about what the U.S. really stood for, caught the country's attention. Naturally there were truths to the tale but this suddenly unveiled acute provincialism was taken as the gospel truth of "life in the sticks." Franklin P. Adams, the influential New York columnist F. P. A who made observations from his "Conning Tower," yearned for the ever-evasive "Great American Novel." "For a prominent position on the all-American team we nominate Sinclair Lewis, author of 'Main Street,' a high achievement. Mr. Lewis's pictures of Gopher Prairie…[are] a fine piece of imaginative poetry, and his recording of the commonplace conversation is perfection of satirical reporting." Adams later would declare the novel "the best book I have read in as long as I can recall."[20]

Lewis and Harcourt, Brace & Company roared. The author may have appeared to be running against American norms, but in reality he struck sensitive mainstream nerves that resulted in his work, and his persona, being the talk of the town and the crossroads burg. The millions to whom the chattering class purportedly spoke—increasingly effective by means of the explosive growth of mass communications—were all ears. *Main Street* made sense—sales enriched the coffers of the house, and the novel emerged a harbinger of plenty more "firsts" to roar out of the New Era. The country was in a state of constant celebration, a lot of it the simple product of ballyhoo, and a lot premised on

---

[20] Ibid, 150. Adams oversaw the romanticized "Algonquin Round Table," waterhole for the artistic and journalistic twenties elite. See F. P. A. [Franklin P. Adams], "The Conning Tower," *New York Tribune*, October 19, 1920, https://www.newspapers.com. Adams inserts a lengthy discourse by a Gopher Prairie burgher, demonstrating Lewis's talent for mimicry and mockery.

substance. Lewis typed away, he kept ahead in the celebrity scramble as he turned out a string of sensations and engaged in a long line of newsworthy personal escapades. Harcourt, Brace & Company's lists expanded, Lewis was ensconced on top of a cultural volcano—all his sales, hundreds and hundreds of thousands, novel upon novel, all his publicity, the generation of top-drawer receipts—all added up to big news. By a bank of measures the twenties was a bang-up decade. And within the racket, there were plenty who were not faring so spectacularly, whose plight was not considered newsworthy; the vast majority of the population working hard at simply getting along was not *it*. But it all was touted as the best of times. Lewis made his fortune—in current terms some three million dollars alone off the publication of *Main Street*.[21]

Literary critic Ludwig Lewisohn twelve years on recalled Lewis's break-out: "Perhaps no novel since 'Uncle Tom's Cabin' had struck so deep over so wide a surface of the national life." Robert Littell, another critic, two years following publication, estimated: "[I]f *Main Street* lives, it will probably be not as a novel but as an incident in American life."[22] Littell proved right, more prescient than he realized. Lewis and Harcourt pressed on to launch a rash of *incidents* which deeply identified American life itself, promulgated the country's vision of itself. With the 1922 publication of *Babbitt*, both an indictment of and a challenging paean to America's rising, business-oriented middle class, Lewis hit an even more sensitive nerve. *Babbitt* sold like hot cakes and was promoted like toothpaste; again a movie, again the title character quickly established itself within the nation's lexicon—to be a babbitt carried a lot of weight, good and bad. In 1924, Harcourt, Brace & Company rolled out *Arrowsmith* which again rocked the literary world, selling 100,000 copies the first month. The novel would continue to sell well, but not as well as *Main Street* and *Babbitt*—perhaps it was too high-falutin' with its focus on science and medicine. It was far less caricature; possibly Lewis's finest writing, its deeper "novelistic tendencies" may have detracted from the message. The storyline was a more

[21] Lingeman, 156. A quarter-century later, well beyond three million.
[22] Ibid.,162.

defined call for "America at its best." Academic and literary critic Harold Bloom noted decades later, "*Arrowsmith* has enough mythic force to compel a young reader to an idealism of her or his own."[23] An indictment of the commercialization of science and medical practice, *Arrowsmith* earned Lewis the 1925 Pulitzer Prize in literature. In a defiant rejection of the award, a tale of purported motives unto itself, the author further rocked those in the nation who paid attention to such matters. All the newspapers, metropolitan to small presses covered this latest Lewis scandal; given the increased commercialization of and popular interest in the literary scene (a heyday of literary magazines and journals), those paying attention were plentiful. The controversy was a market-street coup, further raising Lewis's "sensational" profile.

In 1926 Harcourt, Brace & Company staged Lewis's next commentary on the passing scene: "*Elmer Gantry* hit America like a Sunday punch in the jaw." Lewis, always notable, became certifiably notorious. He and Harcourt played the public and critics for all they were worth. Lingeman appraises their game:

> Harcourt's publicity strategy was to erect a fire wall between the controversy over the novel's subject (which ought to boost sales) and its literary merit (which ought to buttress Lewis's artistic reputation). As he explained to his author, "We are taking the line that the book is a great novel in the best tradition of English fiction, so that the inevitable scrap about it will heat up between the two groups of readers and go over the publishers' and perhaps to some extent, the author's head. The ad prepared for publication day was minimalist: it announced "Sinclair Lewis's Eagerly Awaited 'Preacher Novel' ELMER GANTRY."

Nothing more needed to be said. Minimalism heightened the excitement, a strategy Madison Avenue increasingly was taking to heart. Religion had become hot in America; two words told the whole story.[24]

The buzz had already commenced with the firm's and author's whispering campaign—"everyone" had picked up in the preceding

[23] Ibid, 257.

[24] Ibid., 300.

months on the news Lewis was taking on religion. The ad played on the anticipation and certain scandal. Once out, the jacket on *Gantry* sealed the deal with a simple attribution: "Lewis was the author of *Main Street*, *Babbitt*, and *Arrowsmith*."[25] Little more needed to be said—the country had become increasingly primed to the latest news.

Harcourt had arranged a first printing of a mammoth 138,000 copies. The Book-of-the-Month Club, recently founded as a commercial outreach to the middle-class, placed *Elmer Gantry* in its coveted main-selection slot. The day following *Gantry's* March, 1927 issue, Harcourt cabled Lewis across the Atlantic in Paris: "SALES ABOUT HUNDRED THOUSAND. NEWS STORIES EVERYWHERE. KANSAS STAR FIVE COLUMNS. REVIEWS VIOLENT EITHER WAY. CLERGY HOT. REORDERS ALREADY. LETTER AND CLIPPINGS MAILED. EVERYTHING LOVELY." Indeed the *Kansas City Star* was in effect the center-fold of the heartland press; and the heartland stood at the center of the book—a searing indictment of American Christianity "in-practice." Lingeman recollects, "The furor over *Elmer Gantry* gathered force like a cyclone and swept the book to the number-one position on the bestseller list, where it remained for most of the year. It sold 'like peanuts at a circus,' said *Literary Digest*."[26]

Gantry was a sparking tornado which generated in its path a firestorm of accolades and scorn. The strategy worked—to an extent; the intent to avoid "the inevitable scrap...between the two groups of readers" in the hope that it would "go over the publishers' and perhaps to some extent, the author's head" did not pan out. Harcourt and Lewis had appeared charmed, New Era success-stories; now they glowed red-hot, and the author was to be singed badly. Harry's hometown, which initially took umbrage at *Main Street*'s misperceived attack on them alone (and soon-enough warmed to its native son's celebrity and the tourist-dollars it generated) had welcomed the *Babbitt* boost to its fortunes followed by the critically hailed *Arrowsmith*. *Gantry* was received

---

[25] Ibid., 301.

[26] Ibid., 301. *Literary Digest* was considered a bell-weather of the national temper, or at least the temper of those who increasingly kept up with this sort of news.

as a lit bag of excrement tossed on the front porch. The Congregational minister, as well as Lewis family counsel, intuited Harry was a greater scoundrel than Elmer the gallivanting, bloviating, sinful, and highly charismatic preacher; *Gantry* offered insight "into the unclean mind of the author"; and conclusively, the sordid work indicated Harry's mind was "dead to goodness and purity and righteousness." Sauk Centre's son had grown up and devolved into cosmopolitan Red, a sensationalist hungering for mammon. The town coalesced around the view its son's irreverence was in part founded upon his disgusting personal life; far from the confines of Sauk Centre righteousness, Harry Lewis had sunk to the depths. Celebrity exacted its price; meanwhile, the author and publishing house cashed in big.[27]

Elmer Gantry was a high-caliber scandal in a decade of contretemps, and it was read everywhere. It quickly soared over the 200,000 sales mark. Harcourt and Lewis opted not to engage in a futile fight when the blasphemy was banned in Boston—a slight surely to guarantee more receipts. Schorer points out Harcourt, Lewis, and company missed no steps courting their national market: "The novel was advertised on five enormous billboards of the General Outdoor Advertising Company in New York, and in May of the following year, when the General Conference of the Methodist Church assembled in Kansas City, on forty-nine billboards including, in the center of the city, thirteen that were illuminated." Every media tool to embrace markets across the country was exploited. The New Era milieu was churning: a conglomeration of a bounty of goods, sales, and jazz; New Youth, New Women, New Negros, new mores—an age of novelty; all was alight with bright "white ways" as the raging electric grid spread its tentacles to all regions; all fueled by sensational news headlines hawking papers and magazines, the pot was boiling over. Bans popped up as librarians, booksellers, town and city fathers drew lines. "Every ban," writes Schorer, "provided the publishers with the least expensive form of promotion." Newspapers bannered the blacklists, making a farce of "the

[27] Ibid., 303.

entire Boston censorship folly" which had gone on for decades. Boston was old hat. Cash registers rang in the news.[28]

Lewis was skewered—and applauded—by the public, reviewers, politicians, editors, and ministers; a great controversy shook the nation already sensitized to the "faith issue" by celebrated media events as the Scopes Monkey Trial and the mesmerizing preaching and antics of the likes of Billy Sunday. In one sense Lewis was at the height of his game, unassailable in his celebrity as a national spokesman. In a more disturbing sense, he was a man increasingly in a bad way—his personal life did not bode well for the future. His marriage to Grace dissolved amidst all the hoopla, his drinking problems reached extremes, his whirlwind courtship and marriage to journalist Dorothy Thompson in May 1928 attracted further attention to his purported immorality—the novelist was spinning like a singed top, embers aloft everywhere and *Gantry* was a whole new level of scandal. The social commentator, always controversial, seemingly had reduced his work and his life to trash. All the glow Lewis projected was now seriously smudged. Always a workaholic, Lewis whirled on publishing *Dodsworth* in March 1929.

The novel capped a literary marathon as the writer made one more New Era effort to be taken with utmost seriousness, given acknowledgement that what he worked at was strong literature, possibly great. His works always were treated with reservations as to "literary quality." *Gantry*, he granted, made for an easy target; beyond the subject matter, Lewis was widely skewered for falling short in his quest to be honored a "man of literature." He was at peace with *Gantry*, no regrets, he never expected literary plaudits for this book. Now he had more to say about the United States, and he wanted to say it well—well enough to garner the respect he believed he had earned in tracking the national saga through five telling novels. *Dodsworth*, the tale of a considerably more refined and thoughtful babbitt who makes it big, a middle-American business tycoon in search of himself, stands to this day as a remarkable capstone to Lewis's decade.

---

[28] Schorer, 473. In the first six weeks sales numbered 175,000. See Hutchisson, 200.

The novel provides one last perusal at what had happened, what was going on with the U.S.A.; not incidentally it reflects Lewis's calm as he remarried and set his life in better order. Samuel Dodsworth is as much in search of the country's character and himself as Lewis. Less controversial by the longest shot from *Gantry*, staid as *Arrowsmith* yet drawing out a more emotive profile of a man in turmoil, *Dodsworth* is definitively less caricature, more "novel" as the literary set would have it. Lewis fittingly in 1929 of all years, six months before the Market Crash signaling the end of the New Era decade, had scored one more bull's eye. The novel is a substantive critique of emergent twentieth-century society and arguably one of his two best written works, the other being *Arrowsmith*. Sales were strong; the novel was well-received—with relief by a bevy of critics. In the future Lewis would publish many novels, good sales overall, and a few bull's eyes in terms of substantial social currency. Certainly he never drew out a cavalcade as consequential as the great five novels of the New Era. Those five had told the story he wanted to convey, for which he was primed and at his prime. It took him a decade, *his decade*—he had succeeded, he had made a deep mark on the national identity.

As a package the five formidable twenties novels comprised Lewis's statement about the nation and his craft; he had hit his stride, he had wanted to be hailed as a writer of note, and he had made a refreshed dash for recognition at the end of the day. Just possibly he had come, too, to understanding himself, as he had sought to comprehend his country. In 1930 Sinclair Lewis arose the first American Nobel Laureate of Literature; this time around he pulled no Pulitzer antics—this honor he accepted. He was at the top of his game. And so commenced the final chapters of his career which would proceed another two decades, but it was a downhill run. But that descent in no fashion should diminish the stature he had achieved.

Hutchisson in his study of Lewis's twenties body of work reiterates Malcolm Cowley's conclusion: "The real task of critics is not to explain the decline in each case, but rather to explain the height and nature of the achievement from which it started."[29] Lewis famously uttered in

[29] Ibid., 3.

response to the award, "This is fatal." He was in a maudlin mood but proved inadvertently prescient: "I cannot live up to it."[30] The award in itself hardly broadcast the end-game—still, he no longer would be in step with the *zeitgeist*. This was the seminal challenge which would come to haunt the author. Lewis's decade, the country's fling with the juvenile excesses and hefty challenges of modernity was over, and he would have little more of relevance to say. The author perceived change in the air, it was a matter of discussion the last years of the twenties, but he did not envision how far away from the decade the country was about to move nor its literature. The Nobel, as so much about Lewis, would prove controversial: did he deserve it; for what exactly—his writing, sociology, currency, worst his crass celebrity? It was the United States' long anticipated Stockholm turn, and Lewis to the dismay of many of the literati of all people stood center stage. While the questionable status of the U.S.A.'s identity remained *au courant*, wasn't Lewis *passé*? The literary scholars, the New Humanists, aspiring Modernists, established Realists, the Marxists, all and sundry scurried to have a say. The novelist of late had been considered decaying wood (and not high-grade to begin with) in their haunts. Their vantage point upon the passing scene, and Lewis all along, was hardly representative of the popular view—the public liked to read the author and valued his outlook. Another Lewis contretemps was in full swing; the literary world was up in arms.

The medal was given singularly for *Babbitt* and compositely for the five outstanding works of the past decade. Lewis, all acknowledged, was hotly read in the U.S.A.; and his work had brought him an international readership. Lingeman writes, "Most observers, at home and abroad, agreed that Lewis, better than any novelist of his day, had mapped the topography of American society." The Swedish Academy in presenting the award purposely signaled that the U.S. had stepped up: Sinclair Lewis spoke for American culture in the twenties, for the volcanic New Era. Erik Axel Karlfeldt, the Swedish critic who made the presentation, summarized: "Yes, Sinclair Lewis is an American. He writes the new language—American—as one of the representatives of

[30] Schorer, 543.

120,000,000 souls. He asks us to consider that this nation is not yet finished or melted down; that it is still in the turbulent years of adolescence."[31] Despite his ever-nagging blues, Lewis was standing tall—swooning in the *zeitgeist*. In Stockholm he did not nurse serious worries over his headliner status, nor the elites harping at his heels. The controversy raged for a month as banner news. And then it was onto the back pages, as any sensation. No problem for the novelist—he anticipated he would continue to write, address what mattered, maintain his position as an interpreter of the American Experience.

In the years to come, while the U.S.A. was hardly finished, it became apparent Lewis had ended his brilliant run. Amongst all the debris to be piled up in the country over the next decade, the literary world chucked Sinclair Lewis; alongside they tossed off all he had accomplished in one ferocious decade. "The real task of critics is not to explain the decline"—appreciate the achievement, Malcolm Cowley had urged. Amid the analysis, praise, carping, and gossip surrounding the Nobel, the *New York Times* took its gauge of the author: "His talents are far from the highest, but when reinforced by the sustained sale of his books…he is the most representative of living American writers." The "newspaper of record" observed the twenties had passed; the Nobel came "when the temper of the country seems definitely to have turned away from the Main Street and Babbitt formula." Malcolm Cowley still had his sights on the whole story: critics must "explain the height and nature of the achievement." Errantly, that over the next century would be misread.

Lewis knew what he was about, his strengths, foibles, what he was after. He had a bead on the rambunctious decade and his country's destiny. As a writer he had read his decade well, and he had successfully translated it to the public. Heywood Broun, one of the *Time's* most

---

[31] Lingeman, 354 and 356–57. Hutchisson points out: "By 1930 eleven of Lewis's thirteen books had been translated into Russian, German, and Polish; seven into Hungarian, Danish, Norwegian, and Czech; six into French; four into Dutch; two into Spanish; and one, *Babbitt*, into Italian and Hebrew." Lewis had been angling with Harcourt the entire decade to land the Nobel; Scandinavian publication was part of the strategy. See 204.

prominent critics, noted in his column Lewis was "old hat," a member of the "old guard," that the "radical cause" was now the literary vogue. New times called for new perspectives; critic Harry Hansen claimed younger writers had located a "new realism." John Dos Passos, about to burst onto the stage with *Manhattan Transfer* followed up by his searing focus on good and hard times, *U.S.A. Trilogy*, blandly set the novelist and his ilk aside: "Anyway, the Jazz Age is dead." The temper of the times turned acidic: Lewis was played out.[32]

The country was a year into the Great Depression. The stock market had tanked, the economy had imploded for a variety of reasons, and the United States of America was collapsing on itself. The New Era, month by grueling month, year following year was swept away, swamped in a disparaged past. Some would come to disparage the thirties as the dirty decade. At the announcement of Lewis's Nobel, Calvin Coolidge dry-panned "no necessity exists for becoming excited. What is important is not what some writer represents us to be, but what we really are."[33] Coolidge had been wrapped tight in Lewis's purported denigration of modern America—the author even had mocked the president in a light-weight twenties novel. The ex-president had no stake in the literary wars, yet it may have been sweet revenge to have the final say. As it was, he, too, was washed away in the deluge. The twenties Coolidge Era had imploded. Still, "what we really are" was dead-on—this is what the newer era's authors would be after. This had been Lewis's ground. Lewis's take had been praised as bordering on the impeccable; now the Jazz Age was a *fait accompli*. American identity was not. Lewis no longer would merit the notice he had long been accorded. The world within which he had thrived had radically shifted. Writers aplenty—Dos Passos, Steinbeck, Wright, Conroy, Hurston, and Gold would tap deep into the malaise of the uneasy thirties, *their decade*. That in no way discounts the fact that for ten years Lewis had stood front and center—because he belonged there. He understood, he probed, he tried to get at just who the American people were, what they wanted for themselves, of themselves. It was never formulaic with the

---

[32] Lingeman, 354–55 and 362.
[33] Ibid., 353.

writer. He was in on the long hunt same as the nation. He, as Americans for centuries, had pondered identity, the country's story. He was a prominent consultant in an era he had fit like a glove; now he was falling out of fashion, marooned in the past, much to his chagrin passing year by year deeper into critically perceived irrelevance. It was a mean insult.

The author was stuck...as the country at loose ends. He knew he had a lot of babbitt in himself, and always said so; he never denied he liked Babbitt—he simply had wanted to make him a better man. He wanted the businessman to mature, rise to a higher standard. He had not; nor apparently had the nation. The criticism, the dismissal, the snide denigration found its mark, and the author hurt. Ernest Boyd in a stinging critique earlier in the mid-twenties observed Lewis dressed to the nines strutting New York:

> Tall, slim and well-barbered; his sandy hair sleeked down on either side of an immaculate parting; his clothes carefully pressed; two inches of shirt cuff showing; his shoes well-shined—Sinclair Lewis looks the personification of conventional elegance, as badly dressed as only the wearer of standardized fashions for men can be.... Sartorially he realizes the ideal of the supporters of nationalized products, "authentic styles for the better-dressed man".... He looks the part of an aggressive, forward-looking, up-standing citizen, a sales promoter of ability, a key man and live wire....

Boyd wrapped up, "His appearance does not belie his activities, for Sinclair Lewis is the drummer of ideas, the sales executive of the new American literature...[J]ust like the hero of a success magazine story." At base, "He has discovered, like so many of his countrymen, that it pays to advertise...Babbitt." And Boyd emphasized just how base it was; no fan of the decade's excesses, he pictured Lewis its poster boy. And now a few years after Boyd had raked over the author, the decade's new literature had become old stuff. Babbitt now that the party had ended faced bankruptcy, and Lewis had run short of currency; his stock-in-trade had become dated. Boyd had nailed "a key man and live wire, who works entirely on leads and full organization support, 80 per cent of whose annual business consists of repeat orders." The nation now was in arrears; an accounting was in order; Red Lewis, as so many washed aside in the "dirty thirties," was at a loss—still, for all his shortcomings no one ever took the author for a charlatan. In the twenties heyday Boyd, for all the flair of his slander had misread the man: Sinclair Lewis was no clown in the Roaring Twenties; the novelist was attuned to his day and spoke—wrote—volumes.[34]

This loss of standing for Lewis bore a particularly cruel quality. Critic Ludwig Lewisohn, long a great admirer (he, too, would part ways) once observed the writer "seemed to have no inner certainty, no balance, no serenity, nothing between heaven and earth to which he could withdraw for quietude or healing. He did and said things that, as I well knew, outraged his true self [and] depressed us all by his clamorous but unmistakable unhappiness."[35] Lewisohn had been perceptive, keying in on what drove Lewis to write as well as he had. As outrageous as he could be, in his personal unease, he caught the nation's attention in the 1920s for what he addressed, for what he and so many seemed to be looking for, for some sort of reconcilable, respectable identity. Schorer summarizes when Lewis published *Our Mr. Wrenn* back in 1915, it was clear that while he was not yet selling, and he had a lot of growth ahead of him, his work already demonstrated he was on to something essential. The young author was praised by reviewers

---

[34] Schorer, 398. Boyd just as well could have mocked Coolidge who Lewis parodied. One of his two less successful twenties novels was *The Man Who Knew Coolidge: Being the Soul of Lowell Schmaltz, Constructive and Nordic Citizen* (New York: Harcourt, Brace and Company), 1928. Fleming, *Sinclair Lewis,* cites most critics forgave "Lewis his two lighter works of the 1920s, *Mantrap* (1926) and *The Man Who Knew Coolidge* (1928): A typical reaction to *Mantrap* was the assertion Lewis had the right to toss off a minor work from time to time, whether he did it to make money or simply to amuse himself." Lewis declared of the work sometimes one needed the cash. See viii. Sinclair Lewis, *Mantrap: A Story of the Northern Wilds* (New York: Harcourt, Brace & Company), 1928.

[35] Lingeman, 309.

> for his realism—the carefully detailed scenes of ordinary life, the ordinary characters and their colloquial speech, the rather good-natured social satire...—in its combination with a prevailingly optimistic point of view, an optimism that, while never denying the existence of cruelty and greed and suffering, was yet capable of sentimental nonsense on the one hand and, on the other, of a rather admirable liberal individualism derived from Wells and best summarized in America by Herbert Croly's book *The Promise of American Life*, published in the very year of *Mr. Polly*. Mr. Wrenn was a large part of that promise."[36]

Ah yes, *that promise.*

Optimism had been a constant: The country's ethos was "make the Experiment a go." As that promise took a devastating hit in the Great Depression, the New Era became the nemesis, in hindsight amongst elite social commentators paradoxically demonstrative of an egregious low point in the nation's quest for higher ground. Lewis was harshly charged in retrospect for having missed the underlying corrosion of the Roaring Twenties; worse, he represented it. He was, looking back—yes Boyd in a sense had been prescient—just another salesman; now thrown back on his heels, never respectable to start. He, who wrote so well of the nation's shortcomings in that decade, remained for many thirties elite observers appropriately *that* decade's poster boy. It was a simplistic revelation.

Two decades later, looking back on his notable run, the novelist was perplexed. He remained, while falling out of step with the distemper of the times, good enough to stay a popular novelist, albeit one not taken so seriously as he had once been. Lewis decried in 1949: "I am the diagnostician. I don't know what to do about anything. I am not a reformer. I really don't care."[37] He claimed he never had solutions, and he had none now. But he had been dead serious the entire time, and he always would be; progress was his mainstay, set the country on the right track. At base

[36] Schorer, 213–14. British novelist Wells sat high in Lewis's esteem; and Wells became a huge admirer.

[37] Ibid., 797; *New York Times* interview on the event of his sixty-fifth birthday.

he was an optimist—he looked forward, argued for growth. He attempted to redirect the country by diagnosing ills with an eye on the American Experiment; he placed his faith in the country's ability, once recognizing its shortcomings, to move on, tinker, work out the solutions as it always somehow found its way. It had mattered that *he* get the larger picture right. In the twenties he was credited for pointing out what was wrong; and many if not most it would seem caught he was, too, encouraging what was right, what was good about the country. For the rest of his career, he was at a loss; in short, he could not take in the problems of the depression decade nor the trial of the second world war and its aftermath. It was not easy to admit. Simply, for Lewis, the fact was *his decade*, his magnificent rise in stature, was over.

In the twenties Lewis took pride he was respected for his insight. In 1950 dying it would have been good if he could have considered that two difficult decades had passed, the country had held together through the Depression, a global war "against evil" had been waged, and the mid-century United States was embarked on a further exhilarating surge along its odyssey, never quite there, never perfection, but striving for it. He might well have contended he had had it right. The country just needed to "keep at it." Shed the excess, get back to restoring high aims—that was what most mattered. The optimism was back: the emerging postwar middle-class surge to prosperity, the acquisition of not only more "better than ever" goods but a reenergized baseline stability was gestating. Lewis always had that faith, that sense the country could pick itself up. And yes, in 1950 problems, some old and some new, needed to be addressed; there were authors, good diagnosticians at work; Lewis by this late date was too worn out to take up the task again. He was no longer the writer he once was, and the U.S. was long past the New Era, his area of specialty. But he had counted. And the arc of progress he beheld held true. Yes, in the words of the Swedish Academy back in the twenties the national adolescence had ended and the country had been whipsawed into a new maturity. That country having tangled through the twenties for a better understanding of itself was better for the effort. Lewis, a formidable twenties figure, had completed his diagnoses and they bore hardy substance, reflection in their day, worthy of reflection long past his day. He had made his contribution. It would have been good if he did sense that his middle-class, all-American diagnosis had held true—the country had in it the wherewithal; it just had to keep taking a close look at itself. There is no evidence he had recognized he deserved to be satisfied—Lewis really never had that in him anyway.

Two generations beyond the crash, few came to recognize the author deserved reconsideration. Author and critic Alfred Kazin would judge Lewis's subsequent work pointless. Most of the elite did, all those years. It was not, Kazin argued, that the later novels were inferior to the twenties work. They simply did not drill down into what mattered. James Hutchisson starting out his analysis says it right: "Lewis simply lost touch with the times. He was a satirist with nothing left to satirize." Really, he was much more—he had gotten America right; and his prognosis for the country held true—this is an experiment that takes constant vigilance. Satire demands freshness, and the novelist no longer attuned to the *zeitgeist*, for whatever the reason, could not keep at it in his best fashion. He was at his best a man of the twenties. He had in that span trumpeted the nation has its flaws and its possibilities. In the postwar decades the country worked at securing the order Lewis most believed in: the United States, middle-class to its core. How did Kazin not get it? Lewis deserved better. Generations further on that remains true.[38]

Lingeman senses that standing at Stockholm the Nobel Laureate could not assuage "his inner doubts or banish the knowledge that he was being honored for work already fast receding into the past."[39] Perhaps so; it is not clear. However, at the end of his life, despite dismissing himself as not caring, he remained a reformer. This was not a world he could reform; to his credit he did try those last two decades to remain current. He practiced what he preached: one had to keep working, improving. It was sad. He continued a search he had launched in the twenties to write the great labor novel. But he never could effectively connect with the working man's world. Even in the thirties when labor became red-hot, he could not intuitively grasp the moment, embrace

---

[38] Hutchisson, 2.

[39] Lingeman, 359.

the cause; he tried repeatedly, but he never would write that story.[40] Dorothy Thompson, after his death, recalled in a letter written to the first Mrs. Lewis, to Grace: "He simply could not write about a world of which he had no first-hand experience. When he decided to drop the project, he explained to me that it was because 'I know it will be phoney. The only class I understand is the one to which I belong—the middle class.'"[41] Exactly (although he hardly was middle-class in most senses of the word)...but after 1929 the evolving challenges to the middle class for which he cared a lot no longer resonated with him. Harrowing times, highly politicized, conflict in the streets, this was not a middle-class story; World War Two, not his sort of story; postwar recovery, no; Communism and Red Scares, no. Lewis was no longer, as his friend and critic Carl Van Doren had once said, "a seismograph of the zeitgeist." And yet the country, by 1950, was indeed back on track, as he always prognosticated was possible.[42]

---

[40] Lewis struggling over the labor novel in 1930 wrote a "fellow, more genuine 'activist'": "I still may do the labor novel some day, but I think it will probably be in very different form from that in which I was planning it. It is not a question of its being more or less radical. It is a question of its being more a novel of character and less one of ideas and propaganda, because the novel of character is really the only one I can do with any success." Schorer notes: "The working class, in whatever state of organization or disorganization, and whatever its aspirations, was not the middle class." See 548 and 527. Lingeman comments on Lewis's political philosophy: "Lewis didn't see himself as a commercial sellout; his broad political sympathies were still socialistic. Ramon Guthrie [another labor activist and close colleague] called him a negative socialist who 'took it for granted that, by and large, politicians are scoundrels and governments more or less consciously contrived swindles to enable small cliques to exploit the masses' but who didn't believe in Marxism and had no theory about what should replace the present system." See 324. Hutchisson offers a strong assessment; see particularly 91–94 and chapter six, "The Labor Novel and the Nobel Prize: 1929–1930," 193–209.

[41] Ibid., 202.

[42] Ibid., 354. Lewis published twenty-one novels. Late in life, blue over his reputation, he remarked, "If my books are read fifty years from now, it's because I did for America what Dickens did for England." Despondent, leaving the U.S. one last time, he considered, "I've given my life to this country in

The novelist was by no means totally out of touch; simply he now could only weigh in as a distanced spectator on a society facing differently nuanced challenges than did the babbitts of the twenties. He was not indifferent—he shared the concern of most over the nation's welfare. His heart was not into the economic or political challenge—never had been a nuts-and-bolts fellow. He had his moments. Alerted to the dangers of fascism abroad and at home, he struck lightning in 1935 releasing *It Can't Happen Here*, a gripping tale of home-grown fascism taking devastating root in a panicked middle-class America.[43] It was

---

the best way, and no one cares." Scharnhorst and Hofer, 311–12. Not quite true: Scharnhorst and Hofer cite in 1998 Modern Library editors chose *Main Street* as the "68th best English language novel of the twentieth century" ahead of amongst other Wharton's *The House of Mirth*, Hemingway's *A Farewell to Arms*, Joyce's *Finnegans Wake*, Conrad's *Jim*, and London's *The Call of the Wild*. In 1999 *Arrowsmith* was ranked 78th best novel of the century "besting Willa Cather's *My Antonia*." See Ibid, 2. Lewis's work continues to make the rankings.

[43] Sinclair Lewis, *It Can't Happen Here* (New York: New American Library), 2005. The novel still grips; sales skyrocketed following the November 2016 election. Lewis scored large sales and respectable reviews for *Ann Vickers* (Garden City, NY: Doubleday, Doran, 1933); *Cass Timberlane* (New York: Random House, 1945); and *Kingsblood Royal* (New York: Random House, 1947). Lingeman argues *Ann Vickers* is his most woman-centered book; it "had more talk about sex than any previous Lewis novel and was laced with controversial plot elements like abortion, adultery, and lesbianism." This was new terrain for an author considered adverse to such topics. See Ibid., 386. *Cass Timberlane* was more a throwback to the plight of the conventional midwestern, middle-class male, but it was well-received; its sales approached half a million; Lewis easily made over half a million dollars from it and magazine and movie contracts. *Kingsblood Royal* was path-breaking as the modern civil rights era was coalescing. While not his expertise, and it showed, Lewis grasped the centrality race would hold in the postwar decades, and it created a sensation in its day. Hence in his wilderness years he occasionally had a perceptive sense of current maladies. None of these works were published by Harcourt, Brace and Company. As was his wont, Lewis had fallen out with Harcourt in 1930. Prominent publishing houses were quick to pick up a cash-cow. He continued to write stories and commentaries for popular magazines, newspaper articles, literary

Dorothy Thompson, ever attuned to foreign and domestic challenges, who raised the alarm for him. The book was artistically adequate; more to the point it excited reviewers taken by its currency and political punch, and it sold big. But that was it—the author had little more to say about current affairs. There was one more noteworthy exception in the late forties—Lewis published *Kingsblood Royal*, which aggressively addressed the issue of racism in American society. Norman Grebstein concludes "he tried in his own way to deal with the turmoil of the 1930s, but too often...his work[s]—so fresh and original in the previous decade—appear self-contradictory, tired, confused, contrived, and even anachronistic." And so, too, beyond the thirties. The exception(s) prove the point: Lewis just needed to find his footing, find a topic he prized; that had been the 1920s.[44]

---

critiques and book reviews, plays and screenplays; he occasionally acted and taught college courses; he lectured. Lewis always was supportive of young writers. He still could garner attention: *Time Magazine* for a second time (the first was in the 1920s) ran a decidedly complimentary cover story on the author upon publication of *Cass Timberlane*. Edmund Wilson observed, having just returned from war-wracked Europe, that the novel was just right to assist him to understand the U.S. Lewis had been so long about "that he has become a familiar object, like Henry Ford or the Statue of Liberty, about which, if one has been living in America, one does not think very much." A dubious compliment, but still he considered the novelist "one of the national poets"—beyond his "notorious faults." Wilson held Lewis's take on the middle-class's prominence in the American story remained strong—after depression and war it might be the tonic the country needed. Lewis for Wilson, then still held some relevance after all. See ibid., 487.

[44] Grebstein, 124. "[W]ith the coming of the Depression, the stable middle-class world based on peace, prosperity, and business as usual, the world to which Lewis was inextricably attached, fell under assault by political, social and economic forces which Lewis was either not fully equipped to comprehend or unable to depict convincingly." "The very affluence of American life, which Lewis had turned to artistic advantage in the 1920s, by attacking it, had vanished.... Babbitt could sustain no further onslaught nor furnish the substance for additional satire." Grebstein addresses the labor manuscripts, "Sinclair Lewis's Unwritten Novel," *Philological Quarterly* 37 (October 1958): 400–09.

Lewis was not just out of sorts with the remaining "news." His personal life remained in turmoil. He and Dorothy had shared happy and fraught years. They had a son, Michael, to whom as with his son Wells with Grace he could not be intimate either within the house or removed from the fractious family circle. His dipsomania along with the insecurities both he and Dorothy nursed, all the more frustrated by dueling careers—hers definitely on the rise and his sinking—created untenable strains and finally divorce. Wells was killed in Europe during World War II. Lewis carried forth, on-the-wagon, off, moving locale to locale, making scenes, continuing his practice of public quarrels with all those around him, and writing. His body was ravaged—he looked decades older than he was; his mind had strayed far from its famed acuity. Late in the game, in 1950, he took one last go searching for that illusive equilibrium, landing in Italy. He died in Rome just short of his sixty-sixth birthday.

Lewis's death received considerable attention in the United States and overseas, the obituaries measuring his career in the light of decline. He died rich, only further fortifying some critics' dismissal of the materialistic arc of his work. Schorer, having barely tolerated Lewis through eight hundred-plus pages, cruelly chronicles his final collapse: Lewis had settled in a marbled faux palace, a monstrous relic of Fascist Italy in the hills above Florence—"a kind of joke among Americans in Florence, being at once so ostentatious and impractical"—perched high above the Plain of the Jesters, where in the Renaissance "troops of traveling buffoons and jongleurs camped at night...." Lewis's life was not always a pretty picture, but he was no buffoon. His ashes, Schorer reports, were shipped home where a small gathering came together to bury "our latter-day jester" in Sauk Centre.[45] On his gravestone, his

---

[45] Schorer, 777 and 788. Schorer never camouflaged his distaste. Gore Vidal, not the most empathetic of figures, wrote scathingly: "[I]t would seem impossible that a mere biographer could effectively eliminate a popular and famous novelist; yet that is exactly what Mark Schorer managed to do.... Schorer's serene loathing of his subject and all his works is impressive in its purity, but, at the end, one is as weary of Schorer himself as of Lewis. I once asked Schorer, an amiable man who liked to drink almost as much as Lewis

final epitaph was simply carved, “Sinclair Lewis, Author of Main Street.” A lot more could have been said. Perhaps though that was all that needed to be said—after all, all for which he might have been further noted stemmed from that initial burst into the national consciousness.[46]

Lewis died January 10, 1951. John Farrar, editor of *The Bookman*, back in 1922 dismissed the newly released *Babbitt* as second-rate; he assaulted the novelist for shortchanging his talent demonstrated in *Main Street*, selling out to crassness and a lust for wealth. He prophesized, “If he died suddenly, you would find written on his heart, in blinking electric bulbs of letters, those two magic words.” He got the gravestone right, but he misconceived its import: Lewis never sold out. *Main Street*, indeed, was the first huge novel; and all the others huge as well in the twenties built upon its theme. Farrar misread *Babbitt*; the novel was true to the author's literary charge as he conceived it. However, Farrar was right in that it all ultimately came back to main street—"what America was all about” is exactly what Lewis continued to tackle in *Babbitt*, *Arrowsmith*, *Elmer Gantry*, and *Dodsworth*. Farrar claimed back in 1922 Lewis knew he was just a main streeter at heart. Yes, he had that right, too.[47]

---

did, why he had taken on a subject that he so clearly despised. The long answer was money; the short, too.” It does not sound as if Lewis, as a fictioneer might have it, had been queried (as always posed in the Sunday *New* York *Times* “Book Review's” interviews with authors) “If you had a chance, what three figures would you invite to a dinner,” he would choose Schorer and Vidal—or maybe he would just to stir things up. Gore Vidal, “The Romance of Sinclair Lewis.” *New York Review of Books*, October 8, 1992. http://www.nybooks.com.

[46] Lingeman, xxiii.

[47] John Farrar, “The Literary Spotlight,” *Bookman*, September, 1922: 54–59, www.unz.com. Farrar by the end of the decade had a more nuanced view of Lewis's strengths.

THREE

AMERICAN IDENTITY

Sinclair Lewis singularly was more than the Author of Main Street. Through the 1920s he contributed to the genesis of twentieth-century American identity. He was one among many cultural voices; his work was seminal to what in essence was a centuries-long national discussion. The multi-faceted dialogue primarily was engaged by and about Christian white males, assessing an America traditionally foreclosed to the voices of an array of "others." Still, those who endeavored to make the U.S. work, fulfill its promise, all along despite their own shortcomings and the country's, moved society toward a more progressive vision of that "city on a hill"; and still there were too many who did not have a chance to weigh in, and still do not. There are plenty of lessons to be learned. James M. Hutchisson, studying Lewis's formidable twenties novels, demonstrates contextually how Lewis "selected usable materials and shaped them, through his unique vision, into novels that reached and remained part of the American imagination."[1] Lewis worked with what he knew, and readers responded to what they recognized. In the decades following the end of World War Two and into the first quarter of the twenty-first century, Americans have become increasingly enriched by the recognition that other, equally genuine perspectives, unearthing the ever elusive "story" must be heard. All by rights must have a say in any national dialogue and all by it should profit. Cultural historians over the same period have come to understand how complex this process, this American Experiment, remains. Sinclair Lewis in the early-twentieth century, hardly alone, stood forth, and stood out ferreting out what the United States was up to. The author prized history, he studied it, and he applied it. He proved to be in the end a spot-on cultural historian, as E. M. Forster had recognized.

---

[1] James M. Hutchisson, *The Rise of Sinclair Lewis, 1920–1930* (University Park: Pennsylvania State University Press), 1996, 4.

The New Era at base rested on an amorphous middle-class ideal: the good life—the new American Standard. It would be reiterated in the depression-wracked thirties as the American Dream—in crisis, in need of resuscitation. Lewis understood the U.S. to be what historian Alan Brinkley describes "a vision of middle-class prosperity and stability.... a dream of personal achievement and fulfillment—an individual, not a social, dream."[2] This in effect always was the rub: the dream of individuals shared by a competitive society with a purported social conscience, a faith in community—tricky philosophical terrain for a noble endeavor. The American Promise: Lewis was no philosopher, no ideologue—he just believed his countrymen and women had it within them, amidst the bursting bounds of their society, to secure a "good life." Richard Lingeman notes, "His advice was perfectly sound but left Lewis open to the criticism that was to dog his entire career: that he could only complain and had nothing better to offer."[3] That critique, Lewis as scold, simply is not supportable. Lingeman is well aware his advice was on-the-mark. The novelist projected before the public a reflection of the country-at-large—perhaps at times a fun-house distortion, but it made an awful lot of sense. He gave millions something to think about: the U.S.A. could do a lot better by living up to its ideals, or just as well his ideals—there existed a lot of overlap between the two. Yes, as he acknowledged, he was weak on specific solutions, but he could get at the nub of the matter. His countrymen were destined to progress to loftier heights. The diagnostician has as much to contribute as the theorist.

America for a clutch of centuries has held itself aloft with a self-defined epochal air. Whether in myth or reality, and the two easily merge, the United States has been fashioned a land of diverse opportunities by any number of groups, leaders, activists, commentators, artists, and ordinary men and women. The U.S. took on a retooled identity in the twentieth century. Decimal markers always deceive, but historians

[2] Alan Brinkley, *Culture and Politics in the Great Depression* (Waco: Markham Press Fund, 1999), 5.

[3] Richard Lingeman, *Sinclair Lewis: Rebel from Main Street* (New York: Random House, 2002), 132–33.

agree a mammoth urban-industrial order clearly emerged by the turn of the century. By the 1920s twentieth-century America as we have come to understand it had reached maturity—or advanced adolescence, keeping with emergent sociological and marketing norms. The U.S.A. manufactured lots of goods and hopes. "America" appeared cross-cut by an energized competitive spirit, a variegated commitment to community, and distinctive strains of confidence and fear; it was contoured by small-town ideals, increasingly urban norms, and a tangible claim of classlessness nestled within an intangible sense of homogenizing middle-class identity. By the early twenties a majority toasted, albeit illegally, a New Era, energized by a triumphant ethos which soon would be dubbed an American Way of Life, a huge middle-class success story.[4]

Middle-class identity audaciously was in the making. A century later it purportedly remains in streamlined production, and as always occurs, hits rough patches. With good reason as the middling demographic sinks in size given diminishing opportunities the past half-

---

[4] This analysis first appeared in Edward Gale Agran, *Too Good a Town: William Allen White and the Emerging Rhetoric of Middle America* (Fayetteville: University of Arkansas Press, 1998) followed by *Herbert Hoover and the Commodification of Middle-Class America* (Lanham, MD: Lexington Books, 2016). The metamorphosis into a twentieth-century order is drawn by complementary studies proliferating particularly across the end of the twentieth century and the early years of the twenty-first. For a cross-section: Robert H. Wiebe, *The Search for Order, 1877–1920* (New York: Hill and Wang, 1967); Lawrence Goodwyn, *The Populist Moment: A Short History of the Agrarian Revolt in America* (Oxford: Oxford University Press, 1978); Daniel T. Rodgers, *The Work Ethic in Industrial America, 1850–1920* (Chicago: University of Chicago Press, 1979); T.J. Jackson Lears, *No Place of Grace: Antimodernism and the Transformation of American Culture, 1880–1920* (Chicago: University of Chicago, 1994); Richard Wightman Fox and T.J. Jackson Lears, eds., *The Culture of Consumption: Critical Essays in American History, 1880–1980* (New York: Pantheon Books, 1983); Kathleen G. Donahue, *Freedom from Want: American Liberalism and the Idea of the Consumer* (Baltimore: Johns Hopkins University Press, 2003); Joan Shelley Rubin, *The Making of Middlebrow Culture* (Chapel Hill: University of North Carolina Press, 1992); Meg Jacobs, *Pocketbook Politics: Economic Citizenship in Twentieth-Century America* (Princeton: Princeton University Press, 2005).

century, many argue the assembly line has broken down. This always has been an element of the continuing saga as social and economic forces push in a national tug-of-war.

Middle-class identity: decidedly rooted in an older story, one of real opportunity enmeshed within a frontier mythology. Americans, the lore passes, march toward new horizons. By the turn of the century, the country had definitively moved on beyond its rough-hewn origins. The 1890 census broadcast the news, and a host of commentators wrote the obituaries for the passing frontier. For historians and the educated, Frederick Jackson Turner's 1893 address *The Significance of the Frontier in American History* signaled the possibilities of a new ideological vantage point on western progress which as always was grounded upon congeries of older truths and myths. The frontier, geographically corralled, remained in Turner's view a vital if ephemeral asset to the nation's future. Richard Slotkin, *The Fatal Environment: The Myth of the Frontier in the Age of Industrialism, 1800–1890* assesses the role of the frontier as an idea. He advises a "process of mythogenesis, breakdown, cooptation, and mythic renewal informs the history of culture." The scholar views the frontier not only as a still viable concept, but essential to American identity: myths are regenerative, current, and ideologically laden; they are "central to the cultural functioning of the society that produces them."[5]

[5] Frederick Jackson Turner, "The Significance of the Frontier in American History," in *The Frontier in American History*, ed. Frederick Jackson Turner (New York: Henry Holt and Company, 1921), 1–38. Richard Slotkin, *The Fatal Environment: The Myth of the Frontier in the Age of Industrialism, 1800–1890* (New York: Harper Perennial, 1994), 25 and 16. See especially chapters one and two. Patricia Nelson Limerick reasserts the frontier's ideological vitality in her confessional, "Turnerians All: The Dream of a Helpful History in an Intelligible World," *American Historical Review* 100 (June 1995): 697–716. Continuous study attests to resilient interest in the myth. See Richard W. Etulain, ed., *Does the Frontier Experience Make America Exceptional?* (Boston: Bedford/St. Martin's, 1999) and Allan G. Bogue, *Frederick Jackson Turner: Strange Roads Going Down* (Norman: University of Oklahoma Press, 1998). For "new western" historiography see Clyde A. Milner II, ed., *A New Significance: Re-envisioning the History of the American West* (New York:

Bright horizons: a new middle class was establishing itself across a national domain—the ideal of a vast middle-ground American demographic dates from the early-seventeenth century. Robert Wiebe midway through the twentieth century took note: the middle class at the end of the nineteenth had stretched beyond traditional geographical contours; association was coming to trump location in a sophisticated commercial complex; status, once closely bound by local ties, not only was fluid, it flowed through newly established national structures—the American Bar Association, the American Federation of Labor, the Women's Christian Temperance Union, the National Association for the Advancement of Colored People—scores of continental organizations. James Oliver Robertson assesses what this came to mean in less structured but far-reaching terms: middle class "does not signify the self-contained, middle order of a structure with lower and upper orders—as it does for Europeans." It is more similar to the Chinese Middle Kingdom. "For Americans, the 'middle'—whether middle class, Middle West, or middle American—is a large, solid, geographical center of almost limitless extent. Around and beyond it are other, haphazardly arranged areas of varying, but entirely peripheral, importance." America's middle-class culture was coming of age—bursting britches, slipping on modern garb. People knew it when they saw it but it was not easy to define. Most agreed as all along across U.S. history middling standing was a coveted commodity. By the end of the first decade of the new century, a novel, expansive, opportunity-laden frontier was in process of settlement.[6]

Oxford University Press, 1996) and Robert V. Hine, John Mack Faragher, and Jon T. Coleman, eds., *The American West: A New Interpretive History*, 2nd ed. (New Haven: Yale University Press, 2017). Stephen Aron, "The American West Reprised, Revised, and Revived," *Reviews in American History* 28 (June 2000): 245–50 surveys the field a century following Turner.

[6] For a complementary re-examination see Kenneth Cmiel, "Destiny and Amnesia: The Vision of Modernity in Robert Wiebe's 'The Search for Order,'" in Stanley I. Kutler, ed., *American Retrospectives: Historians on Historians* (Baltimore: Johns Hopkins University Press, 1995), 294–310; Ian Tyrell, "Robert Wiebe's *The Search for Order*, Fifty Years On." *Journal of the Gilded Age and Progressive Era* 17 (April 2018): 397–411. Myth research emerged a

Cultural historians during the last quarter of the twentieth century took note of what had evolved. Slotkin observes, "Since even a shattered mythology preserves elements of the cultural past, the new mythology will inevitably find connection with the old: indeed, the readiest way to renew the force of a weakened mythology is to link new ideology to the traditional imagery of existing myth." This was highly contested terrain, a hugely staked power game—nothing new in United States history. Increasingly myth-making took on a clear-cut twentieth-century identity.

> If we choose to study national popular culture, we should see it not as a national folklore but as the myth medium of the victorious party in an extended historical struggle. It has come to represent the mythology and ideology of those groups or classes whose political and economic concerns and cultural predilections have by and large dominated and directed the course of American social, economic, and political development—entrepreneurs and corporate directors, salesmen and promoters, entertainers and purveyors of grand ideas.

---

century beyond Turner. Slotkin, *Fatal*, assesses the wider field, 536 note four. Memory research arose. See David Thelen, "Memory and American History," *Journal of American History* 75 (March 1989): 1117–1221; Mike Wallace, *Mickey Mouse History and Other Essays on American Memory* (Philadelphia: Temple University Press, 1996). James Oliver Robertson, *American Myth, American Reality* (New York: Hill & Wang, 1980), 260 is provocative. A strong complement to Wiebe and Robertson's views of shifting outlooks on community is Thomas Bender, *Community and Social Change in America* (Baltimore: Johns Hopkins University Press, 1982). For American middle-class history see Robert D. Johnston and Burton J. Bledstein, eds., *The Middling Sorts: Explorations in the History of the American Middle Class* (New York: Routledge, 2001). Johnston observes while "a considerable tradition of historical study of the American middle class has developed in postwar America," work remains "where we might next proceed in our studies of that great beast that so defines the United States." It is "a call to our higher democratic selves." See 296–97. See Bledstein's introduction confronting challenges to establishing middle-class identity, 1–25.

The grandiosity of the game was a narcotic to the powerful and resonated with all who endeavored "to do well."[7]

Historians for generations have plotted the field, vetted the players. Lawrence Levine and Warren Susman worked to come to terms with a twentieth-century culture that at moments appeared a craze of competing realities. Levine warns it is no simple task to study what emerged—a commodified landscape:

> It is a mistake, then, to divide the world up too easily into reality and representations of reality. The latter—the representations—when they become embodied in theater, tales, radio, movies, become forms of reality themselves. I don't mean by this that audiences necessarily "confuse" them with reality. Indeed, I think the opposite is more often true. Rather, the entire setting constitutes an important form of reality in which many essential things are realized: lessons are learned, values enunciated and repeated, modes of behavior scrutinized, social institutions and their effects explored, fantasies indulged.[8]

Susman lays forth what materialized in the first four decades of the century: a culture of abundance mediated by communications and organization revolutions; a new middle class the recipient of the goods; public opinion shaped, values and personalities molded. "The concept of the average was born…."

> For a culture that originally had enshrined individualism as its key virtue, interest in the average was now overwhelming. The Average American and the Average American Family became central to the new vision of a future culture…. Increasingly, this statistical culture…was invested as well with the sentimental aura that went with the more mystical notion of the people. If the people seemed pleasingly poetic and the average

---

[7] Slotkin, *Fatal*, 25 and 30.

[8] Lawrence W. Levine, *The Unpredictable Past: Explorations in American Cultural History* (New York: Oxford University Press, 1993), 312–13. Warren I. Susman, *Culture as History: The Transformation of American Society in the Twentieth Century* (New York: Pantheon Books, 1984), 213.

> American suitably scientific, both versions of the idea nevertheless regarded society as a single entity.

It appeared, on average, sustainable.[9]

Poetry, science, and seduction: T. J. Jackson Lears contends a whole value system was giving way, a broad shift "from a Protestant to a therapeutic orientation within the dominant culture."[10] Roland Marchand, *Advertising the American Dream*, points out advertisers "recognized a much larger stake in reflecting people's needs and anxieties than in depicting their actual circumstances and behavior. It was in their efforts to promote the mystique of modernity in styles and technology, while simultaneously assuaging the anxieties of consumers about losses of community and individual control, that they most closely mirrored historical reality—the reality of a cultural dilemma."[11] Somehow goods could substitute for community and individual empowerment. In the twenties and thirties Madison Avenue emerged supreme to explain it all and ultimately with reassuring material markers over the next half century negotiated the sale. Lynne Dumenil in *The Modern Temper* summarizes: "The twenties are a critical period for these transformations, for the decade embodies much of what constitutes consumer culture: the cornucopia of material goods; an occupational and corporate structure that limits individual autonomy; and a shift in behavior and values away from the Victorian 'production' ethos

---

[9] Susman, *Culture as History*, 213. The role of popular culture was extensively discussed. See "AHR Forum," *American Historical Review* 97 (December 1992): 1369–1430. Hegemony simultaneously entered the debate. See Lears, *No Place*, especially xvii-xviii and 10. Lengthier, see T.J. Jackson Lears, "The Concept of Cultural Hegemony: Problems and Possibilities," *American Historical Review* 90 (June 1985): 567–93.

[10] Lears, *No Place*, xviii.

[11] Roland Marchand, *Advertising the American Dream: Making Way for Modernity, 1920–1940* (Berkeley, University of California Press, 1985), xxi. See Pamela Walker Laird, *Advertising Progress: American Business and the Rise of Consumer Marketing* (Baltimore: The Johns Hopkins University Press, 1998) and Charles F. McGovern, *Sold American: Consumption and Citizenship, 1890–1945* (Chapel Hill: University of North Carolina Press, 2006).

of work, restraint, and order, toward one that embraces leisure, consumption, and self-expression as vehicles for individual satisfaction."[12]

The advertisers had been around for generations. Now they were cashing in big-time on an amalgamated, nationalizing ethos. They hardly were alone. The people, whether some emergent average, single

---

[12] Lynn Dumenil, *The Modern Temper: American Culture and Society in the 1920s* (New York: Hill and Wang, 1995), 57. See Marina Moskowitz, "Public Exposure: Middle-Class Material Culture at the Turn of the Twentieth Century," in *The Middling Sorts: Explorations in the History of the American Middle Class*, eds. Robert D. Johnston and Burton J. Bledstein (New York: Routledge, 2001), 170–84. Moskowitz argues individual and national character were at stake for concerned Progressive Era Americans more so than brute access to products as they sought "a standard of living that was defined by aspiration rather than income." See 184 and 172–73. "Material goods and the organization of the physical environment were a means of expressing an increasingly shared national experience; with the social mixing in public spaces, they were also a means of introducing the tenets of that experience to those not yet sharing it. Spaces and the objects within them were freighted with, and thus carried, significant values of middle-class life...." Moscowitz, *Standard of Living: The Measure of the Middle Class in America* (Baltimore: Johns Hopkins University Press, 2004), especially the brilliant introduction, offers a synthesis of twentieth-century identity issues. For an assessment of the arrival of consumer history see David Steigerwald, "All Hail the Republic of Choice: Consumer History as Contemporary Thought," *Journal of American History* 93 (September 2006): 385–403 and two responses similarly excellent—T.H. Breen, "Will American Consumers Buy a Second American Revolution?" *Journal of American History* 93 (September 2006): 404–08 and Lizabeth Cohen, "Escaping Steigerwald's 'Plastic Cages': Consumers as Subjects and Objects in Modern Capitalism," *Journal of American History* 93 (September 2006): 409–13. Steigerweld concludes "consumer interpretations of American history have come of age"; they establish "consumers can stand as central characters across the span of the nation's past." All the more important, consumption "might well be the defining thread of American life." Naturally, "The act of consumption...cannot carry the weight of history.... Yet we must take account of consumption as a universal activity, especially those of us in twentieth-century American history who cannot give a persuasive account of our time unless we recognize mass consumption as the center of our sociopolitical system." See 385 and 401.

entity, or host of sub-entities was a long-sought commodity in the democratic-capitalistic marketplace. Identity itself was now up for grabs; the attention of *the people* had been coveted not only by merchants but politicians. Susman studies bevies of hunters after *the common man* ranging from entrepreneur Henry Ford to novelist Willa Cather, emerging filmmakers to consensus theorists, eugenicists, too. No protagonist beyond Madison Avenue would play a greater role than the politician in reaching out for the average.

In the beginning of the century progressivism struck a relatively high civic note. Experts at communications and organization, middle-class reformers sought out votes. John Whiteclay Chambers II outlines the broad agenda:

> In diverse ways and with divergent goals, the progressives sought to modernize American institutions while attempting to recapture the ideals and sense of community that they believed had existed in the past. They battled conservatives, radicals, other reformers, and often each other. But despite their disagreements and difficulties, progressives played a major role in helping Americans to adjust to new conditions and create new institutions for coping with the challenges of the time. They took the lead in establishing a social agenda for modern America.[13]

Susman argues progressivism represented a new cultural amalgam as "it proposed as a social 'and' political end the opportunity for each man and woman to know some experience that was creative and satisfying, an aesthetic experience that was the consequence of communal and political life." "This kind of vision," he claims, "was strikingly new as a political goal in America."[14]

---

[13] John Whiteclay Chambers II, *The Tyranny of Change: America in the Progressive Era, 1890–1920*, 2nd ed. (New York: St. Martin's Press, 1992), 133.

[14] Susman, *Culture*, xxii–xxiii. Progressivism has been the subject of debate for a century; bibliographies abound. Daniel T. Rodgers, "In Search of Progressivism," *Reviews in American History* 10 (December 1982): 113–32 remains an excellent resource for a selective bibliography and strong insights. See Robert M. Crunden, "Thick Description in the Progressive Era," *Reviews*

Progressivism was a novel politics of sorts and has survived the century. Certainly the language, the therapeutic ideal, the amalgamation of community and identity, the aesthetic, the packaging has had staying power. Daniel Rogers argues the words mattered, they always had: "For it is largely through a string of words—be they 'freedom,' or 'equality,' or the 'sanctity of property,' or the claims of race—that individuals separated from normal sight of each other are shaken into

---

in American History 19 (December 1991): 463–67; Bryant Simon, "One Side of Main Street," *Reviews in American History* 22 (September 1994): 461–67; and James Livingston, "Why is There Still Socialism in the United States?" *Reviews in American History* 22 (December 1994): 577–83. For an incisive discussion (and bibliography) of progressive studies see Robert D. Johnston, "Re-Democratizing the Progressive Era: The Politics of Progressive Era Political Historiography," *Journal of the Gilded Age and Progressive* Era 1 (January 2002): 68–92; Johnston, "The Possibilities of Politics: Democracy in America, 1877–1917," in *American History Now,* 3rd ed., eds. Eric Foner and Lisa McGirr (Philadelphia: Temple University Press, 2011), 96–124; Johnston, "Influential Works about the Gilded Age and Progressive Era," in *A Companion to the Gilded Age and Progressive Era*, eds. Christopher McKnight Nichols and Nancy C. Unger (Hoboken, NJ: John Wiley & Sons, 2017), 437–49. Compendiums of perspectives abound: Glenda Elizeth Gilmore, ed., *Who Were the Progressives?* (Boston: Bedford/St. Martin's, 2002); Ballard C. Campbell, ed., *The Human Tradition in the Gilded Age and Progressive Era* (Wilmington, DE.: Scholarly Resources, 2000); David B. Woolner and John M. Thompson, eds., *Progressivism in America: Past, Present, and Future* (Oxford: Oxford University Press, 2015). Monographs abound: John Milton Cooper, Jr., *Pivotal Decades: The United States, 1900–1920* (New York: W.W. Norton, 1990); Nell Irvin Painter, *Standing at Armageddon: The United States, 1877–1919* (New York: W. W. Norton, 2008); T.J. Jackson Lears, *Rebirth of a Nation: The Making of Modern America 1877–1920* (New York: Harper Collins, 2009). Maureen A. Flanagan, *America Reformed: Progressives and Progressivisms 1890s–1920s* (New York: Oxford University Press, 2007); Ellis W. Hawley, *The Great War and the Search for a Modern Order: A History of the American People and Their Institutions 1917–1933*, 2nd ed. (Prospect Heights, IL: Waveland Press, 1997); Patrick D. Reagan, *Designing a New America: The Origins of New Deal Planning, 1890–1943* (Amherst: University of Massachusetts Press, 1999); Alan Brinkley, *The End of Reform: New Deal Liberalism in Recession and War* (New York: Vantage Books, 1996).

consciousness that their grievances, ambitions, angers, and desires are not peculiarly theirs, but, at some slightly altered level of generalization, the material of politics. Abstract generalizing talk makes private matters public." Rogers laments the crass corruption of progressivism in a nationalized political arena. The Progressive Era, running roughly from the 1890s through World War One (and stumbling through the postwar decade to be reinvigorated by the demands of the Depression) was a golden age for wordsmiths: "[N]o one looking back on the years before the First World War has failed to be struck by the vigor, the massive confidence of the era's appeal to ideals. The big, highbrow words which had fueled political argument so long went out not with a whimper, but unexpectedly, in full career." Politics in the process was mauled by the huge business interests, and the whole lexicon became nonsensical: "It is the story of how, in a world transformed by admen, propagandists, and public opinion shapers, among men shaken by these hucksters into a deeply skeptical attitude toward words of every sort, a mud-stained term of opprobrium swallowed up the whole of politics." Progressivism, at base, fell prey to commercial culture. Progressive politics is still with us—baked in, as American as apple pie—but the substance of the vision has become depressingly entangled within the claptrap of the marketplace and the vicissitudes of social change.[15]

The U.S. always was openly contested terrain: lands, markets, ideas, ambition, opportunity; classes, interests, and individuals mixed it up. The People, Rodgers cites, always held its own in the linguistic contest. Progressivism was heady, all hailed the citizenry, "our coveted allies," as questions of individualism and communitarianism were knocked about.[16] Robert S. McElvaine explores the extenuated American tug-of-war between the two ideals, arguing the load-bearing 1930s, coming on the heels of the surging twenties, would witness

[15]Daniel T. Rodgers, *Contested Truths: Keywords in American Politics Since Independence* (New York: Basic Books, 1987), 4 and 178–79; 3–16 summarizes his take on words. Rodgers impressively treats the Progressive Era; see in particular chapters four and six. Rodgers, "In Search" makes a provocative argument for language as a means to probe the elusiveness of the movement.

[16] See Rodgers, *Contested*, especially chapters four, six, and epilogue.

possibly the last great struggle with individualism clearly emergent as victor. But the ground had been significantly tested some twenty-five years earlier. McElvaine considers early twentieth-century middle-class reformers: "There can be little doubt that most of these people sincerely wanted the 'uplift' of the lower classes and a better, more honest, just, and moral society.... Much of what passed for progressivism was pushed by people who saw themselves as altruistic—they wanted to do good for others, not themselves." He contends, too, it would serve their own good: within the secure bounds of a period of prosperity and optimism, "it was possible for the 'better sort' to attempt to guide the discontent that had been so evident among farmers and workers into acceptable channels....Thus, while progressivism had important working-class, farmer, and corporate components, its dominant form represented a 'cautious uprising of the better classes.'" Strategic positioning: "Improvements were not to be won by the struggles of the lower classes, but to be bestowed as gifts from the moral, disinterested people above them." The beneficiaries would "know to whom they should be thankful." No one was to doubt who had secured for whom the blessings of individualism, community, the fruits of middle-class American democracy.[17]

Alas, all did not go as well as intended. Journalist William Allen White, one of the most well-read of the progressive progenitors of middle-class faith, looked back in 1937 from deep within the Great Depression contemplating the shambles he and others had made of their efforts. Questioning what had gone wrong, he espied progressives had sought corporate regulation, a more equitable distribution of wealth, better housing, wages, education, women's rights, and most important

---

[17]Robert S. McElvaine, *The Great Depression: America, 1929–1941*, rev. ed., (New York: Times Books, 1993), 9–10 tracks a devolving tale: "The middle" remained the key player in the 1930s ideals struggle, whereby a decade of communitarian hope ended in a selfish sell-out of the lower order by the middle class heavily enabled by the Roosevelt Administration. Rampant and crass individualism tangled with more communal impulses over the following decades. McElvaine at the end of the century lost faith in a communitarian renaissance.

self-respect; the reformers had tried to do more than bridge class differences. They were seeking something admirable: "The thing we were trying to do from the days of the first Roosevelt and during the dark years that followed Wilson, through Harding, to Hoover, was to brace up the human spirit in those social and economic areas where class differences were cruelly marked and wickedly depressed." But this lofty, middling goal, this boosting of human spirit, the ideal of a vast, secure, and caring society, one that saw beyond self to community had been swamped: "We forgot our objective.... We began to think that the whole trick could be done by distributing toothpaste, automobiles, radios, bathtubs, parks, playgrounds, high schools, libraries, extension courses and canned soups to those who hitherto had been denied these sweet boons." What people needed, what the nation stood upon, was stronger than goods; a benevolence of spirit was essential. This, in short, was what the United States of America was really all about. This, in short, at that dismal pass, was what the nation clearly lacked.[18]

Individualism and community, a socially and politically triumphant middle-class ethos that somehow rings hollow—is it that hard to strike a meaningful balance beneficial to all concerned parties? Yes; it may well be symptomatic of a relatively open and expansive society. The conflicting questions of the good of the individual and, or the community may produce an unstable political environment in which citizens perpetually must address the fundamental question whose interest is really at stake? What is it that everyone seeks out, for one and all, for everyman and everywoman, for everyone? David E. Shi surveys the playing out of "plain living and high ideals" in an expansive landscape, yet another take on the Middle Kingdom where Americans for four centuries sought out a time when "'habits of life were simpler; the interests of men less mixed and varied; there were more common sympathies, more common and controlling traditions and associations.'" Shi sees "the simple life" as a "personal ethic." But when ineluctably push comes to shove, as individual and communal needs clash, as myths and realities run their courses, as *progress* ensues, it all becomes complex, and we must look at ourselves more closely, beyond the personal,

[18] Agran, "*Too Good,*" 150–51.

socially as a community: "[I]deas in the abstract are inert; they tell us little about the mystery of daily living. To bring texture—indeed, to bring life to the study of cultural beliefs—requires going beyond symbolic analysis; it entails examining how people have struggled to translate myths into practice." Hence, "the people" arrived of mixed mind in the twentieth century and the first decades of the twenty-first to face a challenge which encompasses examining how the illusory myth of a classless America transposed itself not so simplistically into the comforting, expanding, and yet unsettling realm of practical middle-class identity.[19]

Within this formative landscape, Sinclair Lewis struggled to encase that middle-class identity, to make it real, to make it work. Whose interest is at stake; yours, mine, which group interest—the people, our country? The novelist amalgamated his self-interest, trying to find himself, with everyman's; he proclaimed a middle-class society could provide for all needs—absolutely in-step with the national ethos. There was a place for a simpler life in a complex new century, in a nation of riches, comfort, and opportunities to fulfill one's ambition He tried to find it for himself and for the country he adored. In the 1920s at the height of his powers Lewis sought to direct his nation, *the people*, toward the simple truth of a self-respecting Middle American ethos. There was no great mystery of daily living; the texture of everyday life could be comforting, not a desultory slog; the myth could be put into rich practice. One need only to untangle the complexities, part and parcel of an on-running experiment.

Lewis probed and prodded in *Main Street, Babbitt*, *Arrowsmith*, *Elmer Gantry*, and *Dodsworth*. He never defined the illusive solution, nor was he satisfied he had definitively resolved through his fiction the ideal course for the country. The sum-product of his five great novels, a directive toward a self-respecting Middle American ethos that worked, fell short of resolution—there was more to it; always, there would be more to it. That in essence was the long story. Lingeman

---

[19] David E. Shi, *The Simple Life: Plain Living and High Thinking in American Culture, 1850–1920* (New York: Oxford University Press, 1985), 173 and 7; quoting Charles Eliot Norton.

again testifies: "His advice was perfectly sound but left Lewis open to the criticism that was to dog his entire career: that he could only complain and had nothing better to offer." But the novels never aimed for a quick cure—they were a summons to progress. The novels raised definitive questions as Americans sought a means to identify themselves and articulate exactly what they were after. Sinclair Lewis stood firmly in the cultural mainstream. He construed a diagnosis, both reasonable and compassionate, for a country that for a variety of reasons found itself ill at ease. The first step in annealing a malady is to uncover the hurt. The cure, Lewis argued all along, was within ourselves: it all was simply a matter of working full-out to extend the American Promise. Lewis decades earlier had taken up David Shi's charge: "[I]deas in the abstract are inert; they tell us little about the mystery of daily living. To bring texture—indeed, to bring life to the study of cultural beliefs—requires going beyond symbolic analysis; it entails examining how people have struggled to translate myths into practice."

FOUR

MAIN STREET

Sinclair Lewis had a good eye for the New Era. He knew a lot of the excitement was ephemeral, the product of calculated sloganeering—ballyhoo as it was tagged. He knew, too, it had reflected substance, huge changes were in the offing. Securing "the good life" was an enduring struggle. It was the essence of the American success story, another frontier—and he revered the pioneer ethos. He wanted to make it all work. Critic Edmund Wilson, despite Lewis's thirties fall from grace, recollected in 1945 the twenties chronicler, still at work, had his "notorious faults" but remained "one of the national poets."[1] Sheldon Norman Grebstein, in Lewis's defense, in 1962 lamented, "He wrote the novel as *history*; we prefer the novel as poetry"—Grebstein believed a great author had been short-changed. He recalled Bernard DeVoto's proclamation in the forties Lewis was "the best novelist of his decade." DeVoto had become a fierce critic of the author: The country had moved on; the scholar and historian considered Lewis had fallen out of step. But he had written *Main Street*, *Babbitt*, *Arrowsmith*, *Elmer Gantry*, and *Dodsworth*; De Voto acknowledged in his day the author had chronicled a crucial passage in the national saga. Grebstein cites scholar Harlan Hatcher looking back reckoned Lewis's New Era work the most stimulating of that decade: "By the sheer energy of his mind he helped the modern American novel into maturity and recognition." Critic Henry Seidel Canby concluded long after Lewis's heyday, "He was the

[1] Richard Lingeman, *Sinclair Lewis: Rebel from Main Street* (New York: Random House, 2002), 487. Wilson was in a sentimental mood, having discovered the country in a troubled state as he returned from war-wracked Europe in 1945. He found just released *Cass Timberline* well-written but a novel of the past. What warmed Wilson was Lewis's recall of classic virtues, midwestern identity, basic tenets.

most powerful novelist of the decade when American fiction in general matured in scope and in art."[2]

Sinclair Lewis through the twenties took up key elements of a changing landscape. The country, the countryside, its small towns, the burgeoning middle-sized cities, the towering metropolises tugged at him; so also the denizens with all their charms despite their dubious quirks. He liked growth—the benefits of electricity; the power of corporations, innovation in the sciences; and he prized the rhythms of everyday life. He queried, too—how was all this working out? Denizens across the continent were "moving to the city." Empowered by the frontier ethos, he perceived the U.S. remained on its monumental trek. He did not see himself a pioneer, at least not blatantly so; but he was strongly drawn to the pathbreaking, guiding progressive spirit; he admired those reformers, out to nurture the American Experiment, fulfill the American Promise. Carol Kennicott on Main Street caught the spirit; George Babbitt comically, pathetically, yearned to see himself a twentieth-century Daniel Boone; scientist Martin Arrowsmith was a genuine trailblazer; Elmer Gantry was a clown, ready to assume whatever guise works—ecclesiastical frontiersman would do fine albeit his aim was hardly progressive; finally, Samuel Dodsworth, a titan of industry, in search of new frontiers, espied an opportunity to rebuild American communities, to create that simpler life he perceived Americans craved. Alfred Kazin, a generation following the novelist's remarkable decade, asserted Babbitt "had entered as completely into the national imagination as Daniel Boone."[3]

Lewis never said out-and-out he was out to rebuild community, but that is what he was promoting in the twenties. It hardly is surprising he ends his decade-long sprint writing *Dodsworth*. He would contend to the end of his life he had no new solutions, he was simply a

---

[2] Sheldon Norman Grebstein, *Sinclair Lewis* (New Haven: College and University Press, 1962), 164 and 166.

[3] Kazin cited in Gary Scharnhorst and Matthew Hofer, eds., *Sinclair Lewis Remembered* (Tuscaloosa: University of Alabama Press, 2012), 91. Definitively no Boone; still, the businessman's innocent aborted dreams was one of his charms.

diagnostician. But what is one without the other? Samuel Dodsworth in his can-do fashion had diagnosed the country's problem and set out to reconstruct a simpler American way of life—he could be a community-builder, just a beginning, but "what an adventure it would be" he and his mate chanted. In the 1920s Lewis found his footing: Carol, George, Martin, Elmer, and Sam spoke to America; their voices, with a chorus of secondary characters chiming in, across a boisterous decade resonated with a public that seemed to get what these folks were aiming at (again, the exception proves the rule—Gantry spoke, and they were revolted). The American people tread a path of change: where it headed, how it squared with American Destiny, here was a gnawing query afloat in a dizzying decade.

Prior to the twenties, Lewis had written in an inchoate fashion about the country, the people, their values. Grebstein considers what was to come was in the air: poets Pound, Sandburg, and Frost; novelists London, Wharton, and Dreiser offered fresh, challenging perspectives on the national tale. Still, "most American readers continued to prefer writing which was traditional in its forms and which was affirmative, optimistic, and romantic in its tone." Booth Tarkington, Harold Bell Wright, and Zane Grey were favorites. And Lewis in his first works wrote their way. Mark Schorer points out, however, prior to the Great War in the writer's short magazine stories and first seven novels there were signs where he was headed. He had acquired with the short stories a wide audience which "demanded the explicit, the demonstrated, the heavily documented, the overdrawn and the broad." Schorer senses the promise: "The style, like the man, was made."[4]

The New Era arrived. Lewis had his doubts. On the cusp of *Main Street's* debut, Richard Lingeman observes he was hesitant "realism did not appeal to readers; moreover, the trade wisdom was that novels about small towns didn't sell."[5] He had read a draft to friends in

---

[4] Grebstein extensively reviews the early work in "Romance and Affirmation: The Early Novels," 37–60; quoted 37. Mark Schorer, *Sinclair Lewis: An American Life* (New York: McGraw-Hill Book Company, 1961), 238–41; quoted 241.

[5] Lingeman, 146.

Washington: "Dean Acheson recollected that he and many others warned Lewis that no one would buy such a novel 'because the American public…would not pay to be made fun of.'"[6] Of course, they slapped dollars down once *Main Street* hit the marketplace. Acheson, a rising foreign affairs specialist, perhaps did not know the hoi polloi, could not sense the rising zeitgeist. Lewis did: People were conflicted; so also was the protagonist of Lewis's smash novel. *Main Street* was subtitled *The Story of Carol Kennicott*. Carol wrestled with a conundrum.

Lewis, also conflicted, sought to solve a riddle. Charles Breasted, close to the author as he wrote *Babbitt*, queried, "What about Carol Kennicott, isn't she a portrait of you?" Lewis responded, "Yes," of course "Carol is 'Red' Lewis: Always groping for something she isn't capable of attaining, always dissatisfied, always restlessly straining to see what lies just over the horizon, intolerant of her surroundings, yet lacking any clearly defined vision of what she really wants to do or to be."[7]

In *Main Street* Lewis took on the plight of the small town; as well, he perceived national angst. Main Street was the venue; Carol's struggle with convention, herself, and most people around her was the story. Reform was on the decline; still, woman's position remained on the ascent. Women made up a huge contingent within the Progressive Movement; perhaps a woman's hand was needed—Carol Kennicott was sure of it. What would later be termed Middle America had settled into a shared identity with the newly coined Middle West—representative of rural regions, small towns, bedrock values, enterprising cities "on the make," but "provincial." The country as a whole was a bit frantic, propelled into the twentieth century, into a still ill-defined, modernizing world. Carol was isolated, caught between two universes, one appealing, modern and one appalling, provincial, in need of her helping hand. Here, in the purported plight of small-town America might be located what ailed the Republic as a whole, and a way forward might be suggested.

---

[6] Ibid., 142. Lewis gravitated to the elite despite insistence he was a common sort.

[7] Scharnhorst and Hofer, 103.

The aspiring novelist questioned his prospects, the market, but smartly ran with his instinct and Alfred Harcourt's encouragement. Americans were primed for realism but now with a refreshened focus. Contrary to trade wisdom this small-town novel with a more critical perspective instantly caught fire. The public seemed amendable to laugh at itself, at least wide swaths of it; and at the same time apparently it was prepared to give a reasonable amount of thought to "what seemed to be going on." Across the country were plenty of people inclined to take a look at themselves. That lengthening gaze with the prodding of Sinclair Lewis would span across the tumultuous decade.

Carol, Mrs. Dr. Will Kennicott gazes a lot, and purposely. She is not easily humored. She steps off the train from Minneapolis with her new husband. Gopher Prairie, a midwestern burg, is Will's hometown. Her husband is loving, supportive, staid, and by Carol's measure going to rot in a backwater—she had her ideas. James M. Hutchisson points out Lewis may have had his qualms about his subject matter, but it was "a propitious historical moment."[8] The author, despite worry about public reception of such meaty material, had reflected in the spring and summer months of 1920 that *Main Street* would be the beginning of good fortune: America was stuck; he would drive it out of its rut. Carol Kennicott would be the ticket.

Grebstein argues Carol early-on was clued in: "The lesson is that constriction of habits and imagination makes for constriction of the soul; in short, small towns mold small people."[9] But it was much more than an issue of lackluster burgs, a time-honored pastoral venue on the decline. What was to be coined in the novel and gain renown as the "village virus" could crop up anywhere; it was not a matter of the individual, nor place. Gopher Prairie became a national synecdoche for narrowness, for a particularly American variety of provinciality. "The satire in *Main Street* is effective because most of the time," Hutchisson assesses, "Lewis shows rather than tells, letting the difference between expectation and reality manifest itself without authorial commentary—

---

[8] James M. Hutchisson, *The Rise of Sinclair Lewis, 1920–1930* (University Park: Pennsylvania State University Press, 1996), 43.

[9] Grebstein, 65.

often by letting the villagers reveal their startling banality through dialogue."[10] Yes, Lewis's specialty—all those takes on the passing parade over the years, observing, scribbling, honing his mimicry. His emergent style suited what ailed Americans—what so many seemed to crave; there was an unease in need of definition. Grebstein:

> The very characteristics which later critics turned against him—his simplicity of theme, the weight of his detail, his didactiveness, the emphasis on environment rather than character, the crude vigor of his style, his faithful transcription of American idiom and sharp portraiture of the surface of American life—made Lewis famous, read, and effective.... Lewis broke through the layers of public indifference and the hostility toward unpleasant novels."

The scholar takes the author's measure: "He had, after an arduous apprenticeship, arrived.[11]

Alas, so too had Carol Kennicott in Gopher Prairie. Her take on the world will be particularly destabilizing for her and the community—and the country as a whole. Main Street was not pretty, far from quaint, and its hominess could claw. It all was tediously drab, draped by mediocrity, cloaked with convention, stuck, and a bit mean. Convention for Lewis will always be the devil in the works. Facing down Main Street, Carol has the progressive reform bug; coming from the Twin Cities, enlightened, she is filled with modern biases. She would inoculate the village virus, give it a shot of her own antibodies. She ponders upon landing in the hamlet, having taken an initial thirty-two-minute stroll, what lies ahead:

> Main Street with its two-story brick shops, its story-and-a-half wooden residences, its muddy expanse from concrete walk to walk, its huddle of Fords and lumber-wagons, was too small to absorb her. The broad, straight, unenticing gashes of the streets let in the grasping prairie on every side. She realized the vastness and the emptiness of the land. The skeleton iron

---

[10] Hutchisson, 33.

[11] Grebstein, 73.

> windmill on the farm a few blocks away, at the north end of Main Street, was like the ribs of a dead cow. She thought of the coming of the Northern winter, when the unprotected houses would crouch together in terror of storms galloping out of that wild waste. They were so small and weak, the little brown houses. They were shelters for sparrows, not homes for warm laughing people.[12]

No, Carol is too big for such constraints; *she* will rise to the challenge; and yes, she will be absorbed, to an extent compromised; but she will fight a heartfelt, daunting, exasperating—and she is endlessly exasperating—battle for the town's soul.

Carol speedily is introduced to Will's friends and associates, the "best people on earth." They fall short of her expectations, and so does Will. Throughout the novel she fights what she sensed upon entering the town; she turns on Will: "'Why do these stories lie so?…Lies about marriage…And this town—O my God!…This junk-heap!'" All her causes, her initial crusading, fall short: beautify Gopher Prairie; edify the townspeople; aid the dispossessed; side with the despised lower-class, especially the immigrant Swedes and Germans, against the bourgeois elite; and stand up as a citizen. "She was a woman with a working brain and no work." Destined to live as Lewis asserts in a "Doll's House," she longs for "a room of her own."[13]

---

[12] Sinclair Lewis, *Main Street: The Story of Carol Kennicott* (New York: Penguin Books, 1995). Carol's problematic survey is laid out, hilariously and poignantly, 29–34. "Dahl & Oleson's Meat Market—a reek of blood"; "A fly-buzzing saloon with a brilliant gold and enamel whisky sign across the front. Other saloons down the block. From them a stink of stale beer, and thick voices bellowing pidgin German songs or trolling out dirty songs—vice gone feeble and unenterprising and dull—the delicacy of a mining camp minus its vigor. In front of the saloons, farmwives sitting on the seats of wagons, waiting for their husbands to become drunk and ready to start home." See 31. Naturally, the inhabitants gather in their own eye-full peering upon Dr. Kennicott's bride on her stroll.

[13] Ibid., 25, 76, and 156–57. Carol and Will's blow-outs frame spousal quarreling well: "She suddenly saw the foot-board of the bed as the foot-stone of the grave of love." See 152–59; quoted 152. Lewis, well-versed in domestic

Everywhere Carol turns is ugliness. Aboard "No. 7, the way train, grumbling through Minnesota," the railroad stripped of its romantic gloss, the bride is tormented and ponders the fruits of the American Promise:

> This is no smug Pullman attached to the train, and the day coaches of the East are replaced by free chair cars, with each seat cut into two adjustable plush chairs, the head rests covered with doubtful linen towels.... There is no porter, no pillows, no

---

struggles, captures marital fights in stinging passages throughout his twenties novels. In its way, *Main Street* is a feminist stab. Lewis often feints in that direction. Carol as all his female protagonists reflect women's concerns, but they never are the issue in the bulk of his work. He does respect strength and character, and female characters display both, but also weakness. He most persuasively makes the case for women's rights in a powerful statement by Carol toward the end of the novel. See 379. Schorer, 242–44 argues he made his first serious foray into women's issues in 1917 with *The Job: An American Novel* (New York: Harper, 1917). Lewis's best-seller *Ann Vickers* (Garden City: Doubleday, Doran, 1933) can be considered his most woman-centered work. His instinct for writing about sex was generally considered stunted—a good deal less so in this novel. *Ann Vickers* makes a strong argument for strength. However, Malcolm Cowley in his review espied ambivalence: Ann "is a feminist and Lewis is really hostile toward feminism. Ann is a reformer and Lewis has learned to distrust reformers." This is provocative but too simple. See 386–87. Lewis lays out an impressive array of reform-era works as he reviews Carol's reading list; see 238. See Nan Bauer Maglin, "Women in Three Sinclair Lewis Novels," in *Modern Critical Reviews: Sinclair Lewis*, ed. Harold Bloom (New York, Chelsea House Publishers, 1987), 103–18. "I came to the conclusion that, yes, Sinclair Lewis was consciously exploring through fiction the choices and pressures that women felt personally and socially during the first third of the twentieth century." *Main Street* with *The Job* (1917) and *Ann Vickers* (1933) add up as "all three novels present acute historical insight into what life was like for women." See 103. Women's literature specialist Maglin integrates into her analysis solid history as the modern feminist movement gets its legs. The three novels she writes in the seventies "are historical documents which preserve for us the struggles of women in our past to solve some of the very same problems that still exist in society today." See 118.

> provision for beds, but all today and all tonight they will ride in this long steel box—farmers with perpetually tired wives and children who seem all to be of the same age; workmen going to new jobs; traveling salesmen with derbies and freshly shined shoes.

Not a pretty picture; it is devastating; and Mrs. Doctor Will Kennicott is condescending: "They are parched and cramped, the lines of their hands filled with grime.... They do not read; apparently they do not think."[14]

They are *all* tired in *Main Street*; Carol, too, will be worn bare. Soon enough a disgruntled townsman, a refreshing friend, fills Carol in on the Gopher Prairie prospect: "The Village Virus is the germ which—it's extraordinarily like the hook-worm—it infects ambitious people who stay too long in the provinces. You'll find it epidemic among lawyers and doctors and ministers and college-bred merchants—all these people who have had a glimpse of the world that thinks and laughs, but have returned to their swamp."[15] And they are apparently satisfied, even worse, self-satisfied in their capitulation. What is a progressive twentieth-century woman to do? This is the heartland.

Carol is not heroic, not an accomplished crusader—and she is flighty and moody—but she feints at noble charges. She had been tutored in college to expect more; she, after all, was a twentieth-century woman, a progressive:

> Here—she meditated—is the newest empire of the world; the Northern Middlewest; a land of dairy herds and exquisite lakes, of new automobiles and tar-paper shanties and silos like red towers, of clumsy speech and a hope that is boundless. An empire which feeds a quarter of the world—yet its work is merely begun. They are pioneers, these sweaty wayfarers, for all their telephones and bank accounts and automatic pianos and co-operative leagues. And for all its fat richness, theirs is a pioneer land. What is its future? she wondered. A future of cities and

[14] Lewis, *Main Street*, 17.
[15] Ibid., 140–41.

> factory smut where now are loping empty fields? Homes universal and secure? Or placid châteaux ringed with sullen huts? Youth free to find knowledge and laughter? Willingness to sift the sanctified lies? Or creamy-skinned fat women, smeared with grease and chalk, gorgeous in the skins of beasts and the bloody feathers of slain birds, playing bridge with puffy pink-nailed jeweled fingers, women who after much expenditure of labor and bad temper still grotesquely resemble their own flatulent lapdogs? The ancient stale inequalities, or something different in history, unlike the tedious maturity of other empires? What future and what hope?

She is a neophyte, and she wants to learn—"Carol's head ached with the riddle."[16]

Doctor Kennicott's young wife (her pronounced identity) is up against it. Early on she confronts Mr. Elder (Lewis put great effort into names) at a party, an evening of fun by everyone's lights, and she is a spoiler. She spritely steps out of place: "defied decency by sitting down with the men...." She sets Elder off with an "innocent" query, "Do you approve of union labor?" He lays it out straight:

> "Me? I should say not! It's like this: I don't mind dealing with my men if they think they've got any grievances—though Lord knows what's come over workmen, nowadays—don't appreciate a good job. But still, if they come to me honestly, as man to man, I'll talk things over with them. But I'm not going to have any outsider, any of these walking delegates, or whatever fancy names they call themselves now—bunch of rich grafters, living on the ignorant workmen! Not going to have any of those fellows butting in and telling *me* how to run *my* business!"

If Carol harbors any doubt:

> I stand for freedom and constitutional rights. If any man don't like my shop, he can get up and git. Same way, if I don't like him, he gits. And that's all there is to it. I simply can't understand all these complications and hoop-te-doodles and

[16] Ibid., 21–22.

> government reports and wage-scales and God knows what all that these fellows are balling up the labor situation with, when it's all perfectly simple. They like what I pay 'em, or they get out. That's all there is to it!"

Well, not yet.[17]

Carol, not to be sidetracked, parlays, "What do you think of profit-sharing?" Elder takes off:

> "All this profit-sharing and welfare work and insurance and old-age pension is simply poppycock. Enfeebles a workman's independence—and wastes a lot of honest profit. The half-baked thinker that isn't dry behind the ears yet, and these suffragettes and God knows what all buttinskis there are that are trying to tell a business man how to run his business, and some of these college professors are just about as bad, the whole kit and bilin' of 'em are nothing in God's world but socialism in disguise! And it's my bounden duty as a producer to resist every attack on the integrity of American industry to the last ditch. Yes—SIR!"

The burghers nod along "solemnly and in tune, like a shop-window of flexible toys, comic mandarins and judges and ducks and clowns, set quivering by a breeze from the open door...." Gratefully, the talk returns to fixed channels. And the most fixating these days are motor cars and roads. Druggist Dave Dyer takes the wheel:

> "Yep. I get good time out of the flivver. 'Bout a week ago I motored down to New Wurttemberg. That's forty-three——No, let's see: It's seventeen miles to Belldale, and 'bout six and three-quarters, call it seven, to Torgenquist, and it's a good nineteen miles from there to New Wurttemberg—seventeen and seven and nineteen, that makes, uh, let me see: seventeen and seven's twenty-four, plus nineteen, well say plus twenty, that makes forty-four, well anyway, say about forty-three or -four miles from here to New Wurttemberg. We got started about seven-fifteen, prob'ly seven-twenty, because I had to stop and fill the radiator, and we ran along, just keeping up a good steady gait—"

---

[17] Ibid., 45.

Gopher Prairie's social set is back on safe ground.[18]

The anger and the banality all come through. This is Gopher Prairie's upper crust. This is Lewis at the top of his game. Through hundreds of pages Carol pursues a "perfection" which her husband discounts, then tolerates, then fights: her rebellion froths and then curdles before him. He is determined, he will see it through, *she will learn.* Will is rock-solid; Carol recognizes his majesty, the local doctor tending to everyone's travails, his hard work at all hours under all conditions. Will, she knows, represents the best, but they all are compromised. This is a good land; but it has fallen short of its promise. Their whole bunch falls short, and they supposedly are the leaders, the talented, destined to show the way. And both Carol and Will know they are falling short of their vows to one another. The veil is shorn, the rawness protrudes.

There are marital ups and downs; beyond their quarrels, Will and Carrie as he calls her, inch toward flirtations and love affairs; they have a child; and they have become adept at pressing one another's buttons. Penultimately, they separate. Something has to give. And it is Carol. She bolts for Washington to do her bit in the Great War, for the greater community: "Do you realize how big a world there is beyond this Gopher Prairie where you'd keep me all my life.... I'm—I'm going! I have a right to my own life." And, "So have I to mine!" flashes Will. "I have a right to my life—and you're it, you're my life! You've made yourself so. I'm damned if I'll agree to all your freak notions, but I will say I've got to depend on you. Never thought of that complication, did you, in this 'off to Bohemia, and express yourself, and free love, and live your own life' stuff!"[19]

Carol embarks on a quest. She seeks resolution, not only for her marriage but for the greater whole—and her own well-being. She has seen it all in Gopher Prairie: deaths and births, prejudices and scandals; lessons on the purported dangers in socialist nostrums; the constant tutorials regarding the perceived challenges to the pampered bourgeoisie poised by the lower classes; and along the way a down-to-earth education in the daily struggles of working men and women. Carol takes

[18] Ibid., 45–46.
[19] Ibid., 379–80.

in a bushel full of the warp and woof of life. And she weighs it all out: Her caste works plenty hard, too. And they are not bad, often kind, only so insular. And it is not "all bad." Gopher Prairie denizens high and low have their playful escapes, they sing paeans to midwestern sunsets and rich rolling fields, they take pride in their plucky resistance to frigid winters; they all like a laugh. This is tough terrain; these are, basically, good people. But their lives do not match up to the promise of their glorious land. For Carol, it all is too much. Maybe she can suss out a plan of action out there in the teeming world where ideas are still churning. After all, she is a college graduate, a progressive; and there are plenty just like her beyond the horizon.

Will's "little woman" makes it to the nation's capital, mingles with those she considers better informed than herself—and they are—and thinks a lot. For close to two years, making her way into a considerably more cosmopolitan crowd, engaging a variety of reform causes, distanced from Will and provincialism, struggling to make sense of it all, the world as well as home, Carol "comes to her senses."

Thirteen months into her journey Will visits, and he tries to make his case theirs. Cleverly and thoughtfully courted by her patient husband, Carrie responds to his solid reasoning: marriage, providing for one another, supporting one another; her love for him, family, and home; possibly even a soft spot for Gopher Prairie which she herself has started to conclude measures higher in her estimate "having seen Paree." It is a matter of common sense, a matter of compromise, a matter of digging in and working for the marriage and a greater common good even on the fringes of the battlefield. This, too, is progress.

Carol follows Will's lead: be reasonable. Gopher Prairie is a good spot, it holds promise, and so, too, do they. "I've come to a fairer attitude toward the town. I can love it, now." And she can make a difference: "Her active hatred of Gopher Prairie had run out. She saw it now as a toiling new settlement. With sympathy she remembered Kennicott's defense of its citizens, as 'a lot of pretty good folks, working hard and trying to bring up their families the best they can'.... She saw Main Street in the dusty prairie sunset, a line of frontier shanties with solemn lonely people waiting for her...." Hence, "Though she should return, she said, she would not be utterly defeated. She was glad of her rebellion. The prairie was no longer empty land in the sun-glare; it was the living tawny beast which she had fought…." The fight was good, her small victories, her work to make Gopher Prairie a more decent town, more attractive, caring, a truer community of shared interest—all her projects—she had brought light to Gopher Prairie, she had made it "beautiful by fighting." It always was about the fight, this was what *it* was all about, this is the *America* she had come to understand; never prepared to rest content, she recognized she could continue to do her part.[20]

Carol Kennicott comes to terms with the fact that the Gopher Prairies of the world have values, too, that count. But not too fast—Will has insisted she work it through; they must play for the long run, his wife was entitled to a room of her own, now design it. Months later, still in the midst of wartime exigencies in the capital, Carol has reached resolution. She has debated back and forth, taking all sides in an argument about life, her life, their life. She has seen the promise of progressive Washington, and she has seen its many shortcomings: "Always she was to perceive in Washington a thick streak of Main Street." Will on his visit had asked for time to get to know each other again, to take her not on a "second honeymoon" but a "second wooing": "I guess I never appreciated how lucky I was to have a girl with imagination and lively feet to play with." He, too, has worked to understand the wider world, and Gopher Prairie, and his wife's determination. He still, as she, can learn. "I just want the chance to chase around with you." Early into that first reuniting he gets them away from the confines of the capital, out of the wartime hot-house, finding time, alone, for one another. Away on their jaunt, trying to work it all through, Will is reasonable, Will makes sense, and Carol struggles to strike an accord. Finally she questions, "Shall I go back to Gopher Prairie with you? Decide for me. I'm tired of deciding and undeciding." "No," Will responds, "you've got to do your own deciding." Leave her to her room.[21]

Will catches the train home. Carol continues to work it through, to establish her role in a world she wishes to alter—but what, where is

[20] Ibid., 398.

[21] Ibid., 384 and 395.

her place? She settles; it all is a compromise. Decisively opting to move back to Will and their homestead, she sums up what she has learned and what is its cost. The Gopher Prairies of the world have not won. "I have won in this: I've never excused my failures by sneering at my aspirations, by pretending to have gone beyond them. I do not admit that Main Street is as beautiful as it should be! I do not admit that Gopher Prairie is greater or more generous than Europe! I do not admit that dish-washing is enough to satisfy all women! I may not have fought the good fight, but I have kept the faith." This story, then, has come to its end. Carol is home again. Will has the final word, responding to Carol's triumphant declaration she kept the faith: "Sure. You bet you have.... Well, good night. Sort of feels to me like it might snow tomorrow. Have to be thinking about putting up the storm-windows pretty soon. Say, did you notice whether the girl put that screwdriver back?" And that's apparently that...the last words in the novel.[22]

Well, that's what? As with all five of Lewis's twenties blockbusters, the reader is left hanging. No surprise—Lewis always is adrift as he journeys through life. Determination, compromise, rationalization, even resignation are always at play in his work. Where is one left at the end of the day—or at the end of Main Street? What is in store for the U.S.A., its promise? The novelist's ending, Carol's resolution, reduces to an admonition there is work to be done, she has come home to do it, and she will continue to progress, small as her steps may be—and Will can rest content. Progressivism, in short, wins out. Or does it? It all is left hanging. And doesn't so much? Lewis sets out, in the end, to further fortify the case he argues.

There is more to be told; Lewis reads more into the conundrum, the promise...not only for the couple, but the country. On a bright autumn day, driving home from an outing on a "duck-pass between two lakes," having received her first lesson in shooting the light-weight twenty-gauge shotgun Will had provisioned, Carol once more ponders her passage: "She looked across the silent fields to the west. She was conscious of an unbroken sweep of land to the Rockies, to Alaska; a dominion which will rise to unexampled greatness when other empires

---

[22] Ibid., 406.

have grown senile. Before that time, she knew, a hundred generations of Carols will aspire and go down in tragedy devoid of palls and solemn chanting, the humdrum inevitable tragedy of struggle against inertia." The preface to *Main Street* long before laid it out four-square:

> *This is America—a town of a few thousand, in a region of wheat and corn and dairies and little groves.*
>
> *The town is, in our tale, called "Gopher Prairie, Minnesota." But its Main Street is the continuation of Main Streets everywhere. The story would be the same in Ohio or Montana, in Kansas or Kentucky or Illinois, and not very differently would it be told UP York State or in the Carolina hills.*
>
> *Main Street is the climax of civilization. That this Ford car might stand in front of the Bon Ton Store, Hannibal invaded Rome and Erasmus wrote in Oxford cloisters. What Ole Jenson the grocer says to Ezra Stowbody the banker is the new law for London, Prague, and the unprofitable isles of the sea; whatsoever Ezra does not know and sanction, that thing is heresy, worthless for knowing and wicked to consider.*
>
> *Our railway station is the final aspiration of architecture. Sam Clark's annual hardware turnover is the envy of the four counties which constitute God's Country. In the sensitive art of the Rosebud Movie Palace there is a Message, and humor strictly moral.*
>
> *Such is our comfortable tradition and sure faith. Would he not betray himself an alien cynic who should otherwise portray Main-Street, or distress the citizens by speculating whether there may not be other faiths?*

Here then is the climax: God's Country; destiny fulfilled.[23]

Lewis had at the start laid down the gauntlet. There is a message here. It is heresy even wicked to question it. Comfortable, we are sure in our faith. Any cynic is an alien in our midst—why distress the citizenry by pondering the possibility of another truth? Carol by the end of the novel, hundreds of pages on, argues she will carry on, she is not defeated; after all, "I have kept the faith." "Sure you bet you have…." What is the ending here? The doctor has the little lady back, secure at

---

[23] Ibid., 404–05; Facing Page.

home? Or, Will has come to a reckoning with his New Woman? She will have her projects; he can rest assured he has won in the short run, she is back in Gopher Prairie; yet he need not despair over the considerably lengthier long run? Perhaps he shouldn't be too sure. The "struggle against inertia" will continue, but it will not be for naught: A hundred generations of Carol need not "go down in tragedy."

Prior to going to bed, the page before Lewis laid out another scene. That same autumnal evening, after the duck hunt, looking down with Will upon their recent, second offspring, a baby girl, Carol ponders more:

> "Do you see that object on the pillow? Do you know what it is? It's a bomb to blow up smugness. If you Tories were wise, you wouldn't arrest anarchists; you'd arrest all these children while they're asleep in their cribs. Think what that baby will see and meddle with before she dies in the year 2000! She may see an industrial union of the whole world story. She may see aeroplanes going to Mars."

This all comes in the last pages: Carol, then, resolves she is a builder, and it is a big project: "I haven't even started." Is this, then, the seminal message? It is a long haul. "'Yump, probably be changes all right,' yawns Kennicott."[24]

The End? Can it be ambivalence? There is no *answer*, there is no definitive resolution? Lewis, too, will fight on—again, as he had answered one friend's thought, aren't you really Carol? Indeed he was. Through the twenties he was not ambivalent; he would push the question further: Could this be all? *This is America?* A dead-end—simply put up the storm-windows? Or look further abroad? "She was conscious of an unbroken sweep of land…a dominion which will rise to unexampled greatness…." This always remains Lewis's vision. He has aimed to leave the reader pondering. That is the goal. This is not to be the end of his journey. Could he chart the way out of the cul-de-sac, well beyond Gopher Prairie? Well, he has just started. *Would he not betray himself an alien cynic who should otherwise portray Main Street, or distress*

[24] Ibid., 405.

the citizens by speculating whether there may not be other faiths? No—he is not an alien, not a cynic, he considers himself a believer. And if he could not map out the exacting pathway to a dominion rising to unexampled greatness in one go, would he simply have failed? Could prodding—could Carol's, as Will puts it, "fretting and stewing and experimenting" matter? Lewis's confidence in himself drove all he did, all he wanted to do. And he was insecure…just as Carol. But he would proceed. In the final analysis, prodding was the point.[25]

Sinclair Lewis ends in discouragement or encouragement? He leaves it to the reader. He always will, novel after novel. If nothing else, he strives to strike the balance: causes for discouragement yes; and reasons for encouragement. As for himself, in 1920, at the start of his meteoric decade, he was heartened by the response to his book. The reviewers excitedly embraced *Main Street* and its bright author. Lewis scholar, Martin Bucco in his 1995 introduction to the novel summarizes: "Like Wells in England and Booth Tarkington in America, a confident Lewis wanted to write about individuals dreaming and striving in the large context of national aspiration and struggle." The reviews and reader interest sparked a firestorm: "Sinclair Lewis's incendiary *Main Street* lit up the literary skies in 1920." The myth of America fulfilling God's will for His chosen people, Bucco argued, had been blown sky-high: "More than any anti-village fiction before it, Lewis's post-World War I satiric anatomy shattered the myth of the Middle West as God's Country." The author "turned the phrase 'Main Street' into an active part of the American vocabulary, a term in the English language denoting not only Gopher Prairie but the cultural conformity of dull, smug, narrow-minded small towns everywhere."[26]

---

[25] Ibid.

[26] Martin Bucco, introduction to *Main Street: The Story of Carol Kennicott*, by Sinclair Lewis (New York: Penguin Books, 1995), vii–xxi, quoted x and vii. Village literature, adoring as well as scathing, was long an American staple. Lewis, as Grebstein notes, produced "the first book to become popular which attacked a beloved native institution." See 73. Schorer contends the negative portrayals had never been able to hold a candle to the positive portrayals of the village—Lewis turned that equation upside-down: "Although

The reviewers knew Lewis had reached a country-wide audience. Main Street stretched to the cities, to the metropolises—the country needed, he believed, to get the word, and it did in fact awaken. Franklin P. Adams, who in the decade ahead would tower over the Algonquin Round Table, the witty New York circle that helped set the agenda for the twenties chattering class, hailed *Main Street* for speaking to the country as a whole, the long-awaited Great American Novel. Heywood Broun, New York columnist and influential editor, tagged the novel "almost disconcertingly good." He as others had his caveats, but the bulk of Manhattan's literary elite and the intellectuals heaped praise. Still, there were those qualifications which would hang about Lewis to his death. Francis Hackett in *The New Republic* sang the virtues of the "pioneer work," but he also called Lewis out for cardboard characterization, for creating "types." *The Dial* found the satire merciless and brilliant, but noted the novel had "more social than artistic implications." There was the rub: *Main Street* spoke to a greater American dilemma—but was it literature, was it great? Lewis was not to have a pass, although this criticism represented just an irritation at this point; over the coming years, it rubbed the author raw.[27]

---

there had been a forty-year history of 'debunking'...no novel had smashed the myth of the friendly village or the shell of middle-class complacency." See 287.

[27] Quoted in Lingeman, 150–51. Of particular interest (and fine writing), see Heywood Broun, "Books," *New York Tribune*, October 22, 1920; https://www.newspapers.com. See too Heywood Broun, "Books," *New York Tribune*, October 20, 1920 https://www.newspapers.com. Also F.A. [Francis Hackett], "God's Country," *New Republic*, December 1, 1920, 20–21; www.unz.org: "Can you imagine Henry James deposited for five or six years in McHenry, Illinois...?" "The immense interest of *Main Street*," for Hackett, is "his village is not a special village.... It is, as he himself says, a representative specimen, standing for something to be found anywhere and everywhere in the length and breadth of the Middle West....And in being grasped with such cruel fresh firmness as Mr. Lewis's the whole nation may be felt to squirm." Lewis should be proud: "Main Street is pioneer work.... [T]he light...is on the whole natural, honest, and oh so amazingly illuminating." In a brief note in the *Dial*, Lewis is credited for having "dug his hands into the richest soil of

The word spread across the country; this book had to be read. Of course, judgments were pronounced beyond the cultural hubs. Harcourt advised Lewis "the provinces like it but lack the nerve or sense" to say so. But that was at first. The smaller locales tended to attack, but voices increasingly arose from more sizable towns and from heartland cities. Vachel Lindsay, an acclaimed regionalist, wrote Lewis he would have everyone back in his hometown of Springfield, Illinois read and discuss the book. William Allen White, revered as the spokesman for Middle America, wrote Lewis from Emporia, Kansas that he was buying ten copies for gifts, he wished he could buy a thousand, he wanted the Kansas legislature to make *Main Street* a required text for students. The Sage of Emporia broadcast the reverberating cultural implications.[28]

They all did. Ludwig Lewisohn in the *Nation* reminded the author he must move on. "Our literature and our civilization need just such books as *Main Street.*" He challenged him to live up to "the responsibility which his talent involves." This included the admonition to reach a higher writing standard; a left-handed compliment, sure; despite it he acknowledged Lewis after early stumbles had stepped up. Joseph Hergesheimer, one of *The Saturday Evening Post's* most prominent writers, contacting Lewis from his farm in Pennsylvania, professed unqualified praise: "The detail and labor are stupendous and felicity open to no question." Fellow novelist Charles Norris urged write more, he had a most promising future in the arts. The novel, with its ever-mounting sales, not only spoke to denizens across the continent but to Lewis's delight abroad. Britain's best-selling authors heaped plaudits: Hugh Walpole, H. G. Wells, and John Galsworthy weighed in. Galsworthy observed, "Every country, of course has its Main Streets, all richly deserving of diagnosis, but America is lucky to have found in you so poignant and just and stimulating a diagnostician."[29] The consensus

America and his fingers are a little grubby." See "Briefer Mention," *Dial*, January, 1921, 106; https://books.google.com.

[28] Lingeman, 151–52.

[29] Ibid., 152–53; Lewisohn's unsigned "The Epic of Dulness" appeared in *The Nation*, November 10, 1920, 536–37. "To produce such authenticity of

resounded. Back in the States, another aspiring novelist wrote Lewis's was the best American novel: "The amount of sheer data in it is amazing! As a writer and a Minnesotan let me swell the chorus—after a third reading." F. Scott Fitzgerald signed off, "With the utmost admiration."[30]

H. L. Mencken, whose views Lewis prized, in his vaunted *Smart Set* found *Main Street's* characters "not only genuinely human but also authentically American." He weighed in on the "literature" brouhaha: "The virtue of the book lies in its packed and brilliant detail." Mencken found the characters cardboard-like, but what does that matter? "This attempt is extraordinarily successful."[31] Amongst those critics with a beef about the literary heft of the work, faulty character development kept cropping up. Schorer discusses at length the criticism and totes up: Lewis with *Main Street* became the voice of "a literary generation." "American culture seems always to have had a literary spokesman, a single writer who presented American culture and American attitudes toward its culture, to the world." Lewis was the twenties ticket. Was Sinclair Lewis a bona fide great artist? Schorer writes no, but he provided something possibly more significant:

> Have we enjoyed a cultural irony more absurd than this, that it should have been Sinclair Lewis who emerged to fulfill Walt Whitman's cry for a "literatus"? Whitman had called for a

---

speech once or twice would be merely clever; never to miss it in four hundred and fifty pages is magnificent." He particularly noted the multitudes of characters were anything but two-dimensional: [T]hey detach themselves from the page and are in space, smelling of flesh and hair, cloth and letter." Lewis is neither "didactic or prophetic." "He has notes toward an 'American Credo'...that should be inscribed on tables of brass as both record and warning." Lewis lays out truth and lets the readers speak: "His method is undeviatingly creative; he is secure in the knowledge that to show things truly is to show them up." See https://books.google.com.

30 Schorer, 275.

31 Lingeman, 153. For the rapturous review see H.L. Mencken, "Consolation," *Smart Set*, January, 1921, 138–44, "It is an attempt, not to solve the American cultural problem, but simply to depict with great care a group of typical Americans."

> popular prophet, a maker of democratic images that would elevate and amplify the democratic life which was falling short of its promise. Sinclair Lewis emerged, no mystagogical orator of the sort Whitman had in mind and he himself was, but an image maker certainly, stridently drawing for Americans the picture of their crass, petty, hypocritical, and barren lives.

The foremost Lewis biographer concludes, "The phenomenal success of *Main Street* demonstrated that American democratic culture had received, at precisely the right point, what American democratic culture above all wanted."[32]

Grebstein, again:

> From 1920 to 1930 Sinclair Lewis was, beginning with *Main Street*, a writer who compelled the attention of both his country and the world. The very characteristics which later critics turned against him—his simplicity of theme, the weight of his detail, his didactiveness, the emphasis on environment rather than character, the crude vigor of his style, his faithful transcription of American idiom and sharp portraiture of the surface of American life—made Lewis famous, read, and effective.

The debate would continue for one hundred years, now: great literature, astute sociology, second-class scribbling, anthropology? Some reviewers—not all—would turn Lewis's style harder against him as the decade went by. Still, the twenties would be his. He would be haunted by the criticisms through the twenties and to his end—and he would unabashedly dismiss them *and* earnestly attempt to address them. It was never easy for the author. Nevertheless, in 1920, to all those who paid attention, he had as Grebstein writes, arrived: "America's intellectuals and a good part of its thinking citizenry had become introspective, self-conscious, and self-critical; Lewis had caught the wave at its crest."[33]

---

[32] Schorer, 270–71. For Schorer's analysis of the response to *Main Street*, see 269–97.

[33] Grebstein, 73. Hutchisson discusses shortcomings: "Although nearly all critics agreed that *Main Street* was undoubtedly one of the most important books of its age, they faulted Lewis for a lack of depth in his characterizations.

The tide was in. Lewis wanted to go the distance. He thought a good deal more self-consciousness was in order, for himself, for them all. The suddenly acclaimed novelist would ride the swell, churn up a surge of introspection, speak of, to, and for the United States and its admirable experiment.

In employing his gifts for satire and verisimilitude, Lewis had not concerned himself with the inner lives of his characters. Instead, he presented them as types and defined them in terms of their surroundings and their possessions—'cheap motorcars, telephones, ready-made clothes, silos, alfalfa, kodaks, phonographs [and] unread sets of Mark Twain.'" Ludwig Lewisohn amidst his praise commented *Main Street* was short on "spiritual significance." See 46.

FIVE

BABBITT

A brilliant illustration graces the July 9, 1925 *Life Magazine*, a popular humor publication. An expansive globe fronts an intense blue sky. Main Street crowded with motor cars and town folks sweeps the planet. The thoroughfare is lined by a drug store and dry goods emporium; opera and movie houses; a five-and-dime; fraternal societies; a gas station and more. Business is good on Main Street, pedestrians busy (many literally on the run), automobiles packing the avenue—the road leads straight across America. This is the "Old Home Week" number: country and small-town denizens were being humored in the twenties—more to the point mocked. Joshing rubes and rusticity was not new; the U.S.A. had for a long time done so, all the more as the country moved away from its rural roots. Or had it? Mockery was increasingly directed as well at the presumably up-and-coming residents of the rising cities, particularly in the heartland—this was the laugh *Life* was after. Farmers and town folk were movin' on up—Main Street merged onto the newly paved highways which shot off toward more fashionable domiciles. "The city" had since the Civil War become an explosive phenomenon, increasing exponentially in size and influence. The city was more complex in composition, the citizenry seemed to represent a new breed, a new way of life—all very modern. Most cities—not "sophisticated" New York, Chicago, and the few others feinting toward cosmopolitanism—however housed folks disturbingly similar in spirit to their "bumpkin cousins." They had moved out but not so much up from *Life's* point of view. These urbanites were, as those left behind, hale, hearty, and optimistic; and similarly they were mean and narrow; in essence, they expressed a brand of upmarket provinciality. They took themselves as more sophisticated than those they left back in the country, those upon whom they liked to compare themselves. This emerging hoi polloi was self-assured; they all had landed on a far superior sweep of Main Street; they had reached the pinnacle, twentieth-century civic life. What could be better? Right, laughed the Old Home Week number.

Life knew, and so, too, Sinclair Lewis. The people, the country, the experiment, could do a lot better. Americans across the board had an awful lot in common. The July 9, 1925 issue was a send-up pure and simple; the author was in on the joke. Humor can carry a sting; the magazine was making a point. Those who read *Life* were scoffing at these "others," as they had in 1920 and '21 reading *Main Street*; in 1922 they immediately took up *Babbitt*. The author, on the heels of *Main Street*, set out to expand his assessment of the country's dilemma; it was a straight shot from Gopher Prairie to Zenith, a rising urban center he placed somewhere in the middle of America. By 1925 *everyone* was in on *it*: the very words "Main Street" and "Babbitt" had become embedded in the national lexicon; Lewis in 1924 again caught the country's imagination, or fascination, with the third mammoth splash, *Arrowsmith*, which extended the saga to the canyons of Manhattan. Red Lewis was a scourge...with a point.

In 1922 with *Babbitt*, generally considered the most singularly influential punch the novelist delivered in the twenties, once more the novelist took on the role, as he had prefaced *Main Street*, of the alienated cynic; or as he saw himself a bona fide patriot out to protect the country. Part of the "national" conversation (which was becoming more a reality given the explosive development of mass media) was the decline of the town, the rise of the city; old values giving way to new, the urban business set dominating the country economically, politically, socially, and culturally. Sheldon Norman Grebstein argues, "Lewis's greatest fear" stemmed from the probability that Gopher Prairie's philosophy of dull safety shall conquer all America and then the world...."[1] The "village virus" had taken on modern garb in the typical American city—it did not cover up much of the real McCoy. Main Street for Lewis three years on stretches to Zenith, a middle-sized, middle-American city, the habitat of George Follansbee Babbitt. What could be better? *Babbitt* opens with a vision: "The towers of Zenith aspired

[1] Sheldon Norman Grebstein, *Sinclair Lewis* (New Haven: College and University Press, 1962), 67.

above the morning mist; austere towers of steel and cement and limestone, sturdy as cliffs and delicate as silver rods. They were neither citadels nor churches, but frankly and beautifully office-buildings."[2] Aspiration; austerity; sturdiness; modern and tastefully artistic to boot. Here among these totems stands George F. Babbitt, American businessman—a realtor to be specific.[3] Actually, at this moment he is home, asleep, just about to be awakened at seven-twenty: "It was the best of nationally advertised and quantitatively produced alarm-clocks, with all modern attachments, including cathedral chime, intermittent alarm, and a phosphorescent dial. Babbitt was proud of being awakened by such a rich device. Socially it was almost as creditable as buying expensive cord tires." George Babbitt had arrived.[4]

Main Street had been certified a genuine sensation. Critic Robert Littell had prophesized "if *Main Street* lives, it will probably be not as a novel but as an incident in American life."[5] *Babbitt* in 1922 was an aftershock of monumental proportion. All was not well with Babbitt. He does aspire, he feigns austerity, he'd like to think of himself as sturdy; and he knows, not-so-deep-down, he is delicate; he has genuine feelings and doubts. Babbitt dangerously approaches a major crisis. He has lost confidence in himself and his world. Lewis embarks, for some one hundred pages on a journey through George's day. This is followed by a long year of accumulating mini to middle range crises—another couple of hundred pages. In the end, in the nick of time, George finds resolution as Carol Kennicott in compromise—his is a good deal less annealing for the reader than hers. Carol expressed a faith in keeping at it, sticking to exercises in improvement, and she has a trust in the next generation to carry

---

[2] Sinclair Lewis, *Babbitt* (New York: Penguin Books, 1996), 1.

[3] Babbitt takes pride in the professional, modern rendering of his trade: a realtor, more than simply moving property, possessed an acknowledged American skill—he traded in and on the "good life." Proud of his modernity, status-conscious George had long before ditched the antiquated Follansbee for the sleeker model "F."

[4] Lewis, 3.

[5] Richard Lingeman, *Sinclair Lewis: Rebel from Main Street* (New York: Random House, 2002), 162.

forward the charge. One can locate a slight promise in Carol and Will's twentieth-century progeny and a certainty to their mother's commitment to keep to the grindstone—*they will make it better*. She has compromised, and there is nothing all that bad about it; the United States progresses premised upon its innate talent to reach compromise in the name of the common goal to perfect the Experiment. Carol Kennicott has it in her to build a launch pad for her boy and girl—especially her girl. But *Babbitt* concludes on a far less promising note. The future again rests with the children, yet Babbitt's faith in them, especially his son, offers no hope at all for George other than kidding himself there could be redemption for the errant path he, the boy's model, has trod. It is all-too-probable it is too late for Babbitt and his offspring. It is possibly too late for the United States of America. The country seemingly had become compromised beyond its own good. The postwar decade roars ahead, and it is disturbingly disruptive. Lewis had once more set out to prod the nation forward a long more secure path.

Lewis writing *Babbitt* in part was out to demonstrate to the public and critics not only his condemnation of the new order, its brassy bourgeois template, but on a personal and professional level he needed to testify to his own anti-bourgeois credentials. He knew he had ended *Main Street* in doubt. He apparently had over-compromised Carol, or he had been compromised? "He was," writes Richard Lingeman, "nagged by a sense of unworthiness." He had hit a rich vein, and he was now a wealthy man, but to some critics he was simply part of the problem: "The Bolshevik in him worried that there was something suspect in his book appealing to so many Americans." He wrote literary soulmate Joseph Hergesheimer: "But I agree with them.... Hell's sweet bells, here is divine comedy! An earnest young man, Yankee of physical type, comic and therefore the more humorless, writes a long book to slap the bourgeois—the bourgeois love it, eat it! It would make an excellent short story."[6] He could mend the damage: *Main Street* was a bestseller, he had it made, it had made him; freed from bourgeois pursuits he could write a great novel and show everyone, including himself, he was no sycophant to the middle class. But he was middle class to the

[6] Ibid., 163

core. The idea that Red Lewis had a scrap of Bolshevik in him was in the cant of the day pure poppycock.

The author had earned his tag: he was a class-striver. Still, with *Babbitt*, he would target the bourgeoisie. Robert Littell in the *New Republic* observed the institutions of the city, the world of business, the service clubs, the churches, the papers and banks "conspire to make and keep George F. Babbitt, an ordinary, decent-hearted, soft, average, mediocre American business man, a slave to their own vulgar, noisy, cheap, insincere, illiterate standards of life, by offering him their usual rewards of specious good-fellowship, an ugly but comfortable home, an automobile, and a perishable popularity."[7] Lewis is relentless taking on repeatedly, humorously, sometimes exasperatingly the troubling elements of everyday upper-middle class urban life in the first years of the 1920s. The author's mimicry is perfect, and he unleashes it on a public ready to lend an ear, at least to the extent to hear out the shortcomings of others— "everyman," naturally, considers himself (and herself) superior. This is the village virus.

As always with Lewis's twenties novels, everyone agreed the protagonists are imperiled. Their journeys strike a nerve. Along with the author, readers were taking an entertaining, albeit serious look at themselves and their set. Babbitt himself is getting good at recognition: he

---

[7] Robert Littell, "Babbitt," "The New Republic," October 4, 1922, 152, http://www.unz.org. "[I]n a city the dragon which rules over a small town vaguely, if really enough, becomes an army of dragons with a lot of heads, and the dragons all have names and live in identifiable caves...." Littell recognizes Lewis has moved into deeper territory. He unearths a contagion hardly limited to the small town; but as he digs deeper, Littell believes he oversteps, he is too harsh, too heavy-handed. He wonders if the denizens of the Zeniths of America will see themselves and rise in anger at the author as did the citizens of the Gopher Prairies. "Babbitt is hideously true to the worst things in America." But he argues, there is more to the people than the crudeness Lewis cites so well, "a genuine if not always effective kindliness...." Lewis could be heavy-handed, but he portrays heartland America to be fundamentally decent—hence, capable of nurturing its better angels. Plenty of readers embrace George, a genuinely kind, if hapless and ultimately hopeless compatriot, as still one of their own.

can forever identify what is wrong with others, even occasionally with himself and his society; but he can go only so far. The situation is serious: "Main Street," conceded Littell, "was a complaint, Babbitt is an indictment."[8] George Babbitt errs looking too closely—he sees himself as having taken a wrong turn, compromised by corrupted social values. He finds himself lost, with no way out. He must succumb to social pressure, accept his lot, if he is to live at all, as he has become all-too-accustomed to doing in a most comfortable manner. Babbitt has overstepped, and it scares the dickens out of him.

From the get-go, George concedes he is washed up, wrung out. The real estate game, the Boosters Club, his family and friends, God and nature, cigars and motors, booze and sex—they add up to nothing. Emptiness pervades Babbitt's life, his soul is shot, as much as he flimsily is in touch with it. The first chapter, as he wakes up to take on the day, lays out all the elements of despair. The next six sketch in intense detail what constitutes one day in George F. Babbitt's life. The remainder of the novel tracks his unpromising trajectory toward surrender.

Many of the issues in *Main Street* thread through *Babbitt*, but certain concerns take on a more tactile texture. All five of the twenties bestsellers dabble in marriage, blowhards, and hypocrisy; rural idylls, pioneer dreams, and signs of modernity; endlessly dulling small talk; politics, religion, fads; materialism, consumption, and the farce of advertising; and the automobile (at first treated on Main Street as an extraordinary artifact, by the late twenties Lewis represents it as an ordinary, albeit still admired—and gussied up—totem of the New Era; and he queries in the end perhaps it has become a monstrosity). Each novel highlights its own takes on the evolving society and culture.

Babbitt of the five twenties "tell-alls" is Lewis's most spot-on, heavily supported send-up of the rot that has set in. All is not bad by any means, but somehow the good has been twisted into the ugly. George has arrived: reared on another Midwestern Main Street in another Gopher Prairie, he has climbed to the respectability of Floral Heights, a new subdivision, the crown jewel of aspiring Zenith (which assuredly stands in for Cincinnati). Motoring into the expanding

---

[8] Ibid.

factory district, George marvels "through South Zenith, a high-colored, banging, exciting region: new factories of hollow tile with gigantic wire-glass windows, surly old red-brick factories stained with tar, high-perched water-tanks, big red trucks like locomotives, and, on a score of hectic side-tracks, far-wandering freight-cars from the New York Central and apple orchards, the Great Northern and wheat-plateaus, the Southern Pacific and orange groves." Zenith has arrived; it reigns supreme over the national bounty.[9]

Babbitt marvels at his hard-earned good fortune. He matters—he is a real estate man. He knows little of architecture and urban planning, but he knows the tricks of the trade (legitimate and acceptably illegitimate as Lewis puts it). He is riding an expansionist wave and making good and better money. He does not work nearly as hard as he trumpets to all who can be bothered to listen (snidely, for they sense they all do not work nearly as hard as they contend). His house mirrors the good life; five years old, it is "competent and glossy."

> It had the best of taste, the best of inexpensive rugs, a simple and laudable architecture, and the latest conveniences.

---

[9] Lewis, 60. For another expansive city tour, see 27. Lewis's observations are acute. "He admired each district along his familiar route to the office: The bungalows and shrubs and winding irregular driveways of Floral Heights. The one-story shops on Smith Street, a glare of plate-glass, and new yellow brick; groceries and laundries and drug-stores...Billboards with crimson goddesses nine feet tall advertising cinema films, pipe tobacco, and talcum powder. The old 'mansions' along Ninth Street, S. E., like aged dandies in filthy linen; wooden castles turned into boarding-houses...." "He felt superior and powerful, like a shuttle of polished steel darting in a vast machine." See 46. See 86–91 for detail of the "real city" at night: "At that moment in the city of Zenith, Horace Updike was making love to Lucile McKelvey in her mauve drawing-room on Royal Ridge...." "And at that moment in Zenith, a cocaine-runner and a prostitute were drinking cocktails in Healey Hanson's saloon on Front Street." "At that moment a G. A. R. veteran was dying." "At that moment in Zenith, three hundred and forty or fifty thousand Ordinary People were asleep, a vast unpenetrated shadow. In the slum beyond the railroad tracks, a young man who for six months had sought work turned on the gas and killed himself and his wife."

> Throughout, electricity took the place of candles and slatternly hearth-fires. Along the bedroom baseboard were three plugs for electric lamps, concealed by little brass doors. In the halls were plugs for the vacuum cleaner, and in the living-room plugs for the piano lamp, for the electric fan. The trim dining-room (with its admirable oak buffet, its leaded-glass cupboard, its creamy plaster walls, its modest scene of a salmon expiring upon a pile of oysters) had plugs which supplied the electric percolator and the electric toaster.

Electric wiring is the rage. Lewis concludes "there was but one thing wrong with the Babbitt house: It was not a home." Still, it stands "a master-piece…right out of Cheerful Modern Houses for Medium Incomes." It suited Babbitt's sense of urbanity, his acquired tastes…but it does not reflect fulfillment so much as a showcase for a vapid happiness.[10]

---

[10] Ibid., 12–13. Lewis's compulsion for accuracy never falls short. Bathrooms were the height of modernity, fully displayed: "Though the house was not large it had, like all houses on Floral Heights, an altogether royal bathroom of porcelain and glazed tile and metal sleek as silver. The towel-rack was a rod of clear glass set in nickel. The tub was long enough for a Prussian Guard, and above the set bowl was a sensational exhibit of tooth-brush holder, shaving-brush holder, soap-dish, sponge-dish, and medicine-cabinet, so glittering and so ingenious that they resembled an electrical instrument-board." See 2. For more detail on Floral Heights interiors, see 81–82. James M. Hutchisson demonstrates the author's meticulous research on *Babbitt* and the other twenties works. Maps, interior lay-outs, idiom and cadences, Lewis was extraordinarily thorough in getting surveys right. He wrote Harcourt in July, 1921 that he had started *Babbitt*, "I think he's going to be a corker." He had in hand notes and an outline: "With *Babbitt*, it became Lewis's habit to write such an outline before he wrote the first draft. These outlines represent the storyboards that film directors use to frame sequences of camera shots: like a director, Lewis blocked each section of the action in his plot, scene by scene. It was as if he viewed these preliminary stages of research, note-taking, and planning as a kind of artistic workshop…." All assembled, "characters, plot, and settings and deciding on his theme and tone, he joined these elements together," hastily wrote a draft, then a string of revisions. See *The Rise of*

George is somewhat at a loss amongst his acquisitions. Babbitt "had enormous and poetic admiration, though very little understanding, of all mechanical devises." Electric flat-irons, electric bed-warmers, his new cigar-lighter for his car, all the novelties "were his symbols of truth and beauty." "Regarding each new intricate mechanism—metal lathe, two-jet carburetor, machine gun, oxyacetylene welder—he learned one good realistic-sounding phrase, and used it over and over, with a delightful feeling of being technical and initiated." He does, all his compatriots do. As in Gopher Prairie, they cherish their gift for gab, and it is unceasingly bland, at times verging on nonsensical, and laced throughout with superficial testimonials to solid Republicanism, the virtues of the Republic, and the Ideal Citizen. George bellows: "That's the type of fellow that's ruling America to-day—in fact, it's the ideal type to which the entire world must tend, if there's to be a decent, well-balanced, Christian, go-ahead future for this little planet!" "Once in a while I just naturally sit back and size up this Solid American Citizen, with a whale of satisfaction."[11] Well, yes, and no; deep down, satisfaction is not guaranteed. Sour notes endlessly run the gauntlet of the ever-gabbing men-folk: problems with the business cycle despite the triumphs of capitalism; "bolshevist" unions; "professional" challenges in the offices; problematic New Youth, their own children in particular; the immigrant "infestation." Endless discourse flows in search of a channel, a means to navigate around the obstacles to their general welfare. Sprinkled throughout are racial and ethnic slurs, mean gossip, and the dirty joke. None on close inspection appears so satisfied. Most do not look further. George does so too much. It is a dangerous misstep.

From the get-go—and they are all forever bloviating about pep, initiative, zip and bang, getting ahead of the curve, "the originality of 'spill-of-speech,'" the keen edge in making the sale—Babbitt's daily life is a slog from start-to-finish of depleting frustration. In his palatial bathroom…

Sinclair Lewis, 1920–1930 (University Park: Pennsylvania State University Press, 1996), 65.

[11] Lewis, 60 and 162.

> He hunted through the medicine-cabinet for a packet of new razor-blades (reflecting invariably), "Be cheaper to buy one of these dinguses and strop your own blades,") and when he discovered the packet, behind the round box of bicarbonate of soda, he thought ill of his wife for putting it there and very well for himself not saying "Damn." But he did say it, immediately afterward, when with wet and soapy-slippery fingers he tried to remove the horrible little envelope and crisp clinging oiled paper from the new blade.
>
> Then there was the problem, oft-pondered, never solved, of what to do with the old blade, which might imperil the fingers of his young. As usual, he tossed it on top of the medicine-cabinet, with a mental note that someday he must remove the fifty or sixty other blades that were also temporarily, piled up there."

George faces endless challenge; it is demeaning. Where is the meaning in his life?[12]

Lewis is marvelous at sketching the endless minutiae of everyday life in the dawning twenties. Any middle-class urbanite would have recognized his or her routines, humored by exacting detail—and they did, as this was the author's most admirable talent, his dissection of the American Standard. But the bigger picture is not missed. Paul Reisling, Babbitt's dearest friend and a most unhappy man, one day lays it out straight. Their urbane environs were hardly up to snuff; and for all their snorting and ballyhooing, Paul knows this would not be news to any of their clan. With Paul, George can break away from the trivialities of his existence, "talk some real sense." Generally eager to listen, he is resistant to Paul's straight-talk this day; but he takes it in, he knows there

---

[12] Ibid 108 and 5. The men's room at the Zenith Athletic Club (whose members were disinterested in athletics) was subject for close scrutiny, another gem of modernity. "They grinned and went into the Neronian washroom, where a line of men bent over the bowls inset along a prodigious slab of marble as in religious prostration before their own images in the massy mirror." Ibid., 51–52. Lewis delightfully sends up the design of the club: the entrance was "Gothic," the washroom "Roman Imperial," the lounge "Spanish Mission," the reading-room "Chinese Chippendale," the *pièce de résistance* the half-timbered dining room with its "Tudor leaded casements." See 52.

is a lot more to be said—he feels "out of sorts" himself. But Paul is in a considerably more precarious position: at the end of his rope, his marriage a trap, he huddles with his oldest friend in the corner of their club. George struggles to maintain the standard as Paul unloads:

> "I do draw the line at having to sympathize with Zilla because she's so rotten bad-tempered that the cook has quit, and she's been so busy sitting in a dirty lace negligée all afternoon, reading about some brave manly Western hero, that she hasn't had time to do any cooking. You're always talking about 'morals'—meaning monogamy, I suppose. You've been the rock of ages to me, all right, but you're essentially a simp. You—"
>
> "Where d' you get that 'simp,' little man? Let me tell you—"
>
> "—love to look earnest and inform the world that it's the 'duty of responsible business men to be strictly moral, as an example to the community.' In fact you're so earnest about morality, old Georgie, that I hate to think how essentially immoral you must be underneath. All right, you can—"

But he's not out to pound George; moving on, Paul spews his disgust—"this beastly joke they call 'respectable life....'"

> "And business! The roofing business! Roofs for cowsheds! Oh, I don't mean I haven't had a lot of fun out of the Game; out of putting it over on the labor unions, and seeing a big check coming in, and the business increasing. But what's the use of it? You know, my business isn't distributing roofing—it's principally keeping my competitors from distributing roofing. Same with you. All we do is cut each other's throats and make the public pay for it!"
>
> "Look here, now, Paul! You're pretty darn near talking socialism!"
>
> "Oh yes, of course I don't really exactly mean that—I s'pose. Course—competition—brings out the best—survival of the fittest—but— But I mean: Take all these fellows we know, the kind right here in the club now, that seem to be perfectly content with their home-life and their businesses, and that boost Zenith and the Chamber of Commerce and holler for a million

> population. I bet if you could cut into their heads you'd find that one-third of 'em are sure-enough satisfied with their wives and kids and friends and their offices; and one-third feel kind of restless but won't admit it; and one-third are miserable and know it. They hate the whole peppy, boosting, go-ahead game, and they're bored by their wives and think their families are fools—at least when they come to forty or forty-five they're bored—and they hate business, and they'd go— Why do you suppose there's so many 'mysterious' suicides? Why do you suppose so many Substantial Citizens jumped right into the war? Think it was all patriotism?"

There is a problem here, and George can't stop working it over.[13]

Lewis lays forth a comprehensive scenario vivid in all its trivialities, substance, and absurdities. Some critics and readers would cry enough, he hit his mark time and time again, and again; more to the point, the greater part of the public and reviewers gobbled it up, the truth laid bare. George is a tired businessman. He departs for work: "He kissed her—he didn't quite kiss her—he laid unmoving lips against her unflushing cheek." He uploads himself into his automobile, his cherished symbol of success: "To George F. Babbitt, as to most prosperous citizens of Zenith, his motor car was poetry and tragedy, love and heroism. The office was his pirateship but the car his perilous excursion ashore." Every detail matters, too much to him: "Among the tremendous crises of each day none was more dramatic than starting the engine. It was slow on cold mornings; there was the long, anxious whirr of the starter; and sometimes he had to drip ether into the cocks of the cylinders, which was so very interesting that at lunch he would chronicle it drop by drop…." The lunches, the dinners, the business meetings, it was all talk. And hustle: "As he approached the office he walked faster and faster, muttering, 'Guess better hustle.' All about him the city was hustling, for hustling's sake. Men in motors were hustling to pass one another…. Men were hustling to catch trolleys…. Men in dairy lunches were hustling to gulp down the food which cooks had hustled to fry.

---

[13] Ibid., 56–57.

Men in barber shops were snapping, 'Jus' shave me once over. Gotta hustle.'"[14]

George's good wife, Myra, alone at home, is equally beat: "She had creases from the corners of her mouth to the bottom of her chin, and her plump neck bagged.... She was in a petticoat now, and corsets which bulged, and unaware of being seen in bulgy corsets. She had become so dully habituated to married life that in her full matronliness she was as sexless as an anemic nun."[15] Myra will have her moments, even minor rebellion—Lewis does not short the women's lives; they are repeatedly portrayed to be exercises in "uselessness."[16] Myra, in frustration, ultimately takes a feeble stand for her role, interests, self—still another senseless aggravation for George. The children, meanwhile, lack direction. Verona, the eldest, recently graduated from Bryn Mawr, is bent on reform, even socialism—but knows little about it and finally settles into a conventional engagement. Ted and his high school mates are snappy dressers, well-versed in the lingo of twenties youth; they run to parties, mad on fun. But Ted is heading nowhere. He pitches at the family dining table a correspondence course in mechanics (after all, it was boosted on a matchbook, must be something to it they all agree)—loves to tinker with engines—but is directed by his parents to "State." The university, "that great department-store," after all turned out George, "a sound and standard ware."[17]

---

[14] Ibid., 20–21 and 138.

[15] Ibid., 6.

[16] For a rant on uselessness and modern couples discussing the issue, follow the party conversation's nagging, fraught comments amongst fashionable courses, illicit drink, and indigestion, ibid., 109–10. Lewis dabbles in women's issues through the novel.

[17] Ibid., 61. For Verona's politics and Babbitt's florid retort, see ibid., 14. For his shocked take on the young set's antics see Ted's party, 202–05. For Ted's interests and society's follow the family roundtable pondering a new motor: "They went, with ardor and some thoroughness, into the matter of streamline bodies, hill-climbing power, wire wheels, chrome steel, ignitions systems, and body colors.... Babbitt as a boy had aspired to the presidency, his son Ted [Theodore Roosevelt Babbitt] aspired to a Packard twin-six...." See ibid., 65–66. The novel is filled with motorcar commentaries, much more

George is a joiner. And he knows the score—or does he?

> Just as he was an Elk, a Booster, and a member of the Chamber of Commerce, just as the priests of the Presbyterian Church determined his every religious belief and the senators who controlled the Republican Party decided in little smoky rooms in Washington what he should think about disarmament, tariff, and Germany, so did the large national advertisers fix the surface of his life, fix what he believed to be his individuality. These standard advertised wares—toothpastes, socks, tires, cameras, instantaneous hot-water heaters—were his symbols and proofs of excellence; at first the signs, then the substitutes, for joy and passion and wisdom.

But they all join in, they all carry on. There is no alternative—or is there?[18]

George gets grievously side-lined and nearly flies off the tracks. Bosom-buddy Paul lands in prison for shooting his wife; life hits its nadir. "Babbitt returned to his office to realize that he faced a world which, without Paul, was meaningless." He seeks release; disgruntled, he runs a downhill path toward the less respectable environs of Zenith

---

so than *Main Street* where all is new, rather innocent: "She noted that he was the only person in the motorized town who still took long walks." See Lewis, *Main Street: The Story of Carol Kennicott* (New York: Penguin Books, 1995), 303. By *Arrowsmith* and *Gantry*, cars are of little note, a matter of ordinary life. *Dodsworth* returns to focus more on the iconic invention which has revolutionized life and just possibly is ruining it.

[18] Ibid., 85. For joiners's appreciation of the challenges of effective advertising, see ibid., 106–08. For club gatherings, convention antics, drinking practices, smoker-car discourses see ibid., 181, 230–35, 144–45, 94–104,153–57, 124–30. Catch George and his entrained buddies on race: "The old-fashioned coon was a fine old cuss—he knew his place—but these young dinges don't want to be porters or cotton-pickers....We ought to get together and show the black man, yes, and the yellow man, his place. Now, I haven't got one particle of race-prejudice." Another chimes in: "Thank the Lord, we're putting a limit on immigration. These Dagoes and Hunkies have got to learn that this is a white man's country...." This is the wisdom of Koplinsky, in all certainty a Jew. See 129.

society. He flirts, he arranges an assignation, he starts running around—and then aground—with a younger, bohemian set (whom he comes to understand to be as pedestrian in their values, gossip, and sin as others). George gets political, first as a celebrated party campaigner, then as a dangerous rebel. He renews a friendship with an old classmate, the purportedly radical lawyer Seneca Doane. George starts spouting out to his fellow-boosters surprisingly off-beat observations. He seems less the squire amongst the peasantry and more the rabble-rouser, not to mention an increasingly inebriated womanizer. Babbitt is not all that sure what he's saying or doing; he knows something, everything, is amiss; his manner of life was "incredibly mechanical":

> Mechanical business—a brisk selling of badly built houses. Mechanical religion—a dry, hard church, shut off from the real life of the streets, inhumanly respectable as a top-hat. Mechanical golf and dinner-parties and bridge and conversation. Save with Paul Riesling, mechanical friendships—back-slapping and jocular, never daring to essay the test of quietedness."

Lewis surmises: "Whatever the misery, he could not regain contentment with a world which, once doubted, became absurd."[19]

George's friends and fellow clubmen initially humored, patient with his antics, grow annoyed. They want him back in the fold; in a last-ditch effort, anxious that he has not agreed to join The Good Citizens League (out to establish the Open Shop—a gambit to put down worker unrest), they take "Georgie" on. The G.C.L "was secretly a struggle against all union labor"—and George knows it. He recognizes his friends are out to keep him in line—there is no secret about it. They sit him down and set him straight—he faces banishment from the "Clan of Good Fellows," not to mention financial ruin. Myra worries and George rails: "I know what the League stands for! It stands for the suppression of free speech and free thought and everything else! I don't propose to be bullied...." Babbitt is trapped, and he is feeling justifiably paranoid all eyes are on him. Which way to turn? "He heard them

[19] Ibid., 240, 208–09, and 261. For identity as a burgher overseeing the village from his downtown tower, see 28–29.

whispering—whispering. The independence seeped out of him and he walked the streets alone, afraid of men's cynical eyes and the incessant hiss of whispering." George Follansbee Babbitt has reached the nadir of his rebellion.[20]

Then Myra sickens. Friends, business associates, estranged brothers of the G.C.L., Zenith doctors (whom George has been insulting) rush to the family's aid. Babbitt is repentant. He realizes what counts: friends, community, family. He's safely back on track. And he is close to tears as he once more is encouraged to join the G.C.L.: "Within two weeks no one in the League was more violent regarding the wickedness of Seneca Doane, the crimes of labor unions, the perils of immigration, and the delights of golf, morality, and bank-accounts than was George F. Babbitt." And, expeditiously, George and his realty firm once more are cut in on some "legitimate corruption" vis-à-vis Zenith's traction company…lots to be made on "property transactions."[21]

George, then, has settled. It is the end of the novel, the end of his rebellion. He has his doubts: "He was conscious that his line of progress seemed confused…. He felt that he had been trapped into the very net from which he had with such fury escaped and, supremest jest of all,

---

[20] Ibid., 346, 343, 331, and 336. The fictional G.C.L. reflects postwar reaction and organized repression by the likes of the Chamber of Commerce and American Legion. See 306–07.

[21] Ibid., 345. Spokesman for the virtues of his profession, George throughout remains incurious regarding urban challenges: police corruption, prostitution, business chicanery, unions, small business struggling against retail hegemony; progressive architecture, long-term urban planning, education, et al.—and proud he is "not too reasonably dishonest." "In nothing—as the expert on whose advice families moved to new neighborhoods…was Babbitt more splendidly ignorant than in the science of sanitation. He did not know a malaria-bearing mosquito from a bat; he knew nothing about tests of drinking water; and in the matters of plumbing and sewage he was as unlearned as he was voluble. He often referred to the excellence of the bathrooms in the houses he sold. He was fond of explaining why it was that no European ever bathed." Ibid., 37–41, quoted 40. In his next novel *Arrowsmith*, Lewis does a wholesale expose of the progressive interest in public health which has become in itself corrupted.

been made to rejoice in the trapping." Well, there was time: "I'm going to run things and figure out things to suit myself—when I retire." At the least he has that feint ray of hope: he has, he considers, returned to the fold more liberal in his sentiments and more sensitive to what matters in life. Above all, Myra is alive; he has his friends; heck, he's a booster again; it is heartwarming to be considered worthwhile in others' eyes—no matter how far he descends into their claptrap. "[F]igure out things…when I retire": a contrived rationale that would fool no one, including George. And it is a contrived plot-end. What if, after all, Myra had not been on her deathbed? Would George have had the wherewithal to remain a rebel? And what would that mean, anyway? *What* did he stand for, where was he headed? And now that he has postponed figuring things out, well, what's left for Babbitt? The reader is left with the same sense of defeat George faces: "'They've licked me; licked me to a finish!' he whimpered." There is no satisfactory resolution.[22]

There is no question that George finds genuine solace with family, friends, and community. "Instantly all the indignations which had been dominating him and the spiritual dramas through which he had struggled became pallid and absurd before the ancient and overwhelming realities, the standard and traditional realities, of sickness and menacing death, the long night, and the thousand steadfast implications of married life." He "crept back to her" and peace: his friends and community embraced him, he "felt that he was swinging from bleak uplands down into the rich warm air of a valley pleasant with cottages."[23] There is no argument with the strength of such sentiments. But this never was the issue. In customary Lewis manner, there is no clarifying singular resolution of the ultimate conundrum, the shortcomings of American society and culture. Is George licked or not? He has forged a compromise; but what is it worth? It seems a fraud—"licked me to a finish." Anxiety lurks beneath the satisfaction. This is no practical resolution even as tentative as Carol had embraced. Lewis will scribble on, and never uncover a direct remedy. Critics and scholars always will wrestle with its

---

[22] Ibid., 352.

[23] Ibid., 338 and 344.

"absence"; he never could arrive at *the resolution*—the murkiness haunted his writing, the criticism stung. His wife Gracie objected: his aim was straight; get people to *see.* He knew the country. Therein lay the resolution, the path to salvation. Know ourselves; take action; fulfill the nation's destiny. This is an Experiment. There is substantial Promise. The author knew this would not satisfy his critics; nevertheless he was committed to demonstrate it should not be a conundrum—he was not offering any specific remedy beyond the overwhelmingly necessity to take a good gander and make a difference. He believed he could, that he did—but he struggled getting that aim, that success across—too few put as much weight on it as he. His novels, the fate of his protagonists, always lay in doubt. This for the author was *the issue*—inherent in the nation's trek toward perfection *was doubt.* That is what drives experiment. For the critics, there had to be certainty.

Lewis serves up one final chapter to *Babbitt*; herein arises another insight into George's denouement and with it a clearer yet still murky hint of what Lewis was pursuing and how he viewed it. It raises a seminal issue which appears to have escaped plenty of readers of his day, a fistful of reviewers (but not all), and most literary scholars: Lewis knows what he wants to say but possibly does not have the courage to follow through on it. He believes long-term, tentative steps can lead to reform, a return to foundational values, resolution of the country's Promise—specifics are not his forte; and radicalism is not in his make-up. He is embarrassingly bourgeois—a mainliner. Could he just say he accepts the established order? He simply but significantly wants to enable people to see and to act; fortify the order. Unfortunately, he failed to make that clear. Instead, Lewis leaves George's fate hanging: he cannot create a real rebel, and George, representative of the babbitts, hardly seems destined to see the light, at that crucial minimum take some tentative steps toward real reform. Why doesn't Lewis outright claim he is middle-class and he has faith the middle-class will carry the United States forward?

Lewis suffers his own doubts regarding his ability to act on his personal misgivings—perhaps he queries who is he to set the charge, initiate *the way out*? He is under fire for caving, for at heart being bourgeois. One evidently must be more radical. Just to determine we always, experimenting, are left in doubt is not a satisfying conclusion. But it is Lewis's; and if he is embarrassed to just say so, so be it. But he is never comfortable saying it, and projects the embarrassment when on rare occasion in exasperation he declares I am a babbitt—to say he is a more rarified brand of a babbitt but not bourgeois will never work. He is stuck: Sinclair Lewis is a bourgeois American. To complicate his situation, he accepts the critique, feels obliged to answer it, concedes there is this weakness in his work; or simply the author has not the nerve directly to challenge the critics' sense always there must be resolution. And yes, he is bourgeois, and he takes no shame in saying so—he is an American who is not an apologetist; and he advocates changes are in order. The question then hangs over the writer: is he so compromised, he's just George, maybe some long-away day he'll figure it all out? Is he also irreparably compromised? Lewis is sufficiently aware that he tries to slip the knot with an addendum, a laugh at "resolution." He showcases one last crisis whereby George apparently is not finished at all; and yet on closer scrutiny he is done-in. A few last pages underscore the author's frustration and add no more clarity than this will always be part of the human condition, and the nation's, too.

Ted and Eunice, the girl next door, have eloped. George, Myra, big-sister Verona and her formerly radical but now practical-minded fiancé, little-sister Tinka ("the only pleased member of the inquisition"), and Myra's mother and father (George's no-bull real estate partner) need to lay down the law. Once the renegades are stirred out of their bridal loft, Ted's boyhood bed, they have to face off "society." Firing at the newlyweds all they've got from all directions, George steps forward and takes control: "Ted, come into the dining room and we'll talk this over." He evidently is not licked, he remains a man in charge of his fate—more to the point, his boy's. Babbitt goes up to his son, places his hands on his shoulders: "You're more or less right. They all talk too much. Now what do you plan to do, old man?" Ted is taken aback: "Gosh, dad, are you really going to be human?" George stumbles: "Well, I—Remember one time you called us 'the Babbitt men' and said we ought to stick together? I want to. I don't pretend to think this isn't serious. The way the cards are stacked against a young fellow today, I can't say I approve of early marriages. But you couldn't have married a better girl than Eunice. But what do you plan to do? Course, you could go right ahead with the U., and when you'd finished—" Now it is Ted's turn to rise to the occasion: "Dad, I can't stand it any more. Maybe it's all right for some fellows. Maybe I'll want to go back some day. But me, I want to get into mechanics. I think I'd get to be a good inventor. There's a fellow that would give me twenty dollars a week in a factory right now." But George had gone to the U., he had been amongst the up-and-coming of his parochial day, he is a college man; and he had wanted to study law, side-tracked by his reluctant marriage to Myra. Ted was to complete the odyssey, it was his, their destiny. Maybe not: "'Well—' Babbitt crossed the floor, slowly, ponderously, seeming a little old. 'I've always wanted you to have a college degree.'" Then he catches himself:

> But I've never—...practically, I've never done a single thing I've wanted to in my whole life! I don't know's I've accomplished anything except just get along. I figure out I've made about a quarter of an inch out of a possible hundred rods. Well, maybe you'll carry things on further. I don't know. But I do get a kind of sneaking pleasure out of the fact that you knew what you wanted to do and did it. Well, those folks in there will try to bully you, and tame you down. Tell 'em to go to the devil! I'll back you. Take your factory job, if you want to. Don't be scared of the family. No, nor all of Zenith. Nor of yourself, the way I've been. Go ahead, old man! The world is yours!"

Babbitt concludes: "Arms about each other's shoulders, the Babbitt men marched into the living-room and faced the swooping family."[24]

What does one make of such a conclusion? Babbitt is not licked as he appeared before this addendum is inserted—or is he again fooling himself? Are readers to kid themselves into credulity? Where does Lewis stand? Whatever doubts one is left with as to the final outcome of the Babbitt family crisis, the reader is definitively left hanging—figure it out. Figure out, as well, that Lewis is talking about the national

---

[24] Ibid., 353–55.

condition, the challenge to the country. The true protagonist in his novels is the United States of America: "The world is yours!"

Naturally, to his credit, and to admiring readers and critics, George stands by his son. There are many angles here. Why did reviewers, latter-day scholars, and presumably contemporary readers not *en masse* raise the question—why is this final word inserted? Few mention the addendum at all; some are thrown off and fall into awkward interpretations. Many are quizzical whether Babbitt's penultimate resolve as he returns to the fold in effect offers hope; some charge it is a hollowed-out victory, a doomed compromise. They take this on with some earnest—Babbitt's dilemma. A few see Ted as the prodigal son who will make good his father's dream. Most tellingly, hardly anyone takes serious notice of this last chapter. Perhaps they might have if the author had been straightforward about what he was advising—take a strong look at the state of the union.

Or, is Lewis in effect mocking the whole question as to what has to be answered: "What is the resolution?" Leave it to the reader to see that on his or her own: "We cannot have a singular resolution; we are entangled in a great experiment." Lewis pretty much makes that point without being explicit. We have our doubts. We must live with them. And we must progress; there are choices to be made; where they lead, we shall see; and naturally, moving down the pike, make more choices. That is the individual's challenge and the nation's—seeing, doubting, acting, always moving toward improvement. Yet, Lewis does not say it as "simple" as it could be said. What's up?

He just can't do it. Hence, the final episode: What is the point of it? George on occasion can be strong enough; but is there any sign he and Ted have the wherewithal to man the line against the likes of family and society? Really stick to it? No reviewers, critics, scholars seriously have tackled that question. George has already compromised himself—some argue hope for him, but weakly. Now, purportedly a more substantive ray of hope takes on life with Ted's display of courage? Again, a few critics firmly stand by that. Perhaps, after all, what Lewis in effect is saying to the critics is look at these two: What possible resolution do they represent? Perhaps Lewis not having the backbone to say there lies no hope there, that he radically perceives the whole capitalist system must be altered—which he does not believe—slides in this last "word," and in effect leaves a slippery suggestion: "Can't you see, there is no easy resolution?"

Here then is a possibility that the author has a last laugh on everyone. "I won't say it, but I'll prod you to ask yourself what could be the resolution?" Seeing none, is it not then apparent that one must just keep at it? That the United States, a fundamentally middle-class nation (in aim if not yet in majority numbers) has a job to tackle.

One assumes most have to see Ted setting out in the world, to make his mark, to make a difference, is farcical. Lewis knows exactly what he is saying here. Yes, the cards have been stacked for the privileged offspring; but Ted holds a losing hand. College may well be a compromise for the boy, but if he can stay the course he'll be holding a strong hand if he sticks to it; he'll be well-established, the lawyer his father had wanted to be. His father's son, the family's pride, will not be content. All then must instead back him in his dream to be an automobile mechanic. "The world is his"—but does this track spell contentment? One would hope. However, this jazzed-up grease monkey, this mechanic-cum-inventor, he's headed for the New Era factory. Did Lewis see this as redemption? The workers, he has already acknowledged, are cowed by the ownership class and prize upward mobility. Ted is going to invent—what? There never has been a sign he could concoct much more than a cocktail. Ted has come across as a fun-loving twenties teenager (a term coming into vogue), and he has never expressed any interest in reading, studying, current events, civics, work beyond getting ahead through a college course pitched on a matchbook cover. He has nowhere demonstrated skills beyond tinkering with car engines, let alone leadership talent—he never knows where he is headed; suddenly he is enlightened, ambitious, smart to make it big his way? There are here notable sentiments—father and son standing together, at their best facing life. The boy striking out on his own, in his own way. No one questions the value of factory work—except George, Myra, and their whole clan, not to mention dispossessed factory workers and those who rule them. George is loving, and he is endearing; and he remains a fool. He's banking on Ted. If this is Ted's future, it hardly reflects the credo of the day, substantive twenties optimism, upward mobility, the good life, all can be middle class—or more. Lewis in effect is shouting, "We are left doubtful."

Ted is embarking on his own sojourn, but in certainty it will terminate on the factory or just possibly his own garage floor; one could not count on this lightweight rising to anything more than a supervisory role, perhaps minor management; nor is he the Henry Ford type. And that is okay. But the idea he will rise higher in society, this boy has the wherewithal to charge ahead to new heights, is a misfire. Those who accept Ted's ultimate success as the point Lewis is making miss the real point. Lewis's addendum, Ted and Eunice's uprising, is stillborn—if anything, Lewis was having one last laugh at us all, and himself in particular, or a moan. An optimistic end? No. A pessimistic end? Yes, if in the sense one must have a clear-cut resolution. Carol Gopher Prairie at a minimum has seen the light: compromise and move ahead. But *Main Street* terminated with a good deal more hope in Carol's chances; George and Ted Babbitt's stories end with a lot less so.[25]

What then is Lewis up to here, ending the novel on this note? Whatever he intended for it, or feared to say leaving the story with father and son marching back to take on the family as well as the society, the sad fact is no one took much note of the ending. No one was laughing. Surely because it was so lightweight, so hard to accept that it pointed anywhere ahead, there simply was no discussion about it beyond the passing note. Classic in a sense: Lewis has an expertise playing

---

[25] There is more to our knowledge of George's trajectory that helps to solve for the curious "what happens?" Babbitt crops up in different novels. He drops her into *Arrowsmith* with little fanfare; briefly as well, nothing different. In *Dodsworth* he reappears an acquaintance of Dodsworth, the Zenith automobile mogul who ultimately more than any of his protagonists has a firm grip on exactly where he is headed. Yet in *Dodsworth* there is no hint George is Dodsworth's astute fellow-crusader; he means little to Dodsworth. Lewis appears slyly to be reminding readers George never will alter course. There remains, however, the possibility he is saying, yes the father comes up short, but what about Ted? Nothing evidently. By default—not a word on the promising son, Lewis has no spot for Ted in the progressive arc of his saga. How easy it could have been for Lewis, if he intended Ted to succeed, to slip him in as a big wig in the Dodsworth auto works? It never was in the cards.

with doubt—maybe he really did seriously write in the last scene to make the point there always will be doubt. Maybe he was saying figure it out—if you cannot, so be it. But the fact remains the author was going to set the record straight with *Babbitt*: "He was nagged by a sense of unworthiness." His success with *Main Street* was "divine comedy." His critics he had declared were right…"if the damned book has sold so well, I must be rotten." I'll have to show them, he might have thought. Well, the second book's sales as its predecessor were gigantic. People liked what they read, but they were far from radicalized, far from rallying around specific tonics for the problems at hand. Of course, there is no denying readers and critics got the picture. The author wants readers to take in what ails the nation. He offers diagnosis; they liked the book, a lot. Critics wanted resolution; they are left with doubt, but seemingly do not see what Lewis wants them to see: doubt who we are, do something about it. Hence, Lewis must face, supremist jest of all, that if he'd yet once more only pleased as he put it the nincompoops he had assailed, he had told an engaging tale but no one felt the sting of the challenge, perhaps it is true that his work was bourgeois to its core. Wouldn't it have been easier to simply say that? Explain himself better; expand on his aim more satisfactorily? He had endeavored to prove he was worthy, he had come down hard on the establishment, there was real danger in the land—no one got it? It is unfortunate the author could not accept that in diagnosing, in sketching the broader American Promise must be salvaged, he had done his part—the Experiment must continue, progress will ensue. As always, the country would work its way through. Perhaps ironically, Lewis was simply swamped in doubts about the country and himself that he could not stand up and say what exactly was on his mind. Again, he was the first to argue I am a babbitt. He ought to have taken a stand more firmly behind that fact.

Lewis was a man uncomfortable with own identity, bourgeois to his nines. In his own estimation he might well be as compromised as much as his protagonists. Perhaps the reviewers, the critics were right, he did not have the literary chops. Having attempted to set the record straight, to go beyond *Main Street* and lay out the challenge the nation faced, to paint a dire end-portrait in *Babbitt*, he had fallen short. Lewis could not publicly spell out the personal and professional dilemma.

Bookman editor John Farrar, while commenting favorably upon *Babbitt*, argued there was farce here, even tragedy. Farrar deduced that for all the novel's strengths in the end he was disappointed: "So Main Street, the insulted and injured, has won out after all. It has taken Lewis into its materialistic camp. It has made him worship, against his surface will, perhaps, its own kind of success. He 'belongs' now, does Sinclair Lewis." Lewis for Farrar had cashed in, the hearty promise of *Main Street* ended in a bourgeois dead-end, no serious resolution to the problems at hand. This was a grave misread of the novel and the author's intentions. Still, Farrar correctly uncovered he offered no exacting resolution, nothing radical, just keep plugging along as he saw it. The critic must be credited with digging deeper than almost everyone else.[26]

For all the accolades, Lewis accepted he had fallen short. The remaining big three novels of the decade, *Arrowsmith*, *Elmer Gantry*, and *Dodsworth* forthrightly would expand on his argument: the United States has problems and it must have the wherewithal to work its way through. But he never clearly states that is what he is all about. And, that is the American story. To his credit he seemed to acknowledge along with George it is complicated: "He was conscious that his line of progress seemed confused."

Try as the author would, he would remain haunted by the charge he was not a solutions man. John B. Koblas succinctly caught, using Lewis's own words, the unhappy conundrum he could not escape: "Lewis related that he was a member of the middle class, that there would always be a middle class, and that he would always write about it. Yet he confessed to a friend that he regretted in his own essential ways that he was so middle class."[27] Really, all along, there was the dilemma; even back in 1922 he was on record: "Damn it. You can't realize how much of Babbitt there is in me—in all of us. Along with his Rotarian, right-thinking notions there was much that was fine and lovable." Babbitt was not all that bad, or at the least Lewis wanted to believe so. What was good from his perspective was that the middle class, the

---

[26] [John Farrar], *The Bookman*, "The Literary Spotlight," www.unz.com.

[27] John B. Koblas, *Sinclair Lewis: Home at Last* (Bloomington: Voyageur Press, 1981), 136.

United States, had it within itself, had proved over centuries it had the know-how to carry on—this the author never doubted. He even wrote it—but for all the heft of his work, he never outright put it this way. His personal and professional lines of progress seemed to have dictated he never could.

Perhaps Lewis garnered satisfaction that the reviewers (and if he lived longer, later critics and scholars as well) reached a consensus that Lewis in *Babbitt* had hit his target dead-on, he got America—it appeared to be enough, of a sort, and yet they still questioned his literary credentials. The reviewers of *Main Street* and *Babbitt* unanimously perceived the strengths of his observation skills. He painted a comprehensive picture, but was this literature? It was without any doubt a best-seller. Still, they wanted more from the author.[28]

Lingeman notes, "The reviews were dazzling, including the key ones by May Sinclair in *The New York Times Book Review* and Owen Johnson in the New York *Herald*. Burton Rascoe in the New York *Tribune*, John Farrar (surprisingly despite his qualms) in *The Bookman*, Upton Sinclair in *Appeal to Reason*—all pronounced *Babbitt* superior to *Main Street*." Johnson wrote Lewis, be he novelist or sociologist, had written something "revolutionizingly significant." And Johnson caught Lewis wanted readers to take note: he "educated the great reading public to a willingness toward self examination, a receptive mood, which induces a genuine literature." He is matured in observation and analysis of a "complicated America." Still, in the end Johnson does not see a novel; in "friendly criticism" he urges a most-capable Lewis to become

---

[28] Advance sales were impressive; encouraged, Harcourt ran an 80,500 copy first printing. See Lingeman, 209–214 for the book's success and perceived shortfalls. Ever the capitalist, Lewis from the get-go knew he would create a sensation, and would profit. Hutchisson recalls: "Lewis agreed to a 'joint gamble' with Harcourt whereby one-third of his 15 percent royalty on all copies of *Main Street* sold would be used to advertise the novel. Lewis and Harcourt had the same arrangement for all his novels. Redistributing part of the profits from his novels to advertising kept Lewis's name almost constantly in the public eye." See 56.

that novelist.[29] There was that catch: many still questioned the author fulfilled the demands of a novel—proper literary style, sound character development, a satisfactory resolution. Lewis read his reviews closely. There was this: H. L. Mencken saluted his pal with a first-class review, challenging the negative critiques. "Mencken writes that the central character 'simply drips with human juices.' He takes joy in the fact that 'there is no plot whatever, and very little of the hocus-pocus commonly called character development.' Babbitt is clownish, but he is not merely a joke; 'there is more than mere humor in the novel, there is 'searching truth.'" But this was the nub of the matter. What does one do with that truth? No plot, no character development? Where does it lead? *Where* Mencken balked? Read the work—no resolution? The work is complete: "He is America incarnate, exuberant and exquisite. Study him well and you will know better what is wrong with the land that we live in than you would know after plowing through a thousand such volumes as Walter Lippmann's 'Public Opinion.' What Lippmann tried

[29] Lingeman, 209. Sinclair noted, "For though nobody will recognize himself in George F. Babbitt, everybody will recognize somebody else." May Sinclair, "The Man From Main Street," *New York Times Book Review and Magazine*, September 24, 1922, https://timesmachine.nytimes.com. See Owen Johnson, "Sinclair Lewis as a Polemicist, *New York Herald Tribune*, September 17, 1922. Rascoe, perceiving it inevitable Lewis would project his sights beyond Main Street to a broader venue, was taken aback by his "extraordinary literary development" in less than two years. He saw *Babbitt* as much more than *Main Street*, as art, "one of the finest social satires in the English language." Burton Rascoe, "A Mirror of Mediocrity," *New York Tribune*, September 17, 1922. Farrar as referenced had that curious reaction. He considered the new release fell short of *Main Street*: "The truest thing ever said about Lewis—it was also the highest praise he ever deserved, was that 'Main Street' was one of the milestones in the discovery of America." He does not mean the novel itself but the exposure, what everyone always knew but had never so well-telescoped—Middle America in all its smallness. As for *Babbitt*, he was as critical of its perceived literary weaknesses as he was of *Main Street's*—he does not give the novel the time of day beyond brief notes. Crucially, he believed Lewis had sold out to all he condemned in *Main Street*. Still, he granted there was hope, Lewis could produce superior art. See [Farrar].

to do as a professor, laboriously and without imagination, Lewis has here done as an artist with but a few vivid strokes." For the cynical Mencken, *that* in the end was the story, full stop.[30]

Mencken concluded, "I know of no American novel that more accurately presents the real America. It is a social document of a high order."[31] There was agreement there was truth in the depiction of the overarching dilemma. Novelist John O'Hara would recall: "All the other novelists and journalists and Babbitt himself were equally blind to Babbitt and Zenith and the United States of America until 1922. Do you know of anyone since Fielding who made such an important discovery-creation?"[32] Novelist Rebecca West in Great Britain perceived in Babbitt a "bonehead Walt Whitman: "Stuffed like a Christmas goose...with silly films, silly newspapers, silly talk, silly oratory...."[33] The British edition included an introduction by novelist Hugh Walpole; he noted *Main Street* had repelled English readers because Americans were "ugly in speech, in background, in thought," and *Babbitt* was the same with the exception that the reader who stuck with it would be rewarded: "English readers will be making a very serious mistake if they miss this book. As a work of art it is fine, true, complete, and understanding. As a piece of life it is yet finer...."[34] H. G. Wells, the anointed British dean of realism whose opinion possibly meant most to Lewis, sensed something further had been reached. Lingeman writes that for Wells, Lewis "had *got* the typical American businessman as no one had before, in all his vulgarity but also in his groping for something better." Ah, as Mencken argued, is this not a demonstration

[30] Lingeman, 210; H. L. Mencken, "Portrait of an American Citizen," *Smart Set*, October, 1922, https://library.brown.edu. Lippmann was a formidable commentator on society and politics in the first two-thirds of the twentieth century.

[31] Lingeman, 210.

[32] Ibid.

[33] Schorer, 344.

[34] Lingeman, 210. See Hutchisson, 229–31 for Walpole's full introduction. Lewis was pleased that sales in Britain well outsold *Main Street*. Harcourt had recommended Johnathon Cape as a young publisher with a good notion of promotion. Lewis made the contact. See Lingeman, 192.

of sufficient resolve if not thorough resolution? West agreed with Wells, writing it was hopeful, ultimately those in the United States of America had what it takes: "There is in these people a vitality so intense that it must eventually bolt with them and land them willy-nilly into the sphere of intelligence; and this immense commercial machine will become the instrument of their aspirations."[35]

For the author, however, for all the grasp such reviews demonstrated, there remained the bugaboo "art." Neither West nor Wells considered *Babbitt* a "great novel." Still, West argued Lewis had "art"; *Main Street* had fallen short; it "had not that something extra and above the logical treatment of its subject—'that peacock's feather in the cap,' as Yeats has called it—which makes the work of art." *Babbitt* "is saturated with America's vitality which makes one obey the rhythms of its dance music, which gives unlimited power over audiences to their actresses.... And combined with this, Mr. Lewis has an individual gift of humour, a curiously sage devotion to craftsmanship, and a poetic passion for his own, new country." Most strikingly, West perceived what Lewis was after, something broad and deep. The Old World was a restrictive environment, where the up-and-coming bourgeoisie had little to look forward to: "But there is for Babbitt a certain advantage; or perhaps in the transitional and blundering state of affairs revealed in this book, it should be called a certain opportunity. He moves in a setting so vast and so magnificent that surely it must ultimately dictate vastness and magnificence to the action it contains." What a riddle—art, but not sufficient creativity to be that "great novel?"[36]

What a smash-up. Where plot and character might be hocus-pocus to Mencken, others believed Lewis had either done the job, made art of some measure as Walpole, Wells, and West assessed—and Mencken—or not. Resolution? West sees prophesy and in it a testament to art: a resolute people will find its way—at least clear direction. Then there is Ernest Boyd. He considered *Babbitt* "aimless and negative." Lingeman, in treating Boyd, argues the critic indicts the novel for

---

[35] Ibid., 210.

[36] Rebecca West, "Notes on Novels," *New Statesman* (October 21, 1922), pp. 78–79.

"lacking a countering vision of the good, true, beautiful—of what might redeem Babbitt and America." The scholar notes in conjunction with such criticism there arose charges "Lewis was too much a Babbitt himself to offer anything better, that his satire did not bring to bear an independent standard of values." What was he after, what had he achieved? What constitutes an independent standard of values? Lewis corrupted; society as well; to call it out but not argue a resolution is to fall short? To not establish a vision true, good, beautiful…redemption in and of itself? Again, West saw none of this; Lewis in *Babbit* had struck a grand representation of a vast and magnificent *opportunity.* Yes, Lewis could be excused if he wondered what exactly were they all trying to articulate?[37]

As Lingeman, other scholars weighed in, having read the novels, the reviews, and the work of fellow Lewis students, all sensing something is amiss and trying to straighten it out. They all, as Lewis's contemporaries, seem unsteady, but determined. Lewis baffles. Hutchisson notes reviewers believed Carol in *Main Street* at least offered a glimpse of hope by the end, that she, unlike George, had enough sense to see the distance before her and the difficulty to overcome the malady that haunted the Gopher Prairies; that she had a viable perspective, in their words (which come up a lot) an independent set of standards to fall back on, a grasp what America might be after. There was *that promise.* Hutchisson notes Edith Wharton (Lewis dedicated *Babbitt* to her) wrote she saw George had no capacity to reflect on his plight, to come up with a worthy response as he was "in and of Zenith up to his chin & over. Sinclair Lewis is obliged to do the seeing and comparing for him." Apparently Wharton detected the author indeed possessed an independent standard of values.[38] Yet, bewilderingly Hutchisson in his introduction to the Penguin Classics edition of *Babbitt* expresses some hope in Ted: "Lewis implies that the next generation…will not make the mistakes that the present generation has."[39] So, Theodore

---

[37] Lingeman, 211.

[38] Hutchisson, 89.

[39] James M. Hutchisson, introduction to *Babbitt* by Sinclair Lewis (New York: Penguin Books, 1996), xxvii.

Roosevelt Babbitt has high standards? That is a stretch too far, and why imply it? Just say it—Lewis often was charged with an irritating ability of saying exactly what was on his mind. Wharton, as Hutchisson states, did not see hope in Babbitt; how could Lewis, then, in Ted? That last chapter only served to trip Hutchisson up.

Lingemann, Grebstein, and Schorer as well get knotted up reading the novels, the reviews, fellow researchers' analyses. For all and sundry, across the decades, art continued to pose a gnawing tangle. Latter-day scholars trying to work out the conundrum cannot avoid landing themselves in a debilitating net of contradictions. Not their fault—contemporaries were unsteady, and the multitude of takes on Lewis ever since the twenties represent a daunting challenge. For example, Hutchisson points out Ludwig Lewisohn in 1922 contended Lewis had not fully deciphered the causes of Babbitt's despair; his art suffered.[40] Grebstein on the other hand decades earlier than Hutchisson, had dug further. He writes scholar Max Geismar in 1947 noted Lewisohn was sure of Lewis's artistic shortfalls in 1922—and he was. Hutchisson, however, errs in arguing Lewisohn had not hit upon the cause of Babbitt's anguish. Lewisohn had not minced words. Geismar in 1960, Grebstein relates, in *Saturday Review*, urging a reconsideration of Lewis's literary contributions, recognized Lewisohn had grown in his appreciation, and this should be read into the story. Lewisohn a critic, in 1932 declared the novelist had achieved with *Babbitt* "high artistic achievement." The critic Geismar argues found Lewis conveyed through Babbitt and his compatriots a "sense of fear and dread"; he "compared Lewis with Molière and Dickens."[41] He is correct. Ten years had passed; Lewisohn back in 1922 was certain what Lewis was after—Babbitt's despair was accounted for throughout the novel. Lewisohn, naturally, as Geismar had located in 1947, had every right to change his view about what constituted art. He argued in 1922 *Babbitt* far exceeded *Main Street*, and the praise was high. Compared to *Main Street*, "There is a higher concentration of substance, a more scrupulous testing of style...." He cites "the essence of Rotarianism" which Lewis has made "eternal and

[40] Hutchisson, *Rise*, 88.
[41] Grebstein, 83.

perfect for our delectation and the terror and laughter of posterity." "What is certain is that to us the book represents a deed of high cultural significance and that the future historian of American civilization will turn to it with infinite profit, with mingled amusement, astonishment, and pity." Lewisohn had no problem seeing Lewis was doing literature *and* history in 1922 but "art" initially tripped the critic up. Lewis had moved beyond the "quietness, rudeness, and bickering" of Gopher Prairie to "the granite arched and nickel-plated splendors of sound business, great hotels, cottage-colonies, boulevard systems, and up-to-date offices," and what he located rung despairingly hollow. Beneath the author's "virtuosity" lay "his sense of the tragic in life, his steady closeness to those permanent values by which he condemns the bright and busy scene he delineates." Still, as Hutchisson points out, in 1922 Lewisohn definitively did not perceive "high artistic achievement": "It would be futile to attempt to inquire into the absolute aesthetic value of such a book as ['Babbitt'] nor would the enquiry be important." Ten years passing, Lewisohn thought differently. A decade of stirring developments and full-scale economic and social collapse gave him a higher sensitivity to what makes art; history can be part and parcel of the analysis. Lewis had detected how off the rails the American Experiment was slipping. It is good Geismar caught the change in perspective; it is excellent Grebstein went further in search of what was being said.[42]

In 1932 Lewisohn's perspective had been altered. He had been right to claim in 1922 the enquiry as to art was beside the point. He now perceived a bold stroke: Lewis seemingly had done something entirely new, and now, if one wished to enquire, it did qualify as art—now amidst collapse it made full sense. As any historian and literary scholar of the period knows, the entire perspective had changed amidst the upheavals of the Great Depression. Lewisohn ten years later espied his error, reconsidered aesthetic value; acknowledged there was more to art than they all had perceived. Now, *Babbitt* by his reckoning was the height of achievement as a remarkable historic document.

---

[42] L. L. [Ludwig Lewisohn], *Babbitt*, "Nation," September 20, 1922, 284–85.

Historical insight counts; so, too, historical perspective when assessing literature. This, importantly, is not to fault Hutchisson; his research focused on Lewis's twenties novels (still, it is hard to understand how he could have overlooked Lewisohn's clear detailing of the sources of Babbit's misery). Yet this does serve as a reminder Lewis can entangle frustrated readers, reviewers, critics—the huge bulk of material "all-things-Lewis" can be tricky to decipher.

Lewis is a knotty topic for any scholar to address, and the resources are tangled. Lingeman shares Hutchisson's misread: "Ludwig Lewisohn, who fervently praised the novel, complained that Lewis had not adequately plumbed the causes of Babbitt's desperation." Again, Lingeman adds many reviewers damned the author: "Lewis was too much a Babbitt himself to offer anything better, that his satire did not bring to bear an independent standard of values."[43] Many is an exaggeration, but yes, reviewers harped on the lack of independence, the lack of values Lewis projected. But not Lewisohn. He placed the author's preoccupation with values front and center; of interest, he also declared Lewis was not propagandizing a particular "independent standard of values," just telling it like it is. He credited the novelist was crystal-clear what needed to be achieved—back to basics, permanence, the serious business of making a good life, for all...high standards. Bottom-line, Lewisohn without question saw what was destroying Babbitt—he all along credits the novelist for discerning the dark truth.

To press the case further, the difficulty for scholars clearly to read Lewis, correctly, to the tee, to interpret the reviews, the criticism across decades without error is to misinterpret the challenge. Lewis was perplexing; a different sort of style, complex insecurities, a driving ambition, a willingness to challenge. Commentators contradicted themselves; and scholars, too; they took on occasion to argue with one another. Lingeman correctly notes Robert Littell contrary to Lewisohn in 1922 had detected art in *Babbitt.* At the same time, Lingeman points out the critic had found the picture of American life incomplete, good in mimicry of Mencken's booboisie, deficient in offering no "redeeming spiritual vision." Littell had written "Babbitt is hideously true to the

[43] Lingeman, 211.

worst things in America" but possesses "a genuine if not always effective kindliness...."[44] There was in his view more to a novel than jest, vulgarities; a more complete, less satiric accounting was in order; a deeper vision fitting the United States must be plumbed. Littell, however, had hit on what Lewis was conveying: In a world gone amuck George Babbitt was at base a good fellow. Doesn't Lewis offer evidence in *Babbitt* he, the author, possesses spiritual vision—George, a representative American, has resources to effect change? The country's primary tenets regarding fairness and opportunity remain intact, to be plumbed. Lewis speaks out, and he offers direction. Lingeman knows his subject well...it seems he would have sensed and commented that Littell had misinterpreted the author's purposes in writing the novel (as well as *Main Street*).

Schorer also weighs in arguing for some contemporary critics, "The implication was...that the book had no values beyond Babbitt's own, and that satire, comic and critical as it may be, must found itself on positive standards that are clearly there even if they are not stated."[45] Well, are they there or not? Lewis seems clear, he is committed to an overarching vision, and he details how it is threatened. Schorer notes positive reviews, and he who can be so hard on Lewis thought *Babbitt* a work of great substance. He reads Wisconsin regional novelist Zona Gale's letter to the author: "*Babbitt*" is an infinite book....You are as good for life as you are for fiction." Schorer notes, too, Englishman Somerset Maugham read Lewis closely. Earlier "Maugham recorded in *A Writer's Notebook* that, traveling in the United States, he was baffled by the middle class, he simply did not know what it *was*, but reading *Main Street* enabled him suddenly to conceive it." Maugham in Bangkok wrote Lewis he had now read *Babbitt:*

> I think in many ways it is a much better book than *Main Street*. It seems to me a more complete and rounded work of art; of course I read it with interest and amusement, but, as you will not be surprised to know, also with horror.... I thought I knew from *Main Street* what the man was like in his high stiff collar

---

[44] Ibid., 211–12. For Littell, see note 8.

[45] Schorer, 344 and 350–51.

> and ready-made suit of clothes whom I saw in the smoking compartment of a Pullman, but now I know that this was only an optimistic sketch of him. After reading *Babbitt* he stands before me in all his fleshiness.

Schorer sums up: "Not for Somerset Maugham alone, but for all Americans and for readers everywhere, the novel had brought into focus an image of American culture, partial as it may have been, that enabled them for the first time to see it, understand it, and criticize it." Schorer contends, drawing on other critics, "Lewis had provided a critical focus for the avant-garde no less than the middle-brows." If Lewis's art was discounted by the upper-crust critics, so be it: "[T]hat was because he was the Babbitt of art. But could he have created one if he had not been the other?" No, the scholar concludes: "[H]e alone was able to see it." Clear as day, Lewis had his commendable standards. He had prodded—can't one *see*?[46]

Despite Babbitt's overwhelming commercial success, the acclaimed author was on the defense. A consensus had developed that the aspiring novelist was hard to figure out. He craved the respect due an artist; and the whole idea that he should abide by standards held up by the literary critics, or anyone, in any realm of life, might well have seemed inane to a man who considered he was an independent sort—what are *the standards* and what ranks higher than independence of thought? Lingeman observes, "Lewis would often say that he was a satirist and not in the business of prescribing remedies (though he had plenty in mind)." Did he? Not exactly, as making a list, proposing programs. If one accepts that exposure, pure and simple, offers up a demand for remedy, that mountains of wrongs *had to be righted*, then okay. Lingeman appreciates Grace Lewis's counter: "Hal is not a medicine man. He has no remedies to offer. Who would take them if he did?" The scholar argues, "Awareness was Lewis's 'program.'" Grace had it right: "He believed that Americans would get more out of life "if we would only try to SEE. So he tries to force our eyes open.'"[47] Lingeman here is clear as a bell. Life, to begin with, would acquire greater

[46] Ibid., 350–51.

[47] Lingeman, 212.

depth if we might just *read*, take the not-so-veiled hint we have it within us to be true to the country's Promise.

Well, did Lewis have remedies or not? What did he aim for in art; what did he want for the United States; where did he stand, what were his values, and were those ours? Did opening eyes signify art? Was *Babbitt* a novel? Lingeman has no doubt: "Artistically, *Babbitt* is Lewis's finest achievement, a seamless blend of realism and satire." Babbitt is not simply a caricature, he argues, he is human, and it shows. Lingeman, hence, after pondering all the assessments, comes roaring to Lewis's defense finding high art in George's representation; and then bewilderingly muddles the argument. The puzzle never ends. He writes: "Awareness was Lewis's 'program.'" George, he reads, "recovers his soul, returns to "comfy" Myra and stands by courageous Ted. Hold on—Lingeman reads the future that Lewis did not write at all? "The father comes to approve the son's values—in this case, Ted's becoming a factory mechanic, going on to engineering school, perhaps, and creating a dynamo worthy of Chartes." Whoever suggested an engineering school? Not Ted, not George. Lewis? Hardly; at best George, defeated, still had his son, and he stood by him; but at best, as George in moments of clarity perceived, Ted was a weak reed. And yes, he was a kind father; Lewis knows that counts as well. And Babbitt had enough sense to at least intend to do better. There is no easy resolution to the human condition. But awareness, Lingeman is correct, counts a lot.[48]

Lingeman stands with most all of us; who doesn't want it to work out well for Babbitt? But "he saves his soul" does an injustice to the author's intention. Lewis baffles—this is the bottom line. And perhaps here is profundity: the entire idea of the nation's destiny is a conundrum. On a final note, Grebstein similarly considers *Babbitt* a powerful social commentary and a successful novel: "While the book lacks proposals upon which to build the foundations of a new society, its impact upon its own time was very great." Strangely he, too, sees promise in Ted, in George's kindness: "The children must determine the future, and they must do it by heeding their own desires, by defying the world and doing what they want." The foundations of a new society then are

[48] Ibid., 214.

laid by the Ted Babbitts? Lewis never argued that; quite the contrary; he had for certain been more confident Carol Kennicott's children *might* do well. It all is a tangle; and a stimulation to further analysis.[49]

Lewis deserves reconsideration. As intended, *Babbitt* offers a challenge—peril stalks the novel, well beyond George Babbitt's ken. Lewis believes he has a stirring tale to tell. Given the nation's promise, grasping its trajectory, who would not be moved? Lewis is cocksure he has his standards. And he could reach the Babbitts and the critics. He had to do better. Hutchisson, beyond getting tripped up in spots, knew for sure what lay at the author's core:

> His fame as a public figure notwithstanding, Lewis knew that *Babbitt*, like *Main Street* before it, had been praised largely on social instead of artistic grounds. More than ever, he was now determined to demonstrate to his critics that he could write nonsatiric material—that he could perceive not only hollowness in modern man, but genuine integrity as well. Therefore, when he needed to choose a topic for his next novel, he looked for one that would be suitably idealistic. He told Alfred Harcourt that this next book would be "not satiric at all—rebellious as ever, perhaps, but the central character *heroic*."[50]

Heroism: Perhaps here the novelist would find salvation for himself and the United States. Idealism lay at the core of all he was trying to affect. He would put to rest the question whether Sinclair Lewis was a man of literature. As he urged his countrymen and countrywomen, he would keep at it. With *Arrowsmith* he would profile an epochal American with the wherewithal to find a way through the maze.

---

[49] Grebstein, 85 and 83. For his treatment of *Babbitt*, particularly see 73–85; for Schorer's primarily 343–57; for Hutchisson's especially 79–90. Lingeman excellently explores the issue of satire, character, and type 192–97.

[50] Hutchisson, 90. America's challenge? Lewis remains relevant. It is an ongoing experiment. See Scott Tong, "100 Years of Sinclair Lewis' 'Babbitt.'" https://www.wbur.org. December 27, 2022.

SIX

ARROWSMITH

"Perhaps it is futile to approach any Lewis novel as a work of art. Certainly, if *Babbitt* cannot be thus approached, none of the other novels can be. And generally speaking, artistic considerations in 1922 were of far less importance than the fact that, once more, Lewis had precisely hit upon a current mood and given it popular definition." Mark Schorer assays the essays in the iconic Harold Stearns's *Civilization in the United States* published by Harcourt Brace & Company the same year as *Babbitt*. He espies an exacting similarity between the writer's work with the collection of seminal observations of the national condition: "In one novel, Sinclair Lewis had simultaneously dramatized the conclusions of thirty American minds."[1] He hitches his definition of art (he elsewhere switches it about) to currency, to relevance, placement within an exacting discourse, context of its own period. Bully to Schorer. He's back to Lewisohn: "It would be futile to attempt to inquire into the absolute aesthetic value of such a book as ['Babbitt'] nor would the enquiry be important."[2] But this would not be enough for Sinclair Lewis. He, as Babbitt, was purportedly deficient in "spiritual gifts"—somehow not the artist. He had to refute the rebuff. E. L. Doctorow, in his afterword to a late-twentieth century edition of *Arrowsmith* assumes, "Sinclair Lewis's faculty of self-observation, like that of all writers, was more likely to probe the claims of his critics than the praise of his admirers."[3]

---

[1] Mark Schorer, *Sinclair Lewis: An American Life* (New York: McGraw Hill Book Company, 1961), 355–56.

[2] L. L. [Ludwig Lewisohn], *Babbitt*, "Nation," September 20, 1922, 284–85.

[3] E. L. Doctorow, afterword to *Arrowsmith*, by Sinclair Lewis *Arrowsmith* (New York: Signet Classic, 1999), 452.

Lewis was sensitive to the perceived wisdom; he knew what was considered "literature." He appreciated the accolades; he read the caveats; he took stock. He took in plenty of praise. Philosopher and essayist George Santayana considered *Babbitt* a "true classic"—"the prophetic intention is evident, although no suggestion of the direction appears in which salvation may come." Santayana discounted direction and, or the importance of salvation, asking "is America really so helpless and distracted?" He had just read the novel, in 1931, no less, hardly a year strong on direction or salvation. The Depression deepened beyond anyone's forecasts. For Santayana, eyeing the U.S.A in turmoil, reading Lewis made great sense; he some nine years earlier had been prophetic; now the American Experiment was in free-fall. Marxist Leon Trotsky, after reading the Russian translation of *Babbitt*, observed: "I find *Babbitt* curiously interesting and instructive although it is too bourgeois in character. In the last analysis, however, Babbitt, the man, is no more bourgeois than your John D. Rockefeller, J. P. Morgan or Henry Ford."[4] For Trotsky, proletariat rebellion was in the offing; the novel had merit; there was no hope for the bourgeois experiment. He and Santayana recognized Lewis was not a solutions man; both understood that he had long foreseen where the United States was headed.

Lewis for them may have lacked an answer for the United States, but he was dead-on regarding future calamity. Of course, the author did see a path forward: stick to principles. Through the twenties, he proposed the American population needed to get back to grass roots. The country was an experiment; the population had lost sight of the promise it held; all can do well, all deserve the opportunity to "get-ahead," to be secure; fairness, freedom works. Take a close look; take action; get the capitalistic, democratic nation back on track—the "system" is in a state of rot. Through his first two twenties novels he sought to demonstrate, despite the problems he cited, there was something of the heroic to be plumbed within bourgeois America. Carol Kennicott perceived it; George Babbitt clung to the possibility he could rise to that stature, be a hero. The critics were not wise to the intention. For all his strengths in social exposure, Lewis had yet to serve up a concrete

[4] Schorer, 352.

resolution; his works fell short in meeting the literary standard. Lewis was determined in his next novel to avoid being amorphous, write resolution, artfully articulate it. He would answer the naysayers. James M. Hutchisson has it right. Turning to his next novel, to *Arrowsmith*, Lewis was determined all-the-more "to demonstrate to his critics that he could write nonsatiric material—that he could perceive not only hollowness in modern man, but genuine integrity as well." He signaled Arthur Harcourt this book would not be satiric; rather it was to be "suitably idealistic"; "rebellious as ever, perhaps, but the central character *heroic*."[5]

The American Pioneer: for Lewis, here lay a heroic model *par excellence*. Carol fancied herself a pioneer; George blathered on about frontier instincts. His idealization of Joe Paradise, his backwoods guide up in Maine, caves on itself when he asks Joe if he could do anything, what would it be? "For the first time Joe brightened. He chewed his cud a second, and bubbled, 'I've often thought of that! If I had the money, I'd go down to Tinker's Falls and open a swell shoe store.'" Joe, half-Yankee, half-Native, had come a cropper. George had gone to Maine with hope: "If he could but take up a backwoods claim with a man like Joe, work hard with his hands, be free and noisy in a flannel shirt, and never come back to this dull decency!" In its stead he slinked back to Zenith: "Thus it came to him merely to run away was folly, because he could never run away from himself." So much for Babbitt, Joe, and antiquated frontier instincts: "Moccasins—six-gun—frontier town—gamblers—sleep under the stars—be a regular man, with he-men like Joe Paradise—gosh!"[6] Babbitt's fate is sealed—no six-guns, he was less the border ruffian, more the twentieth-century realtor wheeling and dealing in Middle America. There was no escape. Still, Babbitt retained the wish for salvation—as did Carol, so also Lewis; could there be more than an inkling of what the author was trying to say? Pioneers counted, and the novelist counted himself in. Pioneering to be clear

---

[5] James M. Hutchisson, *The Rise of Sinclair Lewis 1920–1930* (University Park: The Pennsylvania University Press, 1997), 90.

[6] Sinclair Lewis, *Babbitt* (New York: Penguin Books, 1996), 263 and 267.

was progressive, the American tale. He could not be pigeon-holed as a writer, which perhaps he appreciated; but at the same time he wanted to be considered a man of literature. With *Arrowsmith* he would take another shot at it. He, after all, was a trailblazer—his novels were applauded for their social bent; he more intentionally would address the country's destiny; and it would be art.

The author fancied himself some sort of pioneer (he described himself a product of old Yankee stock), always feigning to blaze his way tracking whatever fancy currently caught his interest, hailing the invigorating nature of the mythic frontier, including periodically striking out on genuine efforts at getting back to the woods as the tonic that would restore him—until he got fed up and hurried home. But he continued to believe, to his personal and professional credit, he could move ahead; writing, he could develop a character, a twentieth-century man who could cut a swath through all the social and cultural palaver. Lewis appreciated the frontier spirit of the country. Richard Lingeman writes, "Lewis is saying Babbitt—and with him America—must acquire the spiritual, artistic, and moral traditions that will harness its technology to humane purposes." The country shall progress. With *Arrowsmith* Lewis set out to profile an epochal American; his protagonist was to portray what it takes to find a way through the twentieth-century maze of the American Experiment.[7]

How is that new frontier charted? That is what Carol pondered. George Babbitt was a lost cause. But Martin Arrowsmith would succeed or at least reach considerably higher ground—always the country's driving ambition to seek perfection. So, too, would the author reach a loftier perch. Lewis would out-gun the critics and write that superlative novel. *Arrowsmith* would not have the gargantuan impact on American culture that the eye-popping *Babbitt* had rendered, but it would far surpass it as a greater literary work if not reach the heights to be proclaimed "the great American novel." It would in a more substantive manner prod Americans to "see" what they had in them. It was for Lewis in its design a noble effort; albeit he ultimately would deem the

---

[7] Richard Lingeman, *Sinclair Lewis: Rebel from Main Street* (New York: Random House, 2002), 214.

novel unsuccessful in satisfactorily resolving in that one fell swoop the American Dilemma he pondered. Again, he did not have "the solution." He pointed the way; eventually he would have to trust, especially after his fifth stab, the impressive *Dodsworth,* that with the five great twenties novels he had reached a consequential achievement. Unfortunately, being who he was, he never reached that satisfaction. When he had completed *Arrowsmith*, Lingeman notes a writer to *Atlantic Monthly* declared Lewis had demonstrated he was "no longer the composer of superlative jazz. He had shown himself an artist, sincere, powerful, restrained."[8] The reviewers, the critics, the scholars to the contrary never reached consensus he had achieved *art.* In the end, they would applaud *Arrowsmith* and then *Dodsworth* as the novelist's finest writing. But there would be no consensus Lewis was a literary man.

Martin Arrowsmith would not be the hero who resolved the national dilemma, but he underscored where the nation's malady lay and just which way it had to turn to free itself up, to live up to its own promise. To Lewis's credit, while with *Arrowsmith* he did not in the end offer a neat resolution, critics and scholars clearly caught the message: the United States was in peril. This was a huge step forward. And it would be further hammered home by the darkness of *Gantry*—the country was sinking deeper into disarray; and then followed up by *Dodsworth*, building on the idealism expressed in *Arrowsmith*, portraying a country which could find its way back to its fundamental premise, all deserve a fair shake—still, not a singular *resolution*, not *literature.* Lewis had given all he had in him, and he considered himself in the end underappreciated.

Arrowsmith demonstrated that Lewis could be a masterful writer. Once more, "More than ever," pointed James M. Hutchisson, the novelist "determined to demonstrate to his critics...that he could perceive not only hollowness in modern man, but genuine integrity as well."[9] And this he accomplished; Martin Arrowsmith, of those five twenties protagonists, was a man loved by Lewis's readers and the critics. He was not taken as a savior on a white horse, to be dutifully followed, but

[8] Ibid., 255–56.

[9] Ibid.

a man to emulate, a fellow citizen pointing the necessity to get back to basics.

Toward the end of *Babbitt*, Lewis takes an anxious glance at the problem at hand, embodied in George's safe-house, the "Good Citizens' League":

> To the League belonged most of the prosperous citizens of Zenith. They were not all of the kind who called themselves "Regular Guys." Besides these hearty fellows, these salesmen of prosperity, there were the aristocrats, that is, the men who were richer or had been rich for more generations: the presidents of banks and of factories, the land-owners, the corporation lawyers, the fashionable doctors, and the few young-old men who worked not at all but, reluctantly remaining in Zenith, collected lusterware and first editions as though they were back in Paris. All of them agreed that the working-classes must be kept in their place; and all of them perceived that American Democracy did not imply any equality of wealth, but did demand a wholesome sameness of thought, dress, painting, morals, and vocabulary.[10]

America's destiny had become dislocated. Angst stretched well beyond Zenith. The ruling-class in the towering canyons of the great cities was going to ruin as well. Tolstoy read Lewis closely: "In the last analysis, however, Babbitt, the man, is no more bourgeois than your John D. Rockefeller, J. P. Morgan or Henry Ford." This would have to change. Lewis landed on a heroic figure who effectively shouted out the decay for the danger it signaled. One Harcourt Brace magazine pitch pictured the novelist's latest accomplishment: "Sinclair Lewis's greatest novel" sits atop the map of the United States: "Right Thru The Heart of America"...an arrow pierces the heartland ballyhooing "Arrowsmith."[11]

Martin Arrowsmith appears an unlikely hero—just another product of another midwestern Main Street. It shares it terrain with the region's growing cities: Zenith, as Lewis pictured it in *Babbitt* is "large," one more of the "commercial cities of a few hundred thousand

---

[10] Lewis, *Babbitt*, 346.

[11] Dennis Morgan, MD, "Dr. Arrowsmith Hangs Out His Shingle," *Sinclair Lewis Society Newsletter*, Spring 2021, 29 (Spring 2021), 1 and 11–16.

inhabitants, most of which—though not all—lay inland, against a background of cornfields and mines and of small towns...."[12] Martin moves about the Middle West, he fights against "something," many things, which bother him. He migrates to the top, to the metropolis, first through a series of middling domains, a jump then to "second-city" Chicago, and soon enough he is ensconced high in Manhattan—always wrestling with his own bourgeois success. He is a doctor, more inclined toward scientific study than practice. His journey—personal and professional—begins in Elk Mills, "a dowdy, red-brick village, smelling of apples" where his pioneering folk had landed (a descendent of Boone, no less); his father owns the New York Clothing Bazaar; young Martin assists the "town doc" and falls in love with the "adventure" of medicine.[13]

In the early years of the century Martin ventures off to the small, aspiring University of Winnemac. Twenty-some years ahead, 1924 to be exact, Lewis clues in the reader Martin's once-provincial school has arrived: "Its president is the best money-raiser and the best after-dinner speaker in the United States; and Winnemac was the first school in the world to conduct its extension courses by radio." The "U's" aspiration had been fulfilled, a Midwestern gemstone. Lewis country: "The state of Winnemac is bounded by Michigan, Ohio, Illinois, and Indiana, and like them it is half Eastern, half Midwestern." It possesses an air of industry, brick, Sycamores, and Revolution-Era lineage; and it is "Midwestern in its fields of corn and wheat, its red barns and silos...." Winnemac...the cutting edge of progress.[14]

---

[12] Sinclair Lewis, *Babbitt*, 1.

[13] *Sinclair Lewis, Arrowsmith*, (*N*ew York: Signet Classic, 1998), 1.

[14] Ibid., 6. Martin is American as apple pie. So, too, Lewis; writing in a xenophobic era he telegraphs with pride the hybrid nature of American breeding. He disdains "100 Percent Americanism," infectious among a strident minority in the early-twenties: "Martin was, like most inhabitants of Elk Mills before the Slavo-Italian immigration, a Typical Pure-bred Anglo-Saxon American, which means that he was a union of German, French, Scotch, Irish, perhaps a little Spanish, conceivably a little of the strains lumped together as 'Jewish,' and a great deal of English, which is itself a combination of

The university represents everything with which Lewis is at odds—and yet cannot shake. Nor easily could Martin. The future looks dim:

> The University of Winnemac is at Mohalis, fifteen miles from Zenith. There are twelve thousand students.... The University has a baseball field under glass; its buildings are measured by the mile; it hires hundreds of young Doctors of Philosophy to give rapid instruction in Sanskrit, navigation, accountancy, spectacle-fitting, sanitary engineering, Provencal poetry, tariff schedules, rutabaga-growing...the style of Matthew Arnold...and department-store advertising.

In short it is what the people desire, or have bought into, and they have been bamboozled:

> It is not a snobbish rich-man's college, devoted to leisurely nonsense. It is the property of the people of the state, and what they want—or what they are told they want—is a mill to turn out men and women who will lead moral lives, play bridge, drive good cars, be enterprising in business, and occasionally mention books, though they are not expected to have time to read them. It is a Ford Motor Factory, and if its products rattle a little, they are beautifully standardized, with perfectly interchangeable parts. Hourly the University of Winnemac grows in numbers and influence, and by 1950 one may expect it to have created an entirely new world-civilization, a civilization larger and brisker and purer.

A mill turning out respectable but at base shoddy goods: the U represents the American trajectory. One cannot refrain from whistling Pete Seeger's lament of the country's post WWII expansion into "Little Boxes, all built the same...."[15]

The university's students vary little from all of America. Lewis wanted to stand up to the mediocrity of "sameness"; with Martin

---

primitive Briton, Celt, Phoenician, Roman, German, Dane, and Swede." See 2.

[15] Ibid., 6–7.

Arrowsmith he does. Both have a point to make: *they* decidedly were *not* bourgeois. They *were* pioneers. The disturbing trajectory of the country had to be altered. Martin is ordinary by most surface measures. He is bright, and he wants more of life. He is far from perfect. As he moves about and up he tries to find himself, some meaning in his life, in life. He has fun, ambitions, passion; he can enjoy the finer things; he aligns himself with an array of women who often fall short as does he. He develops good friendships; he is, for the most part, ethical. As a boy he had begun to question, to challenge: "When he lifted his head to listen, his right eyebrow, slightly higher than the left, rose and quivered in his characteristic expression of energy, of independence, and a hint that he could fight, a look of impertinent inquiry...."[16] Hence, whether in Elk Mills or at the university; as a general practitioner in Wheatsylvania, North Dakota (another Gopher Prairie); or as a public health official in Nautilus, Iowa (a small-scale Zenith with lofty ambitions) Martin runs across the Lewis middling cast and lifts that eyebrow. He even encounters a George Babbitt crony in Zenith (as well as the Dodsworth Theater, the namesake of Lewis's 1929 novel...all one saga). It was all of a pattern: questions were to be raised. Martin and his good wife Leora (an independent sort herself, one of Lewis's strongest twenties women with her head screwed on tight) contend with the mediocrities of life. Lewis, while trying to break free from satire, at numerous points still cannot let go, and as in *Main Street* and *Babbitt* he can overwork the caricatures, albeit only occasionally problematic in *Arrowsmith*. He tries hard to take that closer look at what ails society and what can resolutely be done about it.[17]

Martin and Leora keep moving on, and they ultimately land in the big leagues. Martin is an eager protégé; he wants to work with those

---

[16] Ibid., 2.

[17] While critics would tire of Lewis's send-ups of American shortcomings, find them inartistic, readers in all likelihood found the hilarious caricatures of American types insightful, fun, not so tedious as the critics would charge. They read novels as they chose, across a long span of years; unlike latter-day scholars, they did not read them together, in part perhaps accounting for no sense of being over or underwhelmed by Lewis's style.

who appreciate the purity of the scientific quest. He finds mentors. He errs, he is seduced by wealth, he trudges forward, all the while burdened by the commercialization of medicine and his own mixed ambitions. He lands at the heart of American industry, finance, and science, in Manhattan at the McGurk Institute, a stand-in for the Rockefeller Institute, a twenties totem of American progress. Lewis is taking on the professions, modernity, the sciences—he is the scion of a medical family, he has a stake in a lofty vocation he considers gone bad. His choice of medicine for his projection of American miasma is significant. He is intensely proud of his father and his brother, dedicated Minnesota doctors of the old-school; he wants to ensure he can diagnose the problem at hand.

Martin's medicine is impersonal. He looks at people in the abstract, he aims to be a doctor of a newer, objective sort: public health, in its promising early years, is his principal field of endeavor. He has not been satisfied with general practice, nor will he ever be, even as a silk-stocking physician raking in the bucks. Public health turns out unfulfilling, hobbled by the same old problems: blowhards, commercialization, politics, lack of vision, corruption, material garbage. Finally he believes he has risen above all that, ensconced in the top-most floors of the McGurk Institute, free to pursue pure research in the name of the public good. He finds the Babbitts reign supreme—Elk Mills, Wheatsylvania, Nautilus, Zenith, Chicago, all roads lead to where else, Manhattan. Martin always remains frustrated about which way to turn and how he can get off all the country's *Main Streets*.

Put to the ultimate test of who he is, what he wants, what matters by way of a desperate journey to a plague-ridden Caribbean island, Doctor Arrowsmith faces disaster.[18] He loses both Leora and his cherished medical partner fighting the scourge—they die miserably as islanders fall everywhere. Martin breaks faith with pure science and opts for today's needy, for humanity. At the cost of pristine, experimental technique, he brings about relief for the stricken, administering the

---

[18] Lewis tracks this island adventure (adventure always is a big draw in his work) in an exciting and compelling fashion, carrying his readers far off from his and their familiar haunts; as always he did his research onsite.

serum he has developed to any-and-all who need it—testing protocols be damned.[19]

Bereft personally and professionally, Arrowsmith returns to New York and his disappointed bosses at McGurk—purer science, better publicity, and more profits would have been the more beneficial course. In the clutches of the rich, he remarries into the highest echelon of society. This is no remedy for his ills. At McGurk and in his own home, he recognizes there is no respect and support for what still matters to him: his quest to pursue pure science, to safeguard human health, to be both a scientist and a public health advocate, to combine the sanctity of research with a genuine concern for the common good. He throws it all up and finds salvation as far away from the capitalist-democratic conundrum as he can get. In puritanical fashion he opts to reside relatively outside this world, hardly be of it, retain the most minimal supply connection. He replicates the first chapter in the Puritan saga, the

---

[19] With the global pandemic breaking out in 2019, renewed interest cropped up in *Arrowsmith*. Dennis Morgan, MD in his 2021 "Dr. Arrowsmith Hangs Out His Shingle," notes a *Science* review of the day: "In *Babbitt*, he was the pathologist [the very term Lewis would later claim for himself] at the necropsy table with Mr. Babbitt on the slab. In *Arrowsmith*, he is an artist[.]" In 1944 *Saturday Review of Literature*, celebrating its twentieth anniversary, announced its readers's choice of Lewis's book as the leading novel of the interwar period. See 16. The 1931 film was a major production. See Ralph Goldstein, "Arrowsmith Endures in the Pandemic," *Sinclair Lewis Society Newsletter* 29 (Spring 2021), 1, 4, 6. David J. Eisenman, MD, in *JAMA*, the American Medical Association organ's website *Arts and Medicine* June, 2020 advises: "'You should read *Arrowsmith*,' I have long told aspiring clinicians-scientists I interview…that recommendation is even more timely and broadly relevant…." He adds, "[T]he delight and comfort we might take from seeing a send-up of our professional communities in great literature turns unsettling given the persisting challenging behavior and unknowns that transverse the century…. It is indeed humbling to see history repeat itself…." See Anonymous, "*Arrowsmith* News," *Sinclair Lewis Society Newsletter* 29 (Fall, 2020), 18–20, quoted 18. In the *Los Angeles Times* a month later, Michael Hiltzik noted he took up Eisenman's recommendation: "It was a revelation." "Like all great novelists, Sinclair Lewis was writing about his own time, and teaching us about our time too. We should be reading him again." See Ibid., 19.

classic genesis of American tale. The religious sect, first attempting to separate from the world but ensure the supplies keep coming in (and products going out) later would further compromise to its ultimate materialistic detriment. Martin is not a compromiser—at least any longer. Martin embarks as his New England forebears on a confounding "errand into the wilderness."

Arrowsmith plunks for an unrealistic option: try as he might, there is for Lewis no clear-cut path to resolution. There is no place for Martin in society except beyond it. An eccentric, he will find peace in the woods. He heads out with his closest friend, fellow McGurk renegade Terry Wickett, who shares his passion. As the novel wraps up, the two could be neither happier nor more alienated from society.

For Martin, this may be paradise, but it never could work for the novelist or for most denizens of the United States. Lewis could not function well alone—nor for that matter maintain a permanent relationship or domicile. Darting off on solitary road trips, sometimes by himself, sometimes with another by his side; or on failed treks into the North Woods, always crawling back—nothing measured up in life to what he sought except literally to move on. For Lewis there could be no satisfactory accommodation living in the world or distanced from it. He was a public figure, a celebrity, and he savored the limelight, and he was burned by it; his distillation of literature was subject to attack, purportedly unworkable as art, not up to standards. And he often was unhappy with himself and others; and too insecure to toss aside the attacks on his personae. Martin may find peace by a wood-side fire, but how could this work for Sinclair Lewis—how, for that matter, could it serve as a resolution for a country, a people? Martin along with Terry may make the great discovery, attain scientific triumph, bring good news to society, but away from the corrupt world they would have to stay—there was no refuge within a society which could still corrupt. Lewis as his custom could not even assuredly resolve Martin and Terry's end-story. The reader as always is left hanging, albeit Martin and Terry's prospectus appears to be more promising than either Carol's or George's; or Lewis's, stuck in the world that discomforts him.

Yet Martin Arrowsmith was a strong American if "odd man out." If any Lewis protagonist could solve the conundrum to retain the purity of experiment, he seemed to represent the best chance. But he always would be stranded, estranged from society. Ultimately the author was going to have to recognize, find a means, a protagonist who, if society was to progress, had to keep at reform from within, a long-run exercise without end—the human condition—for that he would later create Sam Dodsworth. Lewis was a common-enough fellow as he always declared: there was no way he could drop out of society, and no way he could maintain content within it. He was no hero; but more to the point, heroic Martin was no answer in and of himself. Even Joe Paradise was not content; the frontiersman perceived he'd be best off to come down from the mountains and run a shop, a modern man. Lewis laughed that Joe expected he would find contentment in his little shoe store in his little town. But to his credit Joe, tending to his store, might find his way, make his own social contribution within the world, right behind the counter serving others. Most of us, Lewis contended, were babbitts.

Arrowsmith accomplished much artistically. It was Lewis's strongest work to date—but it had not done the job for the country's presumed plight. If high art demanded high resolution, the novel had fallen short. Lewis's prose was beholding to his search for a way for the U.S to find its way home—resolution must be located amidst the hubbub of ordinary life. Again, Lingeman concludes: "Lewis is saying Babbitt—and with him America—must acquire the spiritual, artistic, and moral traditions that will harness its technology to humane purposes." This had to be a communal project. This *was* the "way home"; society is an experiment. Martin Arrowsmith saw the country had fallen short—he had all the qualifications to set it straight—but he was not a community man. Importantly, he set a high moral standard for which all Americans had it in them to strive—in this he was heroic.

Sheldon Norman Grebstein, full of plaudits, argues *Arrowsmith* "has no compromise in the end."[20] Yes, but this is no answer for the

[20] Sheldon Norman Grebstein, *Sinclair Lewis* (New Haven: College and University Press, 1962), 95.

broader environs. What sort of broader canvas has been etched? Can hope premised on flight constitute art if social resolution is left aside? Social life demands interaction which in turns calls for, to work well, compromise. Hutchisson takes another tack; he argues Lewis was an artist by broad measure. *Arrowsmith* proved it: "The commonplace perception of Lewis is that he attacked fraud, but his satiric stereotypes were counterbalanced too rarely by characters of integrity and his novels were based too much on destructive criticism that did not offer hope for improving human institutions. Whether or not that judgment is valid, at least *Arrowsmith* rebuts it."[21] But where does hope hedged on an errand in the wilderness leave one? Where does that lead *everyman*? *Arrowsmith*, contrary to Hutchisson's analysis, does not rebut the critics. He is right that Lewis was an artist with a broad outlook; his back-to-basics argument, resurrect founding principles, restore proven values, take action makes sense—but that was not the ruler his critics had in hand. They demanded exacting solutions. Lewis, by ensuring Martin does not compromise, consequently compromised Lewis's own effort to bring about change—it just was not workable for the community. *Arrowsmith* might have been more satisfying to critics if the protagonist simply made his discovery in the woods, returned to society prescription in hand, triumphant, hence the happy ending. Sinclair Lewis was too engaged to opt for that unreasonable conclusion.

Lewis knows better. There would be no global revelation as to right and wrong, all is well that ends well. What in essence does Lewis offer? Something truer to the real world. Living literally in the wilds (Puritan New England, no less), Martin and Terry, dedicated to the purity of science and the quest for a better world, set up a primitive lab, their Walden. Both are gifted, committed scientists who despite all the temptations put before them by a corrupted world hold to their search for good. But they live as frontiersman in a primeval setting. If Carol's resolution was tepid, and Babbitt's not credible, this end for Martin Arrowsmith, and Sinclair Lewis, however noble in intent, is incredible. "No compromise" is not the American Way. Even if their experiments might lead to a great discovery, what then? They deliver it to the world,

[21] Hutchisson, 124. Doctorow, afterword to *Arrowsmith*.

as the author suggests...but they never could return, stay in the world. Surely the McGirk Institutes of the world, materialistic at base, will undercut their mission. The power of the bourgeois reigns supreme. What, then, has Lewis concluded?

E. L. Doctorow in his "Afterword" to the 1998 Signet Classics *Arrowsmith*, writes Lewis had sought to establish "a new figure in his fictional landscape, a romantic composed of his own DNA, a fellow not perfect if he was to be real, but in one way or another disposed to fight his way to a level of existence higher than those around him." For Lewis "the path to a transformed culture was Science, the purest product of the Enlightenment, a calling fresh and clean. Enter Martin Arrowsmith."[22] Yet in the end, aiming to rise higher than those around him, Martin retreats to a cloister. This cannot work. Lewis, the humanist, once again could not make the case *Arrowsmith* offers "the resolution." The novel works on so many levels—but the ultimate goal, to move society forward, to find a means for ordinary men and women to be extraordinary, for the country to fulfill its destiny, to resolve this ever-modern dilemma, fails in the end to convince. It was not, in plain Progressive Era parlance, *pragmatic*. Surely Lewis could not believe it himself. Surely he realized he had yet again failed to live up to his own expectations. Whatever he believed, he read what the critics had to say; to an extent it was plenty satisfying; but it was not what he had aimed

[22] Doctorow, 452–53. Martin, clearly, in finding his refuge, remains an imperfect human being. He abandons his wife and newborn son. This appears to be no problem at all—Lewis did the same with wives and sons. Grebstein notes, "To do one's work, as Lewis structures the situation, means to neglect family and friends, and to be hard, tough, honest, and crude. Furthermore, the man who does his work and is responsible only to its demands, is inevitably and necessarily hard to like." He is "fundamentally motivated by a great love for mankind, but it is well-disguised, even totally hidden, under a cynical and tough exterior." This cannot inspire. Oddly, one of the great strengths of the novel is its power of inspiration. Another tangle to be resolved—emulate Martin, but stay within society? See 93–94. For more of Grebstein's analysis of *Arrowsmith*, see 85–96. Hutchisson and others contend that Arrowsmith serves as a character of integrity; where does family neglect register?

for; there was no roaring consensus he had met the standards of art the literary world demanded.

Questions stalked the writer. The reviewers and critics while full of praise were not sure just what to do with the latest work; the bugaboo clung, it could not be art for the resolution did not fit the overarching dilemma. Scholars looking back as well are laudatory; they are more sure-footed as to the novel's artistic merit, yet they contradict themselves and stumble. They insist on addressing the matter of art and tangle it up with the shifting debates over literary credibility. They carry forth beyond the contemporary debates over Lewis's credentials the same old battle—it is an unnecessary contretemps which overshadows and distorts their interpretations of the author's entire body of work. Is this art? Yes, but no, they contend: *Arrowsmith* is "more artistic," yet it has no "resolution"; they fail to see it as one more step for Lewis, through his novels, toward fleshing out just what constitutes a workable resolution beyond the literary quarrels over *literature*. Martin, say the scholars, is a strong character, plenty of heft to him, but he cannot just flee the world he aims to reform. There is the conundrum. Critics demand compromise from the author despite the fact some argue Carol Kennicott was too compromised, and George Babbitt all the more so. Lewis ensured Martin did not cave, but that for some critics rightly proved a stumbling block of its own. Martin remains in the woods; so, too, in conclusion, does the reader, left alone to figure out how all this will end. Lewis, true to his craft, has left the novel hanging: what is to become of Martin, the experiment he and Terry work on? What about the country, the broadest issue?

Scholars have had their take. To their credit they work diligently, but Lewis is a tough nut. The author had taken a huge step forward. Doctorow argues seeking to be "serious," to be a "novelist," to develop character and plot, to discount satire, he tapped into a world he knew as well as "the middle class." Taking on science, medicine, "Lewis was claiming credentials as a true novelist—something his earlier work had not earned for him." The critics "were happy to grant the claim, seeing in the book an artistic maturity, a composition of shadows and dimensions, and moral complexity that his out-and-out satires lacked."[23]

Well, this was not exactly so. The reviews reflected a hesitancy to declare the author *that close* to art; they treated the novel as a worthy effort which ends with a serious stumble. Grebstein catches this as he cites no compromise in the end—a problem for those in and of the world. Still, "Both the novel's pervading idealism and its sober factuality overweighed its satire and brought it success, without the success of scandal." "The tone and movement of the novel," Grebstein argues, "are swifter, surer, more inspired than in either of his previous triumphs." "All in all, *Arrowsmith* shows Lewis's growth as an artist; it is the best novel of his great decade, and it is among the better American novels written in this century."[24]

Without question in 1924 the praise in the U.S. (and Britain) approached unanimity despite caveats, despite disagreement as to what had been accomplished. Schorer notes Arnold Bennett, to whom Lewis dedicated the book, gave H. G. Wells, another Lewis idol, a copy: "To H. G. Wells, this reassurance of the long admiration of Sinclair Lewis…." [25] No one doubted he had produced a worthy work, it was an important step, but there was not assurance it was a towering achievement. Joseph Wood Krutch wrote in *Nation* it was "better" because it was "essentially truer."[26] Again, *Atlantic Bookshelf* declared Lewis was "no longer the composer of superlative jazz. He has shown himself an artist, sincere, powerful, restrained."[27] Robert Morss Lovett in *The Dial* sensed loss, missed some of the jazz, but he hailed the twentieth-century light cast on the medical profession and society: "[I]f he

---

[23] Doctorow, 454–55. John J. Koblas, *Sinclair Lewis: Home at Last* (Bloomington, MN: Voyageur Press, 1981), charts the extended medical lineage in Lewis's family. Focusing on medicine, he did write of a world he knew well. See 27–28.

[24] Grebstein, 91 and 95–96; for Hutchisson, see 91–124, especially 94–110. Schorer, too, generally praises, see 414–20.

[25] Ibid., 414.

[26] Ibid., 414.

[27] Hutchisson, 122.

has sacrificed the reality of fiction [resolution], it is in the interest of the reality of a public cause which gives largeness of view and significance to *Arrowsmith*."[28] The *Literary Review* in a brief mention countered "the humanity of it outshines the science."[29] So, by one measure it sacrifices reality, but gives the real story about medicine and society's flaws; and by another the science plays second fiddle to the humanity of the work, the greater problem, the human condition. Despite its implausible resolution, Sinclair Lewis seemingly had at least delivered increased satisfaction to a swath of critics: he had at a minimum risen closer to the stature of an artist.

What about Martin? This, naturally, is the crux of the art contretemps. And he is addressed. Arrowsmith was a hero; the doctor, however, remained stranded in the wilderness, and the author had to be queried. Lovett caught this, pointing out Martin "takes refuge in a sort of hermitage of research among the Vermont hills." For all the astute attention to the medical profession and for Lovett to America's broader ailments, in taking up the public cause the novel tripped over itself ending in "an air of unreality." Still, "Arrowsmith is an important step in the campaign to de-bamboozle the American public and relieve its institutions of bunk." In "An Interpreter of American Life" the reviewer concludes, "If Mr. Lewis attracts his great audience by the sense of reality...and the careless humour of his approach, he holds it by a sense of the importance of what he has to say." Lewis and Mencken "are, in this day and generation, the most read and considered interpreters of American life." Lovett eyes Lewis closely: he credits the progress the novelist achieves by way of *Main Street* and *Babbitt* and determines *Arrowsmith* makes another incisive mark. He hints at that broader perspective Lewis is after. Lovett does not bother much with art—the sociology for him is paramount and within it the humor dead-on. "Humor is the form in which the American takes his cathartic—the Biglow Papers, Josh Billings, Artemus Ward, and Mark Twain, for examples." Lovett, in the end, is far from declaring the work a

[28] Robert Morss Lovett, "An Interpreter of American Life," *Dial*, June, 1925, 515–18, quoted 518.

[29] Lingeman, 256.

masterpiece, but he believes it must be a seriously considered a literary contribution.[30]

Lovett feints toward the art contretemps; others were to have more of a say, and the verdict was a mixed bag. For Lewis, the critics mattered, the issue clawed. One hopes he coveted reviews such as Lovett's. Lovett read *Arrowsmith* as a portion of a saga, the public well-being. Possibly it was more important to treat it as not a singular novel. Perhaps it is not about art in the sense of immediate gratification, but as an organic product of something bigger, less restraining. Lewis in the end had had no choice; Martin's resolution was a solitary achievement; he could not succeed; but Lovett senses his countrymen could; that was their choice to be made; it was not for the author, nor Martin, to lead the charge. Lovett detected something new was at work here.

Grant Overton, in a gorgeous review of *Arrowsmith*, wrestles with the art issue and offers up in the process a brilliant profile: *The Salvation of Sinclair Lewis*. He sets the author's character against his celebratory and controversial status in American society and arts. Lewis was the rage, and Overton tracks the dilemma this presented for the author, his critics, and his popular audience. Only a quarter of the review addresses *Arrowsmith*; it is full of praise. Overton never addresses the issue of resolution or much of the story line at all. Is it a novel? He believes so but finds the question uninteresting. *Arrowsmith* is a great assessment of the medical world and twentieth-century maladies. He ranks Lewis high amongst prestigious twenties novelists who possess "a love of an idea, of an attitude toward life, of sufficient intensity to color the writer's work." Lewis has an idea about the United States; Overton recognizes this novel carries on beyond the realms of the Gopher Prairies and Zeniths. He pegs the novelist a knock-off in the most complimentary way of his hero H. G. Wells "who also writes with the idea-tendency and the attitude who similarly teems with lifelike portraits." He classes both in the tradition of Dickens yet possessing a much broader focus on life: "The same incurable restlessness belongs to both men; the same superb discontent with everything as it is; the same passionate warmth and width of human interest." Art? This is something

[30] Lovett, "An Interpreter of American Life."

different, something new; why not call it art? Lewis is a character, a national celebrity—? Is that a problem?[31]

Surely readers less wrapped up in the "question" thought Lewis was an artist (if they thought about it at all). Readers in the twenties understood; "SEE" as Grace Lewis had importuned; they were reading, and he resonated. Lewis was considered one of the foremost interpreters of American life. This was not wholesale satire; this was that *wholesome, American story,* worth being told. Scholar Harold Bloom in the late-twentieth century surmises: "*Arrowsmith* has enough mythic force to compel a young reader to an idealism of her or his own."[32] Really, considering the country and its self-designated pilgrimage, what could be more American, to the point, especially for Sinclair Lewis? Nurture idealism, one novel after another.

Doctorow claims the reviews of *Arrowsmith* hardly recognized Lewis was addressing the spread of the malaise he had chronicled in *Main Street* and *Babbitt*: "The critics of Lewis's time largely failed to note that the Lewisian critique of our culture was no longer restricted to the midwestern provinces or the commercial men populating them, but, bestowed now, generously, over all our geography." They do not see that Martin's "detestation becomes nationalized and the plague of Sinclair Lewis's curse reaches into every nook and cranny of our social construction."[33] But no reader, critic, then or since, could miss this. Doctorow, acknowledging all were swept up in the majesty of Martin's sojourn, fails to credit readers' depths of perception. Critics, not all but enough, recognized the broader picture, the deeper problem. With that understanding many dismiss Lewis's conclusion as unworthy of the challenge at hand—but they hail he expertly describes the problem. Lewis's dissection courses through the novel as in *Main Street* and *Babbitt.* Having already charted the dilemma with Carol Kennicott in Gopher Prairie, followed up with Babbitt in Zenith, Lewis in *Arrowsmith*

---

[31] Grant Overton, *Bookman*, "The Salvation of Sinclair Lewis," April, 1925, 179–84, quoted 182–83, www.unz.com. Note the striking Bertrand Zadig illustration of Lewis, 181.

[32] Lingeman, 257.

[33] Doctorow, 456.

tracks the contagion's threatening trajectory; he reminds readers opening with Martin in a prairie village, onto other Midwest habitats, then to Chicago, and finally New York that this is a dilemma continental in its sweep, even global. Doctorow correctly notes by literary standards Lewis was criticized, and he agrees that he wasted his latest shot, but readers and critics caught his thrust. He telegraphed resolution exists, and it demands a long, patient, arduous struggle. Try as we will, there is no escape.

All three novels leave the reader in limbo. How is progress to be accomplished? The country possesses a promise which it trusts can be fulfilled. Few of us have Martin's option; rather, we carry on—after all, America is an *experiment*. This is fundamental. Carol returned to plow forward in Gopher Prairie. Even George aimed to do better, be better. It should be clear that in sending Martin out to the wilderness, Lewis turns to that old Puritan dilemma, a cry in the wilderness will not do, that the only way to progress is to stay in the world and continue to work, and *try* not to be corrupted in the process. The novelist's conclusion wasn't off-track at all—maybe in tracking Martin's into the woods, he was pointing "stay in the world." It is the only way to reasonably progress. And perhaps, Lewis inadvertently backed himself into that position. There would need to be more said.

Doctorow concludes his "Afterword" on target: "But withal, Sinclair Lewis, a genius of unappeasable anger and mirthless derision, wanted, urgently, to shine his light upon us. Who can say it is not illuminating. And who can say of life in America today that the Arrowsmiths aren't few and the Babbitts aren't many? Lewis's fierce moral nature was the source of his greatness and that is what we close the book on, as we do with any prophet who tells us what we don't want to hear."[34]

In the final analysis, the Pulitzer Committee set out to grant Lewis its annual award in literature. Lewis, true to himself, possibly intent on "scandal and sales" refused the honor purportedly based on principle. It did not matter—*Arrowsmith* hit its mark. And as was his wont the author remained uncertain—he still was not applauded as he saw it for

[34] Ibid.

his high art. The bottom line, which it would have been best for the novelist to focus on, was everyone sufficiently got what he was after—the plaudits were aplenty. At the outset of the tale Martin's lifelong preoccupation was laid forth: he "saw no one clear path to Truth but a thousand paths to a thousand truths far-off and doubtful." The theme would be reiterated again and again. As Martin, Lewis would continue to try to figure it out, it gnawed at him that he could not convey his truth, or his many truths in a way which foreclosed on the criticism he was insufficiently resolute. He says of Martin he would "try to find (but never to succeed in finding) the Why that made everything so."[35] The world may not bend to one's theories, Martin is told—that does not make the theories wrong. Sinclair Lewis should have taken those simple but paramount lines more to heart.

In *Elmer Gantry* and *Dodsworth*, the last two great twenties novels, the author would take two more cracks at the conundrum. Could he squarely serve up a resolution to America's twentieth-century dilemma? Was a final comprehensive statement possible? In *Gantry* he seemingly had given up the ghost—and it is important to recognize his personal life was in shambles. Yet the novel represents a key step toward sorting through the dilemma. It offers absolutely no resolution, ending on a considerably somber note, but it takes readers deeper into the country's challenge. Without question *Gantry* has its flaws, and Lewis fails to shine a hopeful light on the path ahead; all is darkness, and salvation seems to be slipping fast from the nation's grip. It is a damning indictment of the state of the union. Additionally, it is so harshly set forth (and there is the humor) that Lewis can only hope it gets people to see a path to salvation remains. Progressing further with *Dodsworth*, the author regains his footing, finds a surer path to a variegated truth, to the knowledge *truth* cannot be fully resolved. Lewis in his final twenties novel will deliver his most comprehensive exposition as to what ails the United States.

Historian of Medicine Charles E. Rosenberg decades later revisited *Arrowsmith*: "Martin Arrowsmith is a new kind of hero, one appropriate to twentieth-century America. Journalists and historians

[35] Lewis, *Arrowsmith*, 18, 52.

tirelessly inform us that the 1920s were years of intense and aggressive materialism. Yet Arrowsmith is quite obviously a hero not of deeds, but of spirit. His scientific calling is not a concession to material values, but a means of overcoming them....It is this quest which provides the novel's moral structure." *Arrowsmith* represented a significant stride for the artist. For Sinclair Lewis "the essence of heroism, the gauge of a man's stature, lay in the extent to which he was able to disengage himself from the confining pressures of American society." He struggled with it and succeeded as best he could.[36]

Sinclair Lewis, following *Arrowsmith* with the shattering *Elmer Gantry* and then the triumphant *Dodsworth*, again would pull arrows out of his quiver and take his aim "Right Thru The Heart of America." Harcourt and Brace along with their celebrated author knew what they were about and the audience they courted. From the beginning, setting up the new publishing house, they had set their sights. Richard Lingeman said it: "Harcourt had an ear for the zeitgeist." And so, too, of course, his partner.[37]

---

[36]Charles E. Rosenberg, "Martin Arrowsmith: The Scientist as Hero," in *Modern Critical Reviews: Sinclair Lewis*, ed. Harold Bloom (New York: Chelsea House Publishers, 1987), 41–50, see 41 and 48. Repeatedly, physicians share how much they respect the novel they read in their early days, and how much it speaks to them to this day. *Arrowsmith* garnered new readers during the pandemic of the 2020s.

[37] Lingeman, 126.

Harry Sinclair Lewis at four months, 1885.

Courtesy Saint Cloud State University Archives

Sinclair Lewis graduation photo from Yale, Class of 1907.

Courtesy Saint Cloud State University Archives

Grace Hegger Lewis and Sinclair Lewis
were inveterate motorcar travelers, 1916.

Courtesy Saint Cloud State University Archives

Sinclair Lewis's reputation on both sides of the Atlantic as a dashing, well-tailored man-about-town was cemented in the Roaring Twenties.

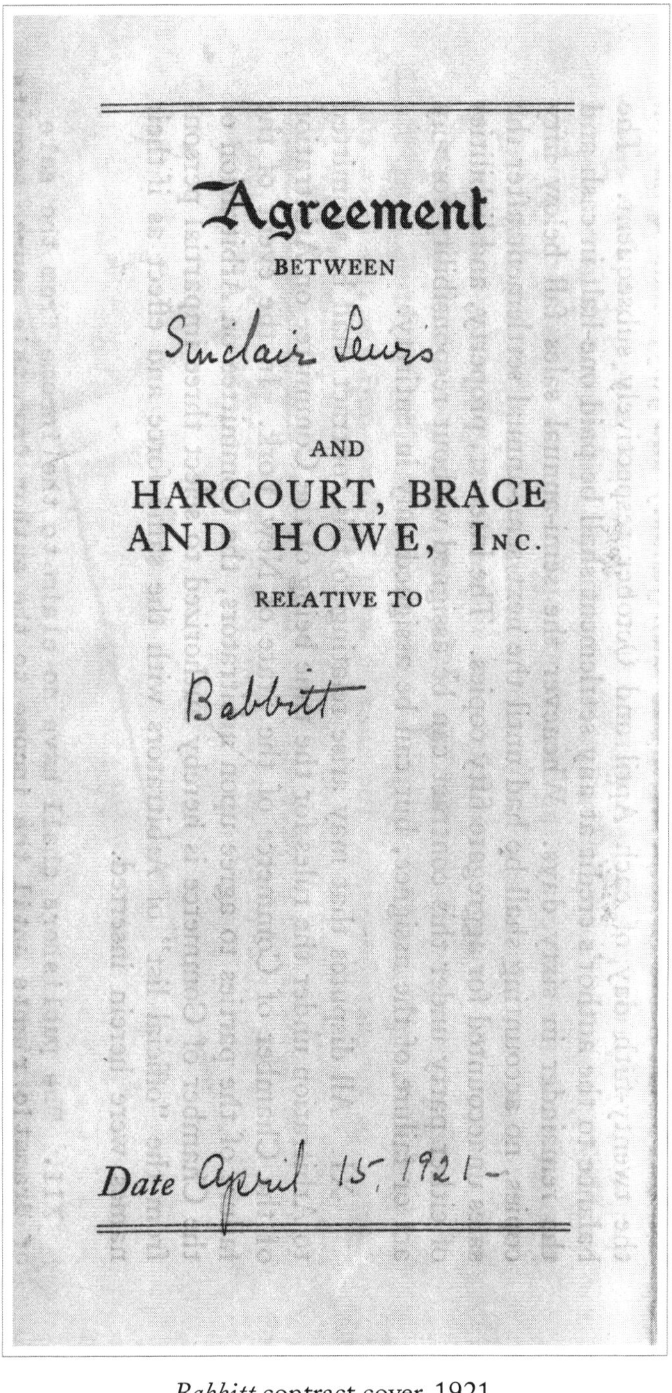

Agreement

BETWEEN

Sinclair Lewis

AND

HARCOURT, BRACE AND HOWE, INC.

RELATIVE TO

Babbitt

Date April 15, 1921 -

Babbitt contract cover, 1921.

Courtesy Port Washington Public Library

In consideration of the mutuality of this contract, the parties agree to all its provisions, and in testimony thereof, affix their signatures and seals.

Sinclair Lewis

HARCOURT, BRACE AND ~~HOWE~~ Company, INC.,

Alfred Harcourt, Pres.

Donald C. Brace, Treas

Babbitt contract signatures, 1921.

Courtesy Port Washington Public Library

Sinclair Lewis was heavily reviewed throughout his career following the publication of *Main Street*. This Bertrand Zadig woodcut highlighted a huge piece on *Arrowsmith* in Great Britain's *The Bookman*, April 4, 1925.

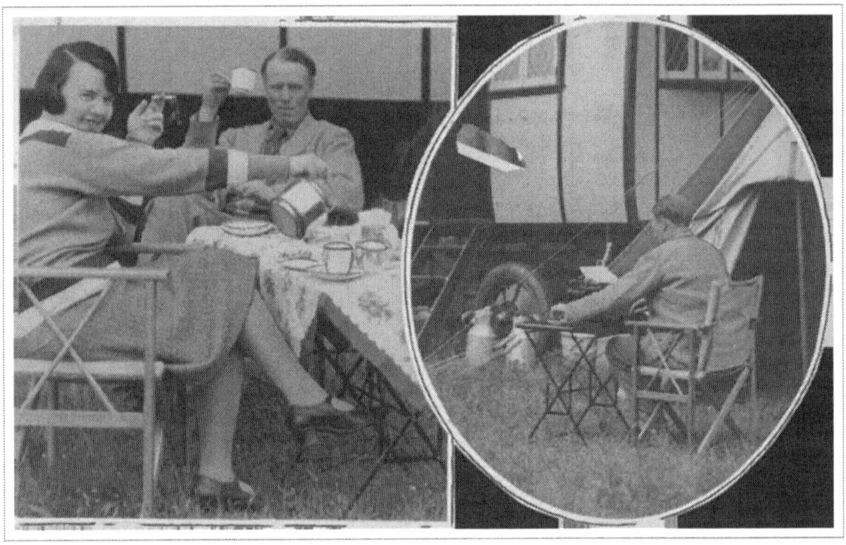

Sinclair Lewis and Dorothy Thompson caravan camping on honeymoon in England, 1928. Lewis possibly is at work on *Dodsworth*.

Leonebel Jacobs lithograph of Sinclair Lewis, 1937.

Courtesy Port Washington Public Library

Al Hirschfeld lithograph, circa 1940.
The cartoonist chose to highlight the five great novels of Lewis's decade.

Courtesy Port Washinton Public Library

Sinclair Lewis, 1949.

Courtesy Port Washington Public Library

Sinclair Lewis died of a heart attack in Florence, Italy, January 1951. Lewis was buried nine days later on an intensely cold day in the family plot in Greenwood Cemetery, Sauk Centre, Minnesota.

Courtsey Edward Agran

SEVEN

ELMER GANTRY

E. L. Doctorow observes in his "Afterword" to *Arrowsmith* the novelist's intention was direct: "Sinclair Lewis's faculty of self-examination, like that of all writers, was more likely to probe the claims of his critics than the praise of his admirers." Lewis never was consistent in depicting his angle of vision. Doctorow writes, "In the controversy surrounding *Babbitt*, he defended himself as a "romantic," thus echoing Sherwood Anderson's insight that Lewisian satire was, behind its cynicism, a cry of disillusionment." Disillusionment indeed is in Lewis's work: "Expecting his countrymen to be more than they were, looking for a resonant truth and righteousness, Lewis had found an American spiritual life that could elicit from him nothing more than bitter derision." Nothing but derision is over-the-top; and disillusionment is not the defining motif of his work, nor for that matter is romanticism. Doctorow concludes that in publishing *Arrowsmith* "the writer finds himself further down the road." This he has right—he searches out *resonant truth and righteousness*—this marks all five of the twenties novels. And he weaves in threads of idealism. Lewis never could, and to this day cannot be pigeon-holed. In his day some critics considered he was something altogether new, while most threw up hands in dismay. The novelist had a lot to say, emphasizing different angles in his twenties novels. Indubitably, if one considers the conclusion, *Arrowsmith* contains hope but reflects, too, disillusionment—no one is left with a strong bead on how all of this is going to turn out. Martin Arrowsmith, Doctorow determines, is "a romantic composed of his own DNA, a fellow not perfect if he was to be real, but in one way or another disposed to fight his way to a level of existence higher than those around him."[1] Martin persisted. As Doctorow sights, the novelist stuck to the

---

[1] E. L. Doctorow, afterword to *Arrowsmith* by Sinclair Lewis (New York: Signet Classic, 1998), 452.

road; he always aimed to get *there*. Having reached the heights of *Arrowsmith*, he moved on to *Elmer Gantry*, a harrowing turn in the road.

Lewis's perspective in *Gantry* on the surface leaves little room for faith he or the country could achieve a "higher level of existence." It is difficult to pin down what exactly motivated his next attempt to get at the United States, beyond keeping at it—his life was a shambles and this weighed in heavily. Perhaps, given his state of mind, he might have concluded, "To hell with the critics…to hell with it all." *Elmer Gantry* offers no specific resolution for what was wrong with the country; nor does it leave the reader hanging—the state of affairs is grim. Elmer is dangerous, and the end note is dire. Doctorow would have been more on-spot if he had argued not that Lewis's entire body of work was premised on disillusionment for again it was not; one need only read *Elmer Gantry*; herein alone lies "an American spiritual life that could elicit from him nothing more than bitter derision." Lewis in writing the novel made a smart decision. Deep in personal agony, he needed to plow ahead; writing was all he had, it was what he most identified with as what was good in him and for him. *Gantry* on the surface and deeper down proves out, in its despair, the literary journey Lewis takes in the decade was premised on contrasts: Here is your United States; make of it what you will, but it has such promise. Beneath the surface gloom he lays out in *Elmer Gantry* (and if read closely it runs deep) the dystopian novel argues the country must plow ahead. The United States faced an eleventh-hour challenge; keep an eye on that American Promise, work the Experiment, secure the nation stays on track. Deep in personal crisis, Lewis appears to have tossed aside optimism. However, he had his sights set: He had to write; and he was right. Climbing out of his misery, the novelist through *Gantry* would land himself and his readers beyond darkness in a more buoyant spot along the progressive road. It was all a journey. *Elmer Gantry* got Sinclair Lewis to *Dodsworth*.

Dodsworth hence is an affirmation of persistence and optimism; it blares righteousness. *Gantry* is a dystopian wail. Following the rousing reception to *Arrowsmith*, turning to this next project, as his wont the author was preoccupied with the maladies that ailed the country. He is indeed disillusioned with the state of the union. His crumbling personal life surely feeds his take the country is in a bad way. There is no romance in *Elmer Gantry*; there is no attempt in *Gantry* to write that great novel, to answer the critics with a resolution of any sort beyond "hail, the hour is dire." The protagonist, standing as a man of God, offers zero promise to everyman. Martin Arrowsmith credulously found salvation in the woods, solace at "a level of existence higher than those around him"—Elmer Gantry was a creature of the gutter and brought all down with him.

Doctorow contends Lewis in searching out a hero for *Arrowsmith* determined he "could not be an artist, lest his author be subject to grandiosity, he could not be a priest or a minister, because as a later work, *Elmer Gantry*, would argue, there was dubious salvation in that."[2] Lewis had played with the idea of writing a church novel for years; he had in *Babbitt* and *Main Street* mocked religion for its commercialization and provinciality. Whatever he had in mind all along, the 1927 publication of *Gantry* dropped a bombshell: the world was in desperate need of saving grace. There seemed to be little hope, the country at its nadir; there might well be no salvation for a society gone amuck. *Gantry* was bad news and scandal galore. But it met Lewis's personal and professional challenges; he had to keep writing and he landed on this thoroughly disreputable product of Heartland America.

Lewis writing *Gantry* was in turmoil. His relations with Alfred Harcourt, as always the course ran with associates and friends, were deteriorating. The publisher increasingly found the house's cash cow troublesome and querulous; by 1931 the two would part company. Lewis's marriage to first-wife Grace ended in calamitous, public fashion—not a surprise on either count. The author's father, Doctor E. J. Lewis, who figured prominently in his son's life, died. The chaos was thrown all the more into relief by heavy drinking. It all played out in Lewis's more-than-usual frantic approach to his writing, and a bevy of souring relations. Critic Ludwig Lewisohn picked up on the perilous drift in affairs after a nasty encounter with the novelist at a party "drunken and ribald (vulgarly ribald) out of sheer despair...putting on a show." Lewis "seemed to have no inner certainty, no balance, no serenity, nothing between heaven and earth to which he could withdraw

---

[2] Ibid., 452–53.

for quietude or healing. He did and said things that, as I well knew, outraged his true self [and] depressed us all by his clamorous but unmistakable unhappiness." Lewisohn on the occasion tossed the author out of his apartment.[3] So Lewis lay in his waste while the controversy around his literary eminence stewed overhead—and, yes he persisted.

Elmer Gantry is a powerful novel, an intriguing story, courting controversy at every turn. Lewis and Harcourt, as always, were out to make a mint. Once completed, Harcourt pulled out all stops to promote in that age of ballyhoo the latest work of "the author of *Main Street*, *Babbitt*, and *Arrowsmith*." Harcourt, Brace and Company released the book in March, 1927. They exploited another innovative New Era enterprise, The Book-of-the-Month Club; the literary merchant made *Elmer Gantry* its March selection for its bulging middle-class clientele. A giant first printing of 138,000 copies had been arranged and adroitly publicized. Harcourt hounded journalists with press releases prior to (and following) publication, and he provided them copies of the book. One pre-publication promotion described how the firm had prepared for the bombshell event: "What It Means to Manufacture the First Edition of *Elmer Gantry*" reeled off the numbers—binding, paper, ink—boldfacing in a number-crazed era the greatest first printing in the history of the American novel. One hundred thousand copies were on the shelves the first day of sales; almost all were grabbed up. Harcourt and Lewis got just what they bargained for. The publisher cabled Lewis in Paris: "News stories everywhere. Kansas [City] Star five columns. Reviews violent either way. Clergy hot. Reorders already....Everything lovely." It continued month upon month, Harcourt and Lewis ginning up scandal and sales. Harcourt wrote Lewis at the end of March, "The publicity on *Elmer Gantry* is amazing, and it still keeps pouring in. We keep a daily bulletin of sales here, and it is very amusing to watch it catch on in one territory after

---

[3] Richard Lingeman, *Sinclair Lewis: Rebel from Main Street* (New York: Random House, 2002), 309.

the other. We are advertising it, of course, in every conceivable way from here to the Pacific Ocean."[4]

The book was first-class scandal, a banner headline bouncing across the U.S.A. Few critics commented on the writing—the great American novel was not at issue. The house and author had had a plan, but how well had it been conceived? Harcourt had put to Lewis, "We are taking the line that the book is a great novel in the best tradition of English fiction, so that the inevitable scrap about it will heat up between the two groups of readers and go over the publishers' and perhaps to some extent, the author's head."[5] Harcourt envisioned he could separate the publishing house from the controversy, jack up sales, and at the same time further bolster Lewis's literary credentials. However, it was immediately apparent the story read the same for everyone: Elmer, a piece of work, captured the nation's attention, and so did the author, and they were inseparable. The issue of art, by default in the view of critics, had been scrapped.

---

[4] James M. Hutchisson, *The Rise of Sinclair Lewis, 1920–1930* (University Park: Pennsylvania State University Press, 1996), 159–60. Within ten weeks, two hundred thousand copies exchanged hands. *Gantry* topped the best-seller lists through July. Banned in Boston and Kansas City, the story blazed as newspapers spread the outraged word. Harcourt fueled it with massive advertising. Lewis was threatened by readers with lynching, with the electric chair; a New England cleric recommended jailing for at least five years. Harcourt picked up an Ohio paper's account of a domestic tiff and sent out a press release: "Trouble in the home of Leo Roberts...began when his wife brought home a copy of *Elmer Gantry* and he burned it. Roberts was ordered to a private sanitarium for a short rest, after his wife...charged him with lunacy." Ibid., 160. Mark Schorer expands, "The novel was advertised on five enormous billboards of the General Outdoor Advertising Company in New York, and in May of the following year, when the General Conference of the Methodist Church assembled in Kansas City, on forty-nine billboards including, in the center of the city, thirteen that were illuminated." The spell in that hyper-active decade could be commanding. See *Sinclair Lewis: An American Life* (New York: McGraw-Hill Book Company, 1961), 473.

[5] Lingeman, 300.

Elmer Gantry was a despicable (and occasionally lovable) character. *Elmer Gantry* was outright scandal. It was an incisive, if hardly balanced, assessment of the state of religion in the United States in the 1920s. Over the top, as always a satirical tour-de-force, Lewis had hit his target, and it was a bull's eye. What was he aiming for? He incorporated the to-be-expected small town, midwestern, urban, and bourgeois themes. They built upon the terrain he had laid out of America—even George Babbitt plays a cameo, Lewis at times in the twenties threading in characters and locales one book to another. But overwhelming all was the religious hypocrisy, which had been put on less resplendent display in *Main Street*, *Babbitt*, and *Arrowsmith*. Here it is the whole show—Elmer Gantry, a good-looking, sweet-talking, clever (and dumb at times), cynical, ambitious turn-of-the century country boy is a religious man with an errant, albeit somewhat educated grasp of the gospels, and he possesses a distinctive capacity for sinning personally and professionally.[6] Elmer is not alone. Many have shortcomings. On a journey across decades, he mixes with hosts of parishioners and preachers, and he indulges in a variety of religious persuasions. He rises up from one country church to another (and out of one scandal to another) on to towns and cities; ultimately he achieves the crowning glory, a prominent New York City pulpit. He is canny, he gets what is in the ether, pragmatic to a tee, even exploiting the newest phenomenon radio.[7] Religion, its practices, followers, leaders, teachings, its sects

---

[6] "Though Elmer was the athletic idol of the college, though his occult passion, his heavy good looks, caused the college girls to breathe quickly, though his manly laughter was as fetching as his resonant speech, Elmer was never really liked." Sinclair Lewis, *Elmer Gantry* (New York: Harcourt, Brace and Company, 1927), 6. For Elmer it was all Elmer: "His eyes were friendly, his smile was friendly—oh, he was always friendly enough; he was merely astonished when he found that you did not understand his importance and did not want to hand over anything he might desire." Ibid. 8–9.

[7] "The Rev. Dr. Gantry was the first clergyman in the state of Winnemac, almost the first in the country, to have his services broadcast by radio. He suggested it himself. At that time, the one broadcasting station in Zenith, that of the Celebes Gum and Chicle Company, presented only jazz orchestras and retired sopranos, to advertise the renowned Jolly Jack Gum. For fifty

and divides, its commercialization, machinations, its multitudinous convictions and doubts are sent up on brutal display. Lewis in a self-portrait confessed he may have had "no virtues whatever save a real, fiery, almost reckless hatred of hypocrisy." To be sure there are a number of good pastors in the novel, and they are honest brokers within the corrupt world. But hypocrisy reigns; the novelist had set out on a tear.[8]

Harcourt and Lewis had created a raucous across an easily crazed country. Critics—and ordinary folks—piled on. Hordes took on Elmer Gantry as anything but a representative American and espied Lewis most exemplary of what was wrong with the country. Magazines and newspapers profited. Sales refracted the glow of the firestorm. Hutchisson recounts "pulpit fury raged on for at least a year."[9] Billy Sunday, one of the country's most famous evangelists, spouted, "Oh boy, if I'd been God, I sure would have landed a haymaker right on the old button."[10] Every man and every woman weighed in. Robert Littell wrote in *The Literary Digest* in April, 1927 "The Storm over 'Elmer Gantry,'" the book moved "like peanuts at a circus." Kansas City, a

---

dollars a week Wellspring Church was able to use the radio Sunday mornings from eleven to twelve-thirty. Thus Elmer increased the number of his hearers from two thousand to ten thousand—and in another pair of years it would be a hundred thousand." Lewis always catches the zeitgeist, zeroing in here on the very earliest days of radio, prophesizing where it was headed. Ibid., 399.

[8] Gary Schornhorst and Matthew Hofer, eds., *Sinclair Lewis Remembered* (Tuscaloosa: University of Alabama Press, 2012), 7 consider the self-portrait fanciful; it was one of many and at times contradictory poses Lewis shared with the public. He had done the research—that in itself had proved word-of-mouth fodder for Harcourt and Brace's long build-up to the novel's unveiling. Samuel Harness was a consultant to Lewis: "He came to Kansas City to do the preliminary fashioning of a missile intended for a bulging hornet's nest. He was perfectly frank about it. He gathered a group of preachers of all shades of theological opinion to meet in a series of weekly luncheon-conferences. He demanded that the ministers call him 'Red'; he had their first names at his tongue's tip...." And the Kansas papers printed all his going-abouts. Ibid., 161.

[9] Hutchisson, 160.

[10] Lingeman, 301–02.

totem of heartland identity (and the source of most of Lewis's research), stood affronted speaking for America, disparaging the author. Red-hot with anger one prominent K.C. minister (an early supporter and consultant of Lewis) advertised his forthcoming sermon on *the book* with the heading drawn from the first lines of the novel: "Elmer Gantry was drunk." Harcourt stirred the fires by incorporating Kansas City preachers into his own ad—it was the twenties, all had learned advertising pays. The minister William L. Stidger later commented that Lewis had to have been drunk writing *Gantry*: "Elmer Gantry came out of a mind whose standard of conduct and morals are such that if they were universally adopted or condoned would destroy the institution of marriage, the home, the American constitution, and the church itself."[11]

---

[11] Robert Littell, "The Storm Over 'Elmer Gantry,'" *Literary Digest*, April 16, 1927, 28–29 ran a hefty two pages, four columns, headlined with four photographs: Lewis, "Who started the fuss" with this "moral leper"; Mencken, "Who, much pleased, says that 'Elmer Gantry' is 'the most dreadful and perfect portrait of a man that has gotten between covers since Rabelais painted *Friar John*'"; Billy Sunday, "Who tells us emphatically that had he been the Lord, he 'would have socked Mr. Lewis so hard that there would have been nothing left for the devil to levy on"; and the eminent Baptist reformer Dr. John Roach Straton, "Who says the book is bunk and that Mr. Lewis had no plan or purpose 'save the putrid purpose to besmirch God's prophets and to demean all holy things.'" Elmer in part had been modeled on Straton who led the National Association for Purity in Art and the Press. See 141–43. As for Elmer, Littell remarks, "He is a morally moronic monstrosity given over to the world, the flesh and the devil." The piece references a hash of reviews. One notes Lewis was uninterested in "finding truth," which apparently meant maxims regarding the ministry or art. Littell repeats Mencken's remonstration that Americans may well be saved by Lewis who portrays in *Gantry* as he did in *Babbitt* "danger" which is "as American as goose-stepping or the mean admiration of mean things." He cites Joseph Wood Krutch who finds Lewis sincerely on a quest for an "almost too literal truth." In *Main Street*, *Babbitt*, and *Elmer Gantry* Lewis has "recorded a reign of grotesque vulgarity which but for him would have left no record of itself because no one else could have adequately recorded it." In "Mr. Babbitt's Spiritual Guide," *Nation*, March 16, 1927, 291–92 Krutch surmises it is not *Gantry* that is an aberration in Lewis's twenties work—that had been *Arrowsmith*:

"With 'Elmer Gantry' Mr. Lewis returns to the practice of his own particular trade. In "Arrowsmith" he turned aside in an effort to achieve certain qualities, characteristic of the conventional novel, which his detractors had declared outside his range...." He "adds the third member to his impressive trilogy devoted to the most grotesque aspects of American life." As for art "though there are many who will not be able to read it without the Devil's question, 'But is it art?', it is not likely that any review will answer that question definitively." See too, Littell "The Preacher Fried in Oil," *New Republic*, March 16, 1927, 108–09. Julia Peterkin, "Notes of a Rapid Reader," *Saturday Review of Literature*, April 16, 1927, 725 saw no reason to bother over art as "the literary criticism of this book seems likely to go by the board" awash in the sensationalism and scandalous charges. She declares it is not art because Elmer and the entire entourage lack depth of character. But what does it matter? "No satirist ever was fair, yet if he does not keep some relation to truth, his book goes flat; and 'Elmer Gantry' is not flat." A month earlier, Henry Seidel Canby editorializing in "Vicious Ignorance," *Saturday Review of Literature*, March 12, 1927, 637 and 640, announced he was not about "to enter upon literary criticism of that remarkable book." He leaves it to others as Carl Van Doren in the same issue: "Yet," Canby notes, "no one who reads it can be without reflections of his own, and one at least seems worthy of discussion": "Sinclair Lewis does not attack the church *per se*—he does not even raise the question of the validity of religion." *Elmer Gantry* should not be discussed "as a novel, but as journalism, and that is precisely what it is, high-powered journalism making news of the religious world. We think of Lewis as a modern, but actually his really important books—"Main Street, "Babbitt," "Arrowsmith," "Elmer Gantry"—belong in the Victorian line; the raucous style, the modern scene, the frank rough-and-tumble of the description, conceal the fact that they are not only successors, they are the companions" of those earlier works of Kingsley, Eliot, Twain, Wells in which the authors called upon the intellect to save society, and excoriated, most of all, ignorance." He ponders, "Lewis was too angry in this book to be at his best." He found himself in such a "murky place," a moral morass, "he struck out with little art but the knock-him-down variety." Religion was not the curse—for Lewis, a most ethical man, saw "an affront to right thinking and right living." Carl Van Doren, "St. George and the Parson," *Saturday Review of Literature*, March 12, 1927, 639, www.unz.com, praises: "Sinclair Lewis once more reveals himself as something besides a novelist. He is still the spokesman of a notable phase of American discontent with contemporary America." He did so in *Main Street* and

The public response of the clergy was emphatically negative, although there were those few of the cloth who stood up and took Lewis's side (and a lot more others in private). Stidger would later comment quietly in a letter friends had since advised him "of case after case of preacher friends *I know* who are living Elmer Gantry lives, and *getting by* with it!" Those siding with Lewis were overwhelmed by raging condemnation. Rev. Everrett C. Wagner of New York's West Side Episcopal Church in his sermon the Sunday following publication declared the author had conjured a "shepherd in a sheik's role," and he wrote "like a pig in a parlor." The Congregational minister back in Sauk Centre (who had just buried the elder Lewis) declared the novel lewd beginning to end. The town son, fallen by way of *Main Street* but arisen in estimation amongst his town folk following the successes of *Babbitt* and *Arrowsmith* (and the money they generated in tourism), once more had sunk low, displaying in the pastor's words "his own nature and he out gantry's Elmer Gantry." He charged town boy Harry was out for the money, a best-seller whatever the cost. Many in Sauk Centre agreed: Lewis was irreverent, a man with a disgustingly immoral personal life.[12]

Elmer Gantry *and* Sinclair Lewis were the issue. Rev. John Roach Straton who pastored New York's Calvary Baptist Church (and came to be one of the leaders of the powerful fundamentalist cause of the day) declaimed the characters "figments of a disordered imagination." The remarks were tantalizingly paired in the *New York Evening Post Literary Review* with those of a Lewis novelist friend who determined *Elmer Gantry* to be "the greatest, most vital and most penetrating study of religious hypocrisy that has been written since Voltaire." A host of reviewers who could not get past the protagonist's (and for some the

---

further in *Babbitt*. Oddly, Van Doren makes no mention of *Arrowsmith*, but it, too, fit the pattern. He believes Lewis's anger got the best of his satire in portions of the book; "'Elmer Gantry' suffers as a novel." "Though the total impression made by 'Elmer Gantry' is less than it might have been if it had been held in a firmer satiric grasp, the details are generally striking." Maybe that was Lewis's aim overall for the book—throw it all out there.

[12] Lingeman, 302–03.

author's) repellent character ignored Lewis's valid indictments—albeit it was a selective treatment—of the religious establishment. They, too, conjoined Gantry and Lewis. Kansan William Allen White, a huge Lewis fan and national spokesman, was outraged, believing God had struck the artist dead. Author and scholar William Lyon Phelps charged Lewis wrote *Gantry* "literally foaming at the mouth." Robert Littell saw Gantry as "an effigy rather than a character in a story," one who was "roasted anew in every page with such zest that we end by feeling in this instance that Mr. Lewis is not a novelist, nor a crusader, nor even a propagandist, but simply and solely a witch-burner." But a few, such as Julia Peterkin in *The Saturday Review of Literature*, peered deeper; she pointed out that while everyone debated *Elmer Gantry's* "truth," they forgot to notice it was satire, which by definition was both critical and distorting. Building on such a critique, others argued Lewis's charges were accurate and significant, but he fell short artistically. Elmer Davis in the *New York Times Book Review* took the author to task charging he had abandoned art for propaganda. He offered up that as a study of the "grosser fatuities" of the clergy, the novel demanded debate; it should be read; but in the end, it was not art as the characters were beyond belief. The British, on the other hand, heartily embraced the novel, as they had the earlier Lewis works. Schorer records, "H. G. Wells based his observations of American culture on the novels of Sinclair Lewis, including *Elmer Gantry*, as though they were the most reliable of documents." Whatever might constitute art, no one seems to have doubted they were reading something of value, even if it came down to assessing Lewis's own "deplorable" character.[13]

---

[13] Littell, 28–29; Lingeman, 303–04; Schorer, 475. Elmer Davis, "Mr. Lewis Attacks the Clergy: In 'Elmer Gantry' He Deals a Blow Beneath the 'Bible-Belt,'" *New York Times Book Review*, March 13, 1927, 1 and 22; on the front page, the article (accompanied by a deco painting of Lewis by G. T. Hartmann) offers a striking dissection of the novel, its author, and the times. "Sinclair Lewis, who can write very good novels when he is in the mood, chooses this time to write a missionary tract." "Of these four hundred pages perhaps twenty have been written by Lewis the artist; the rest are preempted by Lewis the preacher, and refinements of character...would weaken his polemic." Still, the ghastly Elmer's "history will alternately make you shake with

Elmer Gantry and Sinclair Lewis had merged in popular and critical estimation; the literary quality of the novel was subsumed by scandal. In *The Nation* Mark Van Doren concluded *Elmer Gantry* was the "sensation of the season," but most of the talk side-lined its worth as literature. The work, however, proved to be a good deal more telling of Lewis's literary talents than most were letting on. Lingeman some eighty years on notes the novel is flawed, but Gantry the character produces an "enduring fascination," and Lewis's mastery of mimicry, satire,

---

laughter and seethe with rage." "If the whole book had been written" by Lewis the artist, "it could have been a great novel; but it would have been a less effective sermon, and Lewis is writing to get his argument over, in language that nobody can misunderstand." "People are going to read it and remember it." Davis recognizes that all the hoopla should reduce to "at the moment...not what about Lewis, but what about the clergy." There are real matters of grave concern considered, if in a highly distorted, albeit absorbing, fashion: there is "an immediate menace to religious liberty in this country" represented by the power of the Methodist Church, with the support of the Baptists. "[T]here are plenty of artists; but no other creative writer has his capacity for minute and patient research" which is the author' most useful talent." In this work he has caught "the raw substance of current American life; too many people have seen it and felt it to permit plausible denial." And there is hope: read the Frank Shallard passages, Davis urges—dismiss Elmer as a caricature, you cannot dismiss Shallard who with his honest earnestness is crushed by the forces Elmer represents. In the end, Frank's wholesale defeat symbolizes what the good forces in the church and society are up against—"contemporary Protestantism owes some explanation." But Lewis the acute sociologist may not be on to a feasible solution; Lewis, for Davis, fights along with Mencken for salvation—but Mencken's solution, along with Lewis's, is not the truth the nation requires; it too lacks democratic substance and tolerance, and its secularized religion is no more sound or sacred—and disturbingly "is likely to be the State church of America within a couple of decades." In this thoughtful piece, Davis as a Baptist tries to sort through all the palaver swirling about the author. Lewis might well be afraid of where he and Mencken and the U.S. may end: "[L]ike Christianity it is a syncretion of diverse elements held together by a fanatical refusal to compromise with older creeds and a firm conviction of its monopoly of salvation." Hardly incidental, Lewis dedicated the book to "H. L. Mencken with profound admiration." Perhaps the next should have gone to Davis.

and humor play well with his "dead-on portraits of the social life of the clergy." Lewis, not all a bad seed, drew from his Congregationalist upbringing in Sauk Centre; he hankered for "the communal bond that Sunday mornings had symbolized in a small town...." Lingeman argues plenty of readers knew there was a lot of truth to what he had to say about the "bad." Lewis focused on church shortcomings, he points out, yet he still repeatedly acknowledged the draw, the power of religious community to bond parishioners to one another. Clearly for the biographer Lewis was neither casting aside faith nor abandoning literary virtue.[14]

[14] Lingeman, 304–05. Van Doren interestingly observes the public's primary interest may have nothing to do with art: "So there will be less discussion than there might be concerning the quality of 'Elmer Gantry.' Yet when have many readers cared for such discussion?" See Mark Van Doren, "First Glance at the Season's Books," *Nation*, April 20, 1927, 441. Rebecca West, "Sinclair Lewis Introduces Elmer Gantry," *New York Herald Tribune Books*, March 13, 1927, 1 and 6, jumped in as well. In another front-page spring review, with another striking portrait of Lewis, a woodcut by Bertrand Zadig, the British novelist wrote lengthily of "one of the most disappointing books that a man of genius has ever produced." She determined this may have been a matter of choice: "The incompetence must be the result of the author's feeling that the enterprise on which he has embarked is not worth while." In art he has failed; as a satirist and societal critic he has fallen woefully short. He is directionless...as is Frank Shallard, "an albino Babbitt." (This is a particularly errant conclusion—Shallard is a powerful, sensible voice.) Lewis, West continues, asked more of Babbitt, "a fervent plea that George F. Babbitt should let the light of his real character shine...." Lewis offers nothing worthy of salvation, "a finer and more complicated mode of thought and feeling"...something of art, of intellect. West cuts to the chase, arguing the author needs to "sit still so life could make any deep impression on him." He needs to re-establish a "standard of profundity," to "give his genius chance." "Why has Mr. Lewis produced a book that in spite of its humor, its research, its bravery, has not succeeded in being the satire he has the wit to plan?" West as so many surely knew Lewis's bad personal state. So bad, for her he offers evidence he is reduced to a defeated Babbitt, overwhelmed by the society within which he lives. She sees nothing radical in this work. It will be controversial but not

There is no full-proof means to gauge national sentiment, and certainly not that of a hundred years ago, but for what it is worth Lewis received many letters of support—albeit not outnumbering the missives damning him.[15] He knew the Baptists, the Methodists, and the controversies within and between the sects. He understood small and large churches; rural, town, and urban congregants; some of his best writing crops up in conversations and debates between religious practitioners who genuinely care about their vocation and their congregations. He studied the Catholics and the Jews as well as mainline Protestants, and he zeroed in on the power and antics of the rising wave of evangelists of the Billy Sunday and Aimee Semple McPherson breed; he possessed a vast library of books on rcligion which he worked closely; he pegged the role of business in religion and the power of the new medium radio; and many figures are recognizably based on well-known religious personages of the day. He had done his homework. And he had plenty to say beyond satirizing folks. He seemed to have struck a good number of "truths." Humorist and social commentator Will Rogers cited one. He wrote in the *New York Times*: "When I am playing in a town and there looks like there is not going to be much of a house, I announce through the papers that that night I will read passages from *Elmer Gantry*, the Baptist sheik, and the house will be packed with Methodist and Presbyterian women. Old Elmer sure had it." So, too, Lewis; and it amounted to more than scandal.[16]

Lewis was not aiming so low as many proposed. He knew he had a story to tell. Why he chose to offer in the end no redemption, one cannot say with certainty—but if one reads novel upon novel, it is clear he saw a country at risk which needed to be put on notice. *Elmer Gantry* swings a sledgehammer. Yes, there were passages which spoke for higher American principles, but disillusion shadows the entire novel.

---

consequential, "this book will not start any great movement toward enhanced sensitiveness of life…."

[15] Hutchisson, 162.

[16] Schorer, 474. Rudolph Valentino and sheiks were elements of the cultural firmament. Recall Rev. Everrett C. Wagner declared Lewis conjured a "shepherd in a sheik's role." All were knee-deep in the churning culture.

Gantry was part of Lewis's twenties storyline, that being one of promise as well as an outlining of shortcomings. *Gantry* represents in the main serious dangers. Lingeman's analysis is of particular interest. He makes the contextual connection, but he does not take it the distance. Lewis was taking on Protestant Fundamentalism, a rising force in the twenties. But the author looked further. Broader Christianity as it was generally practiced certainly was not his prey. Lingeman correctly argues Lewis saw major Fundamentalists were out to gain national power by means of the political arena "to regulate morality, art, and education in America." In the end, Elmer sits astride a New York power-base and dreams of rising as the nation's "moral dictator." This is, beyond religion, a hegemonic concern he minimally raised with *Main Street*, espoused clear-as-a-bell in *Babbitt*, reiterated in *Arrowsmith*; and which he will take on again in *Dodsworth*. Lingeman considers the ending a "dystopic vision of what Lewis saw as the worst aspects of fundamentalism...." It is much more: it is a fully disillusioned view of what has happened to "America." The scholar concludes, "In *Elmer Gantry*, Lewis played Paul Revere, attempting to rouse the country against fundamentalist fascism. Seventy-five years later, in a time of errant televangelists and evolution-banning creationists, his charges against Gantry are hardly shocking." He is right as to Lewis's sense he could serve as a Paul Revere—*the* issue, on the other hand, ran far beyond fundamentalism. A mass of evil forces was at work. The destruction of the republic was at stake. Lingeman could have stressed the considerably deeper concern. Elmer Davis in assessing the novel in 1927 was emphatic. In *Gantry* the critic proclaimed the author displays "the raw substance of current American life; too many people have seen it and felt it to permit plausible denial."[17]

---

[17] Lingeman 306–307; for full analysis see 298–308. For Davis see note 13. Hutchisson perceives having deified science in *Arrowsmith* Lewis "set out to investigate its opposite—fundamentalist religion—and show it to be vacuous and false." Of course Lewis was equally dismayed by science's corruption. See 127. For Hutchisson's entire analysis see 125–63. Throughout his study, Hutchisson does not—it is not his primary concern—distill the personal chaos and its effect on Lewis's work. The exception proves the rule: in *Gantry* he

In both *Babbitt's* Good Citizen's League and in the vision set forth in *Arrowsmith* by one of Martin's New York institute's superiors, the challenge is clear: "Some day we might be able to erect a superstructure of co-operative science which would control not only McGurk but every institute and every university scientific department in the country…."; "[W]hy, you and I can become the dictators of science throughout the whole country!"—hegemonic control was the issue.[18] Lingeman is correct, Lewis feared fascism but he hardly considered religion to be *the carrier* of the disease; the body politic as a whole was considerably ill and susceptible to destruction. The devolution of the American Experiment, bowing down to the power of money, the adoration of conformity, the loss of community; materialism, the bane of selfishness, discounted ethics all for a false sense of individual fulfillment, this was the issue. Lewis foresaw great danger ahead; demagogic ranting was in the air and poisonous. There was more to all his work than sociology, satire, or scandal. Lewis all along was signaling alarm. Whether many picked up on his deep sense of danger to democratic institutions,

---

recognizes its impact on his "darkest" novel and what he considers his most sarcastic; see 129. For the fullest account of Lewis' personal, professional, and psychological struggles, Schorer is the strongest resource; for his assessment of *Gantry*, see 473–83. The weakest analysis of *Gantry* surprisingly crops up in Grebstein, 96–107. He is unusually off-balance as he harshly tackles it and still concludes "it remains to this day one of the two or three best American novels centered on religion." See 106. The scholar raises sharp points amongst which is one most miss—*Gantry* is Lewis's most "naturalistic" work; see 102. Elmer roams a beastly world. But one of the best novels on religion? Grebstein, in 1962, may have been exercising presentism in his analysis. Hollywood clearly did in interpreting the novel when it took on *Elmer Gantry* in 1960. Of all the screenplay possibilities the film principally highlighted the preacher's most fundamentalist and wild episode in the novel—hardly representative of the breadth of the novel (which always is a challenge for filmmakers), but this seems an odd plot choice. But perhaps not: Playing on twenties evangelist Aimie Semple McPherson's still lingering notoriety, early sixties cultural attacks on fundamentalism, and loosening sexual mores, the choice seemed to be a good one to fire up box-office receipts.

[18] Lewis, *Arrowsmith*, 323.

Gantry proved a good read, a strong piece of writing, a clear shot over the bow—in shattering fashion the novel was a wake-up call much was off-kilter in the U.S.A.

It was all part of a pattern—religious reaction was hardly Lewis's most serious concern. It was one more symptom of trouble he had been deciphering all along. With *Elmer Gantry* he opted to be a good deal less subtle about the toxicity in the body politic. In the conclusion of the novel, with Elmer reigning high, the novelist signaled precisely what he had foremost on his mind. This was deep into the eleventh hour. Nothing was left hanging; the country was on a precipice. Whether or not Lewis got that overarching particular across, his readers putting down the book were left with plenty to ponder—the conclusion reeked of fascism.

Yet Lewis as always confounds. Lingeman addresses a minor character, Frank Shallard; he misses the significance he plays for the author: Lewis's alarm that the danger is not the religious establishment but the basest elements he believed it represented. (And naturally, it may be that the readers missed it as well, but that seems difficult to accept.) Americans were losing their footing—and it could get ugly. Surely, Lewis had it in for shortcomings in religious institutions; with H. L. Mencken he found it an engaging topic for discussion and ridicule. Both felt it symbolized something severely wrong with the nation. And religion was a hot issue in the twenties. But within the scope of *Gantry*, the considerably greater matter of concern is expressed by the fate of the conspicuously ethical, somewhat naïve Christian doubter Shallard. The U.S. is on a perilous path, careening toward an un-Christian destiny. Lewis here, counter to Lingeman's perception, places great weight on the character and fate of Frank Shallard.

As a Zenith minister (and long past seminary acquaintance of Elmer), caught up in the religious culture wars of the twenties, Frank ends up literally beaten to a pulp. Elmer, having risen up to be a Zenith leader, opportunistically arranges Frank's banishment from the benign church he leads. Gantry plotting from his more powerful church's perch stokes the anger that drives the Reverend Shallard to his doom. Here is a minister on a worthy quest. Shallard presents no danger to anyone; he does serve as a further punch in Elmer's ticket to far more fame and a move up and out of the Middle West. Early on when the two freshly minted ministers set out from divinity school to spread the word, Frank had a real yearning for truth: "He had no such definite and ecstatic Call as came to Elmer Gantry, but he had always known that he would go on nibbling at theories about the eucharist, and pointing men the way to uncharted plateaus called Righteousness, Idealism, Honesty, Sacrifice, Beauty, Salvation." He is the equal of Martin Arrowsmith, forever in doubt, forever certain there was a greater truth whether it was to be found in a purer science, a sanctified relationship with God, anywhere. As Martin recognized, the world was chock full of truths. Elmer is another character altogether, and Frank pays a hefty price.

Frank's end is harsh. Having once despaired, "I've never been violently enough in earnest to be beaten for the sake of the Lord our God!...Not yet!" his hour comes as he takes to speaking across the country, addressing crowds on fundamentalism, the Scopes Monkey Trial, and the gospel high-jinks of William Jennings Bryan and his ilk. In the Southwest "in a roaring modern city," Reverend Shallard was scheduled to make an address "at Central Labor Hall, auspices of the League for Free Science": "Are the Fundamentalists Witch Hunters?" He was forewarned to steer clear by way of an anonymous note from "The Committee": "If you enjoy life, you'd better be out of this decent Christian city before evening." Noting the fascistic tilt of the religious zealots, he calls out, "That's how these men speak, with so little power—as yet!... Use your imaginations! Think how they would rule this nation...if they had the power!" Frank's earnestness is inflammatory. A "dozen tough young men" enter the hall and look "expectantly toward the line of prosperous Christian Citizens." The signal is given "and the young toughs galloped down the aisle toward Frank, their eyes hot with cruelty, teeth like a fighting dog's, hands working—he could feel them at his neck." Brother Frank is piled into a sedan—might as well have been a Klan Ford—for a ride out in the country. Deciding not to hang him with a tow-rope in a cornfield, the judges draw forth "a coiled black leather whip, a whip for mules." Broken, "his right eye was a pulp of blind flesh," his jawbone exposed, Reverend Shallard ripped to shreds at dawn arises, stumbles to a farmhouse, and is turned away. He is sighted by a motorcycle policeman in a ditch: "[A]s he stooped and saw Frank's half-hidden face, he whispered, 'Good God Almighty!'" Frank, as yet not having been beaten for the Lord, has gone down. Elmer Gantry, upon hearing the news, called his "old friend" and raged: "This is the most outrageous thing I've heard of in my life, Frank!" And that was his final word on the topic, "privately or publicly."[19]

Elmer transgresses to richer pastures, answering a call to pastor a New York congregation; Frank loses his eye sight and any capacity he has to spread God's Word. Shallard is a minor figure in the novel; his message is fundamental, and it strikes home. Mixing fact with fiction, as well as terror, a reader raged in a letter to Lewis: "Some of us who try to live clean lives and hope to leave behind us footprints on the sands of time not to our discredit—consider your book the nastiest—vilest—most immoral piece of writing put before modern civilization. We think that the author and publishers who will put such a book into the hands of the general public deserve the fate or worse! of the preacher Shallard...." Lewis trusted a larger slice of his readership would understand what he was after.

It was fiction, and it resonated. Lewis figuratively got beaten up over *Gantry*. He seemed to shuck it off; he would move on to emphasize in a more deliberate manner what really mattered as he undertook to write *Dodsworth*: getting America out of its fix, a considerably more positive tale. *Elmer Gantry* was a sort of anomaly—a dark work, offering little to no hope, no resolution by a long shot, and yet it brilliantly represented Lewis's determination to hang on against formidable trouble. The novelist clung to Shallard's faith in the good in the world. In *Arrowsmith*, he had a character, a noble (and flawed) scientist, remark to Martin that "the scientist is intensely religious," he seeks purity; "he is so religious that he will not accept quarter-truths, because they are an insult to his faith." In truth, "He is the only real revolutionary, the authentic scientist...."[20] This seeker, Martin's mentor, gets beaten down by enemies professionally and personally. Shallard, not a man of science but of God, is crushed mercilessly, a Christ figure. Lewis had

---

[19] Ibid., 372 and 385–95.

[20] Sinclair Lewis, *Arrowsmith* (New York: Signet Classic, 1998), 278–79.

unveiled in the heart of "God's Country" the epitome of inauthenticity in the saddle. But again, neither fundamentalism nor religion, nor medicine and science had been *the issue.* There was a greater truth, a sanctified civil order must be resolute; a good person had to make his or her way, contribute—a good country had to progress. The author was no revolutionary, no ideologue, and hardly pure by any measure. He knew there could be no heroes to save the day; Martin demonstrated that futile possibility. But the author had faith that the common man and woman had the makings, the resolve to step up and address the community's challenges. He knew the mob mentality. Something was gravely amiss in the U.S., and the powers-that-be had to be revealed and taken down before they unleashed more lethal dangers. The community needed to stand strong...that was the story, stand as one for the individual, stand as the majority for the country.

Frank's story was no aside; nor that of Arrowsmith's mentor. Another "minor" character had similarly been given the task to broaden the discussion in *Babbitt.* The "radical lawyer" Seneca Doane ends up figuratively beaten down as the babbitts of the world outfox him—he is defeated as he runs for mayor on a platform calling Zenith to aim higher. His faith is sturdy—this they cannot take from him. Not science, not religion, he speaks the language of civic decency, and he offers up an explanation of where it can take *everyman.* There is a *promise.* There had been a *revolution.* Time for another *radical* turn, but one back to grass roots—not ideological rigidity. George and Seneca had been college acquaintances; in fact Babbitt in those days actually stood up for progressive-style issues; he and Doane long before shared a concern for "others." Discussing the country with a European critic, Doane speaks a language far from extreme: "Zenith a city with gigantic power—gigantic buildings, gigantic machines, gigantic transportation."[21] He is exploring what's wrong with the U.S., and the critic, an Old-World radical, needs to be set straight. The problem is not size nor bourgeoise standardization which the European attacks. An outsider, he does not get it: First, Europe, too, in the twentieth century is embracing standardization. It is the wave of the future...a product of

[21] Sinclair Lewis, *Babbitt* (New York: Penguin Books, 1996), 89.

the New World. But Europe is small in its ways, unable to fully step up, let alone keep to the greater pace. The United States has made a discovery, it is gigantic, but the country is dangerously mishandling the sizable power it holds. Doane as Lewis is a middle-of-the-road liberal, and he simply espies a better future, an American Dream that can come to full fruition: a land of tolerance, cooperation, and plenty where all are free to come to good fortune in every sense of the word. He is unsure how to bring it about, but he knows it heralds a better day.

Doane makes the argument:

> "Standardization is excellent, *per se*. When I buy an Ingersoll watch or a Ford, I get a better tool for less money, and I know precisely what I'm getting, and that leaves me more time and energy to be individual in. And—I remember once in London I saw a picture of an American suburb, in a toothpaste ad on the back of the *Saturday Evening Post*—an elm-lined snowy street of these new houses, Georgian some of 'em, or with low raking roofs and—The kind of street you'd find here in Zenith, say in Floral Heights. Open. Trees. Grass. And I was homesick! There's no other country in the world that has such pleasant houses. And I don't care if they *are* standardized. It's a corking standard!
>
> "No, what I fight in Zenith is standardization of thought, and, of course, the traditions of competition. The real villains of the piece are the clean, kind, industrious Family Men who use every known brand of trickery and cruelty to insure the prosperity of their cubs. The worst thing about these fellows is that they're so good and, in their work at least, so intelligent. You can't hate them properly, and yet their standardized minds are the enemy."[22]

And these men can fall prey to the more powerful, smoking out their doubts, inflaming their insecurities, grasping for themselves hegemonic control. America for Doane represents a middle-class revolution, one which is pure in spirit and one which must be salvaged. Doane knows he is as bourgeois as his old acquaintance Babbitt, and he feels no

---

[22] Ibid., 89–90.

shame in arguing his case—that was his political platform in his race for the mayoralty. George and his brothers-in-shame can be saved; it's simply a matter of cracking the nut, their standardized minds. Doane's radical European discussant remains skeptical.

Doane has made a heartfelt statement, but there is an inherent flaw which the outsider, the "irreverent" European, sights. Doane argues the boosters of American cities can be mightily taxing, still, he has a notion they are on to something: "Zenith is a better place to live in than Manchester or Glasgow or Lyons or Berlin or Turin—" It is for him, for the world for which he wishes, an enticing vision. "Personally, I prefer a city with a future so unknown that it excites my imagination." The flaw, however, may well be that the babbitts do not have it in them to pull it all off. The European sets Doane straight: "You...are a middle-road liberal, and you haven't the slightest idea what you want. I, being a revolutionist, know exactly what I want—and what I want now is a drink." He has no faith that the better instincts of the bourgeoisie will prevail. Well, who knew what the outcome might be? A middling liberal, the type the European held little brief for, has the will, the strength to show the way? Babbitt can be that American? Sinclair Lewis could not have more starkly raised the question—of course, he just had, through Doane, and he may well have had himself in mind as both weak link and needing a drink?[23]

Lewis often ranted about his self-perceived superiority, but all along he bewailed his shortcomings. He knew all too well he was no radical—never was. Will it in fact take a genuine revolutionist? Sinclair Lewis was simply a middle-roader, and he wanted the country to get back onto a higher track. Democracy can devolve to mobocracy, and plutocracy will take the reins, and reign. This he fears, perceptively, instinctively. Doane speaks that truth.[24]

So where is a middle-of-the-road liberal to turn? Well, that was between Seneca Doane and his European counterpart, and 1922 seemed a more innocent day. Five years on *Gantry* is a best-seller, and the final hour looms. One cannot stand by while a creature like Elmer

---

[23] Ibid., 90

[24] Ibid.

sits serene in Manhattan. The Frank Shallards and Seneca Doanes must triumph. Carol pondered the current condition and planned action. Babbitt demonstrated at least he was willing to question standards. Martin took the issue seriously and opted out. Doane kept at it. And the good Pastor Frank Shallard is eliminated. Can the middle road hold? Lewis was in a bad way; the novel in the judgment of most is far from his best writing, and the strain all around—personal, professional, and social—shows all the more as *Elmer Gantry* races to its climax. At the very end evil is triumphant. Amongst all the muck of *Gantry*, the greater concern, the subtle and not-so-subtle calls to action, a brutal close signifies it is more than late-in-the-day, it is three minutes to midnight for the American Experiment. E. L. Doctorow says with *Arrowsmith* Lewis was looking to demonstrate for his countrymen they possessed a "resonant truth and righteousness," but he could not demonstrate how they could lay claim to it. "And so the novel ends as Martin Arrowsmith, having been educated painfully in the ways of the world, finally achieves a life that is in accordance with his self." Fleeing offered no sustainable resolution for America's dilemma.[25]

Now Lewis had followed up with Elmer, he and his protagonist fully in and of the world. No one, preaches Lewis, can opt out—this is a time of testing. The novel ends with Elmer pondering: "Let me count this day, Lord, as the beginning of a new and more vigorous life, as the beginning of a crusade for complete morality and the domination of the Christian church through the land. Dear Lord, thy work is but begun! We shall yet make these United States a moral nation." And that is "The End."[26]

Grinding to that end, perhaps to signify the crime at work, Lewis inserts a sloppy cops-and-robbers scenario and the biggest scoundrel, Elmer, comes out *clean*. Incongruous with the storyline, Lewis's style of narrative in this scene is not good writing and comes across as slapstick. Nevertheless, the author wants to make a point; he switches back from the hilarity and makes it unavoidably transparent he is dead-serious. Elmer, having evaded a disastrous embarrassment, a come-down

[25] Doctorow, 452 and 454.

[26] Lewis, *Elmer Gantry*, 432.

from which he could not arise, he'd once again skirted scandal and gets the last word. Lewis's statement is not an oddly placed addendum as in *Babbitt* with George having his eleventh-hour epiphany that Ted would save him. Nor are there woods to which anyone can escape. And the crisis has reached well beyond Carol Kennicott's faith that in time, even if it is a hundred years, the country will set itself right. Elmer has an organization, he is a ballyhooed moral crusader, and he prays to power.

Lewis did not need to conclude in this fashion. He'd already, before the last-minute threat to Elmer's position, laid the groundwork which could have ended the novel on a calmer note, albeit the Reverand Gantry was "safe." Lewis seemed to think he needed more than a shot over the bow; he would show where exactly Elmer was destined to land—so close, on the verge, in charge of the nation's fate. The preacher had worked it out clear as a bell. Earlier, just prior to facing his certain scandalous downfall and at the last hour skirting infamy, Gantry had boldly etched his plan—he was about to establish his seat of power. He plotted: "He would combine in one association all the moral organizations in America—perhaps, later, in the entire world. He would be the executive of that combination; he would be the super-president of the United States, and some day the dictator of the world."

> Combine them all. The Anti-Saloon League, the W. C. T. U., and the other organizations fighting alcohol. The Napap and the other Vice Societies doing such magnificent work in censoring immoral novels and paintings and motion pictures and plays. The Anti-Cigarette League. The associations lobbying for anti-evolution laws in the state legislatures. The associations making so brave a fight against Sunday baseball, Sunday movies, Sunday golfing, Sunday motoring, and the other abominations whereby the Sabbath was desecrated and the preachers' congregations and collections were lessened. The fraternities opposing Romanism. The societies which gallantly wanted to make it a crime to take the name of the Lord in vain or to use the nine Saxon physiological monosyllables.

Yes, Elmer concludes, "And all the rest."[27]

The plan for Elmer came from the Lord. To drive his word home, the author punctuates Elmer's dark truth: "We shall yet make these United States a moral nation." Elmer has the final, decisive word. The ailing democratic capitalist dream is not in the end, as with all the novels, a minor plot line at all—the fate of the American Promise remains at the core of Lewis's work; his last words are bold. Sinclair Lewis was not up to writing that Great American Novel when he undertook *Elmer Gantry*; still, in personal and professional despair, he left no doubt he still carried a torch for the country.

The danger Lewis feared was noted by some reviewers, but that take later scholars discounted. Amidst the novel's sensationalism, national controversy over Fundamentalism, and the ever-present quarreling over the author's merits possibly the threat of authoritarianism was lost in the kerfuffle. He had set it up plain and simple: the Republic was on thin ice. In *Gantry*, Lewis demonstrated a penetrating understanding of what ailed the nation, what endangered its promise. Amidst all the hubbub swirling about him, not many seemingly took note of his strident call to action. However, a slice of the public, as with that slice of worried reviewers, seemingly could not have missed the concern Lewis broadcast.

Most critics found the novel wanting; they were scandalized by it, and apparently mesmerized. The bottom line, beyond the immense receipts the book garnered, all the talk about the book overwhelmingly was *the book*. Reasonably, the core point, Lewis's concern for the nation, while still not center-staged, must have drilled through at some level been acknowledged. Again, a small coterie of reviewers commented on what he had revealed. They recognized that *Elmer Gantry* fundamentally remained a call to arms, like the previous three novels. Recall, *Elmer Gantry* was promoted as the latest work of "the author of *Main Street*, *Babbitt*, and *Arrowsmith*." No critic, if reading closely, could doubt Lewis preached reform. The United States of America had problems. To contemporaries the basic line that a fundamental American institution, religion, was in turmoil would come as no surprise. And

[27] Lewis, *Elmer Gantry*, 432 and 409.

focusing on such a combustible topic, it could only remind readers as it did those reviewers of other concerns...the author's forte. But perhaps not. The novel possibly was too outrageous, the expose too daunting. But once more, there were the prominent few who took Lewis in as a whole and understood his gravest concern. *Elmer Gantry*, at bottom, was an impressive piece of work. Sinclair Lewis had stuck to his twenties script.

But how about the scholars decades on as Lingeman, Grebstein, and Hutchisson who see religion as the mainstay of the novel—can't they see more? Understandably, *Gantry*'s laden with distraction. But they study the author, they consider his whole body of work; they read the studies of others; they cite the reviews of the day. If anything, readers, book after book, however spotty their reading, surely picked up at some level Sinclair Lewis's concern for the country's trajectory. They had to know Lewis was saying something, a lot about the United States—and connections could be made. This seems self-evident; the readers were *in and of the twenties*; and yes, maybe they missed the deeper message, action was necessary, fast. That is understandable. The scholars occupy another *moment*. They have before them all of Lewis, all that has been said of the author. One would assume they would recognize that this was the recurrent theme. This was what the *perplexing* author was all about. This is why he *chose* to write his novels as he did. Scholars probe. They have the perspective of time not only to study twenties culture but the history before and following the decade. Can't they SEE, as Gracie observed, what the author was all about? Isn't Lewis throughout the novels waving a banner, displaying the very *standards* they fault him for lacking? He asks for better of the people, the country. He calls out, act on first principles.

A select coterie of distinguished critics certainly picked up on the call, the urgency of the moment. The scholars read them, thoroughly, and yet do not detect the gravity of concern? As noted, Elmer Davis in his treatment in the *New York Times Book Review* observed Lewis caught "the raw substance of current American life; too many people have seen it and felt it to permit plausible denial." Davis, focusing primarily on the religious controversy, argues what is at stake. In "Mr. Lewis Attacks The Clergy: In 'Elmer Gantry' He Deals a Blow

Beneath the 'Bible-Belt,'" the critic pulls no punches. He recognizes where the tale might well end—the implosion of the country's Experiment. Christianity he depicts as a "syncretion of diverse elements held together by a fanatical refusal to compromise with older creeds and a firm conviction of its monopoly of salvation." The nation has run off the tracks—he is pointing his finger not only at the religious institutions, but at the likes of Lewis and Mencken; the more radical reformers can be as harsh as the Fundamentalists. This country is in trouble. Carl Van Doren took a more forgiving tack. He wrote in "St. George and the Parson" in the *Saturday Review of Literature*: "Sinclair Lewis once more reveals himself as something besides a novelist. He is still the spokesman of a notable phase of American discontent with contemporary America." Both Davis and Van Doren cite literary flaws but could not be deterred from the main line. Davis: "Of these four hundred pages perhaps twenty have been written by Lewis the artist; the rest are preempted by Lewis the preacher, and refinements of character…would weaken his polemic." "Literature" is not the issue.[28] Both critics take the writer at his word, do not muddy the water with debates over art. For all the novel's faults, they are in line with E. L. Doctorow's declaration "the writer finds himself further down the road." And the road may well end in tragedy.

Mark Schorer to his credit goes to great length to make sense of the end of *Elmer Gantry*. Long considered the foremost authority on Lewis, the scholar comes up short. In so doing he reflects, despite strengths in an analysis of the author's body of work, what in fact trips up many scholars: a closer look at his treatment of *Gantry* reveals what stands in his way. As with most assessments of Lewis, Schorer's does not contextually place the force of history in the novelist's works, albeit he does address history. In trying to make his literary argument he gets so tangled up in contradictions that he takes Lewis as an ahistorical figure projecting his shortcoming on his characters. The argument flips back and forth on itself as he tries to assess the author's literary

---

[28] See notes 11 and 13 for Davis's extended analysis and others, including Van Doren.

shortcomings in terms of great art, which he dismisses as irrelevant in considering Lewis; meanwhile he declares Lewis's twenties literary contribution pathbreaking. The novelist is a puzzle—but so, too, is the biographer's critique.

In the final analysis Schorer argues, whatever Lewis's state, whatever his motives for taking on religion and so harshly, with *Gantry* he had stretched his satiric streak to its limit. He considers he had lost "that early strain of youthful, idealistic optimism" which was visible in *Main Street*. "In *Elmer Gantry*, any drama exists in the immediate victory of the worst over the weakest (who are the best), or in the conflict of the bad to survive among the worst: all is corrupt." *Gantry* in style is "bare brutality." Where it offers close "essential social observation," and Schorer acknowledges there is no shortage of that, he argues the literary approach is successful. But the novel he contends is overwhelmed by satire: "*Elmer Gantry* is a work of almost pure revulsion. It seems to shudder and to shake with loathing of that which it describes." "The point only is that in no novel does Sinclair Lewis more clearly announce his loathing of the social environment with which he is concerned, and in no novel does he make it more mandatory that we remain within the terrifying limits of that environment." While Schorer returns to the art wars, he totally misses what Davis and Van Doren perceived: Lewis spoke *for* the ill-at-ease nation, not against it. Schorer proposes doom hallmarks his body of work following the optimism of *Main Street*? To the contrary, the author is a progressive in spirit novel following novel. Smiling optimism is not driving him; rather, he is committed to reasonable, pragmatic diagnosis.[29]

Lewis may have reached his satiric limit or over-stepped it, still at the end of *Gantry* he punctuated the real danger facing America. He had not, low as he may have been, given up—fatal entrapment was not his message; avoiding that trap was his beacon. Schorer's confusion in

---

[29] Schorer, 476, 478, and 480. Hutchisson notes, "Several reviewers did observe that the strain of idealism that had appeared in *Main Street*, faded in *Babbitt*, then reappeared in full force in *Arrowsmith* had now vanished entirely...." But these, he notes, were the only comments "on the artistry of the novel or its cultural relevance." He seriously errs. See 162.

part lies in the fact he lost sight of what Lewis was getting at—or, he had misconstrued it, not only in *Elmer Gantry* but in the previous three best-sellers:

> Most novels operate through a conflict, dramatized in a plot, of social and individual interest, and the more sustained the pressures of the plot, the more likely is the individual to be forced into a position of new self-awareness, which prominently contains an awareness of his relation to his society. A certain dynamic interchange has been at work, and the result is that the historical forces which contain the individual's experience have been personalized in his awareness. What is most characteristic of the novels of Sinclair Lewis, and above all of *Elmer Gantry*, is that there are no such dynamics of social action, that we are presented with a static, unpersonalized image—and that *there* lies its horror.[30]

Yet, as just noted, Lewis had in *Main Street* that "early strain of youthful, idealistic optimism"—now Schorer argues Lewis at his core is at sea, no bearings, filled with horror? Indeed, historical forces are at work. Novel by novel, *Main Street*, *Babbitt*, *Arrowsmith*, and now in *Gantry* history is reckoned with; so too currency; optimism is set against evolving social forces; protagonists are self-aware throughout, dynamism marks their steps, even if as with Babbitt he ultimately trips badly. (Significantly, as the biographer well understands, *Dodsworth* will at length demonstrate the novelist's acute sense of historic forces at work.) Schorer declares vis a vis *Babbitt*: "Perhaps it is futile to approach any Lewis novel as a work of art. Certainly, if *Babbitt* cannot be thus approached, none of the other novels can be. And generally speaking artistic considerations in 1922 were of far less importance regarding Lewis's second sensation than the fact that, once more, Lewis had precisely hit upon a current mood and given it popular definition." Indeed self-awareness is the hallmark of his works. Why is Schorer so entangled in contradiction?[31]

---

[30] Schorer, 478.
[31] Ibid., 355.

Schorer makes the case for the artistry of *novelists*: "A certain dynamic interchange has been at work, and the result is that the historical forces which contain the individual's experience have been personalized in his awareness." There is struggle in the three earlier novels: readers are left hanging. In *Gantry* evil in the end remains in the saddle; yes, there has been brutal struggle: "The point only is that in no novel does Sinclair Lewis more clearly announce his loathing of the social environment with which he is concerned, and in no novel does he make it more mandatory that we remain within the terrifying limits of that environment." *Elmer Gantry* does announce the eleventh hour has arrived—and it pushes midnight. In doing so, it follows in a more blatant manner the course paved by the previous novels; Elmer's character throws into relief all the possibilities, the challenges to be overcome, the trust in the American Experiment which mark those novels. Now, with doom descending, Lewis clearly argues it is mandatory we escape the terrifying limits of an authoritarian environment. No one is left hanging—the novel's protagonist contemplates *his* victory; no reader favors dystopian alternatives: of this Lewis was certain.

Lewis is a conundrum; studies reflect the puzzle. Schorer offers excellent evidence that without a strong historical bearing, analyses of Lewis can go awry. Select contemporaries acknowledged Lewis a man of literature and history. Schorer gets so tangled up in the literary conundrums that in wrestling his way through them vis a vis *Gantry* he misrepresents the bearing of history on the author's work. His conclusions cannot help but come up short. To be clear, Schorer's analyses of the author's body of work, of his life, his character offer up plenty of evidence he knows what he is talking about—as do works of other scholars. They know their business; but they do not always know their history; at base they do not give just weight to how Lewis's grasp of history, as well as his acute social and cultural sensitivities, heavily influenced his intention in writing.

To summarize, within his scorching treatment of *Gantry* Schorer argues the author has no grasp of the history about him; he stands stagnant, lost, trapped—as seen in his characters. How remote he stands from the work is evidenced in how disjointed is his argument. He conjoins the characters with the author's purported sense of hopelessness, entrapment. Schorer is correct in saying, "A character so open to self-deception as Elmer is not in a position to estimate the forces that have made him so: to him, society is given, accepted, used."[32] But Elmer is not Lewis. And he is not Martin, George, or Carol—Lewis roots for them. They struggle: they seek to make it work, here, now, in their social niches; they measure themselves against the greater community. They look forward. Elmer is the nadir. The hour is late: Lewis believes in redemption, but he is confounded how to locate it in the world he tracks in *Gantry*. No Elmer, he sees himself in Carol, George, Martin, and plenty of others including Doane and Shallard—he likes them, he praises their awareness, whatever their flaws. But with this unprincipled protagonist, he has nowhere to go; and indeed, he queries if the United States has anywhere to go but down. No doubt the novelist had his misgivings, but he never intended Elmer to be anything but the voice of doom, and he painted him as despicable.

The novels stand strong on their own and they build one upon another. *Gantry* is not an anomaly. Carl Van Doren did not miss the point, and he hardly was alone: "Sinclair Lewis once more reveals himself as something besides a novelist. He is still the spokesman of a notable phase of American discontent with contemporary America." Van Doren stands strong. Yet, Schorer concludes, "That history, perhaps no larger than it is beautiful in our tradition, is nevertheless considerable, and Sinclair Lewis was aware of it even if, because he had no alternatives, he could not let his characters become so."[33] It seems a curious observation: Lewis, then, knows history but fails to share it with his characters; no historical perspective for any of them? Hutchisson, on the other hand, sees more clearly. He notes as the novelist sought a topic for a new novel following *Arrowsmith* it was "a propitious moment to write a satire on the ministry…a moment supplied by the spectacle of the Scopes 'monkey' trial in Dayton, Tennessee, and the controversy over the obscenity case against Herbert Asbury's 'Hatrack,' a story published in the April 1926 issue of Mencken's *American Mercury*."[34] Lewis

[32] Ibid., 478–79.
[33] Ibid., 479.
[34] Hutchisson, 128.

was deep in the cultural mix. Religion was hot; he would make the most of it. Mencken, an enthusiastic Lewis promoter, had long pushed him to write the "preacher novel." (And once published, he considered it excellent: "*Voltaire! Not since Voltaire....!*"). As his pal, he considered religion most representative of "America."[35] For Menken alone amongst the critics, *Gantry* was a superior novel to *Babbitt*. The Baltimore cynic knew his country, its history well. He, counter to Schorer, thought the satire complete. And unlike Schorer, who seems to think Lewis is aware of history—or not—Mencken knew Lewis had the country's history down pat. Religion was one more means to get to the nub of the matter—the United States stood center stage; its historic trajectory was slipping. Lewis was himself in a bad way; yes, it was a propitious moment to further endeavor to find a way out for the country and for himself.

The final word: It can be a muddle. To further muddy the waters, Schorer makes the odd case Lewis had not written with "any literary tradition" in mind; "once more he had created an 'original.'" He also links the novelist back to decades of realism, classes him with Twain, Howells, the greats. It was not, he asserts, a traditionally "religious" novel. Of course not; nor was *Huckleberry Finn* a classic boy's story. At best Schorer contends in *Elmer Gantry* Lewis had developed some sort of "half-truth" world: "As the drama is only half realized," owing to the heavy dosage of satire, "so the social observation is only half true, but in its partiality resides such force as it has." Exactly—Schorer had said, repeatedly, that Lewis's characters had some substance, that his observations were keen as no other in his time, that his work was original, and that there was no problem about this. He took his lead from the likes of Twain who no one doubted had his history down and related it to current matters of interest. Schorer argues all Lewis characters, not just Gantry, are as damned as he is, unable to resolve the dilemma, to somehow get the word out that there is hope. They lack knowledge:

---

[35] Schorer, 483. As Schorer notes, so, too, of course did Tocqueville equate the nation with religion as he recognized the unique "non-political" role religion played –"that when America ceased to be good, she would cease to be strong." Ibid., 481–82.

"The result is that the Lewis character cannot separate itself from the Lewis society; and this, in the dynamics of fiction, means that the Lewis character *has* no character apart from the society in which he is embedded, and that therefore the Lewis society is not a society at all, but a machine, or a parody, or a poetic-satiric vision." "That vision, however impressive or outrageous one may find it, is static, since it lacks a certain reverberating largeness that would animate the concretely conceived situations, a largeness that characterizes all great art, including great satiric art." Schorer is entrapped, entangled by the issues of art which he had set-aside as irrelevant to grasping the significance of Lewis. He undercuts what he espies so well in Lewis: the author was current, a man of his time, who reflected across time.[36]

Lewis never sees himself separate from society; he depicts it with consummate skill and uses his characters to great effect to do so. Schorer strangely ends his study of *Elmer Gantry*: "In all the uproar, there is almost nothing one could call criticism, and there has been very little since." Reading the critics of the day, that is simply impossible to argue—they had plenty to say; and scholars for decades have taken on the novel. The biographer considers *Gantry* up to the early sixties to have been the author's "most neglected novel."[37] By whom? The public and critics were in the grip of *Gantry*—readers all along have found it a mesmerizing read.

Interestingly, E. L. Doctorow observed in discussing his own late-twentieth century body of work heavy in history "novelists have always had to persuade their readers that what they were reading was not fiction [but a] kind of 'urgent truth,' so that the reader could break down the distinction between fiction and nonfiction in his own mind." Novelist Mary Gordon said of Doctorow, "Everything that he wrote was really about a vision of America as it could be..." She identified the hugely popular and highly acclaimed novelist an "idealist." So, too, Lewis can be cast. He was attempting in one novel after another to come to terms with an America which was troubled: this was his urgent

---

[36] Ibid. 480–81.

[37] Ibid. 476.

truth. Doctorow argued, "I think really of myself as a national novelist; I am an American novelist, writing about my country." So, too, Lewis.[38]

Lewis endeavored to send a wake-up call. He demonstrated his arching concern for the country and increasing expertise in establishing his reform vision. He covered the cultural landscape—towns, cities, values, mores, current events, fads, politics, hegemonic threats, sensations of the hour, eternal doubts and dreams. Lewis knew a lot was good as well that something was wrong. Readers took him *at his word.* Lewis had said all along he was a diagnostician. Mencken chimed in he and Lewis had no answers as such. But they did: they beheld their nation, its past and its possibilities. And he claimed he and Lewis were patriots, raising the alarm bells.

Beyond the personal chaos which engulfed the author as he had written *Gantry*, and the furor surrounding the publication, Lewis would try once more in the formative twenties to make his point—he did so profoundly with *Dodsworth* two years later. By the conflicting measures of "art," Lewis produced in *Dodsworth* a work as strong as *Arrowsmith* and for some stronger. As the culmination of an evolving perspective of the United States, if readers chose to see it that way, his way, he demonstrated in the final New Era blockbuster a long-gestating theme: The United States, roaring through the new century, was in trouble; and it could progress, direct itself beyond the problems, get back to its fundamental tenets. *Dodsworth* did not result in Lewis finding contentment despite the fact this capstone to his decade-long effort to tell the country's story received solid support from the critics. But most missed the five-novel accomplishment; little note was made of the holistic nature of his decade's work. There was relief: the novelist had left the pessimism and "trash" of *Elmer Gantry* in the dust. Perhaps the relief did not assuage the novelist since they had not read the whole story, all starting with *Main Street.*

---

[38] *New York Times* book critic Liesel Schillinger recalled the "urgent truth" (on the occasion of Doctorow's 2015 death). Doctorow, often depicted as a historical novelist, took issue with being pigeon-holed, arguing others missed the greater point: "Historical novel is, it seems to me, a misnomer," he said in a 2014 interview. Quoted in Lynn Neary, "Doctorow Wove Fact And Fiction To Imagine America As It Could Be," http://www.npr.org.

In conclusion, and in fairness to Schorer who studied Lewis so long and came to know his so well, the authoritative biographer gets a last word. He concludes *Sinclair Lewis: An American Life*: "He was one of the worst writers in modern American literature, but without his writing one cannot imagine modern American literature. That is because, without his writing, we can hardly imagine ourselves." After all, "In at least five solid works—*Main Street*, *Babbitt*, *Arrowsmith*, *Elmer Gantry*, and *Dodsworth*—the endurable core…he gave us a vigorous, perhaps a unique thrust into the imagination of ourselves." Schorer, half-way through his biography, 334 pages before he comes to this spot-on conclusion to his study, says Lewis spelled out how immersed in his history Elmer was—but he was unaware of its significance. "A character so open to self-deception as Elmer is not in a position to estimate the forces that have made him so; to him, society is given, accepted, used." "That history, perhaps no larger than it is beautiful in our tradition, is nevertheless considerable, and Sinclair Lewis was aware of it even if, because he had no alternatives, he could not let his characters become so." What? Schorer for all his trying just cannot read Lewis straight. He gets so much right about the author and flips it into so much that makes no sense. Perhaps he'd have best titled his opus: *Sinclair Lewis: An American Conundrum.*[39]

---

[39] Schorer, 479.

EIGHT

DODSWORTH

Sinclair Lewis had written *Main Street* as a commentary on the passing scene, the United States as it entered the twentieth century; he had moved on to *Babbitt* to make his most durable observations, concluding the U.S. had entered the New Era following World War One wagering success upon dubious materialistic premises. In *Arrowsmith* he clarified he had another serious matter to explore, the medical and scientific complex, one more component of a corporate rot he saw settling upon the country. Also, he had literary scores to settle. He knew he was doing important work, sarcasm in-and-of-itself was hardly the point. He had plenty to say of substance, and he could say it well. He needed to prove something to the critics and to himself: the country needed to take stock, profoundly change direction, get-a-grip on its destiny; and he had it in him as an artist to point the way. In *Elmer Gantry* he needed to rage as much as guide. What precisely motivated that expression cannot be pinned down; what charged readers to rush and buy the novel is impossible to pin-point but in all likelihood it was the scandal it generated. What is certain is that the country was caught up by the work—as it had been by Lewis's previous runaway successes. Kansans took a big hit in *Gantry*; still they purchased the novel in record-breaking numbers—and a minority testified they recognized themselves in it.[1] *Arrowsmith* had received particularly strong (albeit guarded literary accolades); *Gantry* few to say the most. In 1929, the boisterous decade coming to an end, Lewis dispatched his final twenties work, *Dodsworth*, and what he was after all along appeared within view. No one can precisely say what readers took from it; or what they took from any or all his twenties work. But critics overwhelmingly recognized the novelist was "back on track," beyond anger, bitterness, or whatever they tossed

---

[1] Mark Schorer, *Sinclair Lewis: An American Life* (New York, McGraw-Hill Book Company, Inc., 1961), 483.

at him; and some sensed he was summing up what he had tried to say for a decade—the best they could make out. He had in their readings regained balance and direction. *Dodsworth* has always been considered his strongest novel along with *Arrowsmith*.

Lewis craved "adventure" in life; he expressed it in private, public, and in the novels. He sought as well a sense of security and the satisfaction he had done an excellent job. He never appreciated he had reached it with *Dodsworth*—he never had it in him to be that satisfied. *Dodsworth* turned the trick as far as it could stretch—as far as the writer could take on the national saga. The novel articulates a loving relationship fashioned in a manner absent in the previous novels (Arrowmith's first marriage was a strong step in that direction—his follow-up a bad stumble for both spouses). A more global view of the world at large is present by which to measure the country's own experiment, and Lewis offers an entirely pragmatic suggestion (very American in itself) as to progress. It is hardly suggestive of a final resolution to the nation's dilemma, but the novel throughout soundly drills down on what ails the country and the necessity to address it. *Dodsworth* banks upon the success of the American Experiment modulated back to common sense proportions. A novel more narrowly satiric and broader in substantive reach draws out more complete human characterizations and if not a "solution," a direct charge the country can never stop working toward fulfilling its Promise. *Dodsworth* is the worthy summation of a five-novel compendium.

In the 1920s Sinclair Lewis had reached his peak. His challenge had been to etch in remarkable detail the decade, unveil what had gone wrong and suggest a means to press on: redirect a materialistic society to be more at ease with itself—embrace a secure, harmonious life, simpler, ethically intact. Diagnosis, if sharp, prescient, only went so far. Here he would stretch his perspective beyond the continent to view the country from a European vantage point. SEE—how does the nation stand up against other societies? Satire works, perhaps stronger if it is dialed back. It eases the sting while highlighting the dilemma. The author had to strike the right balance. In *Dodsworth* he accomplishes that end.

Neither the critics nor likely the readers, nor the author perceived with the publication of *Dodsworth* what he was *supposed* to be after he had in fact achieved, as far as he could go. He landed, seemingly, on the recognition that there is no singular resolution, and he would stand by it—the critics be damned; there was the quest for *perfection*, to find the most plausible course to resolution—and that made great sense. That was the core of the American Promise: strive, press the vision. This is *Dodsworth*'s story. This in essence was what the diagnostician through the five novels prescribed. No snap conclusion: It was, however, the best the canny novelist, the accomplished sociologist, the student of culture, the historian had to offer. Few at best recognized *Dodsworth* was a capstone achievement, crowning a decade-long effort to decipher where the nation was heading.

The author offered no conclusive directive, but he did supply a blueprint: get back to the grass roots, pick up the spade, carry on in the best American fashion. The immense catastrophe that struck the nation the same year *Dodsworth* was released seriously muddied the waters. Lewis ended the decade knowing he had not written the great American novel and was not fully acknowledged an artist. Sinclair Lewis's novel, all his twenties work, by the end of 1929 swiftly collapsed into what huge segments of Americans, including the educated and the chattering class, concluded a best-forgotten past; the twenties for many were even shameful.

Dodsworth deserved better. The United States was in trouble. A lot of talk in the late twenties began to emerge in commentary and through the arts about getting back to grass roots. This, naturally, was Lewis's storyline throughout the twenties. Lewis was not an economist; he did have a strong sense of history. He never foresaw full-scale economic collapse; he had offered the sound advice that the nation needed to get its priorities in better alignment. With *Dodsworth*, to his lasting credit, he had with his five novels sealed the deal, he had demonstratively discerned by 1929 "there was trouble in River City."

With Samuel Dodsworth the novelist develops his most balanced protagonist. He stands as a model citizen with a progressive view of the nation's future. He also stands in for the author who has tentatively secured his own sense of contentment, newly remarried and in a good state of mind about his work. Lewis saw himself in all his protagonists, save naturally Elmer Gantry. Sam is an ordinary fellow by Lewis's measure and a most exceptional American—the author without doubt admires this contemplative "joe." Dodsworth recognizes himself bourgeois to the core, deserving of respect, and despite his fallibility still capable of promise. Sam's final say, his personal resolution, is not overwhelming—no more than had been Carol's with whom Lewis similarly identified way back in Gopher Prairie. Unlike Martin, Sam is still in the game, and he has a real chance to succeed in a way no one could see George progress at all—here was a man building community, not just pitching a weak facsimile. Unlike Martin, he was no idealist, out to save the world...he just took on a practical task and worked to get it done. Elmer had absolutely no respect for community, nor practically anyone. Dodsworth struggles and arrives at a stage where he can remake himself, give it his best shot, by doing all he can for community. It is the most anyone could expect—of Sam, Lewis, ourselves, of the American Promise.

Carol Kennicott, George Babbitt, and Martin Arrowsmith, and Elmer Gantry were as critics asserted two-dimensional—but there were plenty of hints of depth to their characters. There was an edginess that critics discounted; it is that edge which drove them to seek resolution. Each was at loose ends in America. Each spoke out, at points thoughtfully, what had befallen them. *Dodsworth* represents Lewis's ultimate twenties statement. Sam Dodsworth takes a consummated stand for himself; in the process he does so for the country. The middle had to hold; within its grip it held a promise the world admired. Sam got the full story.

Sam lands in Europe, and he carries his truth, hardly the deepest, home. He proffers a shake of common sense to his fellow citizenry. He has undertaken, at first haphazardly, and then with greater attention, a study of what ails the old burg, the U.S.A. He takes note of the best and worst of Old and New Worlds. In the end, he determines to plant himself back home, back in Zenith, in the heartland. He conceives he can sow the seeds of an amalgamation of the two civilizations...good, old-fashioned horse sense.

In essence Lewis returns to Main Street. Sam, as Carol a decade earlier, comes home to do the best he can. But Sam is a broader figure, one who can assuredly work the gears. He is a corporate titan who has seen the light of progress, and he has the cash to do anything and everything he desires. Significantly, and it nurtures his contentment, he realizes he can go only so far but recognizes he has what it takes to get *there*. He is a believer: he could turn out a resurgent American Dream just as he had rolled motor cars off assembly lines, if he could just get at its nuts and bolts. Individuals deserved "the good life." Most of his adulthood he focused on the material end of the equation: he invented a car that sold like pancakes. His path-breaking invention, the turn-of-the-century Revelation, practical, available to all, had fit the bill. Now, having completed that task, overseas in restless retirement he makes a discovery: his countrymen needed to get back to foundational truths, a simpler life. Sam is a puritan of sorts but more pragmatic; he has concrete ideas about establishing in the here-and-now a city on a hill. And he is a genuine pioneer, an American original, disillusioned yes, and fired up, eager to build anew. Sam's return to the States, with a new balance to his life, a better sense of direction, affords him nothing grand in theory but something essential to share with the nation. Others Lewis confidently implies should follow his lead.

Lewis in *Dodsworth* engages in an age-old American debate, long knocked about by historians, literary scholars, intellectuals of all stripes, comparing New and Old Worlds, adjudicating a case for or against the American Experiment. Let's take that longer glance he admonishes—just what in down-to-earth terms is the country about? He does so through the mindset not of an intellect but of an ordinary man who finds his ground. Indeed, Sam is not Carol, nor George, nor Martin—indisputably not Elmer. But he has something they were kicking around. Sam has a greater purview of the passing parade, and he possesses a greater opportunity at successfully fulfilling his mission—coming to terms with his life, returning to his love of work; Sam is a champion of American know-how.

Samuel Dodsworth, retired industrial magnate, is abroad in Europe for the season. His marriage is on the rocks. He bumbles about, and ultimately beyond learning so much about himself—and his country—he finds a truer helpmate. They will establish a companionate marriage—a faddish progressive idea, both spouses retain their individualism, working and playing together, and in consultation with a strong supporting cast, they have reached the conclusion, *let's get back to America*. There is room for satire, but it is downplayed in *Dodsworth* (as with *Arrowsmith*). All the targets from *Main Street* through *Babbitt*, *Arrowsmith*, and *Elmer Gantry* come to the fore: motor cars, furnishings, fashions; morality and mores; striving and blustering; class airs, pasttimes, high and low shenanigans; Madison Avenue pranks; and the ominous threat of hegemonic corporatism. And the primacy of ideals threads through the whole story. And, idiocy and common sense. This is who we are. Lewis has a better handle on that by the end of the decade—it's something to take pride in. Rebecca West back in 1922 had said it best: "There is in these people a vitality so intense that it must eventually bolt with them and land them willy-nilly into the sphere of intelligence; and this immense commercial machine will become the instrument of their aspirations." In 1922 she espies: "Mr. Lewis has an individual gift of humour, a curiously sage devotion to craftsmanship, and a poetic passion for his own, new country." Most strikingly, West perceived what Lewis was after, something broad and deep. The Old World was a restrictive environment, where the up-and-coming bourgeoisie had little to look forward to. She is British; Lewis is American: "But there is for Babbitt a certain advantage; or perhaps in the transitional and blundering state of affairs revealed in this book, it should be called a certain opportunity. He moves in a setting so vast and so magnificent that surely it must ultimately dictate vastness and magnificence to the action it contains."[2]

Seven years later Lewis fulfills West's prophecy. This man is broad, and he is deep; Sam Dodsworth packs a magnificent change, the embodiment of the country. At the outset of the novel, Sam generally

---

[2] Rebecca West, "Notes on Novels," *New Statesman* (October 21, 1922), pp. 78–79.

content, realizes he is not content. He sets out looking for something more substantial, some truths he can hold on to, he can live by. He has found, after decades of accomplishment, he is shallower than he had ever thought—and truth-be-told, he admits he never had time nor interest to even consider the proposition. Dodsworth senses as he proceeds that he stands at a crossroads as does his country. In his small way, perhaps a chance to be writ large, he can make a difference. By luck and pluck Sam Dodsworth humbly recognizes he just might point the way, make a lasting contribution to American life. In the process he recognizes he is a bona fide patriot, and he takes pride in the acknowledgment. At the end of the novel he looks west before sailing home, content and optimistic.

Mark Schorer writes all of Lewis's work comes down to "the Lewis character cannot separate itself from the Lewis society; and this, in the dynamics of fiction, means that the Lewis character *has* no character apart from the society in which he is embedded, and that therefore the Lewis society is not a society at all, but a machine, or a parody, or a poetic-satiric vision."[3] He is errant. *Dodsworth* strikes the best balance of Lewis's twenties novels for establishing character—an individual influenced by society but capable of defining in his or her (again, Sam takes up with a woman who shares his outlook) own terms what matters to him alone and as a member of the greater community. Sam offers a whole lot more than a poetic-satiric vision. He is not an automaton, nor is his society a machine—he is trying to reclaim his humanity and the country's soul.

James M. Hutchisson looks at *Arrowsmith*, designed not to be "controversial," not "to stir up a public debate," and concludes, "In the main, *Arrowsmith* is Lewis's quietest, most controlled, and most serious-minded novel of the 1920s."[4] *Dodsworth* is equally serious and

---

[3] Ibid., 480.

[4] James M. Hutchisson, *Sinclair Lewis, 1920–1930* (University Park: Pennsylvania State University Press, 1996) 122. "The commonplace perception of Lewis is that he attacked fraud, but his satiric stereotypes were counterbalanced too rarely by characters of integrity and his novels were based too much on destructive criticism that did not offer hope for improving human

controlled, a novel designed with additional, tempered contemplation. In the final analysis *Dodsworth* is the most settling novel of the five great Lewis works. The story offers not only a particularly rewarding read, but it stands as a personal and artistic statement by the author, concluding his twenties drive to come to terms with his country and himself. And, contrary to Hutchisson's take, Lewis always aimed at stirring up public debate.

The year following *Dodsworth's* release, the novelist received the Nobel Prize for his resonant view of the U.S. It was awarded in part as a testimony to his effort to establish a notable body of work; and as he predicted, more likely as a jest, it would now all be down-hill for him. Never again would he come this close to some sort of resolution of what he wanted to say about the country. He would not, as it worked out, stitch his life together as much as Sam appeared destined to achieve—and no one knows if Sam succeeded in the end; as always it was left open.[5] The story ends on a high note with the entrepreneur and his fiancée embarking on an "adventure," believing it right to journey home and make a new start. America, always in Lewis's view is on an adventure, the national experiment. The theme threads throughout the novel. It is not too much to argue the author had come to hang it all onto Sam: this was the end—of the twenties, of the New Era, of his contemplative five-novel compendium. As it was, it was also the onset of the Great Depression; no one would know how that effected Sam Dodsworth's life; as for the author he never stood at such a lofty height

---

institutions. Whether or not that judgment is valid, at least *Arrowsmith* rebuts it." See 124.

[5] Sam and Edith do reappear in a cameo in 1951 in Lewis's posthumously published *World So Wide* (New York: Lion Library Editions, 1956). Nothing is said about Sam's success back in the U.S.; he seems twenty years on a lost soul. It is hard to decipher why the author even bothered to disinter Sam—unless in his late-life gloom, he chose to present Sam and Edith as directionless, forever sailing back and forth across the Atlantic representative of his own pessimism about the whole affair of the American Promise or his life. This is purely conjecture; all that is known is that Sam and Edith were not in the end content; and the weak novel was more a last gasp than anything else. Perhaps in need of filler, the author dug back to the Dodsworths.

again. A prominent transitional era had reached its end. Sinclair Lewis in the popular imagination had run his course. He hit his full stride with *Dodsworth.*

Dodsworth as all five twenties best-sellers is episodic; it is satiric, and Lewis as usual provides his cast with rants and orations. The novel is in scope his most serious of the decade. All twenties themes play out, but the ones which receive the most attention are instructive. For those who read the novels through the decade, and for those who read them retrospectively years on, those who take the opportunity to consider them as a whole, it is easy to see the saga builds and comes full circle. *Dodsworth* nearly a decade on, from across thc Atlantic, points back to *Mainstreet*, and it all makes sense.[6] But the story does not move backward; the five make up a progressive tale. And the conclusive work strikes one's fancy and challenges one to think about it all. For those who long since, close to a century now, have tried to make sense of the author, *Dodsworth* wraps up the whole story. A tripartite analysis of this novel focusing on the automobile, innovation, and community—cultural totems all—conclusively sets forth not despair but a faith that pragmatic Americans have it in them to make a better job of their shared American Promise. Most significantly the driving topic is the welfare of the United States.

---

[6] Lewis's foci ran the gamut as always. For familiar issues addressed in *Dodsworth*, see as an example the comparative commentary on turn-of-the-century courtship and twenties mores: "They sat talking by the lake at midnight. Out on the dappled water, seen through a cloud of willow leaves, the youngsters in canoes were now singing 'My Old Kentucky Home.' Zenith was still in the halcyon William Dean Howells days; not yet had it become the duty of young people to be hard and brisk, and knowing about radios, jazz, and gin." Sinclair Lewis, *Dodsworth* (New York: Signet Classic, 1980), 11. For more see alcohol practices, 29–30 and 104; the comfort and complacency of the Zenith upper-middle class, 30; the privileged who sail to Europe, 38–41; shipboard amenities and religion, 104. "There is about a ship's bar, any bar of any ship, however small, a cheerfulness unknown elsewhere in life's dark and Methodist vale." Always current Lewis introduces the marvel of air travel to his scan of the decade; see 282–85 full of descriptive passages. Finally, as in all the novels couples squabble, marriages work and fail; see 53–58.

The automobile as the exemplar of American innovation and promise threads throughout the novel. In *Main Street*, *Babbitt*, *Arrowsmith*, and *Elmer Gantry* the growing omnipresence of the "motor" is striking: road improvements, stylistic and mechanical advances, proliferating name-plates as symbols of class distinction; garages, traffic jams, drives, hideaways for drink and sex; and endless conversations on the pros and cons of automobiling as a national pastime all serve as fodder for contemplation—the characters ponder, and the readers ponder. But in *Dodsworth*, motoring serves another purpose. The craze has settled—the car is here to stay and blends into the landscape. It is time to take account. It is, too, much more. It has been Sam's work; it is formative; and it lays at the foundation of his dream for redemption for himself and the country. It is a theme which made perfect sense to readers of the twenties—a symbol of *who we are*. Americans were on the go, hustling—to get where? Social and cultural norms were stamped by the motor phenomenon. And Sam Dodsworth, key to launching the cultural revolution, at length questions what he has wrought.

Sam first appears rolling up in style in 1903: "The aristocracy of Zenith was dancing at the Kennepoose Canoe Club":

> Tonight he was particularly uplifted because he was driving his first car. And it was none of your old-fashioned "gasoline buggies," with the engine under the seat. The engine bulked in front, under a proud hood over two feet long, and the steering column was not straight but rakishly tilted. The car was sporting and rather dangerous, and the lights were powerful affairs fed by acetylene gas. Sam sped on, with a feeling of power, of dominating the universe, at twelve dizzy miles an hour.

A reminiscent reader can hear in the background the romantic charm of "On the Banks of the Wabash" soon to be interrupted by the brassier new song "The Little Ford Rambled Right Along." The narrative runs on— Sam's life revolves around the automobile. He meets Fran at the dance, his wife and fellow-protagonist (playing the fall girl for American shallowness), and Sam shares his dreams:

> "Well, I believe that in twenty years, say by 1923 or '4, they'll be as common as buggies are now! I'm going in on a new company here—the Revelation Automobile Company. I'll get less salary, but it's a swell gamble. Wonderful future. I've been working on my mechanical drawing lately, and I've got the idea that they ought to get away from imitating carriages. Make a—it sounds highbrow, but I mean what you might call a new kind of beauty for autos. Kind of long straight lines."

Kind of streamlined, a long way down the road—Sam is prescient.[7]

The young man is a risk-taker, but he as well is grounded in sound practicalities. He is all-American, a Yale athlete, sociable, moderate in his habits, sufficiently good-looking, and he espies a Zenith beauty: "If she was an angel, the girl at whom Sam was pointing, she was an angel of ice; slim, shining, ash-blonde, her self-possessed voice very cool as she parried the complimentary teasing of half a dozen admirers; a crystal candle-stick of a girl among black-and-white lumps of males." Possessive and selective Fran will never understand the class Sam finds in his motorcar, a vision built for all to share. Fran is a snob; Sam has a lot of "democracy" about him.[8]

The Dodsworths build a good life in Zenith. "It was not till 1908, when he had been married for five years to Fran Voelker and they had had two babies…that Sam Dodsworth came on his real struggle at the Revelation Motor Company." It is a practical test for a young American with foresight:

> "His superiors in the company had equally prized him for his steadiness and industry and fretted at him for being a dreamer. He was crazy as a poet, they said. Not only did he venture to blaspheme against the great Renault-Darracq of car-designing, not only did he keep on raving about long 'stream-lines,' but he insisted that the largest profits would lie in selling automobiles as cheaply as possible to as many customers as possible."

---

[7] Ibid., 9 and 12.

[8] Ibid.,10.

Sam recognizes to hold his own he needs to learn the nuts and bolts—not of mechanics and design, he had that down pat—but "something about the tricks of financing: about bonds, transfer of stock, call loans, discounts to dealers." Sam wins the new day; he brings out "the first four-door model, and he saw the Revelation become the sensation of America for a season and one of its best-selling cars for a score of years."[9]

The Dodsworths grow wealthy, and Sam emerges a nationally admired magnate. He was content: "he was too busy to be discontented; and he managed to believe that Fran loved him."[10] Fran is more materialistic, and she is a social climber. Zenith is too small. She is a good mother, devoted spouse, and she has ambitions. Her desires will create the great schism in Sam's life.

Encouraged by Fran and changing times, Dodsworth accepts a buy-out by one of the newly emergent industry giants, those who are cornering the market on nameplates, design, innovation, business know-how, and sales. "A crisis in life had been forced on him, for his Revelation Company was being absorbed by the Unit Automotive Company—the imperial U.A.C., with its seven makes of motors, its body-building works, its billion dollars of capital." Sam had his doubts, but "the U.A.C. Cossacks were good fellows," his directors were convincing that mass-production on their scale would drive Revelation into bankruptcy, and he was well into middle age: "The U.A.C. could put on the market a car as good as the Revelation at a lower price....If necessary, the U.A.C. could sell below cost for a year or two. But they wanted the Revelation label and would pay for it." Sam is no push-over. He fears the massive corporation would undercut his "creation to which he had devoted twenty-two years." *They* would, in short order, "cheapen and ruin the Revelation and turn his thunderbolt into a standardized cigar-lighter," but he caves and agrees "to their generous purchase price."[11] And in truth, later, Sam acknowledges U.A.C. did not undercut him or *his car* at all—the corporation represented progress; its product, rapidly retooled, was a better car for less money. His

[9] Ibid., 14.
[10] Ibid.
[11] Ibid., 18.

Revelation had outlived its shelf life, the world had moved on, this was progress. He still could take pride in the corporation's contemporary dream motor was built on his chassis.

Having sold out—for dollars and possibly the cost of his integrity—Dodsworth finds himself treated with respect by the new bosses, and he plans to stay on with U.A.C. On the first day of the transfer, having arrived in his "limo," the lame-duck chief executive bumps up against facts. U.A.C. wants Sam to be a player, the game had changed, and they offered him "in." What the dickens, he queries, "that he was turned from a bandit captain to a clerk?" U.A.C. was okay; it was a different age. Sam, more honest, thought further:

> For the first time he admitted that if he went to the U.A.C., even as first vice president, he would be nothing more than an office boy. He could make no daring decisions by himself. *They* had taken from him the pride in pioneering which was one of his props in life—and who *They* were, he didn't quite know. *They* were something more than just...the U.A.C. *They* were part of a booming industrial flood which was sweeping over him. *They* would give him a larger house, a yacht, but *They* would not give him work that was really his own. He had helped to build a machine which was running away from him. He had no longer the dignity of a craftsman. He made nothing; he meant nothing; he was no longer Samuel Dodsworth, but merely part of a crowd vigorously pushing one another toward nowhere.[12]

Sam had been down-sized, just another disenchanted Babbitt. George experienced the occasional brief respite by beating the crowds in his motor—might have been a Revelation (in truth George would have prized a flashier motor). Sam runs a deeper course. He is no company's cog, and he is not facilely assuaged. His discontent, his character, his remaining fight finds purpose—he is more subtly drawn than Babbitt; Dodsworth searching for escape and resolution will fare a good deal better in the end game.

George played a devil for a momentary tear in his motor as well as his affairs, but for Sam, a genuine captain of industry, an American of a

---

[12] Ibid., 22

bolder stripe, an innovator, possessed of a considerably more contemplative personality, this would not do: He could not settle for what befell Babbit. He could not be a glorified office boy. Sam for that matter saw little promise when he's told one day he could be president and that U.A.C. would be a global empire. Discussing his position with the U.A.C. president, he finds he holds a tinny consolation prize: "You'll be tickled to death at getting hooked up with a concern that can control the world-market one of these days—regular empire, b' God...." That, he is told, is "real business." Further, one day he may be president of U.A.C.:

> "Come up to Detroit and see how we make things hum! Come sit in with us and hear us tell Congress where it gets off....I tell you, Dodsworth, to me work is a religion. "Turn not thy hand from the plow." Do big things! Think of it, by making autos we're enabling half the civilized world to run into town from their pig-sties and see the movies, and the other half to get out of town and give Nature the once-over. Twenty million cars in America! And in twenty more years we'll have the bloomin' Tibetans and Abyssinians riding on cement roads in U.A.C. cars! Talk about Napoleon!"[13]

Talk about prophecy; still, global domination is not "Sam." He was not accusatory. He had had his day. He had to settle, be content to retire as Fran wished—follow her lead; or so he grudgingly conceded.

Now Dodsworth has time—to be discontented; and he is lost in repose. While half aware of "who exactly he really was," he had a strong inkling something was wrong: "He was not happy about it, when he let himself think abstractly. But he was extremely well trained, from his first days in Zenith High School, in not letting himself do anything so destructive as abstract thinking."[14] Sam always had had his doubts, insecurities, but anchored by work and friends and family, he had been at home, sufficiently at ease in his own skin. Now he had time to think—and the more his thinking took on the abstract, the more he was at sea, and increasingly he came to recognize he had a good deal to ponder:

---

[13] Ibid., 25–26.

[14] Ibid., 18.

Samuel Dodsworth was profoundly unhappy.

Fran has gotten all she wants. She wants to break away from the mediocrity of Zenith, her empty nest, her friends. The retirees sail to Europe for the extended tour, the be-all and end-all of the Zenith set. Along the way, both in their own way are discomforted. They learn a lot about the similarities and contrasts between Europeans and Americans, the antics of Yankee tourists, the happy and not-so happy expatriates, the snobbery nurtured on both sides of the Atlantic, love and marriage—well-established literary themes. Lewis wants to plumb deeper.

The marriage badly frays, and Fran first, then Sam have affairs; there are partings and reunions, lots of discussions; slowly Sam comes to the realization his marriage is doomed. But he comes to learn much more, especially about himself. Herein lies the crux of the tale, and the core understanding of what Lewis was trying to get at throughout the decade be it in Gopher Prairie, Zenith, or New York; now he locates it in Europe where one can get a more distanced yet telescopic perspective on "America." Dodsworth finds himself more successfully than Carol, George, and even Martin (set aside appalling Elmer). What he finds is that he, and his country, must get back to the grass roots. Sam will return home, and with him will go Edith, his new love, who understands him and wants to build a fulfilling marriage, be part of his "adventure," working always together. They aim to pursue Sam's dream, not to be a global auto magnate, not to be an emperor, not to rule people, twist Congress, but with his own hands once again craft something that counts.

Once, Sam considers, he had "insisted that the largest profits would lie in selling automobiles as cheaply as possible to as many customers as possible." That job was done—perhaps too well, as U.A.C. usurped him and his reasonably sized company: "He had helped to build a machine which was running away from him. He had no longer the dignity of a craftsman. He made nothing; he meant nothing...." But again, he recognized U.A.C. was not evil—the retooled Revelation worked; it was a new marketplace, the world moved ahead, and in terms of dollars and cents, there was demand. But that was not Sam. Money was not the end-goal. If he could start over, if he could create something good, solid...perhaps Sam could craft a way of life that brought out the best in people. Possibly he still could make a contribution, demonstrate he had something of real substance to sell. More was at stake than his well-being: could he recreate neighborhoods, a sense of fellowship, simple, pure; could he generate demand? Could he, could America be not reinvented but streamlined? Was there a less cluttered path for Americans, progress of a twentieth-century sort founded upon rock-solid "community?" Could he, as once he had produced everyman's car, contribute to making the good life work for all?

Hence, following all the back-and-forth in the book on what differentiates the United States from Europe, how a solid American can still take hold of the gears, make the U.S.A. once again a going concern, Sam lights up. He sets out literally to build homes, neighborhoods (just as Carol had set out to do—community work—and as she returns home finds again that goals count plenty in the end). Lewis, all along, had engaged the fabric of everyday life, had observed social norms, mores, values; he had diagnosed the country's ills; he loved its people, his countrymen at their best, and he trusted individuals could be better. He saw himself as a babbitt—not all that bad, after all George simply wanted to be better, to do better despite his failings; Lewis always argued George was at base a kind man. Carol and Martin—good people—tried to be better, to do more, for others. Elmer was the foil, the lost soul who only sank to lower depths as he aspired to more tawdry prizes. Seneca Doane, Babbitt's acquaintance, had seen promise in the country:

> "No, what I fight in Zenith is standardization of thought, and, of course, the traditions of competition. The real villains of the piece are the clean, kind, industrious Family Men who use every known brand of trickery and cruelty to insure the prosperity of their cubs. The worst thing about these fellows is that they're so good and, in their work at least, so intelligent. You can't hate them properly, and yet their standardized minds are the enemy."[15]

People, he knows, are at base good. And then of course there was Frank Shallard's faith lost souls could be saved: "He had no such definite and ecstatic Call as came to Elmer Gantry, but he had always

---

[15] Sinclair Lewis, *Babbitt* (New York: Penguin Books, 1996), 89.

known that he would go on nibbling at theories about the eucharist, and pointing men the way to uncharted plateaus called Righteousness, Idealism, Honesty, Sacrifice, Beauty, Salvation."[16]

Sam also had faith, not an encrusted theology but a sense of the importance of neighborliness, good will, of America's can-do spirit—all deserve a fair shake. He wants to build. He could locate a compromise, one that takes the best of America, and the best of Europe, and builds anew—isn't that at base what the United States was all about? "*They* would not give him work that was really his own....He made nothing; he meant nothing; he was no longer Samuel Dodsworth, but merely part of a crowd vigorously pushing one another toward nowhere." This had been Carol's plaint, George's lament, Martin's bug-a-bear; this would be Sam's bugle call. As a titan of business, he could help to re-make national life. He got America and Americans. He could do his bit. Nudged out? No, Dodsworth had been throttled into the new century; Sam has the grit to keep at the game.

Sam's revelation comes slowly. As he wrangles with Fran, with himself as he takes off on his own he comes up with the nub of an idea. Dodsworth is a highly successful businessman—another babbitt, but for Lewis a classier model:

> Samuel Dodsworth was, perfectly, the American Captain of Industry, believing in the Republican Party, high tariff and, so long as they did not annoy him personally, in prohibition and the Episcopal Church. He was the president of the Revelation Motor Company; he was a millionaire, though decidedly not a multimillionaire; his large house was on Ridge Crest, the most fashionable street in Zenith; he had some taste in etchings; he did not split many infinitives; and he sometimes enjoyed Beethoven. He would certainly (so the observer assumed) produce excellent motor cars; he would make impressive speeches to the salesmen; but he would never love passionately, lose tragically, nor sit in contented idleness upon tropic shores.[17]

---

[16] Sinclair Lewis, *Elmer Gantry* (New York: Harcourt, Brace and Company, 1927), 120

[17] Ibid., 17.

Sam is as discontented in Europe as George was camping with Joe Paradise. Having lost his real passion, his hand-tooled Revelation; recognizing he is caught in a long less-than-satisfactory marriage, he takes the measure of his lot. And as he does so, as he treads the wilderness of retirement, as he struggles with ideas, big and not-so-big, contemplates politics, art, relationships, cross-Atlantic mores, he discusses, listens; he thinks, he explores. He sees something abstract; "he was extremely well trained, from his first days in Zenith High School, in not letting himself do anything so destructive as abstract thinking." Now, he perseveres and reaps a bounty. Sam hopes to get back in the game, a new one for him, fresh and exciting.

Dodsworth hence is not George Babbitt, albeit a distant cousin. George in his ordinariness queried his lot, reaped a whirlwind, and could not face the tumult. Sam is stronger: he can make the break. He is an American titan, an original, and he can make a difference.

> To define what Sam Dodsworth was, at fifty, it is easiest to state what he was not. He was none of the things which most Europeans and many Americans expect in a leader of American industry. He was not a babbitt, not a Rotarian, not an Elk, not a deacon—well yes, a babbitt, but of a stronger breed. He rarely shouted, never slapped people on the back, and he had attended only six baseball games since 1900. He knew, and thoroughly, the Babbitts and baseball fans, but only in business.[18]

Leon Trotsky perceived, "In the last analysis, however, Babbitt, the man, is no more bourgeois than your John D. Rockefeller, J. P. Morgan or Henry Ford."[19] Sam is indeed a babbitt, but a better pedigree. Sam gets something others missed, or would not, or could not grasp. He cannot be one of the U.A.C. bunch, a Rockefeller, and certainly not one of George's pals at the Athletic Club. Nor can he be content with his old comforts, retired, while the world about him speeds on. He is bourgeois; and he is a good man; and he needs to see things straight. He is for Lewis a somewhat old-fashioned American, one who can

---

[18] Ibid., 17–18.

[19] Schorer, 352.

dispense with the nonsense. He is willing, eager, albeit with trepidation at points, to SEE. He wants to return to the arena. Sam Dodsworth is a no-nonsense fellow and in his fashion a good student of life:

> While he was bored by free verse and cubism, he thought rather well of Dreiser, Cabell, and so much of Proust as he had rather laboriously mastered. He played golf reasonably well, and did not often talk of his scores. He liked fishing camps in Ontario, but never made himself believe that he preferred hemlock boughs to a mattress. He was common sense apotheosized, he had the energy and the reliability of a dynamo, he liked whisky and poker and pâté de foie gras, and all the while he dreamed of motors like thunderbolts, as poets less modern than himself might dream of stars and roses and nymphs by a pool.[20]

Sam was all right; and capable of doing good. He had had a dream, and he had made it come true. But his Revelation had gone bad—it had crashed, a victim of modernity run riot. The pioneer magnate needed to get back to basics: common sense works; he had the solidity of a dynamo; like his country, it was time to get back to the job.

Dodsworth comes slowly but surely to the realization the malady weakening America is what Seneca Doane perceived as its glory: standardization. He sees a linkage between standardization and a society in decline, and gives it thought. He has no beef with standardization as a going concern, but the U.S. had run itself into a ditch. Standardization led to a numbness, an inability to think life through, to take it on—standardization of thought was evil. Standardization must be refined. Along with Frank Shallard, Sam shares a call, but it takes some delving to recognize it: "Righteousness, Idealism, Honesty, Sacrifice, Beauty, Salvation." Sam has been caught up short, and he is thinking: not Babbitt's lightweight fantasizing; not Arrowsmith's monkish seclusion. He is Carol, stronger, more capable, and he has resources she never could

---

[20] Lewis, *Dodsworth*, 18. Sam also has his preposterous rituals, as any ordinary babbitt cherishes: As he read his Zenith and Chicago papers in the morning, he "ponderously and thoroughly attended to orange juice, porridge and thick cream, bacon, corn cakes and syrup, and coffee in a cup twice as large...." See Ibid., 17.

attain. And Sam has his feet sturdily planted on the ground. He is not flighty: he lives in this world, and he is of this world. He is a proven pioneer. It sounds pedestrian as he works up a plan, hardly a thunderbolt—but it all starts with tinkering. For Dodsworth a lofty enterprise is in the making—there is reason to his quest; he still has got to figure, run the numbers. He wrestles, he teases out as Lewis's critics would have it his independent standards.

Lewis would like to think there are more countrymen like Sam, like himself—like Carol, George, Martin. He can accomplish what Carol Kennicott set out to do: sturdier, he can create from the ground-up a better community. He can take a sustained look at the hokum as George could not. He can as Martin take satisfaction in progress and the process itself. Sam has all that it takes: common sense, energy, reliability. Dodsworth for the author is stability and progress rolled into one; if he could only put it together, make it work, make something better—Dodworth and Lewis, pragmatists. He is Lewis's common hero, attuned to the conundrum that has haunted him, what had gone wrong with himself, the country. The U.S.A. is good, solid, a self-sacrificing community. How about get back to brass tacks, build a neighborhood, a real hands-on affair? Start with one test-model? Sans Souci Gardens is Sam's second "revelation." A builder, he wants to get at what the United States has lost of its promise. Start anew: security, the good life, ideals fulfilled, it cannot be that hard. Sans Souci Gardens, simply a good neighborhood: build with integrity, take the best standardization has to offer, demonstrate the possibility of retaining one's independent standards, build a simpler and richer life.

For Lewis, in the end, here is the only resolution that is conclusive. It hardly is revolutionary, but he never was a radical. The novelist was, as Seneca Doane's European had charged, a progressive: "You...are a middle-road liberal, and you haven't the slightest idea what you want."[21] Well, finally Lewis has a better idea, and Sam Dodsworth is the ticket. It may not lead directly to "Righteousness, Idealism, Honesty, Sacrifice, Beauty, Salvation," but it was a start. Perhaps more to the point, this was an end, what progressivism was always about—not

---

[21] Lewis, *Babbitt*, 90.

one answer, one program, not one directive how the U.S.A. in the long haul can get the job done. SEE: It starts and it ends "not with one truth but a thousand." *Community* is the core tenet. Dodsworth's goal is practical: build right, create ideal habitats, sell at a fair price, establish beauty within the very idea of neighborhood. None of this represented a dangerous leap into the unknown but good old-fashioned common sense. A middle-road liberal did have a pretty good idea of what he wanted. As Martin, he saw "not one clear path to Truth but a thousand paths to a thousand truths far-off and doubtful."[22]

San Souci Gardens, pioneering, an adventure: Lewis, always proclaiming he had a sense of daring, always on the lookout, searching, always coming up short, finally reached the compromise he could embrace, a reasonable resolution for the nation's malady. It was not glorious. This was pragmatic. This could be done. This had substance; a sufficient middle-ground venture could produce answers, shine the light on what counts. Sam Dodsworth could plant an ideal, substantially nestle it in a suburban enclave, and see that it takes him and ordinary denizens to higher ground. San Souci Gardens: Cosmopolitan, worldly in architectural design; up-to-date with conveniences new-world men and women like to possess; something providing genuine satisfaction, something within which to take pride. A garden community; upper middle-class—isn't that where all should be headed, grounded, content? Sam is hardly inventing something new, just a better model.[23]

Gradually, as he tramps through his travails, and it is a hard trek, Sam's revelation, communities with character can make a difference, takes shape. He had had a few early ideas. Initially, newly retired back in Zenith, he considered that after a few months overseas with Fran he'd sign on for a spell with U.A.C. in Detroit: "When I really make my pile, I'll do something to help turn Zenith into another Detroit.

---

[22] Sinclair Lewis, *Arrowsmith* (New York: Signet Classics, 1998), 18.

[23] Garden communities, urban-planned neighborhoods, representing up-market customers in search of innovative architecture, styled vegetation, safe streets, living amongst "one's own" were coming into to their own in the 1920s.

Get a million people here. Only, plan the city right. Make it the most beautiful city in the world. Not just sit around on my chair in Europe and look at famous cities, but *make* one!"

In Europe, increasingly troubled, still caught up by his inchoate vision, Sam starts building castles. But Dodsworth never has been in the business of fantasy. Early on, he notices English countryside refinement: "To Sam, just now, the millionaire country houses he had seen on Long Island and the North Shore above Chicago—Tudor castles, Italian villas, French châteaux, elephantine Mount Vernons, mansions which he had admired and a little coveted—were raw as new factories beside a soft old pasture." The English countryside, something was definitively different. What was the U.S. missing?

Further on, contemplating: "Sam was silent while the other three hilariously scoffed at America," including Fran. "Sam was thinking, almost impersonally. It was a new occupation for him, and he was a little confused. It had become a disease with both nations, he reflected, this discussion of Britain vs. America; this incessant, irritated, family scolding." The heck with all that—how about some common ground? Sam was breaking that Zenith public-school mold, thinking now in the abstract but with a pragmatic twist: "Of course back in the cornfields of the Middlewest, people didn't often discuss it, nor did the villagers on the Yorkshire moors, nor Cornish fishermen. But the people who traveled and met their cousins of the other nation, the people who fed on newspapers on either side the water, they were all obsessed." Sam is not the compulsive type, nor were the down-home Midwesterners, Yorkshire denizens, those English fishing the seas; but weren't these privileged arguing out the pros and cons of the American way of life versus the European on to something? Wasn't there something the Yankees hankered for nestled in "English countryside refinement?" The British had something going for them. They were not so business-driven; they found amusement in life; and they were genuinely learned, used their time to enquire, to get some insight: "Couldn't there be—weren't there people in both England and America who were...enterprising and simple and hearty" and gay, curious, and credulous as youngsters? Weren't these British enclaves with their air of contentment evidence something works better on this side of the Atlantic? Couldn't his countrymen and women as their British forebears come up with an equally commodious, refined life suited to a new world environment? And those in the cornfields, on the moors, fishing the seas, the common folks, could not they, from such experiments by those who have the time, energy, money to tinker, gain as well—a simpler, richer common life? What, after all, were we after in the U.S.A? Yes, a city on a hill, Detroit rarified—far-fetched but a start. How to go about this?[24]

Sam Dodsworth in his explorations comes across travelers and expatriates, boors, snobs, and the more reasonable, and he detects they, too, recognize the U.S.A. had something as well as more to learn from the Old World. "These men believed, and belligerently announced, America was the 'greatest country in the world,' not only in its resources and increasing population and incomparable comforts of daily life, not only in its energy and mechanical ingenuity, but equally in its generosity, its friendliness, its humor, its aspiration for learning." And they as Sam knew the U.S. was beautiful, and the citizenry in its fashion noble. Broadway's lights were dazzling, New York a city of "a million lights." Factories churned out the good life, a middle-class nirvana in the making. And there always would stand the Vermont maples "like torches" on "autumn afternoons"; the Middle West's corn and wheat fields "talked to themselves," and amongst those rolling fields stood "the tall red wheat-elevators and the spire of the German Catholic Church." What a vision—Sam loved it; Lewis cherished it.[25]

These Americans, far from home, knew something more:

> "Cities of a quarter of a million people with fantastic smoky steel works, like maniac cathedrals, which had arisen in twenty years upon unpeopled sand-barrens. The long road and a rather shaggy, very adventurous family in a squeaky flivver, the new Covered Wagon, starting out to see all the world from Seattle to Tallahassee, stopping to earn their bacon and bread and oil by

[24] Lewis, *Dodsworth*, 29, 77, and 89–90. For a more extensive investigation of conflicting customs and mannerisms between the British and the Americans, an intense debate amongst the chattering classes on both sides of the Atlantic see ibid., 90–98.

[25] Ibid., 93.

> harvesting; singing at night in tourist camps on the edge of wide-lawned towns——"

There is plenty afoot in the U.SA.; something noble, a promise at work. But is it working well?[26]

Self-defined rebels—the expatriates—in old England found they missed something; something in the blood had thinned back home; here it was stronger. One spouts:

> "Well, I'll tell you the way I look at it personally. Strikes me that one-half or maybe two-thirds of the American people are the best fellows on earth—the friendliest and the most interested in everything and the jolliest. And I guess the remaining third are just about the worst crabs, the worst Meddlesome Matties, the most ignorant and pretentious fools, that God ever made. Male *and* female! I'd be tickled to death to live in America *if*. If we got rid of Prohibition, so a man could get a glass of beer instead of being compelled to drink gin and hootch. If we got rid of taking seriously a lot of self-advertising, half-educated preachers and editors and politicians, so that folks would develop a little real thinking instead of being pushed along by a lot of mental and moral policemen. If our streets weren't so God-awfully noisy. If there were a lot more cafes and a lot less autos—sorry, Mr. Dodsworth, you being a motor-manufacturer, but that slipped out and I guess I'll just have to stand by it."

Sam was not affronted; he was provoked.[27]

Dodsworth had had a hand in creating marvels—and he knew the cost. Coming home on his own for a respite from his European burdens, he conjures while laying over in Manhattan a hustle, a bustle which boiled down to unmitigated chaos, the seeming end-product of all that American brain and brawn spawning a vaunted good life that was vulgar:

> Ninth Avenue was insane with the banging of the Elevated; Eighth Avenue was a frontier camp of little shops; Seventh

[26] Ibid.

[27] Ibid., 93–94.

> Avenue was a bedlam of traffic between loft buildings with enormous signs –"Löwenstein & Putski, Garments for Little Gents," and "The Gay Life Brassière, Rothweiser and Gitz"; Sixth Avenue combined the roar of Ninth with the nastiness of Eighth and the charging traffic of Seventh; and when in relief Sam saw the stateliness of Fifth Avenue, there was an inhuman mass of shiny cars from curb to curb.

Inhuman—had he built that? Sam on the promenade deck sailing to the U.S. had imagined all he loved and needed *back home*: "wide streets, clashing traffic, brick garages, the insolent splendor of skyscrapers and, toward the country, miles of white and green little houses where the sort of men he understood played games he understood, poker and bridge, and listened on the radio to the sort of humor and music that he understood. And before every other bungalow was a Revelation car." That Sam knew, this Sam had built—now, back on the home turf, what had it all devolved to?[28]

Dodsworth loved the egalitarian promise of American Democracy. Sailing in, he had marveled as Manhattan loomed ahead, and he had stood transfixed on the deck of his liner: "Then the fog lifted, and he cried, 'My God!' High up shone the towers and spires of an enchanted city floating upon the mist, pyramids and domes glistening in the early sun, vast walls studded with golden windows, spellbound and incredible." Here was the promise, enshrined, American know-how. But there was, too, a gnawing ache as he observed in New York shortcomings. He is yanked this way and that. Once landed, Sam had taken in other sights as his taxi struggled within the clogged metropolis:

> It was achingly hot in the side streets leading from the piers, and appallingly dirty. In front of warehouses and mean brick houses turned into tenements were flying newspapers, piles of bottles and rags and manure. Gritty clouds of ashes blew from open garbage cans, and tangled with the heat was New York's summertime stench of rotten bananas, unwashed laundry, ancient bedding, and wet pavements. In front of the taxicab, making Sam's heart stop with fear, darted ragged small boys (quite

[28] Ibid., 148 and 145.

> cheerful, and illogically healthy); and on the flimsy iron balconies of fire-escapes sat mothers with hair dragging across their eyes, nursing babies who in between sups wailed against the unjust heat. It was, Sam felt, a city nervous as a thwarted woman. (Sam still believed in male strength and female weakness.) It seemed so masculine in its stalwart buildings, but there was nothing masculine in its heat-shocked, clamor-maddened nerves. The traffic policemen raged at Sam's taxi-driver, the taxi-driver cursed all the truck-drivers, and above the roaring of their engines, the truck-drivers cursed everybody on the street.

Lewis the romantic and the skeptic; Dodsworth, too, as well the accomplished pragmatist; neither a great visionary; both can-do sorts—Lewis so wanted to be Dodsworth.[29]

Once out of New York and into the heartland, home again in Zenith, Sam observes how dearly the U.S. had short-changed itself:

> He saw, slowly, that none of his prosperous industrialized friends in Zenith were very much interested in anything whatever. They had cultivated caution until they had lost the power to be interested. They were like old surly farmers. The things over which they were most exclamatory—money, golf, drinking—didn't fascinate them as brush-strokes or wood winds…these diversions were to the lords of Zenith not pleasures but ways of keeping so busy that they would not admit how bored they were, how empty their ambitions. They had as their politics only a testy fear of the working class. (Why, Sam perceived uneasily, the whole country turned the dramatic game of politics over to a few seedy professional vote-wanglers!) To them, women were only bedmates, house-keepers, producers of heirs, and a home audience that could not escape, and had to listen when everybody at the office was tired of hearing one's

[29] Ibid., 146–47. Note Lewis's parenthetical aside regarding male strength, female weakness. In finding Edith, comparing her to Fran, Sam ultimately reaches a fuller appreciation for modern feminism, the promise of "companionate marriage." Lewis plays certain concerns hard while always slipping in those less urgent but important to consider; no surprise, in *Main Street* it is partly the tale of women's position that preoccupies him.

> grievances. The arts, to them, consisted only of jazz conducive to dancing with young girls, pictures which made a house look rich, and stories which were narcotics to make them forget the tedium of existence.

It amounted to a bitter indictment: "They did things, they rushed, they supervised, they contended—but they were not interested."[30]

Europe hardly had the answer. But a lot could be learned. In one of his discussions with a fellow American he met sailing back to the States, a fellow well-grounded in truths, a journalist who traveled the world round, Sam listens. Ross Ireland concludes: "Well, I guess it's all about alike, really—Buddhism in Burma and Henry's flivver. It's all neighborhood gossip, with different kinds of neighbors." Only most live in beastly cities:

> Being a hick by origin, I like cities. I had enough cornfields and manure-piles before I ran away, at fourteen. And from what I heard at lunch, all the other towns in America are becoming about as bad as New York—traffic jams and big movie theaters and radios yapping everywhere and everybody has to have electric dishwashers and vacuum cleaners and each family has to have not one car, by golly, but two or three—and all on the installment plan! But I guess any of those burgs would be better than this New York monkey jungle.

It is a conundrum.[31]

Sam in New York had wandered and wondered: "People running with suit-cases nicked his legs, small active Jews caromed into him, flappers with faces powdered almost purple looked derisively at his wandering and bucolic mildness, a surf of sweaty undistinguishable people swept over him...and at every street-crossing he was held up by the wave of traffic...." In Grand Central Station, within this concrete and marble, sun-streamed testimonial to American pride and accomplishment, he contemplated the contrast with the immensity of Notre Dame in Paris or St. Paul's in London: Why he asked did these edifices "not dwarf and make ridiculous the

[30] Ibid., 180–81.

[31] Ibid., 153.

figures of the worshippers as this vastness did the figures of travelers galloping to train-gates? Was it because the little people, dark and insignificant in the cathedrals, were yet dignified, self-possessed, seeking the ways of God, whereas here they were busy with the ludicrous activities of insects?" "He fancied that this was veritably the temple of a new divinity, the God of Speed." Furthermore, "Of its adherents it demanded as much superstitious credulity as any of the outworn deities—demanded a belief that Going Somewhere, Going Quickly, Going Often, were in themselves holy and greatly to be striven for."

> Here was enthroned "an abstract, faultless, and insatiable God" who demanded more, and more. Dodsworth understood that "with his motor cars [he] had contributed to the birth of this new religion." "He shook his great shaggy head as he looked down on traveling-salesmen importantly parading before bag-laden red-caps, on fagged brokers with clanking bags of golf sticks, on fretful women, contemptuous overdressed women, and sleek young men in white knickerbockers. They seemed to him driven to madness by the mad God of Speed that they themselves had created—and Sam Dodsworth had created."[32]

What hath God wrought?

Ireland, the newsman, took stock:

> Honestly, Sam, I don't get these here United States. We let librarians censor all the books, and yet we have musical comedies like this—just as raw as Paris. We go around hollering that we're the only *bona fide* friends of democracy and self-determination, and yet with Haiti and Nicaragua we're doing everything we accused Germany of doing in Belgium, and—you mark my word—within a year we'll be starting a Big Navy campaign for the purpose of bullying the world as Great Britain never thought of doing. We boast of scientific investigation, and yet we're the only supposedly civilized country where thousands of supposedly sane citizens will listen to an illiterate clodhopping preacher or politician setting himself up as an authority on biology and attacking evolution.

[32] Ibid., 151 and 154–55.

"All the news that's fit to print"—crushing, demoralizing. "Yes, and to have a little more of our American paradox, we have more sentimental sobbing over poor de-uh mother in the movies, and more lynching of negroes, than would be possible anywhere else in the world! More space, and more crowded tenements; more hard-boiled pioneers, and more sickly discontented wives; more Nancies among young men; more high-brow lectures, and more laughing-hyena comic strips and more slang...." And he looks in the mirror: "Well, take me. I'm supposed to be a newspaper man.... I have ideas, and I even have a vocabulary. But I'm so American that if I ever admit I'm interested in ideas, if I ever phrase a sentence grammatically, if I don't try to sound like a longshoreman....Oh, I've learned a lot about myself and my beloved America today!'"[33]

So, too, Sam, a bushelful. Yet as his compatriot, he is ready to defend the U.S.A. on a dime—he worships the promise. So they tear it apart, put it together, try to assess what is right: "Just the same, Ross, I prefer this country to——"; "Hell, so do I! Things I can remember, people I've talked to, knocking around this country." Still Ireland raged, "God.... Luxury! Gold! Everything but self-respect and decency and privacy!" Sam is drained: "I don't want anything enough to fight for it much. I've done about all I ever imagined."[34]

Sam and Ross part; Sam takes the train to Zenith. He is depleted. An old friend, a respected banker, good at talking business, speaks common sense. Elon Richards admonishes you're not beat: "Why not dive head-first into whatever battle seems most interesting?" He expands: "Sam, it's a battle here the way it is in Russia and China. And you, Sam, you old grizzly, can never be a contemplative gazelle. You've got to fight. And think of it! Maybe America will rule the world! Maybe in the end we'll be broken up by Russia. But isn't a world- fight like that better than sitting around...?" Let's talk turkey: "Sam, this American adventure—— Because it is an adventure that we have here—the greatest in the world....And say, do you know, our adventure is going to be the bigger because we do feel that Europe has a lot we need. We're no longer satisfied with the log cabin and the corn pone. We want

[33] Ibid., 155–56.

[34] Ibid., 156 and 163.

everything that Europe has. We'll take it!" "Um," said Sam."[35]

Confused and lonely, Dodsworth returns to Europe and Fran aiming to salvage his marriage. It does not work. As the marriage disintegrates, Sam comes to be friends with Edith Cortright, an expatriate. He shares with Edith all what Fran had frowned upon, all the ways in which he was just an ordinary American, not up to snuff—not European—by Fran's gauge. Fran craves the snuff. Edith shares her own disappointments in life; together they find how much they are alike. Sam is energized; the housing development resurfaces as something he can really see. He had back in Zenith, before the European Tour, excitedly shared the first thoughts about it with Fran. She disdainfully had dismissed him. But once back home, pondering Europe, looking closer at the U.S., and with Elon's prod, Dodsworth had spent his last days in Zenith before dismally heading back to Europe "very busy peering into the Sans Souci Gardens development," his imagined venture into urban renewal. Now, sharing his interest with Edith, he comes alive.[36]

Dodsworth starts working it out:

> To the north of Zenith, among wooded hills above the Chaloosa River, there was being laid out one of the astonishing suburbs which have appeared in America since 1910. So far as possible, the builders kept the beauties of forest and hills and river; the roads were not to be broad straight gashes...but winding byways, very inviting...if one could only kill off the motorists. Here, masked among trees and gardens, were springing up astonishing houses—considerably more desirable as residences than the gaunt fortified castles of the Rhine, the magnificent and quite untenantable museums of French châteaux. They were all imitative, of course—Italian villas and Spanish patios and Tyrolean inns and Tudor manor-houses and Dutch colonial farmhouses, so mingled and crowding one another that the observer was dizzy. They were so imitative and so standardized that it was easy to laugh at them. But they were no more imitative of

[35] Ibid.,161–62.
[36] Ibid., 181.

> Munich than Munich of Italy or than Italy of Greece, and like the rest of the great American Domestic Architecture of this era, they were probably the most comfortable residences in the world…for one who didn't mind it if his Venetian balcony was only ten feet from his neighbor's Swiss chalet, and if his neighbor's washing got slightly in the way of tea on his own lawn.

Sam was taken by the "energy with which roads were being dug, houses rising" and the way the arty street signs swung in the breeze, designating Assisi Crescent and Plaza Reäl. He was hardly a fool: "That there was something slightly ridiculous about mixing up Spain and Devon and Norway and Algiers, and transplanting them to the sandy hills of a Midwestern town, where of late the Indians had trapped rabbits and the rusty-bearded Yankees had trapped the Indians, did vaguely occur to Sam…." But he saw more: There was a strong contrast with the "solemn respectabilities" of older, established Zenith residences. "Here,… he reflected, was all the color and irregularity he had gone abroad to seek; all the scarlets and yellows and frivolous pinks, all the twisted iron-work and scalloped tiles and striped awnings and Sicilian wine-jars he could swallow, along with (he thanked Heaven) all the mass-produced American incinerators, over-stuffed chairs, and built-in garages…." Further, Sam had become enlightened, in a bold, American manner: "It came to him that now there was but little pioneering in manufacturing motors; that he hadn't much desire to fling out more cars on the packed highways. To create houses, perhaps less Coney-Island-like than these—noble houses that would last three hundred years, and not be scrapped in a year as cars were—"[37]

In those last days in Zenith, Sam had sought out the advice of architects, carpenters, and gardeners: "That'd be interesting." He was absorbing all he could, and he was excited. He knew he had zero understanding of architecture: "But he knew a good deal about steel and wood and glass, about organizing companies, about getting along with labor." How could he contribute?[38]

Edith listens and understands. Sam has found a helpmate. Amidst

---

[37] Ibid., 181–82.

[38] Ibid., 182

the shambles of his marriage, the entrepreneur had let his dream languish. Now, sharing more and more with Edith, it has come again into its own. Together, with Edith's insights, Sam begins actively to plan. Sans Souci was not yet *it*—but what could be? Nothing so fantastic; something more pronounced, more grounded, more American was in order. Sam travels Europe, on the run again, fleeing his broken marriage, searching, and he studies: "He was going back to make some such a 'development' as the Sans Souci Gardens, and contemplating it he was becoming conscious that there was such a thing as architecture. Details that once he would never have noticed became alive: hand-wrought iron-balconies, baroque altars, tiled roofs, window shutters, copper pans in kitchens seen from the street."[39] He sketched, he kept an eye out for articles on architecture. An amalgamation, a mix of Old World and New, the American admixture could work again—that's where it had all started, right? Yes, America was grand; borrow, adapt, build anew, its promise was not lost; get to work.

Dodsworth draws up a blueprint. As Fran sues for divorce, Edith patiently puts up with Sam's repeated, tail-between-legs attempts to make it work with Fran, as well as his tangles with guilt, with hurt, with his hankerings for doing more with his life. He meanwhile holds tight to that blueprint. Dodsworth finally gets his bearings: Edith knows him, what is he stumbling about for? He queries, "Could you ever possibly consider going to a place like Zenith to live?" She responds, "Of course. Do places differ so much?" The world is the same all over. But perhaps they can make a better world of it in America, in Zenith, just to start. "Would it amuse you to work on a plan like these garden suburbs?" Edith ruminates. An hour later, she bursts:

> Sam! About your suburbs. Something could be done—not just Italian villas and Swiss chalets—for a town with a tradition of Vermont Yankees and Virginians in buckskin. Why shouldn't one help to create an authentic and unique American domestic architecture? Our skyscrapers are the first really new thing in architecture since the Gothic cathedral, and perhaps just as beautiful! Create something native –and not be afraid to keep all the

---

[39] Ibid., 207.

> plumbing and vacuum-cleaners and electric dish-washers! Dismiss the imitation châteaux. The trouble with the rich American is that he feels uncouth and untraditional, and so he meekly trots to Europe to buy sun-dials and Fifteenth Century mantelpieces and refectory tables—to try to buy aristocracy by buying the aristocrat's worn-out coats. I like my Europe in Europe; at home I'd like to watch people make something new. For example, your motor cars.

The Revelation, his great pride; Sam can only wonder: "Then you would like a place like Zenith, that's growing?" Edith tosses back what any red-blooded American, still with fight, knows: "How can I tell? I'd certainly like the adventure of trying it."[40]

So ends the novel, one would expect. An adventure, but not quite there yet—Sam once more crawls back to Fran. He is not a tough guy. He never will get over her. He and Fran "reconcile," sail for America, and once in New York, having had his final fill of her shipboard nagging, childishness, game-playing, and manipulating, Sam telegraphs Edith, who in pain had seen him sail off. No, he cannot ever fully get over Fran, but he'll be damned if he cannot get beyond her. Edith receives his news with open arms, and Sam hops back onto a liner.

"They were dining at the Ritz in Paris, Edith and Sam, feeling superior to its pretentiousness, because that evening they had determined to return to America, when his divorce should be complete.... They were gay, well-dined and well content." All is not perfect, and it is silly to believe all will be. But Sam and Edith will set out on their adventure. In fact, appropriately, the plan at first is to try another idea of Sam's, closer to the grass roots, to experiment with caravans. All along, Sam has tinkered with the idea (as had Lewis who loved them). It was another American original: "Ritzy motor caravans with electric stoves and radios and everything built in." Trekking, that's the ticket, that's what the frontiersmen were all about. It's a good place to start.[41]

Sam is a practiced manufacturer—there is little doubt he can succeed. He is his native land's past, present, and future. Maybe he'll

---

[40] Ibid., 338–39.

[41] Ibid., 351.

become a caravan magnate. Who knows what "Sans Souci Gardens" might in the end germinate? *If*...it's all ahead. Dodsworth is an American original. Lewis would love to be Sam: "I'd certainly like the adventure of trying it!" Sinclair Lewis never could be Sam, but he did have the satisfaction of writing Sam up, developing this protagonist of strong character and a plan to boot. He could imagine Sam will deliberately follow through to whatever end he chooses. The reader is left hanging, where will it lead, but infused with a sense of real possibility. Lewis always prized imagination. And isn't the American Experiment at its core a trust in imagination?

Lewis writing *Dodsworth* used his imagination to consider "what if." And, what if he, too, could reach such an end, to be fulfilled, satisfied with a job well done? That would be a stretch: he just did not have that in him. Always aching, searching for that greener pasture, the novelist, still, had finally found a reasonable resolution for his fictitious journey. Through the twenties he had probed, worked to decipher ills. Sans Souci if not *it*, the answer, was a start; it represented a simple admonition to the country: observe, take thought, where can this country step forward?

Sam and Edith represent American strengths—together they could build. Through his first four works, Lewis had worked the home turf. With *Dodsworth* he had stretched overseas, undertaken prolonged discussions of the merits, shortcomings, the advantages of the U.S. as opposed to Europe, and just what the older world had to offer to its offspring. There in plush surroundings, Dodsworth had engaged in lofty talk (and not so lofty) of democracy and aristocracy; he was awash in high art and philosophic diatribes, a long way from cars, bath tubs, and vacuum cleaners. He tried to put it together. Sam weighed the value of centuries of accumulated knowledge against the quick acquisition of wealth; took the measure of his homeland's strengths and weaknesses; considered husbands and wives and shattered dreams.

On one occasion, Sam, Fran, and some Old-World acquaintances fall into an extensive conversation of substance, as they could on occasion. Engaged, at first wrapped in stars and stripes, Sam ponders: "This bearded beauty may know something about economics in Germany, but I'll bet he doesn't know anything about the land of the safety-razor." But as has become his wont, he listens closely to this professor, and he learns a lot, and it has little to do with economics. The Old-World denizen proceeds to explain the aristocrat "feels that he is responsible to past generations to carry on the culture they have formed. He feels the graciousness, agreeable manners, loyalty to his own people, are more important than wealth; and he feels that to carry on his tradition, he must have knowledge—much knowledge." "We feel that the real Continental Europe is the last refuge of individuality, leisure, privacy, quiet happiness. We think that good talk between intelligent friends in a café in Vienna or Paris or Warsaw is more pleasant and important than having septic tanks or electric dish-washing machines." And yes, Europe may well be influenced by the U.S; but from the European perspective the rising young man aping his American brother can and must strike the right balance. "He must have—even though he may plan to be a stock-broker or an importer, or sell your automobiles, Mr. Dodsworth—he must have some understanding of music, painting, literature…." Ours, he maintains, is a world designed by an aristocracy, and while the hoi polloi may never be refined, they support an elite class which preserves the best in life; yours, he charges, on the other hand, is more of an amalgamation, a manufactured society. "America wants to turn us into Good Fellows, all provided with the very best automobiles….Europe! The last refuge, in this Fordized world, of personal dignity!" And it is not solely America that threatens: "We are menaced by the whole world." There is Russia which "wants to turn us into a machine for the shaving off of all the eccentricities which do not belong to the lowest common denominator. And Asia and Africa do not t'ink that human life and the sweetness of human life matter." No, this German intellect advises, centuries of refinement cannot be discounted and it should not be displaced by rough-hewn pioneers who have created a "dollar society"…and God save us all from the Bolsheviks. Whereat could it all end?[42]

Sam grasps the argument; he sees many of his own and his nation's shortcomings, but surely there was a formidable middle ground laid in the New World; possibly he could fortify it. "Was it possible that in

[42] Ibid., 227 and 231–33. The lengthy discussion runs 227–41.

some involved, unelucidated way, he himself was a savant in fields not admitted by the academicians as scholarship? (Lewis answering back to his literary critics?) He told himself that in the American motor-world he was certainly not known merely as a peddler and as a financial acrobat, but as the authority on automobile-designing, as the first man to advocate four-wheel brakes. Hm…*did* that constitute him a scholar….?" And there was more to contemplate—perhaps *he* was an artist. "He had created something! He had no pictures in the academies, no books to be bound in levant, no arias nor flimsy furniture named after him, but every one of the twenty million motors on the roads of America had been influenced by his vision, a quarter of a century ago, of long, clean stream-lines!" This, too, was art. Lewis has Sam, his answer to the critics.[43]

Fran, ever the snob, had earlier back in Zenith scorned Sam's Revelation, that "beastly old medium-priced car." She could plunge the dagger. That had been his dream brought to fruition, a car for millions. But now, as he listened, he relocated his pride, and he thought he was not alone, he and others had built an empire. There was much with which to reckon. He rejoined the conversation: New York's towering Woolworth Building has integrity, the Chicago Tribune Building is a sight, and so too a Ford plant. A "prosperous cement-paved powerful country" is not to be mocked. Americans are not yokels: "The kind of pride that you describe, Professor, as belonging to the real aristocratic Europeans, is fine—I'm all for it. And I want to see just that kind of pride in America. Maybe we've gone too fast to get it. But as I wander around Europe, I find a whale of a lot of Americans who are going slow and quiet, and who are thinking—and not all of 'em artists and professors, by a long shot, but retired businessmen. We are getting a tradition that…." Sam stops, embarrassed he has been lecturing. What was he on the edge of—a tradition that can be restored, the American Experiment, the Promise? "110,000,000 people—might be worth studying"; he made his point.[44]

Having restrained himself, Sam turned back to silent conjuring:

---

[43] Ibid., 229.

[44] Ibid., 234–35.

"Could he ever attain scholarship now? Was it too infantile a fancy to think of becoming the first great historian of motors, historian of something which was, after all, more important in social evolution than twenty Battles of Waterloo?" But he was no scholar of that sort. Perhaps he could learn "something of architecture.... Could he really make better San Souci Gardens?" After all, "[I]t didn't hurt a man to be a little proud of some honest thing he had done!" This was something seriously to contemplate:

> "Here I am fifty-two years old, and just this last year or so I've wanted to be more than a money-coining machine.... To be *something*. Though God knows what!... I have been a good citizen! And I have brought up my children! And I have paid my debts! And I have done the job that was first at hand! And I have loved my friends! And now I'm not going to stand back the rest of my life and be satisfied and dead—dead on my feet—dead."

That's not Sam, that's not his people, that's not the U.S.A. He came to Europe, trailed Fran, to find some truth. It would not be hers—he was not about to try to imitate Europeans manners, take up Old World biases, abandon what he knew. Again, he speaks:

> "What most Europeans think of America! Because we were a pioneer nation, mostly busy with farming and cod-fishing and chewing tobacco, a hundred years ago, Europe thinks we still are. The pictures of Americans in your comic papers indicate to me that Europe sees all Americans as either money-lenders who lie awake nights thinking of how they can cheat Europe, or farmers who want to spit tobacco on the Cathedral of St. Mark, or gunmen murdering Chicagoans in their beds."[45]

Americans still were pioneers. Americans still could build: a large middle class was in the making; ordinary men and women were acquiring the security and comforts of a home; they raised families, opportunities to rise existed, and women were gaining all along more of a chance to contribute in a way Europeans were deficient; this was a land of common sense. Sam kept pondering. An admirable foundation had been laid. It had its cracks and fissures. They could be addressed. There were many truths.

---

[45] Ibid., 229–230 and 234.

In Sam, Lewis had created a countryman to whom he could hitch his star. Sam was no artist—or was he? Not a scholar? Not a historian? With *Dodsworth* Lewis had a lot to say about himself as well as his country's promise. Eighteen months following the publication of *Dodsworth* the Swedish Academy declared: "Yes, Sinclair Lewis is an American. He writes the new language—American—as one of the representatives of 120,000,000 souls. He asks us to consider that this nation is not yet finished or melted down; that it is still in the turbulent years of adolescence."[46] Sinclair Lewis had received the Nobel. While the critics had hailed *Dodsworth*, and even—especially following *Gantry*—its artistry, none saw in it the consummation of Sinclair Lewis's body of work, nor was he granted full-throated registry of his competency as a novelist. He remained an enigma, to which the reviewers still were drawn. A puzzle: perhaps the Nobel Committee, as Sam, as Lewis recognized a cross-Atlantic perspective was of particularly good value.

Neither Dodsworth nor Lewis conjured *the solution*; the resolution Sam arrives at offers a partial step ahead, and it may seem small given the big picture. But that does not have to be the end of the story; it is the story. Sam nurtured a hope. The U.S.A. had its traditions; and its optimism. Where had the country gone astray? What was the route out of the conundrum? To keep trying, was that possibly enough, did it really constitute a blueprint? Was this the essence of the American Promise? In the end Sam Dodsworth goes home to America; there's a job at hand. The literati missed it. Perhaps the readers as well—but a careful read pretty well indicates Sinclair Lewis had a good tale to tell.

Looking back on his body of work in the 1920s, one could hope the novelist would be satisfied—he had placed plenty to conger before the eyes of his country. But he was rarely satisfied. Soon it materialized *his decade* was over. He had given it his best shot. "It is my fate," he declared, in his Stockholm acceptance to swing constantly from optimism to pessimism and back, but so is it the fate of any one who writes or speaks of anything in America—the most contradictory, the most

---

[46] Richard Lingeman, *Rebel from Main Street* (New York: Random House, 2002), 356–57.

depressing, the most stirring, of any land in the world to-day."[47] That is the point—the country inherently has its doubts; there is no clear path ahead—yet the Promise remains stirring; so, too, persistence.

Hutchisson notes the acclaimed novelist in Stockholm—despite his early cry on learning of the award that it was over for him, that it would now be all down-hill—may have perceived how tenuous was this moment. Pessimism and optimism: nevertheless,

> "Lewis was in high spirits. In his letters from this period, he spoke of new beginnings and new directions.... [B]ut his career after 1930, although largely a success in commercial terms, would not be as significant in artistic terms as it was during the 1920s. By the time of *Dodsworth*, Lcwis was simply running out of material. When he began to cast about for a new project, he came up empty."[48]

His decade, his great run, had come to its end—but with *Dodsworth*, rich in the material he knew best, he hardly went out with a whimper.

---

[47] Hutchisson, 239. The entire Nobel speech runs 235–46. It makes a strong read, conceptually and stylistically.

[48] Hutchisson, 192

NINE

DODSWORTH RECONSIDERED

Sinclair Lewis never sat back; still, his remaining two decades were a downhill slide. Subsequent work—style, content, and currency—underscores the twenties had been his decade. He had had a lot to say, he did so with his brand of finesse, and he was hailed a national spokesman, agree with him or not. His final take in *Dodsworth*, how to fulfill that lofty American Promise, reduced to garden neighborhoods hardly had much lift in and of themselves—hardly a reviewer noted that particular. Lewis offered a way out for Sam and by a long stretch for the country. Always, the call was muted; after all it was only a restart the author proffered; but after a decade, built upon the foundation of four distinctive novels, *Dodsworth* had in fact made the most comprehensive, final argument. As seminal as it was to Lewis to get the country to act, there was no rush to arms. The message that the United States had work to do was always his line of thought, always the national story, and he was the best-selling author of the decade. It is hard to imagine he could have produced a stronger contribution.

At Stockholm the Nobel recipient identified with his country: "It is my fate…to swing from optimism to pessimism and back, but so is it the fate of any one who writes or speaks of anything in America."[1] In the thirties, his optimism that the country would find its way ran head-on into a social crisis which nurtured pessimism for most. He always identified as middle class to the core. He saw a lot of Sam, a rarified babbitt, in himself. Dodsworth reveled in the glory of middle-class America; he knew he was a good citizen. In the "dirty thirties" the national tale took a dangerous turn; the middle class took a huge hit. Lewis was a masterful diagnostician. In the rush of the twenties, he argued work is ahead; he charted a progressive path. In the end, what

---

[1] James M. Hutchisson, *The Rise of Sinclair Lewis, 1920–1930* (University Park: Pennsylvania State University Press, 1996), 239.

could be wrong-headed? "Righteousness, Idealism, Honesty, Sacrifice, Beauty, Salvation," Frank Shallard in *Gatsby* spelled out what mattered.

Dodsworth as Shallard acted on those precepts. He did not have the pastor's religious bent in mind. He did speak of promise, he did have faith in the national experiment. In the thirties, Lewis's brand of tinkering, moderate in concept, take a look at ourselves, take time, take action, no longer seemed reasonable. More immediate measures, some radical, some conservative, ultimately a middling mix of efforts to keep the country from total collapse were adopted. Bulk up the middle-class social and economic structure, re-gun mainstream progressivism, recapture momentum. By hook or by crook, by God's grace if one wills, by national regeneration, through the right leadership at the right time to seek out middle-ground direction, or by plumb luck—and with war—the United States did reach significantly calmer waters following the Second World War. Here, in a more pacific environment, Lewis's middle-road diagnosis once more made considerable sense—fine tune that American Experiment. But a decade and a half had passed, and Lewis, by the postwar years amidst brighter prospects could not write provocative prose. He had not for the most part since *Dodsworth*. And he was wearing down as his problem with drink continued. Others wrote during the Depression, the war years, and the postwar years searching in their own manner for what ailed the U.S.A., probing what was wrong and right. New challenges to the body politic were in the making. Sinclair Lewis was drained; he had made his point the best he could in the times he most understood. These new days were far from his day. While a lot of what he had said clearly remained pertinent, well, he had said it. Back in 1930 he sensed he had shot his bolt—he had hit a moving target. He was right, the author fell out of step.

The novelist took his work seriously and the country's destiny as sacred. Though that can sound saccharine, Lewis was anything but. In the Roaring Twenties he was not just etching caricatures, nor was he sending up the U.S.A. While he missed his target to get the populace to SEE all he had to point out, to take a longer look at itself, to act according to its better angels, he did get millions to think about it. Lewis may not have broken through his twenties impasse with the novels, stirred the country into concerted action to right itself, but he did draw his compendium to a satisfactory close—he was fortunate to have gotten his word out. His twenties work was not satire run amuck as some charged, and "he only points out the bad" missed the point entirely. His was a persuasive analysis built upon satire *and* caricature *and* research whereby he laid a foundation for understanding to the best extent he could just who we are. Five hefty accumulative statements, *Main Street*, *Babbitt*, *Arrowsmith*, *Elmer Gantry*, and in conclusion *Dodsworth*: each prodded at what ailed the United States and together suggested a lofty remedy—get back to basics, interpret that as you will. To this day, close to one hundred years on, Lewis's prose reads well and true, and he still does not receive full credit for his accomplishment. That is the luck of the draw. That does not mean it has to be the end of the story. To their credit, a select few critics when *Dodsworth* was published saw the novel was the end-note of a saga. They literally declared Lewis's stance as a strong prophet would be honored one hundred years on. They wrote he will still need to be read.

Dodsworth is not America's great novel, but of those five best-sellers across a remarkable decade, *Dodsworth* was by significant measures more of an accomplishment for the novelist than any of the other four—because of the other four. A considerably deeper study of the nation's character, the tale offered resolution of a sort, a strong statement the country had much to address, and the people needed to get to it—that is the American Way. And at bottom—and generally (if often grudgingly) conceded from up on high—it was art.

Dodsworth is well-written, and reviewers of the day offered praise; yet most missed the novel's monumental significance—Sinclair Lewis over an entire decade, a tumultuous era of fundamental social and cultural change, had drawn out five provocative perspectives on the passing parade. Not all, but most readers remain a mystery; still, they also did not in all probability recognize the breadth of achievement, the importance of all five considered as a whole. The critical focus of the reception was narrow. Criticism focused on the purported plot-line—all the analysis of what is right and wrong with the nation was dwarfed by the marriage breakdown. Reviewers easily picked up that Sam was on a journey for himself, to become truer to what he believed constituted a good man. Seemingly the state of the union was not essential to the novel—that he yearned to be a good citizen hardly was mentioned. There is plenty of evidence critics were tired of talking about it, *that decade*; this was common in the national discourse. Twenties diagnoses were getting long in the tooth; and the *pseudo* resolution Lewis offered as always was understated. There was plenty of talk in the late twenties that the New Era had run its course; and snide remarks Lewis had gone stale were on the increase.

Essentially, critics long recognized the novelist spun a good yarn, about us, about the United States—that had mattered a lot, but a tale had been told. Some took comfort the author had found a new direction in focusing on a marriage gone bad. Very few critics over the decade had ever considered thc fivc grcat novels were amounting to a singular statement and so missed the import of *Dodsworth's* wrap-up. The general drift of the criticism did not bother to give *Dodsworth* that much consideration beyond the observation Lewis had turned his dexterous trick yet again (for most "thank goodness given *Gantry*"). Once more he had earned the country's attention and its money. What the novelist was all about beyond that had really become a moot question—Lewis had been around for the entire decade; few cared all that much. He liked to take on the United States, he liked to provide a laugh, he wrote engaging novels. The mold was set: the twenties had a good run, the era had fascinated, and it had cachet; the decade's pizazz spoke to millions, as did Lewis who raised questions; he was a celebrity, what more could the critics add?

James M. Hutchisson, scores of years later, assessing what was up in 1929 writes Lewis's intention with *Dodsworth* was straight-forward: downplay the satire, emphasize character, be more profound, prove himself more the novelist in "quest for self-knowledge." He perceives Lewis liked Sam "whom he half-regarded satirically and half-idealized as a portrait of himself." He concludes there was a fundamental weakness in the novel, a clumsiness in balancing satire and idealism; interestingly, "Lewis could not see this clearly because much of the time he was writing about his own thoughts and emotions."[2] But that always was the case; so much of his work was premised upon self-knowledge

[2] Hutchisson, *Rise*, 190.

informed by an intuitive (and heavily researched) grasp of the world about him. He looked to balance satire and ideals while getting to the heart of the matter—he craved stability; and he perceived the nation did as well. Hutchisson errs: *Dodsworth* represented the most satisfying balance the writer could achieve between style and substance. Many may have overlooked and still do the idealism of the novel's protagonist, but it was sketched in passage after passage, and the more softly peddled satire did not distract from it. Dodsworth's sojourn was as much Lewis could envision for the passing scene, not to mention the whole show...a steady drive toward stability and fulfillment. Life was worthy of satire, and the reader, Lewis believed, receptive to idealism. That admixture appealed to him; he contended it appealed to the country. Hardly clumsy, Lewis had finessed the trick and demonstrated he could view the nation, and its people, in a holistic fashion.

Hutchisson writes, "When Dodsworth was published on 14 March, 1929, it was greeted with none of the rambunctious enthusiasm Lewis had earlier attracted with *Main Street*, *Babbitt*, or *Gantry*, probably because it was not a satiric send-up of American society."[3] It was, just not as blatant, and the novel had plenty of good to say about the U.S.A. The scholar is dead-on the public and critics knew Lewis; those who read him well could easily recognize it was anoth*er* take on the U.S.A.; nothing particularly thrilling about that, just what one expected from the author—and a welcome pivot to optimism after *Elmer Gantry*. As with *Arrowsmith*, critics conceded and some raved his latest effort was so much more *the novel*. *Arrowsmith* similarly had not been met with rambunctious enthusiasm; it, too, had been deemed a more thoughtful work, less satiric, for some a work of art even. Given *Gantry*'s heavy dose of biting satire, caricature, and cynicism, *Dodsworth* was welcomed as a welcome antidote, thoughtful and funny; and a relief. No need for a crazed reception; after Elmer Gantry, Sam Dodsworth was good company.

There were critics on occasion who noted *Dodsworth* a deeper novel than the "cerebral" *Arrowsmith*. After all, the author's idealism in *Arrowsmith* led to Martin hunkering down in the woods. With Sam

[3] Ibid., 190–91.

Lewis positioned himself on more pragmatic ground—and he set his protagonist on a deep dive into "what's up with America." Hutchisson observes, "Many reviewers thought *Dodsworth* augured a maturity in Lewis's development as a writer, but an equal number had mixed or lukewarm reactions."[4] Lukewarm is off-base; it was more a case that after a decade it was nothing to get excited about—Lewis was not being as sarcastic; he was serious; he had a story to tell about the country. None of it was newsworthy.

Hutchisson works hard to grasp what Lewis was after. Lewis befuddles. The best scholars who take on the author stumble.[5] Lewis challenges; he did so throughout the 1920s. At the end of the decade, *Dodsworth* did not clear the air. There were as always a host of takes on what Lewis was now up to. Those reviewers who had been charting the maturation of the author, who had read him thoroughly, remained flummoxed, at times at odds with one another, but a consensus grew that with this novel they had achieved a greater clarity as to how to approach his work. In impressive criticisms they probed deep, some quite personally, to figure out where they stood vis-à-vis his body of work.

In Britain, Ford Maddox Ford, in "Dodsworth by Sinclair Lewis," queried the ever-present dilemma, how does one address this novelist? He underscores he has no interest in the art business. Ford outright contends the novel did not stand alone, it was the fifth in line: "I like *Dodsworth* much better than *Elmer Gantry*...and Mr. Dodsworth much better than Mr. Babbitt as being the more convincing, the more human and, I daresay, more 'felt' by his creator." He acknowledges he was a great admirer of *Babbitt*, but he found him "a little of a Robot" moving in a landscape which was the dominant feature of the novel. *Dodsworth*

[4] Ibid.

[5] Both Hutchisson and Sheldon Norman Grebstein, *Sinclair Lewis* (New Haven: College and University Press), 1962 cite Sam and Edith remain in Europe. For all their strong analysis, this is definitively not the case and further evidence how seriously Lewis could be misunderstood. See Hutchisson, 173; Grebstein, 114.

is more a poem. Ford is adamant he is not in this piece fashioning himself a literary critic. He only wishes to discuss the book as the book. He finds Sam more real against the landscape we all share. Dodsworth suffers, and we with him. *Dodsworth*, in short, "is a great achievement," and it should be read "by the millions on both sides of the Atlantic." The world has promise, and word should be spread: There are "friendlinesses and freshness and attractions" to ponder. "[I]t is a good novel, a good story." He concludes, "This is the real test—more particularly for a book that is going to do good: for it must be read for itself and the moral must sink in unperceived as do the morals that we draw from life itself. To that end, we must identify ourselves with the characters and live in the scenes." He hoped Sam "might have his luck because, subconsciously, I regarded it as an omen that I might have mine." It was, Ford reflected, an old-fashioned read, uplifting after "half a century or so of books besieged these brows. That is the real, unconscious tribute and the real, true, friendly hail!" Old-fashioned, funnily enough, and loaded with sociological insight—Ford heartily approved of its uplifting power. Abjuring literary critique, he considered Lewis amongst the best, whatever for others constituted best. Seems Ford had in mind, in truth, to do a literary critique.[6]

A few weeks earlier, again from Britain, Rachel Annand Taylor in "Dodsworth" hailed the latest novel. She calls out Sam in the end "is wise enough to save his own soul." The marriage is not the story: She finds *Dodsworth* Lewis's "most readable"; he attempts to "divine the state of a nation." Taylor concludes "not through mere intelligence" is this accomplished: "*Dodsworth* is stimulating and mobile and tonic, and altogether good for the brain." Taylor along with Ford clearly was attuned to Lewis's intent. For Taylor, those who considered marriage the focus, had missed the entire point.[7]

Lewis always sold exceptionally well in Great Britain; and not simply because he criticized or sent up the United States. He was taken

---

[6] Ford Maddox Ford, "Dodsworth by Sinclair Lewis," *Bookman*, April, 1929, 191–92.

[7] Rachel Annand Taylor, "Dodsworth," *Spectator* [*Literary Supplement*], March 23, 1929, 485–86.

quite seriously. Novelist and editor E. M. Forster dove deep into the art question. As he does so, par for the course, he, as so many others, gets in a tangle about the novelist—how to "class him." Unlike the vast majority, he hunts what the artist is up to and how much it matters—and he asserts it will matter more as decades, a century passes. He differed with Ford. Sinclair Lewis was something altogether new, not old-fashioned at all. In "A Camera Man" printed in Britain and in the U.S., Forster works hard at deciphering Lewis's standing and determines with *Dodsworth* the writer is on to something entirely novel and welcome—but it does not bode well for his future. He engages *Dodsworth* as part and parcel of a compendium. He pans: "What has happened? What has changed the Greek Confectionary Parlour at Gopher Prairie, where every decaying banana mattered, to this dreary general catalogue?" "The explanation is all too plain: photography is a pursuit for the young. So long as a writer has the freshness of youth on him, he can work the snapshot method, but when youth passes he has nothing to fall back on." Lewis was getting on. Just as the obsession in the New Era with all that was novel—the new woman, new Negro, new youth, cars and morals—had gone stale, so had Red Lewis. But that for Forster definitively does not detract from the decade-long achievement. He embarks on a widely circuitous analysis to reach a novel, so to speak, conclusion.[8]

The British man of literature was on to something. He works hard to suss out *what's up*._The critic mistakenly finds Lewis offering up another "dreary catalogue" of his country's shortfalls. However, he no longer was addressing Gopher Prairie's provincial issues or those of Zenith and Manhattan. He now was in Europe, projecting a light on broader concerns—at the end of the rambunctious decade, he wanted

[8] E. M. Forster, "A Camera Man," *Life and Letters* 2, May 1929: 336–43 and *New York Herald Tribune Books*, "Our Photography: Sinclair Lewis," April 28, 1929, 1 and 6, quoted 6. The emergence of the camera and its place in the arts had during the last half of the nineteenth century become a matter of considerable discussion and continued to be so. See David E. Shi, *Facing Facts: Realism in American Thought and Culture 1850–1920*. New York: Oxford University Press, 1995.

to reach more of a conclusion regarding *These United States*. Forster misses it. Yes, the confectionary parlor had become a mainstay, as had the manners, mores, past-times, foibles, hopes, and fantasies of Carol Kennicott and George Babbitt. Martin Arrowsmith had represented a turn, a good deal less satiric, more thoughtful take on the passing scene. For the American reading public (and the British), *Arrowsmith* was considered a triumph, as it was by the critics; Lewis had gone further, deeper, albeit there was no over-excitement; of course, he muted the satire. *Gantry*, overwhelmingly judged an anomaly, had been taken as a distraction, not cerebral, and its harshness triggered a loud, unwelcoming response. Still, it "had to be read"—hence, the catalogue contained lots of fresh material—clearly as all the controversy swirled. With *Dodsworth*, the author was more stable personally, more determined professionally. He would discount satire, offer substantial analysis of what had gone right and wrong in the U.S. Lewis was not offering a repetition of old complaints; rather he was extending and deepening his analysis. With the fifth successful novel Lewis had reached his final say. Forster grasped something was noteworthy here, and he endeavored to figure out what it was.

Observing the country from a distant perspective, digging deeper into its dilemma, examining the loss of innocence, dissecting the American Experiment, that failing Promise, it all was beyond Forster's ken. This is good work, Forster argues, but the author had lost his punch; his subject matter, the people, the country had moved on, had aged. The critic, for all his criticism of the cataloguing, could not see its decade-long relation to the broader sweep Lewis had sought. The novel is a good tale; it is a good summary of all Lewis had tried to unwrap in the twenties. For Forster, however, nature has taken its course: Lewis during the decade had done something entirely new, and it was grand. He grasps the novelist had had profound influence. His hand with the camera, his eye for the zeitgeist, was impressive; unfortunately, he has demonstrated his is an *art form* limited to the young. Good for readers, provocative to critics, but for the author of such work it was a limited engagement. How long could a cameraman remain novel? One has to be young, the world must be seen as fresh, ready for its close-up. Forster is correct: he predicts Lewis in the years to come will have little to say. Yet, sadly, he sold short how much *Dodsworth* had had to say, that it was fresh, a conclusive step forward in the saga Sinclair Lewis had tried to lay out.

The trajectory of Lewis's aim had been for the most part steady—he knew what he was after. There was over the decade talk of maturity amongst critics. If the cataloguing of foibles in *Dodsworth* at points might seem stale, well, it all had been around for a long while—how long can one savage decaying bananas? Lewis had trimmed his satiric sails with *Arrowsmith*—even *Gantry* was less satiric, albeit so strong in intent that those disapproving took a lot of the substance as satire. And, in truth the author himself may well have been bored of the satire. The major thrust in *Dodsworth* was to set up a strong caricature, a more softly satirized America, and to contrast it sharply against an Old-World portrait. Lewis was back after the *Gantry* "rant," determined, placing his progressive outlook front-and-center. Through Samuel Dodsworth, a man of sound if not fool-proof character, the author aimed to come to terms with where the nation sat at the end of the Roaring Twenties, and how it had arrived there, a far cry from the Puritan vision of an idealized city on a hill. No one knew what the new decade might bring, but everyone knew where they had been. Lewis trusted his readers would see what in its entirety he was up to for ten years. This was the author's final commentary: Promise remained for Sam and the country; as the New Era passed a new decade was in the works.

This was Lewis's argument all along—progress, keep an eye on the prize; *Dodsworth*, by any close read, was far from tongue-in-cheek and not a lament; it had depth, it was humorous, and it was outspokenly optimistic. Really, quite fresh—an achievement of lasting note. Lewis, through five novels, had put the country on *photographic* display. This was the last shot. It had been engaging; and yes, Forster was astute—it was over. But the compendium all along would stand the test of time.

Forster in his view of the author cleverly pictures Lewis a cameraman. His body of work had been a series of photographic glimpses at society; Forster does not say it was a moving picture he unreeled, but in effect that is what he is arguing; the artist served up a country on the move, and in his style, in his art, he was ever-current, ever-intuitive.

Forster struggles with "art," eager to stretch its bounds. He surmises through a series of strong novels Lewis had contributed to an exercise in self-awareness. "America" was the story line. Readers may not have caught the full meaning of what he was after, novel after novel, but they felt his proximity to their way of thinking. There were issues to be addressed. The people were maturing; so, too, Lewis's camera eye: ever more sophisticated, perceptive. He took in the continent as Forster praised, and he projected it five times over in an engaging, persuasive manner.

Forster's brilliant take on the cameraman begins to take on the deeper significance of the extenuated twenties story-line: Lewis's drive to get the country not just to see but to act. Forster knows he has drawn together a valuable archive, but it is over; he does not see how Lewis could go further. He has aged out of his heyday—there is no more to say. He's given us all the shots, across a decade. The decade becomes familiar: "What has happened? What has changed the Greek Confectionary Parlour at Gopher Prairie, where every decaying banana mattered, to this dreary general catalogue?" What a great job, he asserts. But clearly there was no more to say. Lewis no longer, a decade on, was a tribune...a cameraman, and he had been good.

Lewis indeed will fall into steep decline. It had nothing to do with getting old. The novelist, for reasons beyond "youthful" perspective, will no longer write so well. But that will not be because his forte, his literary camera lens belongs only to the young. Forster, of course, has no idea of what was coming down the pike, but the country was about to be thrown off the track and Lewis as well because he could not relate to the catastrophic hit of the Great Depression. The thirties was not to be a decade for observing middle-class peccadillos and deep regrets about a culture in need of long-term reform. Photographers will have a heyday producing some of the most powerful camera shots of the twentieth century. And, a host of writers, not because they are young, but because they are attuned to what's in the ether, as Lewis once had been, will press out impressive literature; some will be following the twenties author's lead, writing with a camera-eye. One easily thinks of John Dos Passos, who, with sweeping *U.S. Trilogy*, caught the nation's attention in an era of tremendous upheaval.

Forster wanted to get to the bottom of the conundrum: "I persist in exclaiming, for what Mr. Lewis has done for myself and thousands of others, is to lodge a piece of a continent in our imaginations." This he had first declared back in 1922. He now considers the author's photographic method, so pronounced in *Main Street* and *Babbitt*, was exemplary, and it remained so. But, thinking it over, a decade had passed; a writer if up to snuff is capable through practice to retain "the freshness of youth"; he or she has direction; on the other hand "photography is a pursuit for the young," it is of the moment. Lewis with his camera eye was no longer up to speed: "It is here that he differs from the artist"—this is a riddle, and Forster persists to solve it. Lewis could only take pictures; photographs with the passage of time take on a sepia cast. Youth wanes. This is it for the man with the camera. He is alert, curious, caught up in the moment. Lewis was a seer and had done justice to his decade. But as a cameraman's subject ages, and as he lives into a newer era, he "has nothing to fall back upon." This decade had been young in spirit, and it also had run its course. This preeminent observer of the twenties had come of age. And it is the end. We'd seen enough of *those* photographs. Good: nothing lasting in terms of excitement, but brilliant in their display—and not much more to expect from Sinclair Lewis. Looking ahead, a new generation of youthful cameramen would catch the subsequent "day." Lewis, by Forster's measure, passes with his decade. No longer does he possess the youth's eye for the zeitgeist. Ah, but the critic sights something equally of import.[9]

The critic underestimated the greater summons to action. Lewis was not just taking shots; he had plenty to tell through his camera's eye; he was a man of words, and he was a top-drawer wordsmith. Forster moves on to query is there more to Lewis's own story? What happens to him, his reputation? E. M. Forster sharply took on the "Lewis challenge." He got a lot right. He worked hard to interpret it and in the process attributes greatness to Lewis. He concludes, in an abrupt about-face, to argue the novelist had brought to light a new form of literature. Yes, with *Dodsworth* Sinclair Lewis had demonstrated there was nothing new in the air for him to write about. But yes, also across

[9] Forster, 1 and 6.

the decade he had done something altogether new in literature. If this is art, so be it, but it is not of the traditional sort. "The artist has the power of retaining and digesting experiences, which, years later, he may bring forth in a different form; to the end of life he is accompanied by a secret store."[10] The critic hails Lewis, his craft. Alas, he has nothing further to contribute.

The critic and renowned novelist queries "What has happened?" While *Dodsworth* is a weaker novel, it is *worthy*. He argues, it simply is the last novel in a string of literary perspectives with a camera-eye bent. And yes, what has happened is that—lo and behold—Sinclair Lewis has told "it all" in his own manner. Lewis has taken a huge step forward, opened a new genre. Interestingly, Forster hardly addresses the novel at all. It is this new photographic practice that preoccupies the critic. He proposes, as Will Kennicott had done for Carol, Lewis had delivered *exposure*: "Brought some snapshots down to show you." This, determines Will, is Gopher Prairie, our country. Forster declares, "That, in substance, is what Mr. Sinclair Lewis has himself done. He has brought down some snapshots to show us and posterity." And there is value, great value in this. He has, through his photographic technique, which is "a very great gift," established himself as a master of the trade. Is it art? By the logic of our view of art, perhaps not contends Forster; but it is vivid, and the master brings it alive, whatever "it is" he chooses to focus on: "I have never been to Gopher Prairie, nor to Nautilus, Zenith or any of their big brothers and sisters," Forster writes, but he has as good have, for Lewis opened to people on his side of the Atlantic the rest of America, the "mud, dust, grass, crops, shops, hotels, railway stations, churches[,] universities, etc." He made the U.S.A. real, not just the cowboys, not just the skyscrapers: "We enjoyed at once the thrills of intimacy and discovery, and for that and much else we are grateful and posterity will echo our gratitude." "Mr. Lewis," the critic concludes, "is a novelist of the instinctive sort." Novelist Forster is taken aback. Indeed, here stands an artist of a different order.[11]

[10] Forster, 6.
[11] Ibid., 1 and 6.

Forster argues Lewis writes with no "superiority and swank (so pleasantly characteristic of the books)…." He offers a close-up take on his subject from an objective stance. His hero was Arrowsmith, and as Martin the scientist, Lewis the author can be classed with "writers termed 'advanced,' with people who prefer truth to comfort, passion to stability, prevention to cure…. His commentary on society is constant, coherent, sincere…." From Main Street through Zenith, all the way to Manhattan, and now with these innocent Dodsworths abroad, the author picks up on a restlessness, "contrives episodes that urge this way or that," and the character under study comes face to face with "a final issue of revolt or acquiescence." But the camera loses its panache. Lewis, Forster regrets, over the years has sacrificed "clear-cut" dissection of episodes and character…too much surface, too little depth. There is little left to ponder. There is little art of the old school. Hence his stance in the limelight is ephemeral—as a fading photograph. Do not expect more of this strength. Unlike older school artists, a cameraman has nothing to fall back upon as storytelling must move on. He is fresh, and he is short-lived. But yes, he is a man of literature—he has given us something new, and it has lasting value. And here Forster finds the key to unlock the riddle—what has happened?[12]

Indeed, Lewis must be classed with "writers termed 'advanced,' with people who prefer truth to comfort, passion to stability, prevention to cure." No, he is not our traditional man of literature. But does it matter? There is posterity, and Lewis is magnificent. Yes: *Dodsworth* does not catch the imagination as the earlier works. But all five together are unimaginably valuable. Forster pushes on; by 1929, "The method remains, but something has died…." But not the works, it appears on closer analysis. Readers have gained a lot: a sincere, close view of themselves. Lewis, as Dodsworth in Zenith, then in Europe, again back in the U.S.A., "trundles" on, summarizes Forster. Their stories are over. Forster has missed, entirely, what the author had been after, what Sam Dodsworth stood for: progress; he, the United States, must have another crack at fulfilling the Promise. Sam; garden communities? Not a lot of punch here—but, Forster declares, Lewis has in fact left behind

[12] Ibid., 6.

a treasure trove: posterity is enriched. Hence, Forster "trundles" to a powerful conclusion: Lewis leaves behind *documents*.[13]

Forster suggests perhaps Lewis will find more to say, but he does not foresee that will occur. The staleness of *Dodsworth* for him says it all. However, Forster predicts Lewis will sit high in the sights of later generations. For "the historian of the future will cease to worry" over the question of art, he will not dismiss him as the critics of his day had done as "superficial." The historian "will pick up the earlier and brighter volumes" within which the author's "genius is enshrined, and will find there not only that genius, but a recording of our age." Lewis loses his spontaneity but not his significance: "If this theory of his development is correct, the later stages of it are bound to be disappointing. However, there the early books are done, safe, mankind's forever, and the longer one lives the less important does 'development' appear." Forster contends what matters is finding our way. This Lewis was after; he offered no resolution, no snap ending. He left the protagonist and the reader hanging. He had not "developed" an ending. But his substantial compendium laid out a story; this is what progress is all about, a storyline. Sinclair Lewis melds literature with history; and Forster espies greatness. For this author, through his work, leaves a rich record of who we were, how we came to be who we are.[14]

All along, the critic surmises, Lewis indeed has a secret store—not to carry forth with his writing, but to pass on to future generations what he had "seen." Forster prowled his way to Lewis's intention all along. Lewis was as much a historian as an artist. His stories become part of the American story. The cameraman, for many the essence of modernity, is not just snapping shots; he is the projectionist, too. The Nobel Committee saw it: Sinclair Lewis as his country was something altogether new.

Forster struggles in his piece. Lewis is not an artist; Lewis is an artist; most importantly, Lewis makes a great contribution, demonstrating art itself always is in play. Foster was not alone in addressing the query at the end of the decade—how does one assess this author?

---

[13] Ibid.

[14] Ibid.

As noted, Ford and Taylor determined Lewis's latest effort was exceptional work—and they appeared to understand more than Forster that Lewis was writing a rich saga. Again, Taylor cuts to the chase; she sees *Dodsworth* is Lewis's "most readable" novel; he attempts to "divine the state of a nation." She concludes "not through mere intelligence" is this accomplished: "*Dodsworth* is stimulating and mobile and tonic, and altogether good for the brain." The British were in Lewis's corner.

American reviewers for the most part praised the work, but did not dig deep as Taylor. A few did, and they were insistent Lewis mattered plenty—of course they did not all agree. H. L. Mencken reading *Dodsworth* argues Lewis had authored a strong work but had forsaken his greatest armament, satire. *Dodsworth*, he charged, too closely resembled *Arrowsmith*, that other serious attempt at art as the elites would have it—it, too, was devoid of what the critic most wanted to hear. Why bother with medicine? He somehow missed *Arrowsmith* was about the entire culture as well as the medical community. Soon enough, however, *Gantry* for him was a colossal achievement...more his fodder. Mencken in his *American Mercury* took on *Dodsworth* and demonstrated just how befuddled all could be over what Lewis was up to throughout the decade. Pretty striking given the general consensus these two "scoffers" were brothers in arms. Nevertheless, Mencken, too, was divining the state of the nation, and he knew Lewis had the same aim—he just couldn't see it in this fifth novel, or its consequential connection with the previous novels.

In "Escape and Return," Mencken, the infamous cynic (still friend of the author but they were drawing apart towards a break), takes a foreshortened view of Lewis's body of work—instead of crediting Lewis for the long view he develops through the five novels, as with *Arrowsmith* he eyes this latest work out-of-place. He likes the dirt and has less patience for the theorizing. "This somewhat somber work, I daresay, will give a great deal of comfort to Lewis's [and his] enemies, who seem to be extremely numerous, especially among rival novelists." His pal gives the elites a feint at their art, but where are the laughs? Fair enough if that was the sole aim; it was not. The novel is not a one-off, and Mencken should be clear on the point—but Lewis gets people in knots. To underscore the Baltimorean's foreshortened view—and he knows Lewis wants significant action, change—Mencken egregiously misinterprets Lewis's goal in the novel: "In brief, what Lewis attempts to do is to depict the disintegration of a marriage." That is like saying with *Babbitt* the author was preoccupied with realtors. Of all criticisms, Mencken so dismissive earlier of the arguments over character in the author's works, now points to Sam and Fran as surface portraitures showing off only "bald externals." He launches a dissection, taking on Lewis the artist, pointing out flaws, as if art suddenly was at issue for him. At the same time, he revels in Lewis's strengths: "There are passages that show Lewis at his best—unctuous, ingenious, penetrating and devastating." "He is, by long odds, the best reporter ever heard of—not, as incompetent critics so often allege, because he is only a reporter, but because he is so much more...." "No novelist in practice among us observes so accurately, or has so vast a talent for putting what he sees into pungent phrases." Mencken knows full well Lewis speaks the language of his audience; readers eagerly peruse what he has to say about them. Mencken relishes the sendups, the satire, the "realism." To highlight the point, the critic with his national following reminds his readers that *Gantry*, awash in satire, had been grand: "There is vastly more than good reporting in such episodes; one senses in them, also, something that is a kind of poetry."[15] So, while not as worthy as *Elmer Gantry*, short on poetry (of all things rarely associated with *Gantry*), the writing in *Dodsworth* "delightfully" hit Lewis's standard targets, and Mencken cheers; just not his style, he wanted more punches. If the elites are pleased, it is no surprise Mencken is not; still, he stands upright supporting his compatriot despite the fact he discounts or totally ignores Lewis's insistent twenties call for action.

The national scold, so sharp at etching the country's fault lines, so supportive of his comrade's decade of work, seemingly had misread the substance of the entire body of work. That is hard to accept; it seems more likely *Dodsworth* just was not what he was after. Lewis is after regeneration, and so is Mencken but that for him is not the storyline that must be told; preferably slashing is more to his liking. In the final

---

[15] H. L. Mencken, "Escape and Return," *American Mercury*, April 1929, 506–08, quoted 506–07.

analysis Mencken makes amends. *Dodsworth* is emblematic of the writer's sojourn: "Lewis's observation is always fresh, trenchant and full of the color of his peculiarly biting and charming personality. Whatever his defects as an explorer of the soul of man, he is at least a master professor of man's behavior." He made "visible the Main Street that all of us knew, and to give a habitation and a name to the Babbitt who was everywhere. He is, in such matters, *facile princeps*. No other contemporary novelist, not even the early Wells, has dredged more memorable stuff out of the illimitable stock of what-everyone-knows." And he does a pitch for art: "The joy of recognition is not the only joy that a work of art can engender, but it is surely one of the most agreeable and satisfying, and Lewis is unsurpassed at evoking it. Put beside him, most other novelists seem to be incarcerated in ivory towers, with the actual world far away." Further, "It is my belief, frequently set forth at length, to the ire alike of sturdy 100% Americans and tender aesthetes, that his work will probably endure, at all events as long as any other fiction of the Coolidge *Aufklärung* endures."[16]

The esteemed, cranky journalist has it right—Lewis, as Forster recognizes, and Mencken as well, snaps a great picture. And it has holding power. His art has a genuine quality, he gets to the nitty-gritty, he spurs recognition. Later generations will recognize its strength. Perhaps Carol and George, as far as satire, represented the author's best work, but they were the building blocks of a study that stretched well beyond a send-up of the folks in the heartland. Lewis, pounding away, was establishing not only the joy of recognition but a challenge to what Mencken feared, as well as Lewis, the endurance of the Coolidge *Aufklärung*. In this light, read across the decade, his "defects as an explorer of the soul of man" shrink away. He is addressing the soul of the country. Mencken, too, lauds Lewis the historian. His work will endure as long as any other literature, and as long as the U.S., endures. He brilliantly concludes: "The opposition to his history, as Lewis sets it forth so magnificently, is psychological, and lies within the cortices of those who voice it so raucously. The trouble with them is that, despite the spread of atheism and antinomianism, they are still authentic

[16] Ibid., 507.

Americanoes, and hence born with a reverence for theologians. It takes at least two generations, and usually three or four, to breed out that folly. The leaders of the anti-Lewis camorra are simply unable to throw it off." They revere an ideal, and they are sore that Lewis attacks it. Americanoes, the reviewers and their like, are not, he attacks, particularly "trustworthy critics of works of art." Give us a few more generations, and the elite bumpkins will catch up with the ordinary Americans also seeking the ideal but a good deal more comfortable with Lewis's exposure of the nitty-gritty. The folks comprehend: "The national talent lies in other directions." Americans do not get caught up in "the false and the true, whether in art or philosophy, but to love and venerate the sweet. The ideal, to them, is always a shade more convincing than the real. If they lacked their gift, then life in the Republic, to most of them, would be unendurable." Mencken is dead set: Sinclair Lewis has caught what the United States is all about, down deep, and why it needs to get to work to be sure it is lasting. Lewis had struck the right chord. Who would have thought Mencken would own up to venerating the sweet American Promise along with the booboisie? Actually, many who read him close surely would not have been surprised.[17]

American readers, in Mencken's estimate, are infatuated with Lewis, the story he unfurls. The booboisie, for all his scathing remarks, are heroic in a genuine American sense—they see Lewis is aiming high, the country is richer for the hunt, for the ideal. The joy of recognition runs deep he prophesizes. Again, posterity will rank the author high. Even more, beyond sharing with Forster the view Lewis's work will count for the ages, Mencken defends the artist of a fresher sort. He does not frame his argument as Forster, but he packs away as much punch: "Lewis has been bathed in more bad criticism than any other novelist of his time and country." He is at base, argues Mencken, that discontented small townsman who looks for a better America, as Carol did in Gopher Prairie, an American possessing "essential rusticity." Lewis he chants, charts the country's maladies through the twenties through those he caricatured. For Mencken, as for many, *Babbitt* remained his best effort—of course, for *Babbitt* was not primarily about George, but about

[17] Ibid., 507–08.

America's spreading rot, and it was the core indictment upon which all the other novels build. Mencken loved the pictures, the grand expose in all its gritty detail. But Lewis reaches for more, he knows. Like Mark Twain, Mencken writes, a "lingering Americanism" haunts him and his works. Twain, too, with all his contradictory impulses, was far from a content man or citizen of the Republic. And here Mencken tries, just as Forster, to make sense then of *Dodsworth*. As Twain, Lewis is entitled to his "intervening"—and "flabby"—"'Dodsworths.'" And, Mencken ends with a salute. He contemplates the likes of Lewis and Twain are on to something as are their countrymen and countrywomen. It is an all-American trait: "The ideal, to them, is always a shade more convincing than the real. If they lacked their gift, then life in the Republic, to most of them, would be unendurable."[18]

Mencken apologizes as he has wandered "into an autopsy on the man, whereas the sole business of a reviewer, if what I hear is true, is with his books."[19] But that, of course, is the issue—Lewis the man was in search of more just as were his characters and the country. Mencken makes no mistake in trying to understand the man—he makes an essential point, even if he missed it in *Dodsworth*, that for Lewis, the human condition was wrapped up in the state of the union. Lewis is tough to get a handle on, but the readers, if even in the abstract, sensed he had it down pat.

Carl Van Doren is more insistent than Mencken there is an underlying continuum of note in the novels. In "Zenith Meets Europe" he is less conflicted about the novel and the artist. Van Doren addresses the positive reception for *Dodsworth*: "Sinclair Lewis, the first satirist of this American age" had reached beyond *Elmer Gantry*; the author writes with "sympathetic insight with which, for the first time, Mr. Lewis follows the workings of a profound, unreasonable, desperate passion in one of his characters." Sam has "a dignity which no other character of Sinclair Lewis has ever had." Van Doren says nothing of Sam and Edith's decision to launch their adventure in America, and he downplays Lewis's multitudinous comparisons between Europe and

---

[18] Ibid., 508.

[19] Ibid.

America. The issue is not for him "what ails the States," it is literature he wants to address, and for art's sake the author is to be commended. Van Doren catches in Sam the larger picture which Lewis's works tried to portray; he may not have grasped the import of Sam's inquiries as to the state of the union, but he plumbs the depths of the author's decade-long intent to get to the knot of the matter. He sighted *art* in a new guise. Lewis probed the human condition against the backdrop of the United States of America, a project in the making.[20]

Van Doren espied the body of twenties work had come into its own. Louis Kronenberger got closer. In "Sinclair Lewis Parts Company With Mr. Babbitt" he declares, "His American Abroad in 'Dodsworth' Is a Bird of Rather Different Feather." "Almost the first thing we are told of Samuel Dodsworth is: 'He was not a Babbitt.'" Lewis sets the reader "on the path to understanding a more complex and more interesting type of American" (albeit Lewis always contended we all are babbitts, but Sam is of a higher order). Sam can only transform himself so far for he possesses "his own peculiar, unmistakable kind of Americanism." Sam represents that "spiritual indigenousness and inbred practical idealism" which will not make him heroic to a tee, but it does make him a better man. Lewis the master sociologist proves "that where Samuel Dodsworth belongs, for better or worse, is in the United States." Of course, that's the story.

Sam lands; so, too, the author. Kronenberg sights: "The interplay of two distinct civilizations...the case for America and the case for Europe, carry the story into that wider sociological field which so interests and so stimulates Lewis's mind." He has traveled far. The work has artistic deficiencies, including repetition—however, that may be essential in that "in a telling way" it contributes to the novel's "solidity and fullness, and gives a kind of emphasis to indicated values which a book of this sort urgently demands." Lewis has lost nothing...satire, focus, an argument, it is all of a package. Kronenberger strikes the right note: the body of work is long in its telling, full of indicative values, urging attention. The final verdict is commanding. The critic does not fully

---

[20] Carl Van Doren, "Zenith Meets Europe," *Nation*, April 3, 1929, 400–01, quoted 400.

grasp the breadth and depth of Lewis's matured interest in "America," but he sees how Lewis has come to this passage:

> Without tackling so genuinely serious and significant a theme as "Arrowsmith," "Dodsworth" is an able book. In approach it is far more humane and unpreconceived than "Main Street" and "Babbitt," to which of Mr. Lewis's other books it is most closely related. Mr. Lewis has learned with time that it is a civilization and not the product of that civilization which should most properly be exposed; the phases of the American spirit and not the habits of an American. In "Babbitt" he proceeded to deal with a type which he understood. In "Dodsworth" he comes to understand it through dealing with it. And by so doing, of course, he comes far more into his own as a novelist, as a creator of individual character and a chronicler of life, without in any way lessening his command over satire and manners. Though working under handicaps of literary equipment, his interest and his knowledge concerning the American scene are great enough to give his work real and valuable meaning."[21]

With this conclusion, Kronenberger gets closer, as do Forster, Mencken, Van Doren; yet, never quite there, any of them. Kronenberger sees no "generally serious and significant theme" as in *Arrowsmith*. This is not right: he writes they all were to a degree preconceived; yes, there is more to the story, all carry forward a singular theme. The repetition is welcome; it contributes, he might say with and through the previous four commanding works, to the novel's "solidity and fullness, and gives a kind of emphasis to indicated values." Indeed, not just one novel, all five solid, full of values. All along, through the twenties, it was about "phases of the American spirit." The fundamental message did not abide solely in *Arrowsmith*—and Kroneberger errs in thinking medicine was the be-all of that novel. A genuinely serious and significant argument runs through all five works: what is to become of the American spirit.

---

[21] Louis Kronenberger, "Sinclair Lewis Parts Company With Mr. Babbitt: His American Abroad in 'Dodsworth' Is a Bird of Rather Different Feather," *New York Times Book Review* March 17, 1929, 2.

Sam is humane, and he is part of a greater story, not in its entirety pre-conceived, but the end goal never was in doubt for the author. Kronenberger concludes that logically Sam comes to understand himself and his American pedigree: "It seems to us that one of the best things about the book is that Mr. Lewis permits logic rather than literary irony to dictate his conclusion." "He has understood and coordinated [Sam], and in the sociological sense (which is Mr. Lewis's ultimate concern) he has oriented him…." Sam, he declares, is a "genuinely important achievement."[22] So, too, the United States, for which Lewis was so profoundly concerned. Sam went home again; he was of the world and in the world. Lewis wanted so much to be like Sam.

One must reckon that if this contemporary critic amidst a select group who dug deep into the writer's intent could get so near cracking the nut, why across a century do students of Lewis, possessing primary documents along with decades of insights, remain hamstrung? Mark Schorer in his treatment of the author makes a passing reference to "Bird of a Different Feather": "Kronenberger lamented the absence of art but approved the substance." This is errant regarding art; worse, Schorer underestimates the substance Kroneberger hailed. Sam came to understand his "American pedigree." Schorer writes, "No reviewers observed the larger significance of *Dodsworth* in the career of Sinclair Lewis and to modern American writing." The mid-twentieth century authority not only cites Kronenberger and misreads him, but draws also on Forster and misreads him. Schorer misses the storyline which ran through all five novels. He argues "Between the end of the war and the beginning of the Depression, a revolution had overtaken American life in manners and morals and all intellectual assumptions, and *Main Street*, *Babbitt*, *Arrowsmith* and *Elmer Gantry*, whatever their aesthetic limitations, had played a major part, probably the major literary part, in the transformation." Schorer lauds Lewis for not his chronicle of the country's passage but shaping its culture. And he overlooks his overarching progressive theme. Lewis he contends refused to cave, retained faith in progress, and he is correct, but with a contradictory twist. Writers, Schorer contends, as Fitzgerald had given up on struggle for a

[22] Ibid.

better order, and at the other extreme were writers with a proletarian bent advocating "revolutionary 'working class' attitudes." Lewis held his literary ground he argues, and then throws out: "In *Dodsworth*, Lewis refused the extremes and turned back to a reassertion of those very middle-class, middle-brow, and Middle Western values that the decade of the twenties seemed to have destroyed forever, and that it had most emphatically modified at least." Lewis turns back? This was his argument all along, and he looked forward. These were the nation's building blocks. Lewis was doing so much more; his eye was not on literary contretemps; he was dead set that a nation in turbulence, adrift in change, must get itself back on track. The novelist, always progressive, advocated take stock and reform—middle-class, middle-brow, and Middle Western values had not been destroyed; he was pushing the country to work them, make them adaptable to twentieth-century challenges. He was not conservative, wishing to turn back the clock; he cherished bedrock values. He was like his protagonists, Carol, George, Martin, and Sam, all adapters. Lewis was mainstream; all his protagonists (of course the Gantry exception) in the twenties took pride in their heritage and worked to keep it current.[23]

Everyone interested in American literature for a hundred years has been trying to determine if the author's work was art, sociology, photography; satire run amuck; a reflection of Lewis's personal foibles, his celebrity—all with no certainty. The vast majority, across the decades, overlooked his deep trust in the American Experiment. What has devolved to a wholesale dismissal of the author by the literary community defies logic. Schorer correctly underscores New Humanists and Proletarian Writers took precedence in the thirties; but so errantly declares Sinclair Lewis "henceforth would seem to be the most old-fashioned of modern American novelists." He was never old fashioned and those who study him should be sure of that.[24]

---

[23] Mark Schorer, *Sinclair Lewis: An American Life* (New York: McGraw-Hill Book Company, 1961), 516–17.

[24] Ibid., 517.

But why did the weakness of his novels after 1929 poison the appraisal of his powerful earlier work? Why, long after the national debacle of the thirties, then the onset of the Second World War, did he remain "old-fashioned?" Naturally, new, "fresher" literary schools took the lead over the next half-century. Still, given the postwar consummation of the triumphant American Century; given the re-commitment to the materialistic values of the twenties of an ever-richer body-politic; given the rise to full-majority stature of a robust middle class; given the ever-flowing social, cultural, economic, and political currents which foster reassessment of the country's values—why do literary scholars continue to miss Lewis's immense value *today*? Posterity's good fortune, Forster argued—a lot of good reading is stored away; unfortunately, in a sense, "stuck in the attic."

That is a good question for those who study literature. They have the training to pursue it. Historians do not miss the connection Lewis has to the ever-rolling here-and-now. Listen to Forster and the others who sensed "lasting worth." Lewis in the twenties was on to a foundational transition in American life; he possessed an instinctive understanding of what awaited the United States in the century ahead. Historians as literary scholars had come after 1930 to dismiss the twenties as "of little account" in the larger history; however as the decades passed, they came to recognize the weight of the twenties, plenty of clues to the nation's progression through the rest of the century. With the postwar development of the field of American Studies, with its emphasis on the riches to be garnered by interdisciplinary study, literary scholars should have awakened to the possibilities of another look at Lewis. Key literary figures of the twentieth century have been revisited, reassessed. Lewis singularly has been left out. Literary scholars should take note of the historian's interest. Schorer wraps up: "He was one of the worst writers in modern American literature, but without his writing one cannot imagine modern American literature. That is because, without his writing, we can hardly imagine ourselves. In at least five solid works—*Main Street*, *Babbitt*, *Arrowsmith*, *Elmer Gantry*, and *Dodsworth*—the endurable core...he gave us a vigorous, perhaps a unique thrust into the imagination of ourselves." Schorer queries, "Could he have consoled himself with this knowledge, had it been his, and he aware?" Probably not—it was not in the author's nature. Still, posterity has been left a gift; Americans can still take full advantage of what Lewis left behind.[25]

[25] Ibid., 813.

TEN

WORDS COUNT

Sinclair Lewis is not old-hat. In the post-World War II decades loads of scholars undertook to study the author. By late-century the numbers were seriously dwindling—disinterest became the hallmark of Lewis Studies. Still, those who persisted demonstrate there is a lot more to be considered.

Late-twentieth century scholars who tackled the author argue this early-century novelist still has heft. Twenty-first century Lewis scholarship, pretty slim, follows their lead; they all make the point words count; Lewis took this tenet as unimpeachable. Yet, in literature classrooms Lewis is barely mentioned, and if so as an aside, or even a snide remark. However, in history, his novels are assigned to be read as primary documents of the 1920s. Students today, a century on, led to read Lewis (or readers who pick up a copy—they remain in publication) of *Main Street*, *Babbitt*, *Elmer Gantry*, *Arrowsmith*, or *Dodsworth* find him current. Historians plumb Lewis; other humanities and social sciences disciplines occasionally draw on his work.

Three collections of literary analyses edited by Lewis scholars attest the novelist ought to be read. Harold Bloom and Martin Bucco published compendiums in the late 1980s. On Lewis's 1987 centenary, literature scholars (and a sprinkling of historians) gathered to reconsider the author; their work was compiled by Michael E. Connaughton. The scholarship the three editors gather together makes a strong case the novelist still commands attention.[1]

Harold Bloom sets about taking a late-century view of the author's "meaning." The scholars to whom he turns are an impressive lot. He initially looks back to the 1920s. T. K. Whipple in "Glass Flowers,

[1] The MLA listing of "Sinclair Lewis" articles runs over 600 entries. Other scholarly compendiums are available, some addressing particular novels.

Waxworks, and the Barnyard Symphonies of Sinclair Lewis" offers a substantive analysis of the author's character and perspectives on life—a first-hand consideration at the novelist's peak.[2] Whipple assesses strengths and weaknesses and Lewis's import to a large audience and the nation. He writes before *Dodsworth* had been published. He traces the road Lewis travelled beyond the prewar novels. Whipple is provocative; surely the scholar would have altered tack if he had had in hand *Dodsworth*. He would have seen more promise; still, his view that Lewis could only go so far proved correct as the author's work diminished in quality after 1929.

Whipple observes, "Sinclair Lewis has said of himself: 'He has only one illusion: that he is not a journalist and "photographic realist' but a stylist whose chief concerns in writing are warmth and lucidity.'" Whipple takes issue with his self-portrait; he tosses in the author as well is no romanticist, no unqualified realist; but yes, a novelist: "Such illusions are not uncommon." He considers the novelist a satirist of the first order, albeit flawed, but he is not or ever will be a consummate artist. He shows he had the potential with *Arrowsmith*. Arrowsmith by escape into the wilderness leaves his protagonist a legitimate hope, something the characters in *Main Street*, *Babbitt*, and the dark *Gantry* do not. "For these folk, who enjoy ample opportunity to do whatever they like and who do not know what to do with themselves, suffer from an obscure but acute dissatisfaction"— as does the nation and Lewis. "No special discernment is needed to detect a self-delineation in Lewis' novels…." Lewis's words count, Whipple contends; yet they spell dissatisfaction. The novelist, he assays, is expert portraying dilemma. He is of huge social importance: his key twenties works to date offer not "a complete portrait of the United States, but he has "rendered more effectively than any one else several of the most conspicuous phases of our civilization." No one "will deny that the United States recognized

[2] T. K. Whipple, "Glass Flowers, Waxworks, and the Barnyard Symphonies of Sinclair Lewis," in *Modern Critical Reviews: Sinclair Lewis*, ed. Harold Bloom (New York: Chelsea House Publishers, 1987), 9–22. The piece is drawn from Whipple's 1928 *Spokesman: Modern Writers and American Life*.

itself in Lewis's portrait, which therefore, though unflattering, may be accepted as on the whole a good likeness."[3]

Whipple argues the writer's acute dissatisfaction with himself and his society is on full display with his, at that moment, latest work *Elmer Gantry*: "Lewis is the most successful critic of American society because he is himself the best proof that his charges are just." He argues he has his personal and professional limits. In all his works, save *Arrowsmith*, he leaves his readers turned against others which only fuels their dissatisfaction (this interpretation is hard to accept). Only Martin has an intuitive grasp of where to turn: "In *Arrowsmith*, his seventh novel, Lewis showed signs of beginning to develop a point of view, an inner standard of measurement"—hope for Martin, hope for himself (those "standards" they all reference). *Gantry* reveals the author unable "to abandon his assumed attitudes and adopt the position proper to the artist, with the self-reliance which can come only from a sense of there being a pivot or point of rest in himself...."[4] Lewis, Whipple asserts, is insufficiently developed as man and artist. *Dodsworth* would have provided him more substantial hope...and possibly a rich reassessment of the author's body of work. As so many, Gantry had clearly discolored the critic's viewpoint.

The critic's reference to dissatisfaction is accurate—it was widespread and lasting after the war. In his view, Lewis's work appeals despite his inability to provide a credible resolution— he voices angst. Whipple probes deep. The novelist is a best-seller; he paints with his satiric brush a revealing portrait of the United States. "In *Main Street* and in *Babbitt* the life of the mind is noticeable only because of the void left unfulfilled"; in *Arrowsmith*, "Lewis has devoted all of a long book to the tribulations of a seeker for truth in the United States and his handling of the theme is masterly." "If in the land which Lewis depicts 'life at its most passionate is but a low-grade infection,' the explanation is not far to seek. This society from the beginning has developed under

[3] Ibid., 9, 14–15.

[4] Ibid., 21–22.

the dominance of one motive: the self-advancement of its separate members." Individualism triumphs; community suffers.[5]

However—for all *Arrowsmith's* strength, the estimable protagonist, too, gives up on community and seeks a hermitage. Then "*Elmer Gantry*"—Lewis has reached dead-end.

> The absence of relief—even comic relief—in *Elmer Gantry* may account for the fact that the book is so difficult to read and, therefore, unfortunately, so much less effective as satire than its predecessors....But perhaps I do *Elmer Gantry* an injustice; possibly the very qualities which make it inferior to *Arrowsmith* and the rest adapt it all the better to the audience at which it is aimed. However that may be, it can be studied with profit as a sociological survey—even if it cannot be read with pleasure as a work of literature—for as a report on the status of what passes as religion in most of the nation it has the virtue of completeness."[6]

The critic concludes the nation's experiment has reached its nadir as has its chronicler. The scholar sees darkness all around.

This is an intriguing critique puzzling out Lewis and his popular draw. Whipple is no fan—but he knows Lewis counts; and the author reflects the scholar's own dismay. Harold Bloom, sixty years on, in pulling together an array of "modern critical views" was smart to lead off with Whipple. Oddly in his introduction to the collection he observes, "Lewis is of very nearly no interest whatsoever to American literary critics of my own generation and younger, so that it seems likely his decline in renown will continue." Why then bother? Why draw together these scholars? Lewis's satire "has no edge in the contemporary United States, where reality is frequently too outrageous for any literary satire to be possible."[7] Bloom, three-score years on, with his expertise in literature and his familiarity with the course of American history since 1929 might have recognized a country hard at work on its own well-being, yet approaching the end of the century reeking

---

[5] Ibid., 11 and 13.

[6] Ibid., 12.

[7] Harold Bloom, introduction to *Modern Critical Reviews: Sinclair Lewis* (New York: Chelsea House Publishers, 1987), 1

"outrageousness," informs a continuum exists—Lewis was prescient. The satire Lewis crafted remains wholly relevant. Satire reigned earlier, and continues to do so. Whipple had the misfortune not to have had the opportunity to read *Dodsworth*. Lewis had achieved a sunnier perch from which to view the country. How did Bloom, with a longer perspective, miss the weight of Lewis's sharp criticisms? The twenties novels are not weak satire; they project serious contemplation; they argue the American Experiment *still* works, but it is hurting. Fortunately, the editor had the good sense to invite an impressive group of scholars who endeavored to make the case for a deep, second look at the author.

Bloom misses what in truth is the robust satire in the last quarter of the twentieth century was no more than what Lewis wrote in the Roaring Twenties. Satire is as American as apple pie, and often reads *au courant*. Bloom grants, "Lewis has considerable historic interest"—why then? He must recognize the novelist detected what makes this country work as well as its shortcomings. Bloom acknowledges *Babbitt's* "winning qualities" and "the surprising *Dodsworth*." Pondering, he considers Lewis " is likely to survive because of his least characteristic, most idealistic novel, *Arrowsmith*." Hence, the scholar picks up on the idealism, the commitment to the American Experiment Lewis expresses? Bloom likes Whipple; he focuses on the development of the individual—George and Martin make sense to him, and Sam is realistic, practical. Lewis he contends was in "search for a truth that could transcend the pragmatics of existence"—this he gets right. In conclusion, Bloom seems at a loss why publish his compendium; but he persists, and in doing so he offers up a cascade of perspectives, trying to "get at" the novelist. Lewis always befuddles.[8]

Harold Bloom smartly chooses an essay on satire which makes the case for the author's lasting relevancy. Contrary to his own view, its author argues, Lewis's satire remains strong in the late-twentieth century. Daniel R. Brown considers "Lewis's Satire—A Negative Emphasis." "It was his satires that made Lewis the most notorious author in the world during his lifetime." He turns to Rebecca West: "To write satire is to perform a miracle. One must hate the world so much that

[8] Ibid.

one's hatred strikes sparks, but one must hate it only because it disappoints one's invincible love of it." West "describes the essential motivation of the satirist and...captures one of the most intriguing facts about the satire of Sinclair Lewis—that is, the characteristic ambivalence toward his subject matter, a paradoxical love and hate for the things he made fun of." Brown reviews the satire across his career in an effort to "clarify some misconceptions which have arisen from looking at his novels separately." Good: study the novels as a compendium. "Satire," he writes, "represents the historical situation." Lewis, considered as a whole, has lasting currency: "It is a serious mistake to dismiss Lewis's novels as charming and quaint books filled with interesting, if outdated, thoughts of American life. His novels give definite insights into the double-think of Americans of the second half of the twentieth century just as they did in the first half of the century." Brown contends the author offered no solution: "Much of the time Lewis did not know what he wanted." This can be debated. Brown, naturally, concedes it provokes its readers, which Lewis saw as a path to resolution. The piece first appeared in 1966, midway in a pivotal decade for a troubled populace. Interestingly, and he is plenty derisive of Lewis, Brown ends, "Sinclair Lewis quite possibly may have a revival if readers once again discover that he captured much that is wrong in American civilization." Brown may not have recognized just how much Lewis *did* know what he wanted, but he captures the arc of his perspective: "Lewis knew the ingrained habits of Americans very well."[9]

Stephen S. Conroy crosses three disciplines examining "Sinclair Lewis's Sociological Imagination." The cultural historian studies the five great twenties novels. "Without question Sinclair Lewis's imaginative frame of reference was sociological."[10] He argues the author knew what he was after and remains current. Twenties critics regularly noted

---

[9] Daniel R. Brown, "Lewis's Satire—A Negative Emphasis" in *Modern Critical Views: Sinclair Lewis*, ed. Harold Bloom (New York: Chelsea House Publishers, 1987), 51–62; quoted 51–52, 54, and 62.

[10] Stephen S. Conroy, "Sinclair Lewis's Sociological Imagination" in *Modern Critical Views: Sinclair Lewis*, ed. Harold Bloom (New York: Chelsea House Publishers, 1987), 71–82; quoted 72.

the strength of Lewis's sociology. Conroy conceives Lewis's novels revolve around the attempts of his protagonists to remake society and to be broken by it, forced by power of conformity to adjust; or escape to a hermitage; or be autonomous, step outside society and take or dismiss elements as one wishes. The historian recognizes the wealth to be tapped in interdisciplinary study and hits pay-dirt; he considers the body of work holistically conceived.

Conroy contends through *Dodsworth* Lewis reaches as far as he can wherein "his hero finds the most satisfactory answer to the demands of his culture. Dodsworth, a good man, will return to familiar ground, but he will be autonomous within it….[H]e will add to his culture and try to change it for the better." He remains in the world but not fully of it. "This is also Lewis's most optimistic novel of the twenties, for it shows him in good measure reconciled to his culture….American civilization can be lived in, Lewis at last affirms, if only one knows how."[11] The scholar considers Lewis as Dodsworth at peace with the U.S.A. and argues his remaining work demonstrates it. This is a strong argument regarding the twenties work; Conroy's take on the later decades output flies off track. He is dead right Lewis believed the individual can thrive within civilization "if one knows how." Lewis tried hard. However, the argument he had become reconciled to his lot, and the country's, as he wrote on to his death two decades later is errant.

Lewis, the scholar paradoxically attests, had come to an early stop; for two decades he repeats the plots and resolutions. Not one novel was fresh—there was "no way out of Lewis's artistic dilemma." He claims Lewis accepts his culture in the sense he will autonomously pick and choose what he wants from it, and he will find a means to add to it, to refine it; hence Sam as opposed to Martin. Good point; however, the idea the novelist had reconciled with society, found a sort of contentment amidst its shortcomings, and he was satisfied with his later decades on-again-off-again quality of writing is totally off-base. That he had made an autonomous, successful stand, is mistaken—more to the point, he struggles on. Lewis in all likelihood was as satisfied as he

[11] Ibid., 81.

could be in 1929: Possibly he did trust the U.S. seemed in a relatively promising spot; he was, and the projection would be plausible. But there is a caveat: Lewis seemed considerably unhappy for a good portion his final decades.

Conroy correctly concludes, "The sociological imagination of Sinclair Lewis, grasping the cultural setting of American life, seeing the drama inherent in the struggle of an individual with his society, and working out in dramatic fashion the possibilities for individual response…is responsible in no small part for the very real worth of the products of Lewis's great decade. But on the other hand, the limited nature of this sort of imagination is also responsible for the sense of *déjà vu* one cannot escape…."[12] How true…in this Conroy is on-spot.

Interestingly regarding Conroy's view that Lewis had reached a plateau of contentment with *Dodsworth*, *World So Wide*, the novelist's posthumous work published soon after his death, offers up another story-line which Conroy somehow misreads. The Dodsworths crop up again, in Europe, two decades on. The novel itself had little to say to interest readers or critics, and the Dodsworths had nothing to add; the author was hardly in the driver's seat, he was running on empty; the couple in all certainty were "filler." If anything, if Lewis meant to let them have a last say, it had to have been remorse: the couple, forever sailing back and forth across the Atlantic are totally adrift, not much to their lives. To add to the novel's generally pessimistic outlook, *World So Wide* starts out with a horrible car crash; a young couple's promising future ends with the wife's death (at least it was not a Revelation). One indeed can make the case Lewis had positioned himself to "autonomously pick and choose" what he would write about, but following 1929 he generally had little to say.

Howell Daniels takes a sharper look at the Dodsworths in "Sinclair Lewis and the Drama of Dissociation." Turning to *World So Wide* he focuses on Sam and Edith as they "reappear as permanent expatriates

[12] Ibid., 82.

in Florence."[13] Right off the bat, Daniels missteps. The Dodsworths never permanently settled on either side of the Atlantic. Nevertheless, Daniels is right, they attain no contentment. And there is more. He observes, as Forster, Mencken, and Whipple had deduced back at the end of the twenties, Lewis could only go so far.

Daniels, Secretary of the Institute of United States Studies at the University of London and a literary scholar, wrote the piece in 1971. He hardly is in Lewis's corner: "The quality of his prose is generally poor, he wrote too much and too quickly, and no writer of this century with claims upon our attention can have published so many short stories of little consequence....Cumulatively, it may be held, his writings testify to an emotional immaturity, an intellectual imprecision and a moral fuzziness." Surprisingly then Daniels in this assessment grants there is something of value in studying a washout: "Yet the best of his novels continue to find new readers...." "[I]f ever a novelist defined a decade and in turn was defined by it then that novelist was Sinclair Lewis and the decade the 1920s." For all his mediocre work, all his limitations, the dismissed novelist continues, for Daniels, to carry a hefty punch. He remains of considerable interest. Daniels provokes, and he confuses the story.[14]

Daniels reflects the challenge Lewis represents. He plumbs the twenties work. He studies disassociation whereby Lewis's characters "must resort to fantasy in order to come to terms with or escape from their society." He evaluates *Main Street*, *Babbitt*, and *Dodsworth*, his "best works of the nineteen twenties." The three demonstrate "the essential pattern...discontent, escape, compromise or defeat." (Odd not to count in *Arrowsmith*.) The protagonists fall short. Daniels probes the ever-present quest in Lewis's work and life: "The hotel rooms and rented houses of two continents suggest that the most permanent form of dissociation is to be found not in his writings but in Sinclair Lewis himself." Yet, "[E]ven in the last year of his life Lewis could say that

[13] Howell Daniels, "Sinclair Lewis and the Drama of Dissociation," in *Modern Critical Views: Sinclair Lewis*, ed. Harold Bloom (New York: Chelsea House Publishers, 1987), 83–102; quoted 99.

[14] Ibid., 83–84.

he loved America still for its promises but he did not like it." He was attached, and detached, a writer at a loss. He embodied, again, "the essential pattern"— discontent, escape, compromise, defeat. He writes of the twenties; he clung to *that* American Promise. Daniels digs out Lewis's 1935 introduction to *Selected Short Stories*: "[He] who has been labelled a 'satirist' and a 'realist,' is actually a romantic medievalist of the most romantic sort." Carol, George, Martin, Elmer, and Sam, and all their compatriots, and Lewis, writes Daniels "tend to be individuals continuously in a state of self-creation, seeking a humanity which their creator is perhaps incapable of providing." Or Daniels points out, speaking of *Main Street*, and projected onto the other four best-sellers, the author's America is "haunted by the consciousness of the past" and, unrequited, "a confidence for the future." The "myth of the frontier" plays "the major role" in his work—and, it cannot be consummated, yet again out of reach in the twentieth-century. Daniels attributes this emptiness for Lewis to "the basic failure of historical insight."[15]

Not the usual charge against the novelist.... Daniels helps to piece together the Lewis conundrum. However, he heavily errs in arguing an absence of historical insight. Lewis picks up on the Promise, the Experiment—isn't that why he remains of value? One hundred years on, that perspective still grabs readers, set against the satire the author so richly provides. Didn't Forster and others in his own day attest to it? Daniels notes Lewis and his first wife Grace once explained *Main Street* "was intended to illustrate Carol's learning 'the great secret in life of being content with a real world in which it is never possible to create an ideal setting.'" Contentment is not Lewis's strong suit. Still, knowing he cannot reach the ideal, he always will stay in the game, push on. Daniels sums up: "The final choice for America," the author asserts, is 'its nearness to the earth.'" In the end, he argues, Lewis could only offer an incomplete attempt "to translate the virtues of an heroic age into contemporary terms."[16] Indeed: at the end, it all comes down to the mundane, to garden communities he might have queried? Be that as it may, Daniels makes no mention of this, but it is relevant to the scholar's

---

[15] Ibid., 86–87,102, 83, and 89–90.

[16] Ibid., 90 and 99–100.

argument. He is mistaken to argue Lewis's fantasy, there were new frontiers, was an antiquated ideal. Daniels fully grasps it is back to grass roots, but totally misses it has nothing to do with resurrecting older times or the insinuation Lewis was blind to the draw of the American Promise. The past is cherished; do not ignore it as the country progresses. The novelist was a contemporary man with a modern point of view. The scholar calls out Lewis for falling short as an artist, but indisputably as an historian he holds his own—again, odd in that the optimism he clings to is missed by this critic who works in an institution stressing American Studies. Lewis got the idea, it all was an experiment—or if one wishes, fantasy. The ideal threads through all the works. The "frontier myth" he believes, remains vital.

Daniels makes strong points, but gets it mixed up. Lewis holds on with a possibly hapless but respectable confidence he *can* sort it out. He has a strong sense of the historic trajectory; and yes, he is a romantic: "The effect of this persistent romantic strain in Lewis's imagination is that characters, who generally speaking have no sense of history, must resort to fantasy in order to come to terms with or escape from their society."[17] Again, the essence of the "Myth of the Frontier." To the contrary his primary protagonists in the twenties novels, even Elmer, have a sense of history—romanticism perhaps feeds it. Sam argues for history aplenty; the nation's progressive track runs throughout the novel. And he and Edith "believed"; so, too, the author: "[E]ven in the last year of his life Lewis could say that he loved America still for its promises but he did not like it." Sounds like American pragmatism, which always has something of the romantic to it?[18]

Yes, Lewis the romantic. Martin Light in "Dodsworth: The Quixotic Hero" observes the novelist by the end of the twenties had "evolved a way to fuse, in one man, the thinker and the builder, the sensitive artist and the practical realist. From this point Lewis must seek new attitudes, new perceptions of life, or forever repeat himself." And he will fail. Light observes the novelist close to death was at work and, "At sixty-one years of age he was still perplexed...." He acknowledges by

[17] Ibid., 86.

[18] Ibid., 83.

1929 he could go no further in his thinking and art; but Lewis had landed in a good enough spot. Dodsworth "knows that his dissatisfaction with America is also a deep dissatisfaction with himself." Of all his characters the scholar points out the author is most akin to Sam. Light gets Dodsworth: "Not since *Main Street* and *Babbitt* has a character in Lewis's fiction been so deeply disturbed, so torn among values, so ready for that conflict of person and society which can result in character growth and change."[19] Sam, for all his struggles, seems sufficiently strong to make a worthy stab back in the United States at fixing things. The novel leaves the reader with a strong faith Dodsworth will succeed. But this is the last word. Light perceives the reader is left hanging. And the novelist: Lewis could not build on the optimism—that does not discount its faith it can be done. Lewis was Sam: disturbed, seeking growth and change, and he was a realist.[20]

Readers, Light contends, are left in 1929, at the end of the novel, despite the admission of dissatisfaction, with this optimistic protagonist. "The last chapters of *Dodsworth* contain…some of the best nonsatiric passages Lewis ever wrote—and his best conclusion of a novel." Still, the novel, so strong, demonstrates the author remains innocent, immature, stilted: "In keeping with his ideas about the strength of the pioneers and the influence of the west wind," Lewis like Sam finds a new calm, but ultimately is simply becalmed. And beyond that, he can never again evoke that sense of peace, of resolution. Upon what does Light base this conclusion about Sam Dodsworth? It cannot be the final words in the novel—overjoyed, he and Edith are going home, to have an adventure. The pair are riding high. Perhaps Light (he makes no reference to their depressing cameo twenty years later) might have referenced *World So Wide* and argued whatever they felt at the end of the twenties, it would be a temporary calm. As for Lewis, yes, he was becalmed, at loose ends at the end of the decade; and he saw himself in Sam. Pioneers, west winds, Light seems to surmise there has to be more

---

[20] Martin Light, "Dodsworth: The Quixotic Hero," in Modern Critical Views: Sinclair Lewis, ed. Harold Bloom (New York: Chelsea House Publishers, 1987), 119–26; quoted 126 and 122

to it. There is. Light did catch there were in the story, not only in the final chapters but throughout, some of Lewis' "best non-satiric passages." The novelist was working hard, always working hard. And yes, maybe there is that *Don Quixote* in his work.[21]

Light gets the novelist had come to the end of the trail. Hardly a "calm," and hardly lasting, but...Dodsworth is his most sturdy protagonist. The scholar queries how any critic could miss that the novel is "one of Lewis's highest achievements." Some of the deficiencies of his heroes, as those of Martin and Sam, "were intended to indicate that typically American heroes 'bumble' and 'clump' as well as stride." Ultimately, "Whatever Lewis wished to leave to the world as the message of the doers, he left best in *Dodsworth*...."[22] Martin Light gets the final word in this collection. There were limits to the American Promise, but what else could one do but give it a further go? Lewis to a "T."

Martin Bucco, in *Critical Essays on Sinclair Lewis*, takes another tack in his compilation. He assembles a rich cross-section of reviews, essays, posthumous tributes, and bibliography. "Even during Lewis's lifetime, critics agreed that he had achieved his best work during the 1920s; then, the Marxists found nothing in his erraticism, the Freudians nothing in his psychology, and the New Critics nothing in his form." All along the author baffles: "[M]ost contemporary critics acknowledge Lewis's ambivalence, his confusion and misdirection. They acknowledge the clash between Lewis the social critic and Lewis the dreamy romantic, between Lewis the novelist and Lewis the journalist, between Lewis the artist and Lewis the entertainer. To some he remains a keen writer of surfaces, to others a supreme fabulist."[23]

Bucco observes by the mid-thirties "more reviewers seemed to adopt Forster's insight"—Lewis was in imminent decline. He does not

---

[21] Ibid., 124–25.

[22] Ibid., 126. Light wrote *The Quixotic Vision of Sinclair Lewis* (West Lafayette: Purdue University Press, 1975), which contains this piece; he also edited *Studies in Babbitt*.

[23] Martin Bucco, introduction to *Critical Essays on Sinclair Lewis* (Boston: G.K. Hall & Co., 1986), 1–27; quoted, 1.

mention that differing from the thirties critics the British author thought Lewis a formidable novelist of the twenties. Lewis could not progress; he will regress as a relevant commentator—but he would leave riches for historians. Forster predicted the definitions of art will be irrelevant—the success of the novelist will endure. Bucco, however, is right where he points how critics found something was missing: "Most reviewers agreed that Lewis ran fast—but the world ran faster." In a twist, Bucco draws on Philip Wylie's 1945 *American Mercury* observation that Lewis's latest work "displays reel after reel of new film in the old technique." Wylie was reviewing *Cass Timberline*—600,000 sold that year; the author appeared, as he once had in the twenties, on the cover of *Time Magazine.* The long-running twenties tale may have become stunted, but the core story was vital. Popular interest remained. Bucco recognizes the novel was "far from his best." It was certainly far from 1929; depression and war had changed the U.S. And yet, using the old method, Lewis once again, for Wylie and Bucco, had served up something new. Not really: *Cass Timberline*, published just at war's end, amidst celebrating and angst as to the future, smacked of nostalgia—and what readers (and movie-goers soon enough) were catching was a tribute to well-grounded (exemplified in Cass's Middle West identity) all-American values—the American Promise still beckoned.[24]

There was another take on the novelist that year which stands as a complement to Wylie's perspective. A lot had changed, but there was something in the aging author to be embraced. Bucco digs deeper; he points out Edmund Wilson praised Lewis in the *New Yorker* in October, 1945 as current. In "Salute to an Old Landmark," eminent critic Wilson located much of what Lewis had considered relevant in the twenties still so—he had he said conjured a fresher read on the author. Wilson wrote in a trying year; for all the relief of the recent victory World War II left the nation uneasy, the future uncertain. Lewis by Wilson's reading elicited wholesome nostalgia with *Cass Timberlane.* The critic believed he spoke for others as he sketched a welcome reminder of who we really were all along. The author spoke well of the United States, its heritage, in *Cass Timberlane*; what he had drawn out

---

[24] Ibid., 7 and 10.

with particular power in the 1920s was still seminal as the country faces big challenges. Lewis always was attuned to rock-bottom values. Praising those traditional values, he was not pushing nostalgia; the citizenry respected his viewpoint; he gave them promise; the author was a progressive. If Bucco had read Forster right (or at all), this was in the cards all along. Lewis would retain his relevancy decades on owing to the foundation he laid in the twenties. "His decade" had concluded; his contribution paid dividends.

Six years later the novelist was dead, but even at the disheveled end Bucco recollects he had one last novel: "At best, reviewers read the posthumous *World So Wide* (1951) as the valedictory of a once-gifted writer." The reviews legitimately were far from effusive; the novel was poor work. Still, the scholar acknowledges Lewis displayed residual credibility. He notes writer and critic Serge Hughes a few months after Lewis died ran a retrospective, "From Main Street to the World So Wide." Looking long back he declared Lewis a disappointment as a storyteller; but he had his strengths. "[T]he novelist's treatment of moral issues far surpassed his solutions." Well, whatever the last novel's flaws, Hughes perceives what the novelist had always been after.[25]

Bucco's final statement indicates, distant from Harold Bloom's dismissive prediction of justifiable, growing disinterest, that he is conscious of Lewis's worth. Bucco concludes "a surprising number of scholars and critics continue to delve into and speculate on the life and writings of this strangely compelling figure in American literature."[26] In drawing forth his compilation, Martin Bucco wishes to gather a sense of what they are finding: "[M]ost contemporary critics acknowledge Lewis's ambivalence, his confusion and misdirection"—but in their quandaries, they find Lewis remains instructive.

---

[25] Ibid., 11–12. *The Times Literary Supplement*, writes Bucco, "regretted the publication" of *World So Wide*. See "Craft and Contrivance" (October 1951), 625. Serge Hughes, "From Main Street to the World So Wide," *Commonweal* (April 6, 1951), 648–50.

[26] Bucco, 17.

The editor prefaces the latest analyses with reviews of the author's work through 1951, setting a strong context for the essays. Two take readers back decades, reflecting the roiling waters within which Lewis tried to stay afloat. In January, 1933, Bernard DeVoto in *Saturday Review of Literature* weighed in. It was the trough of the Depression, the nadir of what would amount to a decade-long catastrophe. DeVoto, historian and editor, reflects despair as he condemns the author to the waste bin: "The truth is that Sinclair Lewis is a warring marriage, a divided soul, a novelist and a satirist forever at each other's throats." He is rough: "He has made his way through the American scene with a naïveté, a simplicity of point of view, a limpidity, and even a shallowness which it is now time to pronounce invincible." DeVoto on the other hand grants qualified due: "He becomes a flaming hate, and out of that hate he has written the most vigorous sociological fiction of our time, in America or anywhere else." He reviews *Ann Vickers*, the tale of an inveterate Progressive Era reformer "that gets things done in the world," and he admires Lewis's writing is at its best in this 1933 novel. But *Ann Vickers* amidst the debris of the Great Depression is totally irrelevant, Devoto argues. He discounts the hope, pragmatism, the optimism which ran through the novelist's work. He reads the novel right: *Ann Vickers* the protagonist is all "can-do"; one would think not a bad reminder for a country on the ropes. But the hour had grown late. For DeVoto Vickers is a relic, as well the author: "Sinclair Lewis was shaped by the Herbert Croly age in American thinking—the pioneer era in Greenwich Village, the days of generous, idealistic thinking about the future in America, the last generation of American hope." Progressivism was no antidote for a country blown off its tracks. Still, for all his faults Lewis "is nevertheless the best novelist of his generation in America. He knows America better than any of the others...."—and those twenties writers he despairs were a poor bunch. What does it matter—the twenties? It is another day: "The shadow of a period is already on Lewis...." His and his generation's optimism must give way in a dark age to "methods more rigorous and ideas more skeptical." The past decade is well past, and so is Lewis: "There you have him. Too much a satirist, too defective a technician, too limited by the intellectual emotional clichés of his generation, too naïve and too earnest...."

DeVoto in all his back-and-forth is consistent in his determination that despite the author's expertise on the twenties Lewis is to be ignored.[27]

Bucco then jumps ahead to Edmund Wilson's piece. In 1945, in a considerably altered environment, Edmund Wilson publishes his "Salute to an Old Landmark." Wilson, as previously noted, reviews *Cass Timberlane*. The critic has returned from war-wracked Europe, he is unsettled; he finds the postwar U.S.A. awash in new priorities, altered values, and angst. He admires the novel's strength, resonant with midwestern values, a place "really lived in and loved." It renews the spirit. It is not Lewis's "hated" Gopher Prairie and his "ridiculed" Zenith, writes Wilson: "[T]he book made me feel, when I read it, that I was back in touch with home again and made me realize that Sinclair Lewis, in spite of his notorious faults, is one of the people in the literary field who do create interest and value, that he has still gone on working at this when many others have broken down or quit, and that he is, in fact, at his best—what I never quite believed before—one of the national poets." Hence, well beyond depression and the nightmare of war, Wilson as DeVoto earlier on reflects where the country stands in each critic's own "moment." The review must have pepped up Lewis. Wilson argues Lewis no longer is hateful, ridiculing as in the twenties. All is well—"morning in America" one might say. No matter: As much as Wilson applauded *Cass Timberlane* for its rich dose of nostalgia, it is, after all, 1945, and Lewis is writing the same old stuff. Hardly a resolution—isn't that always the nub of the matter? Perhaps not at all—Wilson taps into something he sees of great importance. With *Cass Timberline*, as in the past Lewis has reminded his country it has the wherewithal, the heritage, to take charge of itself and its destiny. Nostalgia for *that* is a tonic. Lewis's perspective has merit: "We have had Lewis around, for so long, so consistently being himself, that he has become a familiar object, like Henry Ford or the Statue of Liberty,

---

[27] Bernard DeVoto, "Sinclair Lewis" in *Critical Essays on Sinclair Lewis*, ed. Martin Bucco. (Boston: G. K. Hall & Co., 1986), 57–60. *Saturday Review of Literature* (January 28, 1933): 398 and 59.

about which, if one has been living in America, one does not think very much." Wilson surmises it is time to take stock.[28]

All Bucco's wisely assembled essayists try to get a bead on the "old landmark." Lewis's work, taken at its own value must be revisited: after all, as Forster declared in 1922, the author had lodged "a piece of a continent in our imaginations." National poet or not, Bucco's scholars in consensus trumpet it remains essential to grasp what does Lewis see, what he does know about the United States of America, what he teaches us today. As an icon of a past literary era, he brings much to the table—in both a literary and historical sense. His body of work—especially his twenties masterpieces—are a testimony to the American Promise; as Wilson declared back in 1945, the author effectively argues "in spite of his notorious faults" the United States is a work in progress.

George J. Becker in "Sinclair Lewis: Apostle to the Philistines," first published in 1952, the year following the novelist's death, makes the case the author retains his significance. He revealed much about the nation's underside as it came of age in the first half of the century—and it is not a matter simply of his best novels written in the 1920s. "Sinclair Lewis was filled with crusading zeal. His attack on contemporary society was overt, tireless and hyperbolic. For thirty years, he lambasted, cajoled, ridiculed and threatened without arriving at any definitive diagnosis of what was wrong with his country or his countrymen. All his life, he was seeking the cause of the multiple malaise which he encountered everywhere. He never isolated the virus, although some of his novels filtered very fine." Nicely put, although he did diagnose with precision in the Roaring Twenties. Becker, as often with those studying Lewis, gets in a tangle. Dismissing what most contend, the novelist for the most part had lost his incisive touch after the twenties, Becker correctly estimates he was still onto the American story in his last twenty years. As the nation rapidly distanced itself from the New Era, perhaps he did not run as fast, but his take on what counts in the

---

[28] Edmund Wilson, "Salute to an Old Landmark in *Critical Essays on Sinclair Lewis*, ed. Martin Bucco (Boston: G. K. Hall & Co., 1986), 71–74; quoted 72. *New Yorker* (13 October 1945), 101–04. "Morning in America" was the iconic pitch of the 1984 Reagan re-election campaign.

United States bore repetition. Becker has a misleading caveat: the novelist ran amuck, and that was okay; Becker says he ran about "without indicating specifically what he wanted done." He errs. Again, Lewis's diagnosis all along had been comprehensive; and in effect he offered no specific antidote to the virus but he articulated what he wanted done: stay true to the American Experiment. Becker adroitly sees, "In any event, it is the amplitude of his evaluation, rather than its profundity, which makes him a significant figure in America's coming of age." Huge numbers of citizens read his work; Lewis "played a strong and decisive part in shaping constructive changes." He took on the shoddy civilization, the myths and the tyrannies of business; he spotted the oppressiveness of work itself; he sensed and wrote more than once about chauvinism limiting women. "[H]e found himself amazingly at home in the broad depiction and sweeping denunciation of a whole way of life."[29]

Lewis lacked, argues Becker, nuance, an interest in or means to find a way out. He errs once again; he was plenty interested in both. Becker misses out on Lewis's extraordinary faith in the U.S. finding that way. And the scholar, as is the custom of Lewis critics, seems at loose ends as to how to assess the author's gifts and baggage. For all he argues in Lewis's favor, he believes his satiric writing and poorly developed characters "discredit the novels as criticisms of society….[We] lose sight of the social matrix which forms these human caricatures and find it impossible to believe that they are typical products of that matrix, even though we adopt their names as household words."[30] Hold on—they became household words *because* his renditions, his caricatures, his novels were a means for envisioning that matrix. That Lewis could not resolve the dilemma whole is one matter; that he vividly portrayed it as a whole counts a lot. Becker claims the author helped the nation to understand itself, to come of age—right.

---

[29] George J. Becker, "Sinclair Lewis: Apostle to the Philistines" in *Critical Essays on Sinclair Lewis*, ed. Martin Bucco (Boston: G. K. Hall & Co., 1986), 104–11; quoted 104–05. Originally *American Scholar* 21 (Autumn 1952): 423–32.

[30] Ibid., 108.

Always, however, it is easy to get tangled up in knots. Becker discounts the strength of Lewis's social criticism and his writing; at the same time he signals something important might be missed: "It is interesting, therefore, to find that *Dodsworth* (1929), in which Lewis succeeds in creating a more credible human being, also comes more nearly to grips with those problems of our society which trouble him." Sam, a spirited American, a regenerated pioneer, can give it a genuine try. But Sam was no anomaly—Becker should see he'd been in the works for the whole decade. Sam may not have had a sweeping resolution to society's conundrums, but as those flimsily sketched caricatures as Becker puts it, he perceives a truth: "Sam Dodsworth…is a vindication of his country's promise." He is not Carol, Martin, nor any of the others…he, too, is a work in progress, but he is also something more, he has been "filtered very fine." America is crude, but Sam, renewed, as his country, demonstrates "American life can be a richer amalgam." Sam's adventure, argues Becker, is "the American adventure." In 1930, with his recognition by the Swedish Academy, "Lewis was beginning to give closer and more thoughtful scrutiny to the problems with which he was concerned." No—he had all along been maturing as an observer of American life.[31]

Dodsworth was not an awakening—it was, however, the last of Lewis's most perceptive work and all power to Becker for seeing it. The novelist would have little to add, with two significant exceptions. *Dodsworth* was the effective summing up of all Lewis had tried to probe about his country in the twenties. Surprisingly, Becker locates a growth spurt in the thirties and forties that no one else espies. He concludes Lewis demonstrated he was on to a resolution as he fleshes it out in 1935 with *It Can't Happen Here*. He argues the novelist begins to mature with *Dodsworth*—truly an isolated position amongst Lewis scholars; no one considers the mid-thirties best-seller a sign of maturation. But they admire the work. *It Can't Happen Here* came out in the early stretch of the long decline; it was the anomaly; it was current, a distressing angle on a frightened middle-class America, written as fascism rises overseas and threatens at home. It was not a strongly written

[31] Ibid., 109.

novel, but it packed a powerful message; it raised the alarm, American values were under dystopian siege. The horror Lewis long had feared could in this moment demonstrably take root in the U.S. The theme resonated strongly with the public and the critics. And within that context, in that stirring novel, Lewis did indeed reiterate what he had argued all along: stick with the Experiment, take stock of the Promise. It was a clarion call; the novel's huge success harked back to the years Lewis had been so immediately in touch. After this momentary burst of currency, Lewis in the following years was back to the post-1929 long-toothed themes, unimpressive if occasionally well-written novels. It is important to note that Lewis's sensitivity to the 1930s fascist threat abroad and at home was principally due to his marriage to Dorothy Thompson, the esteemed, pioneering feminist journalist deep into foreign and domestic affairs.[32]

While Becker badly missteps observing *It Can't Happen Here* representative of the novelist's purported post-*Dodsworth* meteoric trajectory, he gets close in understanding what the novel said about the author by a surprising misinterpretation. He gets close to what Lewis propounded all along. But he slights credit to the author for his deep convictions. Becker argues when Lewis describes what will save America in 1935, the protagonist Doremus Jessup "is characterized by the author in terms not applicable to himself." No, a big misstep—Lewis, as he identified with Sam, with Carol, Babbitt, and Arrowsmith, casts his lot with Doremus. He writes of his fumbling, kindly, worried protagonist: "[F]ar from being a left-wing radical, he was at most a mild, rather indolent and somewhat sentimental Liberal...." "Democracy in this country," writes Becker, for Doremus is bedrock—it "has given the ordinary man more dignity than he has ever had elsewhere, but he is not blind to repressive and authoritarian tendencies...." Doremus recognizes there will never "be a state of society which will come anywhere near to perfection." Doremus states, "More and more, as I think about history, I am convinced that everything that is worth while in the world

[32] Lewis in the late forties would address one more current issue with great power. While not his best writing, as Becker recognizes, *Kingsblood Royal* courageously took on racism.

has been accomplished by the free, inquiring, critical spirit, and that the preservation of this spirit is more important than any social system whatsoever." Doremus's faith, like Lewis's, was grounded: "[F]or all cruelty and intolerance, and for the contempt of the fortunate for the unfortunate, he had not mere dislike but testy hatred."[33]

Becker argues Lewis, weak in caricature, unnecessarily satiric "never really had to channel his thought or subject himself to the discipline of a narrow focus." Correct in that he never intended to squeeze his perspective. His eye was disciplined and his view broad. And yes, if you will, he "narrowed" in on what for him counted. Becker might have discerned Lewis was dredging out a widening channel with a clear end in sight. He thought broadly, knew what he was doing in '20, '22, '25, '27, '29, and 1935—the U.S. at its core held a promise. Perhaps it is good to read Becker in *his* context—a key tenet of history. The scholar was writing in 1952 as the nation was threatened with a distorted fear of enemies within amongst real foes without, and as well was starting to address racism (clearly a pointed interest of the critic, alluding to the issue often). The bevy of concerns may well have distorted his take on Lewis (another tenet of the historian, avoid presentism). Becker notes Lewis "always in the back of his mind" beheld that his characters fell short: "the biting reminder that the half-men whom he pictured were not those promised to this Eden—that when the pioneering fathers sailed in thought and aspiration to the far Hesperides, it was a vision of the transcendent man that led them on." Lewis had abandoned that scheme by leaving Martin huddled in the woods. Here was the catch: there was not, could not be a singular transcendent hero. That man or woman would have to be more down-to-earth. So Becker notes the novelist rises to maturity in his writing, *starting* with *Dodsworth*. "Sam Dodsworth…is a vindication of his country's promise." As Becker concludes, "Lewis seemed to discern what his countrymen at large must learn if they are to survive and flourish: growth, though organic, is not automatic." Exactly—what Sam had come to understand. Dodsworth—the end story which had run through the twenties, by way of Carol, George, Martin, and Elmer. Lewis—by Becker's reckoning,

---

[33] Ibid., 110–11.

matured, takes the lead from Sam, his insights soar. Lewis, in Becker's take, arrives at the heights. In 1935 he sights in *It Can't Happen Here*, "yes, we can." Doremus is common enough, and in the end, holding a gun, on the run, in the wilderness, eyeing Fascism in full form, he is transformed literally into a minuteman. "Perhaps Lewis should have learned this sooner." No; he had. Becker, amidst the chaos of the McCarthy Red Scare, clearly feeling the nation at grave risk, sees this novel as the height of Lewis's career. It is the scholar who has taken the "narrow" view. Lewis perceived in those twenties novels the United States was in grave straits. After all he wrote of the Fascist danger from its earliest days. One surely suspects McCarthyism, the rage when he died, was infuriating for the old line progressive.[34]

Becker still teaches a lot. There is reason for lasting interest in Lewis, an author considered an eccentric: hard to peg, easy to quibble with, adept at striking resonant chords, and perplexing. Becker misreads his trajectory but captures the essence of what drove the long narrative. D. J. Dooley in a lengthy account of the genesis and completion of *Arrowsmith* writes of the twenties works, "The systematic nature of Lewis's assault on American life is obvious enough....[A] character standing for a constructive way of life is pitted against representatives of everything restrictive, narrow, hypocritical, wasteful, and stupid in society." Lewis progresses, protagonists take on increasing depth "clearer in their ideas, stronger in their beliefs, and more uncompromising in their positions." But what exactly is the position? Dooley contends in "Aspiration and Enslavement" Lewis even with the estimable *Arrowsmith* "left his standards still in question." Critics and purportedly readers required more. Dooley finds the novelist still "would have to produce a hero registering his notion of the desirable"—more optimism, more of a direction—that old bugaboo *standards*. Ironically,

---

[34] Ibid., 111. Becker also discusses Lewis's 1947 *Kingsblood Royal.* Here again, the author in the final decades could demonstrate a strong sense of what was in the air; the novel takes on racism in stunning terms, if not particularly well written. Its publication fits Becker's theory Lewis is at the top of his game starting with *Dodsworth*, getting him to 1935, and twelve years later *au currant.*

many of those who personally and professionally knew the author well never questioned his standards, albeit they recognized his shortcomings in personal and professional relations. It is curious what a persistent issue this remained; fighting for rock-solid, long-heralded virtues never was enough; a resolute conclusion was mandatory. Hadn't the novelist hammered home with the end of each novel that virtue, albeit challenged, remained a proud standard to unfurl?[35]

Martin is a character "sympathetic to the author." The problem, Dooley contends, is that Lewis is deficient in what it takes to be heroic, and the novel, for all its strengths, is mangled. "In showing what had happened in one field of endeavor, Lewis was describing the failure of the epic dream: America had aspired to be a nation of free individuals, but the worship of material success by the many had forced the few independent spirits to turn their backs on their fellow men."[36] This is spot-on, not mangled. Indeed, the novelist was no hero. He worshipped material success, and he was sorely compromised by it. Martin had been corrupted and ultimately struggled back to get a more righteous bearing; he ends side-lined, his work attacked; lonely in this world, he flees. Martin was the most ambitious character Lewis created. He could relate to Martin's disillusionment, but he *never* could sever himself off from society. Martin, he recognized, did fall short, for what could he accomplish in the woods? This end, argues Dooley, will not work for the readers, and of course it could not for the country. Right in that the author held up no viable, singular resolution. Dooley is wrong though to charge Lewis had no standards; he does, and so, too Martin (and his other protagonists, albeit not the scoundrel Elmer—the exception proves the rule). There is no way out; he was honest with his readers and himself; so he portrayed the good doctor Arrowsmith, not holding in hand *the answer* but perpetually *at work*. Classic Lewis, everyone, as he, is left hanging. Martin, of course, has not given up on his mythic quest. He has not given up on the U.S.A. Lewis knows

[35] D.J. Dooley, "Aspiration and Enslavement" in *Critical Essays on Sinclair Lewis*, ed. Martin Bucco (Boston: G. K. Hall & Co., 1986), 136–50; quoted 136–37.

[36] Ibid., 142 and 146.

fleeing is not a practical response; in the "real world" he himself would carry on, make his standards work within the world the best he could. Too bad Dooley did not consider *Dodsworth*, Lewis' most optimistic take on what one individual *might* accomplish. *Arrowsmith* would be seen as a significantly successful step forward, but does not *Dodsworth* make the case?

Lewis confounds. It's a long-running tale. Back in the twenties, long before John Farrar reviewed *Babbitt* and took Lewis's measure; disappointed, he concluded he had "fallen." "So Main Street, the insulted and injured, has won out after all. It has taken Lewis into its materialistic camp. It has made him worship, against his surface will, perhaps, its own kind of success.... The 'bigger and better bug' has bitten him." Farrar queried, "Is he strong enough to overcome it, or will Main Street's revenge be lasting?" Farrar recognized the author's dilemma even as he curiously missed the damning message in *Babbitt*—and he doubted Lewis's reserves. Lewis, he was correct, never could break free. Farrar concludes he was "the slayer caught in his own mesh, the tamer tamed."[37] Of course, as the decade persisted, Farrar would recalculate that conclusion. Enslavement (as Dooley would have it), but Farrar misses the aspiration Dooley sights would remain intact. Contrary to Farrar's 1922 prediction, in the seven years ahead the author worked hard to break loose, and *Arrowsmith* evinces it. Finally with *Dodsworth*, Lewis believed he had created a bolder soul, one who could remain of the world *and* establish himself an enviable distance from it. Contrary to the critic's view of *Babbitt* and for that matter Dooley's take on *Arrowsmith*, Lewis may well have become entrapped in the culture, he could not make the heroic leap, but he could still reach for an escape from the malaise. He projected himself into his work, but he was never caricaturing himself in a negative light. "In showing what had happened in one field of endeavor, Lewis was describing the failure of the epic dream" sells Lewis short. Martin was part of that running saga. Lewis was a believer.

---

[37] John Farrar, "The Literary Spotlight," *Bookman*, September, 1922; www.unz.com.

Dooley in dissecting *Arrowsmith* digs back reading critic and historian Carl Van Doren's 1933 *Sinclair Lewis: A Biographical Sketch* to pursue the conundrum...what is Lewis up to? He is wise to do so, but he fumbles. Van Doren suggests, "Leather-Stocking and Daniel Boone had in the eighteenth century turned away from the corrupted settlements to be themselves beyond the tumult of mankind." Van Doren spotted "a familiar American pattern of behavior." Into the wilds, but those wilds were retreating, and in the process the Leather-Stockings and the Boones, occasionally confronted with society will have their say, model strong standards. But they were up against progress as it takes its American course. Dooley turns to author and literary critic Maxwell Geismar who in 1949 studying Lewis found Martin Arrowsmith representative of dissent—"perhaps the most vital element in American democracy."[38] The problem, of course, Dooley considers is one cannot find a "refuge from the modern world" that is rational.[39] Martin, scientist, pioneer, *dissenter*, in the twentieth-century is not up to sparring within the world; but in a world so complicated, to which he will not return, what difference could he make? Lewis knew it; and yes, he knew himself. And he knew while he could not escape, he still could bang a drum of his own. Hence, ultimately down the pike the best he could offer—and he was fine—was Sam Dodsworth. Lewis had not fallen short with *Arrowsmith*; Dooley misses he had taken a large step forward toward grounding his soundest protagonist, with his standards, back home, in his real world.

Dooley quotes Warren Beck, another Lewis scholar, who as Geismar in the 1940s homes in on Martin: "He has run off not only with many a reader but with his author, for in glorifying *Arrowsmith* as scientist Lewis seems unaware of what a crude and lopsided human being he

---

[38] Dooley, 146. Carl Van Doren, *Sinclair Lewis: A Biographical Sketch* (Garden City NJ: Doubleday, Duran, 1933). Maxwell Geismar, *The Last of the Provincials: The American Novel: 1915–1925* (Boston: Houghton Mifflin, 1949).

[39] Dooley, 149, endnote 25.

had made of him."[40] Martin, toiling in the wilderness, cannot assist a world in need, he must remain in the twentieth-century milieu if he is going to be successful. The novelist is well aware his protagonist is crude, lopsided (as is he, and he knows it well)—but to dismiss him, as Beck does, as somehow made that way because of science, this would never do for Lewis. He admires Martin's scientific bent; the doctor knows what is up; but he can only go this far. Too bad Martin cannot find the means to "make it work." Dooley sides with Warren Beck, where are Lewis's standards? Intact: He admires medicine, he is aware Martin is a flawed man. But he is a good man. Lewis must drum away, he has his standards; *and* the author stays in his "twentieth-century milieu"—after all, he has done a forceful expose of medicine and science in the early twentieth century. And Martin, in critical and public measure, was hailed as a worthy idealist. For *Dooley*, Lewis fails to satisfy his readers. His final line on *Arrowsmith* reads: "In spite of the excellence of much of the satire and the author's success in fusing satire and novel, [*Arrowsmith*] shows that Lewis could not...give a satisfactory exposition of values." Yes he could; he was a dissenter—American to the core.[41]

James Lea in "Sinclair Lewis and the Implied America" strikes an engaging note that the novelist knew his history; yet at the same time Lea muddles that understanding, where it led. Writing in *Clio*, kudos are in order for this literary scholar's appreciation of the writer's grasp of the country's heritage. Lea however missteps arguing Lewis's work "implied America," that he made feints the country still had promise. The author all along was underscoring the point. The scholar for all his strengths of analysis struggles setting straight Lewis's historical perspective and its significance to his work while making pertinent observations as to just what he was writing all along.

"That Sinclair Lewis recorded the social history of a major sector of the American population in the first third of the twentieth century is a generally accepted literary maxim.... Especially during the decade of the Twenties, the mirror which his novels held up to the material

[40] Ibid., 148. Warren Beck, "How Good is Sinclair Lewis," *College English* 9 (January1948): 173–80.

[41] Dooley, 148.

crassness and spiritual befuddlement of middle-class Americans established Lewis as a forceful cultural commentator, a best-selling novelist and the darling even of those whom he damned." Lewis must be held up as "one of the country's most astute social critics." Lea, however, gets tangled up in the weeds when he declares, "Sinclair Lewis wrote—or, we should say created—another sort of American history as well." He explains: "In the work of most social satirists, criticism of the contemporary world derives in large part from the writer's assumption that there was, or is, or could be a better world. Lewis assumed that there *had been* a better world, or at least a better America, and that his twentieth century had betrayed the potential for freedom and productive happiness implicit in the people, life, and very land itself of eighteenth- and nineteenth-century America." Lea argues disillusionment trumps all, it is "the tonal foundation of Lewis's major works"; the promise has devolved to "America that has been, and that by extension could be, but is being perverted."[42] Reclaiming this promise he contends is a muted affair for the author—"Sinclair Lewis and the *Implied* America." But this is not so: for Lewis it was a matter of carrying on, revivifying that pioneer spirit that had made the United States what it still can be—he had never given up on the nation's history and destiny. Lewis never minces words through his twenties masterpieces—even *Gantry* cries for salvation—the novelist never was creating another history; he had in his hands the genuine article.

Lea studies a number of novels and reads with a keen eye. He assesses *Dodsworth* and concludes all Lewis's novels devolve into disappointment. He catches the pessimistic ending of *Babbitt* where "there is a quiet note of hope as Babbitt encourages his son" to follow his own star; but it is forlorn as "Babbitt disappears again into the crowd of faces—mindless behind their smiles—of Americans who have severed themselves from history." The reader knows, or at least senses, the end of this story: George's star is falling fast, and Ted's is shooting off in a curious direction; disillusionment justifiably hovers for Lea. But

[42] James Lea, "Sinclair Lewis and the Implied America," in *Critical Essays on Sinclair Lewis*, ed. Martin Bucco (Boston: G. K. Hall & Co., 1986), 184–96; quoted 184–85. Originally *Clio* 3 (October, 1973), 21–34.

George had been, to his credit, trying to take a more promising road—there is at least that for the reader who seeks encouragement; and Seneca Doane made the powerful argument for the country's promise. Earlier, Carol's is not a story of pure disappointment; she hails the country's promise, too. Martin carries forth. And then there is Sam. As it goes, they grasp "The March of History."

Lea takes the wrong track that *all* the novels end in disappointment. He does state that *Dodsworth* "moves in a milieu in which the historical past, Lewis's 'Implied America,' plays a significant role." And Lewis has arrived at something important: "Arrowsmith is characterized as Lewis may have characterized himself: a solitary and beleaguered spiritual survivor of the frontier past." But then, "Dodsworth is another admirable frontiersman who has outlived his time." No, Lea is wrong here; Sam won't accept that, nor Lewis—they both are of their time, they both, unlike Martin, are in for the long run, living within the world, fully cognizant of a promising past that can be made present. Pioneering is not lost; it may have as all along taken on a new coloration, but it is still a current coursing through the body politic. Carol knew she was pioneering; George tried to kid himself; Sam in spades makes the case. Even Martin out in the woods is still a believer. There is no break with the past. *Two histories* are not at work. Lea himself argues, "Dodsworth at age fifty is an analogical national soul who has experienced the rigors of regional and industrial pioneering and now—like America in the 1920s—stands at the threshold of a new spiritual frontier and a new self-perception." Yes—one history; Sam sees himself, justifiably, still a pioneer. Lea then turns his argument inside out as he argues it is one history: "Fully aware of his failings, he learns to revel in being 'a most American American.' After despair and self-denunciation, Sam can gloat 'I am real!'" Lea assesses Lewis has projected his "new" historical perspective towards the decades ahead, deep into the twentieth century. The author does not bewail a severed past—definitively for him, there are not two histories at work. It is all of a piece—Sam makes the case he knows what the people know...we can do this.[43]

[43] Ibid., 190–91 and 193–94.

Lea espies in the work up to *Dodsworth* something different. By the end of the book Sam looks determinably forward, anything but disillusioned as Lea argues were those past protagonists who represent the loss of hope in the citizenry. Why, then, argue despairingly, Sam has "outlived his time?" Why claim in the end there is disillusionment? Lewis's earlier protagonists, as Sam, were hobbled; they tried to break out, break away from despair; Sam seemingly succeeds. Not running to the wilderness; rather he and Edith return to Zenith. Where is the "tonal disappointment?" "Lewis assumed that there *had been* a better world...." Yes, but he never questions there still could be. Something is archly amiss in this analysis: Lea argues Lewis sees hope; if one is fully familiar with the trajectory the author has navigated through the 1920s this is not surprising. Nor should it be that he clings with "more passion" to Sam Dodsworth. Hope builds. This had been the story all along: Progress ensues. Sinclair Lewis was taking history's measure; through his novels he was underscoring promise. Sam has not "outlived his time." He does not break from history; he charges, influenced by that history, into the future. One has to wonder what the historians reading *Clio* make of Lee's case for two histories.

To make the analysis more confounding, Lea contends Sam is a "post-pioneer American." He is hardly Babbitt and those "Americans who have severed themselves from history." But he is Babbitt; Lewis makes the claim for himself. The citizenry can and does take stock of its pioneer roots; he and Babbitt do. No history breaks into two. Dodsworth retains a frontiersman's stance, self-built and retooled for the twentieth century. Lea suggests, as all the pioneers, Sam remains an innocent of sorts. So American, right? Carol, George, Martin—all possess an innocence which Lewis and his readership are drawn to. Sam is, too, a dynamo—an embodiment of American twentieth-century progress. He is not finished as he fears: he explores, he rediscovers he has plenty of energy to expend, he can put to work his wholesome can-do talents in the here-and-now, and do something not only for himself but for his country. Lea knows Sam has his limits; but Sam is no post-pioneer. With his garden communities, his plans for the future—which surprisingly Lea takes no note of—he'll start at the bottom, build up, as he always had done, as his country had progressed all along. Grass roots, very American. Recall, he does envision as he retires but contemplates staying with the big corporation which has swallowed him up not the end of his run in Zenith, but the possibility of building a city on a hill—a better Detroit. The course of history runs through his veins. Funny Lea misses this when he concludes Lewis's "vision ranged backward to the beginning and forward to the unknown but hopeful future"; Lewis "planted himself squarely in the twentieth century"; "he warned his readers to look carefully upon these pioneers, for what they did and saw and said would count for something" in the years ahead—their "optimism and expectancy and the nearly equal potentialities for glory and for ruin" were theirs to make history.[44]

Lea glimpses Lewis was making the direct connection, a unique past leading to a singularly promising future. Lewis was trying to convince his readers in the twentieth century they, too, could be frontiersmen. Dodsworth disillusioned; one more novel mired in tonal disappointment? This is a tangle for sure, as Lea relates it, but not one Lewis devised. Making strong points the scholar reads the novel for the most part well; but the premise two histories is corrupt. Americans as Lewis could forge "another sort of American history" which carries on the same, invigorating story—but it is the real thing, not another. Funnily Lea declares, "*Main Street, Babbitt, Arrowsmith*, and *Gantry* and *Dodsworth*, written amidst the fury of the decade in which they were set, described the harvest which the twentieth century was reaping from its own reckless tending of the national garden." Exactly: Carol Kennicott was going to bring beauty, gardens to Gopher Prairie; Sam is out to plant garden communities; America, a new Eden, the Puritans, Martin tangling with a world he cannot be of, he cannot live in, heads for the pastoral woods. Lewis tells one story, reflects one history. No one has severed themselves from the past. Lea at the outset argues "the theme of Lewis's serious books is disillusionment."[45] Not at all—Sam's "homecoming" demonstrates the *tonal* foundation across the works (always with the arguable exception of *Elmer Gantry*) is optimistic. Sam and Edith end taking off back to America on an "adventure." Why, all

[44] Ibid., 194–95.

[45] Ibid., 195–96 and 185.

along, queries Sam, can't the country? Of the five masterpieces of the 1920s, this final say by far is the most forward-thinking, taking the string of novels, and in Lewis's view the United States of America, to a resolute, albeit knotty, always distant end.

Cultural historian Stephen Conroy crops up once more. As in the piece Bloom had included in his collection, Conroy crosses disciplines. Having written "Sinclair Lewis's Sociological Imagination," he takes a second look at the author and a crack at literary traditionalists in "Popular Artists and Elite Standards."[46] *Art* again, but with a more contemporary twist—just what Forster predicted: historians generations on will understand. Lewis provides posterity with a rich gift.

Conroy questions what eats at literary critics; they discount the novelist's credentials as well as other "truly popular artists who happen to be gifted…." He takes on the "exacting standards of the critical aristocracy" not mincing words: "Its Calvinistic division of the world of art into a small group of the saved and a large mass of the damned not only arrogantly dismisses much of true worth, it also results in confusing arguments about writers along the borderline. Sinclair Lewis was not Henry James, yet he was a writer of real distinction. There are a considerable number of authors of comparable stature." He sets out arguing a close read "will lead to meaningful conclusions." "High culture criticism tends to make a dichotomy out of what surely is a spectrum." "Sinclair Lewis is a particularly dramatic example of a marginal writer, one whose acceptance by the public has been high but whose reception by the critics has been mixed." The critics are "white and elite." Conroy clearly is a late-twentieth century historian. "Classbound standards prove to be of limited usefulness in evaluating the careers of writers such as Mark Twain and Sinclair Lewis who were more than (or less than) serious writers of fiction." Of the points he raises, and some are debatable, most compelling is the scholar's view a popular writer of Lewis's stature seeks a wide audience. Yes for the monetary rewards, and the adulation, but more significantly because it is part of his

---

[46] Stephen S. Conroy "Popular Artists and Elite Standards," in *Critical Essays on Sinclair Lewis*, ed. Martin Bucco (Boston: G. K. Hall & Co., 1986), 197–203.

makeup as an artist and, while Conroy does not explicitly say so, for Lewis a concerned citizen. He admires the writer: "He reaches out to the people; he does not callously try to exploit them." The critics he condemns heartily too often hold themselves aloof to the middle class. The author identified himself a babbitt, he thought we all for the most part are babbitts. Lewis takes pride in America's middle class. And the American people, American integrity; he reaches out to his fellow citizens, his equals; he argues if they worked hard toward a more promising future we all come out ahead. Conroy knows what Sinclair Lewis and the millions to whom he spoke were after; the novelist had a gift for common sense.[47]

David G. Pugh in "Baedekers, Babbitry, and Baudelaire" considers the novelist of considerable interest to students. *Babbitt* reveals "the spirit and unspoken assumptions of an era." "[I]s the image of George F. Babbitt, Realtor, still this encapsulated shorthand?" By 1975, the year Pugh published, he questions if Lewis's coinage of Babbitt and Main Street as mainstays in the American discourse still carried some cachet, still popped up in magazines, newspaper columns, social commentaries. (They did and they still do). But this does not matter. Students recognize Babbitt as a living entity. Students, he knows, consider these old-fashioned terms. But students embrace *Babbitt*. Pugh argues over a half century later *Babbitt* still resonates. "Literature is not so much a mirror which *reflects* life realistically as it is a prism or lens which *refracts* selected, condensed aspects of thought and feeling." Explaining why *Babbitt* still works, he queries whether a late-twentieth century reader could catch "some sense of the actual knowledge of the world possessed by the readers at the time of original composition or publication—knowing that it is, indeed, an impossible dream to evoke 100% of it." How rich would that be—actual knowledge as readers of the day took it? He argues it is possible for readers today to catch the drift, and profit from it, for George's "values live on." Lewis's work is a treasure trove. "Any work that has staying power transcends" the limitations passing decades impose. "This refraction exaggerates, as does a convex

[47]Ibid., 197 and 203. Writing for and to the middle class—a reminder of Updike.

mirror such as a shiny chrome hubcap...." Still, it "offers enough internal clues of tone and context to remain intelligible...." One has to hand it to Pugh, keeping that gleam of the automobile Babbitt so loved front-and-center. "How do you tell photographic realism from the satirical warping of the shiny hubcap?" Pugh concedes, "[S]atiric exaggeration, the shaping by genre and formal technique, by literary convention" intensifies and orders our experiences. But how well does that translate, wear scores of years on? What remains of the author's intent? Lewis was, as Forster spotted, something new: an expert cameraman. So yes, his intent to picture America has not tarnished; the satire is taken for what it is: exaggerated, funny, and thought-provoking. Sinclair Lewis wears well with students one hundred years on.[48]

Pugh is a literary scholar. He argues a student needs guidance—he debates what might work and how in the classroom—and herein the historian, *vis a vis* Lewis, by way of Pugh's reasoning, clearly finds him or herself in an advantageous position. The historian, attempting to transmit "what was up" in the Roaring Twenties, capitalizes on Lewis's works. Pugh raises challenging questions for those who teach literature. He never folds in historians, but his analysis makes the point the thoughtful pedagogue has great narrative power. "The ultimate question, then, for investing time and energy in reading...is whether or not the plastic terms, the technique and surface texture of the novels, clear in their own epoch, can transmit to a later time a feeling about values, ennui, a wasteland or a wasted life." Literature instructors have their benchmarks; historians theirs. Pugh queries, "Do the details we notice in reading *order* and *intensify* our own experience(s)?" Literary specialists must speak for themselves; for historians, addressing whether novels can do the job, the answer is resoundingly positive. They read that in their student's absorption in Lewis's novels. Pugh points out what most readers in the twenties and since recognize: the futility of Babbitt's faith in his son's progress. "It is a whimper of and for the main character and the society in the novel...." This strikes home to the

[48] David G. Pugh, "Baedekers, Babbitry, and Baudelaire," in *Critical Essays on Sinclair Lewis*, ed. Martin Bucco (Boston: G. K. Hall & Co., 1986), 204–13, quoted 204 and 206–07.

young. Pugh steps ahead: "How does Lewis show us How We Live Today?" "To make this possible requires revivifying, recreating some of the era of 1910–1922 and of attitudes toward spiritual wastelands and backyard ash heaps then, and also requires paralleling those ash heaps from our own experiences." One uses all tools at hand—students, reading Sinclair Lewis, learn how that works. The thoughtful pedagogue—the historian—with great narrative power constructs the contest.[49]

Historians embrace Lewis. Literary scholars should take note. Those five twenties novels add to the discussion, to the study of the author, of literature of its day, of one continuing American story. Ask any twentieth-century cultural historian; better yet, ask students why they appreciate reading literature in their history courses. The works they read, if relevant, strike true for them. Words count: to say so is hardly a revolutionary act—*the word* has long established itself as a powerful instrument to convey *truths*. Those who value literature, those who study history know their power. Lewis showcases it. As some in his own day foresaw, the novelist's writing would carry its weight to generations ahead. In the decades since the cited collections made their case, Lewis scholars keep at it. There is substantive evidence future Lewis students, deeper into the twenty-first century, will find so much more to say about the author.

[49] Ibid., 212–13. A student charged into my office long ago "jazzed" on Babbitt: "Damn," he declared, "this book is about my dad!" He went on to be a high school history teacher in Kansas.

ELEVEN

A FINAL AUDIT

Mark Schorer published *Sinclair Lewis: A Collection of Critical Essays* a quarter of a century earlier than Bloom and Bucco. In his introduction he writes, "Generally speaking, the writings of Sinclair Lewis have almost never been the subject of serious criticism."[1] This is peculiar given the scholar had just completed the classic biography that incorporated the work of a host of critiques and offered a plethora of his own insights. So be it: There had been no shortage of critiques; but yes, the greater interest without question was significantly to wane. Still, as the eighties compilations indicate, there is plenty to contemplate. In 1985, scholars gathered in Minnesota; Michael Connaughton gathered their takes in *Sinclair Lewis at 100: Papers Presented at a Centennial Conference*. Selected essays demonstrate not only strong research and writing but a sensitivity that history matters. And beyond 1985, strong, provocative analyses of Sinclair Lewis, his work, his contribution steadily crop up. Some spell out the connection between the two disciplines. Lewis, it must never be forgotten, had tremendous respect for historians—as much so or perhaps more than many in his area of expertise, literature.

Sally E. Parry in *Dodsworth* and *World So Wide:* Sinclair Lewis's European/American Dilemma" sums up: "He was a believer in the American dream and all it signifies in terms of the ideals of American democracy—life, liberty, and particularly the pursuit of happiness." He sagely sighted shortcomings: "In his most successful novels Lewis's ironic effects are the result of his realistic presentation of American life

[1] Mark Schorer, ed., *Sinclair Lewis: A Collection of Critical Essays* (Englewood Cliffs: Prentice-Hall, 1962), 1.

in the context of American ideals." Parry takes a closer look at Lewis's last twenties novel and his posthumous 1951 publication.[2]

Parry understands *Dodsworth.* She wrestles with the idea that Lewis, through Sam, sought out a negotiable resolution to his American Dilemma: "This middle ground which Sam hopes to locate is symbolized by the Sans Souci Gardens, a housing development which he hopes will combine the American know-how of building and modern appliances with the precepts of good architecture and decoration from both Europe and America."[3] She argues there is ambiguity in the end: Can Sam make his new life; can he escape his American trap; will the trap close on him yet again? She contends given Lewis's treatment of Europe in his remaining novels, he seems to have concluded the Old World as bedeviled as the U.S.A. White America remained the standard-bearer for all that was possible in the world. Corruption is the culprit—at base materialism runs rampant and spells doom. The U.S.'s shortcomings ooze around the globe. Lewis loses faith, too, in the children—Carol's, George's, and Sam's offspring are not up to the challenge. Some twenty years on Sam and Edith reappear, as Lewis at mid-century beaten: the Dodsworths in *World So Wide* are shells of their can-do selves,

The Lewis specialist suggests the author to an extent is rewriting *Dodsworth*, reflecting disappointment in what Sam failed to achieve back home. Sam's self-pitying profile twenty years later, then, signifies Lewis's own shaky faith in himself and his country. Sam and Edith, as the author, bounce back and forth across the Atlantic in search of a *home* they long for and will never possess; Lewis dies in Italy, one last stop, seeking a safe port. But they say little, as Lewis has nothing to add They carry no heft; they are, after all, just cameos in the novel.

---

[2] Sally E. Parry, "*Dodsworth* and World So Wide: Sinclair Lewis's European/American Dilemma" in *Sinclair Lewis at 100: Papers Presented at a Centennial Conference*, comp. Michael Connaughton (St. Cloud, MN: St. Cloud State University, 1985), 27–34; quoted 28. Parry led for decades the Sinclair Lewis Society based at Illinois State University. The Society is a strong resource for scholars.

[3] Ibid., 30.

Parry espies a glimmer of hope in that the considerably younger protagonist in *World So Wide*, regenerated by his faith in the American Spirit, may fulfill the author's dream and the country's. She argues the novel is a facile work with a facile conclusion, "wishful thinking" at the end of a life, in the novelist's estimation, of wasted opportunities.[4] This youth's promise has little more chance of fulfillment than had Ted Babbitt's. Parry prizes *Dodsworth* as powerful; *World So Wide* is so weak one cannot put stock in it other than to take the measure of the artist's collapse.

Lewis was well aware of the country's faults; the protagonist Hayden Chart cannot resolve the dilemma. Parry argues the novelist at this late date could not confront his loss of faith yet weakly clung to optimism. What would he be left with had he not? Decades earlier with *Dodsworth* he maintained a trust in himself and the United States. The scholar claims he had been by the end of the twenties considerably more honest psychologically and emotionally. Two decades later, it is hard to face reality—"his true feelings." There is no resolution; Parry judges his heart was not in it, he was beat, just as George had once decried his plight. In the end, Dorothy Thompson, his long-divorced second wife, observed the man she knew was "a disappointed democrat." That is the bottom line. Sally Parry knows her subject well. To write about Lewis you need to know the whole story.[5]

W. Gordon Milne in "Lewis's Muted Influence as Artist and Social Commentator" expresses less faith in Lewis's view of the United States all along. "Can a novelist successfully combine social commentary with a skillful technique, or is he inclined to neglect his artistry in pursuit of the 'sociological' picture?" Sizing the novelist up against other writers commenting on the passing scene, he judges Lewis comes up short. Milne demonstrates a strong grasp of Lewis's attempts to understand, deconstruct, and categorize American society and culture. He is overwhelmingly dismissive of his artistry as he discounts it and gives it weight as well (again the contradictions and tangles in Lewis criticism). "What Lewis objects to, in sum, is the oppressively

[4] Ibid., 33.

[5] Ibid.

conventionalized nature of American society, the pressures which prevent one from being a liberal, an individualist, even a simple 'man of good will.'" But the prose, he claims, weakens the argument: "It is difficult to overlook the many weaknesses, for they militate against the staying power of his work." The scholar condemns success, over-kill for clogging Lewis's novels—then explains this is why he always was so readable and remains so. That the author still retains staying power convolutedly is testified to by Milne as he in conclusion reconsiders: "Perhaps we can conclude that Lewis should be read and re-read—after all." For after all, "[S]till his survey of American life passing into a new social order in the twenties and thereafter is a valuable one...." What is one to conclude? Milne is conflicted and unconvincing.[6]

David D. Anderson specializes in heartland twenties writers. In "Sinclair Lewis and the Midwestern Tradition," he is more sensitive to how much Lewis mattered and for that reason still is of import. He recalls the address of Erik Axel Karlfeldt, Permanent Secretary of the Swedish Academy on the occasion of the Nobel decision. Controversy swirled about Lewis's prize: "Yes, Sinclair Lewis is an American. He writes the new language—American.... He asks us to consider that this nation is not yet finished or melted down; that it is still in the turbulent years of adolescence." Surely to Lewis's delight, the Secretary declared: "He has the manners of a pioneer. He is a new builder." Anderson adds, "Whitman and certainly Mark Twain would recognize Lewis's people—or more properly his character-types...." People may be dull, shallow, but perhaps this at base is why they are in the author's opinions "essentially likable, even good." In sum, "Throughout his career and even yet Lewis remains the great paradoxical figure in our literary history."[7]

---

[6] W. Gordon Milne, "Lewis's Muted Influence as Artist and Social Commentator" in *Sinclair Lewis at 100: Papers Presented at a Centennial Conference*, comp. Michael Connaughton (St. Cloud, MN: St. Cloud State University, 1985), 87–93; quoted 87, 90, and 93.

[7] David D. Anderson, "Sinclair Lewis and the Midwestern Tradition" in *Sinclair Lewis at 100: Papers Presented at a Centennial Conference*, comp.

Anderson contends American Literature cannot be fully considered without taking Lewis's formidable measure…"I think, for reasons that are psychological, sociological, and historical rather than literary—qualities that, I suspect, are the sources of his continued popularity…." Lewis dug deeper than he has been credited for by literary elites: "For Lewis's people, the twin images—the shining path and the mournful face, the dream become reality and the faint howls of psychic wolves—compete in the arena of Gopher Prairie, of Zenith, of the world beyond." America's Promise was never easy: "The new dream, however near it may be to reality, threatens to become a nightmare for Lewis's people, just as it had for their fathers who had been threatened by earlier, more literal horrors…." America marches on: "Lewis's twentieth-century nightmare is neither grotesque nor horrifying; it is, like his people, terrifyingly ordinary, at once both glittering with material promise and more spiritually bankrupt than they can imagine." Perhaps we all are "the ultimate culmination of an ambiguous dream in an inevitable American pragmatic reality."[8]

Anderson has a solid grip on Lewis and a firm handle on United States history. He concludes the author had seen the end story: There are no new frontiers, no resolution. Lewis was right: his babbitts are not bad people, we are not. Gloomily, one must surmise the promise they and their descendants still cling to has degenerated into a dulling mediocrity, their lives a mess of diminishing hopes; it is their misfortune, deep down, that they sense it: "Lewis's people live their lives as tragicomic players reading lines they don't understand in a play that baffles them before a set that threatens to overwhelm them." So, too his readers: "But they go on, in determined dignity to the end that has been written for them, to await reviews that can only be mixed." They see themselves in Lewis's novels. Whether that was Lewis's aim, that pessimistic, to offer little light ahead is debatable—Nevertheless, the scholar leaves one a lot to ponder. Anderson knows his literature, knows his history, his country (and writes exceedingly well). He sees

---

Michael Connaughton (St. Cloud, MN: St. Cloud State University, 1985), 253–65; quoted 255 and 257–59.

[8] Ibid., 258 and 260–61.

Lewis a prescient chronicler of the nation's deteriorating trek through the twentieth century. And he recognizes the author's continuing draw: he continues to read well because he remains timely. In this concluding piece in this centennial collection, in the last lines, David Anderson sums up, "Lewis was not a great writer, nor perhaps was he good enough to win the Nobel Prize in literature.... But we continue to remember and read Lewis, and the best of his works, those that have added words to our language, those that give us greater insight into the moral shortcomings of our times and ourselves, those that define the victimization of the individual in a mass society, deserve better of us than we have been willing to give."[9]

Michael Connaughton wisely ends the retrospective with Anderson's testimony to the novelist's longevity: "Lewis remains the great paradoxical figure in our literary history." Perhaps, he might have added Lewis all along proves out the ironies of the American Experiment. Connaughton, giving Anderson the last word, encourages further weigh-ins must continue. And since that centennial conference, others add perspectives. Three articles of particular interest are Martin Light, "The 'Poetry and Tragedy' of the Car in Sinclair Lewis's Novels" published in 1989; Thorunn Ruga McCoy, "Dodsworth's Revelation: Motoring Toward Self," published ten years on; and Paul-Vincent McInnes's early-twenty-first century "Surviving Modernity: Sinclair Lewis and the 1920s."[10]

---

[9] Ibid., 263–64.

[10] Others always will gravitate to Lewis. Political Scientist Steven Michels, *Sinclair Lewis and American Democracy* (Lanham, MD: Lexington Books, 2017) concludes, "Lewis remains a secondary figure in American literature but deserves to be read more widely than he is...." The analysis has weaknesses; still, the scholar covers Lewis's entire career and makes the case for social and political insights. "[H]is voice is needed somewhat desperately"; his "midwestern upbringing perfectly situated him to understand the American experiment, but he found it wanting...;" "Each book serves as a piece of a greater whole.... " See vii, ix, and xii. Within Midwestern History Lewis carries weight. See *The American Midwest: Essays on Regional History*, eds. Andrew R.L. Cayton and Susan E. Gray (Bloomington: Indiana University Press, 2001). Especially read "The Story of the Midwest: An Introduction,"

Thorunn Ruga McCoy in "Dodsworth's Revelation: Motoring Toward Self" plumbs *Dodsworth* scholarship and offers a clever interpretation. She assesses the novelist's use of transportation—a prevalent element in Lewis's America—as a metaphor for Sam's search for self. Lewis and Sam come to the end of the decade: "Effectively, Dodsworth realizes his wrong turns on life's highways, and rather than internalize a 'dead end' existence parked by the side of the road, he seeks to create a new internal combustion engine, the revelation of himself." Nicely put.[11]

1–26. See Jon K. Lauck, Gleaves Whitney, and Joseph Hogan. eds. *Finding a New Midwestern History* (Lincoln: University of Nebraska Press, 2018) and Jon K. Lauck, *From Warm Center to Ragged Edge: The Erosion of Midwestern Literary and Historical Regionalism, 1920–1965*. Iowa City: University of Iowa Press, 2016. Lauck in the latter study writes Lewis's difficulties with the Marxists were preceded by critics' and reviewers' misunderstanding of literature in the twenties. The scholar crosses disciplines and pays considerable attention to Lewis's complex standings—the critics long struggled to place him, grasp his contribution to literature, history, and sociology as modernism took hold. Lewis to this day "defies categorization"; and pointedly, long associated with the Midwest, he did not turn against the region. See 22 as well as 28–32. See, too, Joseph Darda, "The Philosophy of Creative Writing," *Los Angeles Times Book Review*, February 25, 2019, https://lareviewofbooks.org/article/philosophy-creative-writing/. The professor of English and Comparative Race and Ethnic Studies argues Lewis's continuing significance in the literary wars.

[11] Thorunn Ruga McCoy, "Dodsworth's Revelation: Motoring Toward Self. *Midwest Quarterly* 1, Fall 99: 21–32, quoted 21. See also Maggie Bandur, "On the Road Again: A Review of *Adventures in Autobumming* by Sinclair Lewis, n.p.: Omo Press, 2017," *The Sinclair Lewis Society Newsletter* 27 (Fall 2018), 1 and 11–13. Bandur reviews a recent compilation of three motoring pieces published in *Saturday Evening Post*. "[W]hat primarily strikes you…is the excitement and new sense of freedom…." "[P]oignant are Lewis's hopes for the democratic potential of car travel as a social equalizer." And prescient: "Lewis dreams 'Somewhere in these states there is a young man who is going to become rich. He may be washing milk bottles in a dairy lunch. He is going to start a chain of small, clean, pleasant hotels, standardized and nationally advertised, along every important motor route in the country.'" See 11–13.

McCoy offers an incisive assessment of the importance of the automobile to Lewis's understanding of the U.S. and his sense of entrapment in an idyll gone bad. She returns to David G. Pugh's query, "How do you tell photographic realism from the satirical warping of the shiny hubcap?" Lewis knew the difference. McCoy reads Pugh closely. As earlier noted, he nails it: "To make this possible requires revivifying, recreating some of the era of 1910–1922 and of attitudes toward spiritual wastelands and backyard ash heaps then, and also requires paralleling those ash heaps from our own experiences." McCoy responds to Pugh's call to further study the author, assert his currency. Pugh had concluded, "The ultimate question, then, for investing time and energy in reading...is whether or not the plastic terms, the technique and surface texture of the novels, clear in their own epoch, can transmit to a later time a feeling about values, ennui, a wasteland or a wasted life." No material item encompassed it as well as the motor during Lewis's heyday (and since). McCoy argues *Dodsworth* needs to be revisited, scholars need to connect with one another, take advantage of how much we know and how much more we can learn about Lewis and reestablish his standing in American Letters.

The impact of the motor car, first cropping up strikingly in *Babbitt* and picked up again by Lewis in *Dodsworth*, on its own tells a tale. Martin Light in "The 'Poetry and Tragedy' of the Car in Sinclair Lewis's Novels" six years before McCoy had zeroed in on the novelist's fascination with the marvel (he, too, possibly fed McCoy's interest). Light observes the obvious but demonstrates what so many Lewis critiques errantly dismiss: "In the course of fulfilling one of the tasks of a novelist—to dramatize developments that are of significance to a culture—Sinclair Lewis set forth portraits and situations in a fictional pattern...." The scholar focuses on a cross-section of works but dedicates most of his analysis to *Babbitt* and *Dodsworth* as he argues the novelist held a "sympathetic understanding of the meaning of the automobile in American life...." All modes of twentieth-century transportation—"cars, trains, ships, and airplanes—figure into his novels and stories." "He created characters who are equally footloose and dazzled" as he by "the greatest gadgets, devices, and machines imaginable." Lewis captures the "mass idolization of the motor car and mass accommodation to automobility that transformed American institutions and life-ways."[12]

No characters better demonstrate the phenomenon than George and Sam. Cars stream through Lewis's novels but most prominently in *Babbitt* and *Dodsworth*. Light argues the writer catches the citizenry's soaring infatuation with the motor car and the recognition of its maturing, utilitarian ordinariness. The scholar makes a smart stretch and reads the posthumous *World So Wide* into the greater tale of what Lewis was up to, "always in the grip of his wanderlust." Lewis adored the mobility offered by the car, but as in his own life, by mid-century the automobile had run its course. *World So Wide* begins, again, with a gruesome car wreck. This is a long-distance perspective from George's infatuation with the motor, his triumphant entry every morning into towering Zenith, Sam's marvelous invention and mass propagation of the Revelation, and the automaker's erstwhile "sell-out" to the onward march of corporate America. Sam had been propelled to reconsider what he had wrought. The crash in turn, twenty years on, at mid-century, forces the young driver to find the means to recreate a worthwhile life which in the end seems a forlorn hope. The crash may signal Lewis's own sense of mortality or the death of a cherished dream—but it is important to recall this posthumously published novel was a mess; care must be taken not to read too much into it. Still, Light is sharp and concludes:

> Tracing the motif of the car in Lewis's work confirms his remarkable ability to closely observe and precisely record the patterns of American behavior that have also been seen in the wider and larger perspectives of the historian and social scientist. It is noteworthy not only that Lewis showed us the fact of the automobile's role in American discovery, invention, enterprise, dream, and disillusionment, but also that at every stage he effectively dramatized the emotional rewards and emotional costs

---

[12] Martin Light, "The 'Poetry and Tragedy' of the Car in Sinclair Lewis's Novels," *Kansas Quarterly* 21 (Fall 1989): 23–33; quoted 23–24.

> that accompany such involvements, a skill that he has often been chastised for lacking.

Once again, a latter-day Lewis scholar hits pay-dirt and provokes. Light's expertise in Lewis studies and his focus on *Dodsworth* pans out as he surveys and links the parallel trajectories in the author's work and life by means of a cross-disciplinary look.[13]

Paul-Vincent McInnes in 2005 took a long look back and places the novelist four-square within modernism and its debate. In "Surviving Modernity: Sinclair Lewis and the 1920s," he prophesizes the discarded author at the start of the new century, the twenty-first, ascendent. McInnes, a scholar at the University of Glasgow, draws on readings of Lewis, scholarship, and contemporary thought to argue the novelist did arrive at a resolution, one which should be reconsidered today. In the early years of the twenty-first century McInnes makes the case the old Puritan Dilemma, to be in the world but not of it, which long haunted Lewis and American culture, is *au courant*:

> Shunning conformity and the emergence of a new literary modernism, he managed to develop a system which the individual could both be involved in and detached from. His system of survival closely resembles what is now known as decentralisation. Indeed, Lewis typifies Terry Eagleton's assertion, "To be inside and outside a position at the same time—to occupy a territory while loitering skeptically on the boundary—is often where the most intensely creative ideas stem from. It is a resourceful place to be, if not always a painless one."[14]

Eagleton, Arrowsmith's closest friend and colleague, teams up with Martin in the Vermont woods, unable any longer to remain in the world without becoming ensnared. Could a Lewis character do better? Is closer proximity to society in order? That was the author's quandary and McInnes's rich prompt.

---

[13] Ibid., 24 and 32–33.

[14] Paul-Vincent McInnes, "Surviving Modernity: Sinclair Lewis and the 1920s," eSharp 4 Spring 2005:1–15; quoted 1–2; https://www.gla.ac.uk/media/Media_41160_smxx.pdf.

McInnes writes the novelist deservedly attracts renewed scholarly interest: "Sinclair Lewis has become something of an enigma in the American literary canon. Almost completely forgotten until recently, he appears to be having something of a literary renaissance. A gradual increase in critical and biographical output and the recognition of his influence on the work of Philip Roth and other American writers has seen his profile rise in academic circles." That rising phoenix is exaggerated, but McInnes proffers a powerful brief for Lewis's currency based on his twenties work. "His novels attempt to deal with the question of surviving in a protean modern world that was the antithesis of prewar society. Lewis and his protagonists attempt to discover a solution to the problem of surviving the modern condition. From *Main Street* (1920) to *Dodsworth* (1929) Lewis modified and developed ideologies for the individual that ranged from nonconformity and isolation to autonomous structures." McInnes calls scholars to "recognise Lewis's realization of discovery and place him in the tradition of postmodern thought. "Lewis becomes important, then, as his question posed in the 1920s still resonates today: how can the individual live in a constantly evolving and complex world?" Lewis stretches now, firmly on his pegs, into post-modernity? That, surely, would have given him a laugh and a boost.[15]

A century later Lewis would find himself in a world all too familiar. Establishing three phases of development beginning with *Mainstreet*, McGinnes discerns that with *Dodsworth* "we find Lewis fully developing and discovering a system of living for the individual. Lewis's final adoption of an autonomous framework not only marks him as a truly original novelist, but also captures his prescience in matters of twenty-first century intellectual cultural debate." The novelist for McInnes embodies in himself and his work a resolution for contemporary society: "That a man can function and analyse his culture whilst being simultaneously engaged and detached from it, is critical to our understanding of how one survives in a protean and complex society."[16]

[15] Ibid.,1–2.

[16] Ibid., 14.

Whether the author has journeyed this far—the new century's answer man—remains open for debate. Still, how central does he remain? Lewis the individual never found that contemplative sanctuary within the protean, complex society; nor, despite McInnes's claims, probably would Dodsworth with his garden communities and motor caravans. Shining cities on distant hills might be enlightening but never consummated; still, they can provide direction and a sense of comfort in a challenging world. McInnes testifies Lewis's conundrum remains worthy of engagement well into the twenty-first century. "Surviving Modernity: Sinclair Lewis and the 1920s," steeped in the author's twenties work, offers hope that literary scholars will see there is a good deal more to be discerned in Lewis's literature; toss in an appreciation of the perspectives of historians, other humanists, and social scientists, there is that much more to be revealed about the genesis and substance of American culture.

In conclusion, back in the middle of the twentieth century, social and cultural historian Nelson Manfred Blake wrote "How to Learn History From Sinclair Lewis and Other Uncommon Sources." American Studies was still in its exciting genesis; interdisciplinary studies were hailed. Blake's argument runs historians capitalize on Lewis—other disciplines ought to take advantage of their perspective. He contributed in 1964 to *American Character and Culture: Some Twentieth Century Perspectives*: "By combining the study of history, literature, and the arts young people are grasping the opportunity to share in the American experience in all its variety and color." Blake's admonition to take notice of Lewis still carries weight—however, it is striking that in his read it is *Elmer Gantry* which provides "what we may hope to learn of history from literature and the arts…."[17]

Elmer Gantry appears an uncanny choice—*Gantry* of the five monumental twenties works generally is considered by literary scholars to be Lewis's weakest, lacking in style and substance, not in keeping with

[17] Nelson Manfred Blake "How to Learn History From Sinclair Lewis and Other Uncommon Sources" in *American Character and Culture: Some Twentieth Century Perspectives*, ed. John A Hague (Deland, FL: Everett Edwards Press, 1964), 33–47; quoted 33.

the more encouraging, and more balanced, spirit of the others. But of course, as Blake points out, the novel created a sensation and sales were huge. For mid-century readers, what did *Gantry* have to say that elevated the work above the others? Why would the novel cum social study, written "way back then," be an instructional cultural read close to forty years on? Hollywood had recently released the acclaimed "Elmer Gantry," a box-office bonanza. Rising conservative and right-wing opposition to an increasingly triumphant liberal political order and the reemergence to national attention of religious fundamentalism led Blake to the dark *Gantry*. For the educator and his students the novel was timely, prime for study.

Elmer was no anomaly in 1927—he was of prime interest. Readers found something which spoke to them of themselves and their society. Reviewers may have considered the work troubled, scandalous, an angry outburst by Lewis, but readers recognized the milieu; reviewers even in their condemnation never doubted the novel's currency. Decades later, Burt Lancaster as the crusading, dangerous preacher rang true to movie-goers. (No doubt the novel experienced a healthy rise in sales.) Readers throughout the twenties turned to Lewis; and moviemakers as well as playwrights; his works resonated. At the start of the 1960s, Elmer was finally ready for his silver screen close-up. What is it in our own milieus which draws us back? Of course, often nostalgia; but also, just as often it can be recognition "this speaks to me." In the increasingly freed up sixties, what moviemakers had hesitated to venture was now possible—*Elmer Gantry* will sell, once again he will speak to the country. The country had progressed

The novel absolutely spoke to Blake. He concluded it might well work for students. It is not difficult to discern what drew the scholar to *Elmer Gantry*. In the twenties Lewis through his works had diligently built a perspective on the passing scene. Historian Blake assesses: "To those of us trained as specialists in some traditional field of study" interdisciplinary study raises "a challenge to rethink our conclusions and to draw insights from other types of material than those we customarily use." He makes a plea: "In this spirit, let us consider what we may hope to learn from literature and the arts, first in a general way, and then with specific reference to Sinclair Lewis's angry novel *Elmer Gantry*."

Historians shall prosper; literary scholars as well. He recommends Lewis's entire body of work. Blake concludes the historian "prefers to find out about the past from what he calls primary sources—that is, by the evidence left by the actual witnesses and participants of past events." It is a natural: "It is from this point of view that literature and the arts open up the most exciting avenues for exploration."[18]

Literary scholars have plenty to gain plumbing history, establishing the fuller context, probing the breadth and depth of American culture. To the point, Sinclair Lewis may well be far more intelligible to the literary elite if one with a sensitivity to history gives the author his second read. As important, Blake argues historians have much to learn from the expertise of specialists in literature. A joint enterprise is in order; Blake claims it is common sense. He contends America's storytellers, Whitman and Twain, Hamlin Garland and Willa Cather, and so many more have passed on a "sensitive description...a whole great historical episode." It is not a matter of sentimentalizing a more peaceful, bucolic past. America's march was far from smooth. Blake points to Howells and Dreiser's metropolitan tales: "William Dean Howells has left meticulously authentic descriptions of Boston and New York during the 1870s and 1880s. Theodore Dreiser has done the same for New York, Chicago, and Philadelphia during the 1890s and early 1900s." They move us, still. Blake argues it is then in the New Era that Sinclair Lewis arose to shine the light; he did so for readers of his day; it is he to whom we advantageously turn for rich authority as to who we were and who we are today.[19]

Blake knows his history; he knows his colleagues know their literature. He concedes to literary critics "*Elmer Gantry* is a bad novel—awkwardly constructed, intemperate in tone, grotesque in characterization." But to understand the New Era, including the contentious role of the church, reaction, and plenty more, Lewis stands as a primary resource: "[T]he novel's deficiencies as a work of art do not necessarily destroy its interest as a document of social history." And, he argues you

[18] Ibid., 33–34.

[19] Ibid., 35–36.

must not only know the work, but the author; we must be exhaustive in our search for some sense of truth.

> What general judgment can we make about Sinclair Lewis as a witness to American life in the 1920s? Obviously he is far from being a perfect observer. He is a man of many flaws in character. He is lacking in objectivity and judiciousness. He is strongly opinionated and often times malicious in what he writes. But the judge and jury in the courtroom cannot wait for perfect witnesses. They must listen to whatever testimony is offered, shrewdly noting each witness's shortcomings and prejudices and giving to his statements such credence as they deserve. In like manner the historian must deal with Sinclair Lewis, drawing such information as he can from Lewis's rich gifts for fact-gathering and mimicry, but being constantly on guard against his weakness for exaggeration and caricature.

This analysis would have resonated with the author: the call for holistic consideration of his body of work..[20]

Blake propagandizes: "Literature is not the only survival from the past. Every building, every painting, every piece of music created in an earlier age and still in existence has something to tell us about the period of its birth." Blake remonstrates: "All that I am attempting to say is that literature and art have their secondary delights—and one of these is that they hold the mirror to the society that produced them. I am entirely certain that historians should read more novels and poems, look at more buildings and paintings, and listen to more music. I am almost as sure that students of literature and art should read more history."[21]

The historian admonishes, "[O]ne must apply to these unorthodox materials of history the same standards of historical criticism that he would apply to other sources." "[O]ne must learn as much as he can about the author or artist and why he created this particular work." In "How to Learn History From Sinclair Lewis" Blake makes a strong case novelists must be understood within their element. Naturally,

[20] Ibid., 47

[21] Ibid., 47 and 37.

writers, painters "have deliberately chosen their subjects to make the points that they wanted to make." "The question always is, did a particular author or artist set out to prove anything by this particular work?" What more is there to this story? Use all the tools at hand; cross disciplines.[22]

Blake recognizes Lewis despised hypocrisy. And he loved America. He was conflicted personally, and he judged his country similarly disturbed as to its identity. The United States had taken errant turns; it needed to step back and take a long look at itself as it moved forward. Lewis offered up *Main Street*, *Babbitt*, *Arrowsmith*, *Elmer Gantry*, *and Dodsworth*: "This 'hatred of hypocrisy' is probably our most useful key to understanding Lewis's testimony about the social history of his time." Blake advises, "If one can keep his temper and make proper allowances for Lewis's strong biases, he can learn as much about American Protestantism by reading *Elmer Gantry* as he can about middle-class conduct by reading *Babbitt.*" The scholar is adamant: "Historians, I am sure, have no wish to invade the province of other disciplines. We are not suggesting standards by which we think literature or the arts should be taught or judged." We can learn together the "problems and conflicts that beset men in every age…." And women, and a host of "others"—the march continues. Nelson Manfred Blake makes great sense three-score years on as does Harry Sinclair Lewis a century on.[23]

---

[22] Ibid., 39.

[23] Ibid., 43 and 47.

EPILOGUE

John Farrar in 1922 dismissed the newly released *Babbitt* as second-rate. Lewis, he bemoaned, had tossed aside all he held within his grasp so brilliantly illustrated with *Main Street.* He chastised the author for shortchanging his talent, selling out to crassness, seduced by a lust for wealth. The critic prophesized, "If he died suddenly, you would find written on his heart, in blinking electric bulbs of letters, those two magic words: Main Street." He did not expect much value from Lewis here on out; he was wrong. Inadvertently, he was proved right that Lewis's best work, generated in the twenties, could be wrapped up in those two words, not because he had sold out; rather with *Babbitt*, *Arrowsmith*, *Elmer Gantry*, and *Dodsworth* the novelist had extended his *Main Street* indictment to encircle the globe.[1]

Main Street was augmented by *Babbitt*, further fortified in *Arrowsmith* and *Elmer Gantry.* In *Dodsworth* Lewis had circled back to make his definite claim stick that Main Street stretched far beyond Gopher Prairie—that first preface. Throughout the 1920s he pounded out his case the United States of America had promise, that it had to strike a more righteous chord. Cultural Historian David E Shi in *The Simple Life: Plain Living and High Thinking* sets the context in which the author worked. Lewis's quest was an old one—baked into the national saga. He sought to find a way back where "habits of life were simpler; the interests of men less mixed and varied; there were more common sympathies, more common and controlling traditions and associations." That could not be resurrected; and "back then" all was not perfection. This, however, had been the guiding light in the country's progression. *The people* could move forward and strike a better balance in their lives in line with that prospect. It comes down, Shi had argued, to a "personal ethic," one which "entails examining how people have struggled to translate myths into practice." How, he questioned, has

---

[1] John Farrar, "The Literary Spotlight," *Bookman*, September, 1922, www.unz.com.

the illusory myth of a classless America transposed itself into the unsettling realm of practical middle-class identity? This in short is what Lewis tried to decipher: how to encourage middle-class America to live up to the Promise.[2]

Lewis's five twenties masterpieces still promise not only a good read but good history. *America*: it is not a lost cause. That faith has carried the nation a long way. "So Main Street," wrote Farrar in 1922, "the insulted and injured, has won out after all. It has taken Lewis into its materialistic camp. It has made him worship, against his surface will, perhaps, its own kind of success."[3] Lewis never worshipped at mammon's altar; if anything, he knelt and asked forgiveness for succumbing to its charms. George Babbitt was not a simplistic Lewis stand-in. He was a complex character. Farrar totally missed, and it is hard to understand how, that George was what Lewis stood against—measuring one's well-being in dollars and cents. Babbitt recognized, if only for a brief moment, maybe for his remaining years, that he had been beat. Lewis demanded more of the babbitts of America—he considered himself a babbitt; and he sought to demonstrate George and the others knew better, they possessed worthy if displaced standards. Lewis hankered after the prerogatives of wealth; he never worshipped the crass society off of which he made it. He declared repeatedly Main Street wasn't so bad, nor Zenith—and there were the Martins and Sams. He could not abide Elmer Gantry; he warned this ogre represented the ugly end for a noble experiment. He confessed from the start he was Carol, always on the hunt, a journey she expected her children to carry on. Our heritage could be preserved, the American Experiment was not lost. All Lewis's protagonists were complex…the human condition.

Ludwig Lewisohn had another take on *Babbitt* in 1922: "What is certain is that to us the book represents a deed of high cultural significance and that the future historian of American civilization will turn to it with infinite profit, with mingled amusement, astonishment, and

---

[2] David E. Shi, *The Simple Life: Plain Living and High Thinking in American Culture, 1850–1920* (New York: Oxford University Press, 1985), 173 and 7; quoting Charles Eliot Norton.

[3] [Farrar].

pity."[4] Lewisohn got the message, but once more to his credit Farrar had it right that it all boiled down to *Main Street*—why couldn't the United States make it all simpler, make it work just as it might, in the long run, on Main Street? Carol Kennicott had fathomed it well may be a task too far, but she was not about to give up. Lewis shared that deeper faith. Even kindly George Babbitt clung to that ambition, take on reform—more of a whim to toy with, but there was that.

Azar Nafisi, the acclaimed Iranian writer and educator, grew up to love American literature. Ultimately, she emigrated to the United States to escape a country which had become a danger to her family and undercut her aspirations. Now a citizen, in appreciation of all that the U.S. offers, she tries to make sense of thc country's promise. In *The Republic of Imagination: A Life in Books*, Nafisi brings together three artists; one reviewer reads she lays forth her "irrepressible conviction in the power of fiction to show us who we are." "She reminds us," another writes, "that immigrants bring many things to America, starting with a fresh set of eyes."[5] An outsider turned insider's perspective can be insightful—immigrants sacrifice much to have a stab at the American Experiment. Nafisi takes up Mark Twain's *Huckleberry Finn*, Carson McCullers's *The Heart is a Lonely Hunter*, and Sinclair Lewis's *Babbitt*. She knows literature, she long taught its import in Iran, and now in her new home. In *The Republic of Imagination* she definitively links fiction with dashed and ever-lingering hopes. She concludes her assessment of George Babbitt—and Lewis—with the thought, "And that is where the hope lies…the image of the poet…will endure."[6]

---

[4] L. L. [Ludwig Lewisohn], *Babbitt*, "Nation," September 20, 1922, 284–85.

[5] Azar Nafisi, *The Republic of Imagination: A Life in Books*, New York: Penguin, 2014. Excerpted reviews.

[6] Nafisi, 209. Seymour Chwast, "Sketchbook: Heroes and Antiheros," *New York Times Book Review* March 24, 2019 comically illustrates a page-full of iconic figures: Tom Joad, Jay Gatsby, Mother Courage, Ethan Fromme, Jane Eyre, Kunta Kinte, Dorian Grey, Hester Prynne, Mrs. Dalloway, Rip Van Winkle, Capt. Ahab, and Babbitt occupies center position.

"So few American novels have happy endings. Perhaps this is not surprising in a nation whose declaration of independence provides its citizens not with the right to happiness but the right to its pursuit." Even "Babbitt, despite everything and despite himself" proves "that the faint murmur of the heart cannot be silenced."[7] Nafisi does not miss the dismal fact that George rests his hopes on the hapless Ted: "It is a rather feeble and disappointing ending. We are given the satisfaction neither of complacently judging Babbitt as a villain nor of his redemption and transformation. Ted will never be reconciled to reading Shakespeare, but he does choose what his heart desires."[8] That, yes, can be said for Ted, and George allowing his son to do so speaks well of him. But that is it: Ted does have the freedom to go his own desultory way; but it is a sobering thought—one must have the determination to take the right track. Nafisi declares a lot remains to be garnered from reading Lewis. "If we agree with Ezra Pound that 'literature is news that stays news,' then we can safely say that Sinclair Lewis was, despite his poor standing in the literary establishment, the ultimate American novelist. We have to be thankful for the minor miracle that after almost a century, *Babbitt* speaks to us still."[9]

Main Street, *Arrowsmith*, *Elmer Gantry*, and *Dodsworth* resonate all these decades later just as loudly as *Babbitt*. An urgency exists today, Nafisi advises, "to ask new questions, to define not just who we are but who we want to be."[10] Throughout the saga of the American people that urgency has pulsated. It is fueled by the promise of opportunity in every sense of the word. She advises we have long had consultants: H. L. Mencken, Theodore Dreiser, Frank Norris, John Steinbeck, Upton Sinclair, "and of course Mark Twain" are our champions. Azar Nafisi, a newly minted American, clings to optimism: "It can be said that among the true guardians of American morality, its writers and thinkers have been the most steadfast, challenging readers to question complacent norms, to acknowledge injustice and recognize the underside

[7] Nafisi, 209.
[8] Ibid., 208.
[9] Ibid., 159.
[10] Ibid., 14.

of this heaving, thrusting, purposeful nation dedicated to making ever more new things." The promise endures. Read, she urges; read Sinclair Lewis.[11]

[11] Ibid., 158. Nafisi declares Lewis a "real-life model for the adult Huck." See 153; for the *Babbitt* analysis, 149–209. Nafisi's closest friend, also an Iranian escapee, early advised, "You must bring more U.S. history in your book." "How else" she queried, "can you write about American fiction?" See 41–42. Nafisi's commitment to history and literature is fundamental to her understanding of culture, identity, and ideology. She argues Lewis's "literary mission was inspired by his anxiety for America, a sentiment that links him to Emerson and Whitman and, perhaps more than to anyone else, Thoreau…." She quotes John Updike's 2002 assessment of Lewis: "Who in the last century more manfully and systematically attempted to fill the demand, in recent times voiced by Tom Wolfe and Jonathan Franzen, that American novelists cast off solipsism and introverted delicacy and embrace the nation as it exists, in its striving variety and dynamism?" See 157. Yet Updike also severely cut Lewis down: "What has Sinclair done lately to deserve a new, five-hundred-and-fifty-four page…biography…?" Always a conundrum. *No Brakes: A New Biography of Sinclair Lewis*, *The New Yorker Magazine* (February 4, 2002), http://archives.newyorker.com.

BIBLIOGRAPHY

Agran, Edward Gale. *Herbert Hoover and the Commodification of Middle-Class America.* Lanham, MD: Lexington Books, 2016.

———. *"Too Good A Town": William Allen White and the Emerging Rhetoric of Middle America.* Fayetteville: University of Arkansas Press, 1998.

"AHR Forum." American Historical Review 97 (December 1992): 1369–1430.

Anderson, David D. "Sinclair Lewis and the Midwestern Tradition." In *Sinclair Lewis at 100: Papers Presented at a Centennial Conference*, compiled by Michael Connaughton, 253–65. St. Cloud, MN: St. Cloud State University, 1985.

Anonymous. "*Arrowsmith*" News." *The Sinclair Lewis Society Newsletter*, 29 (Fall 2020).

Aron, Stephen. *The American West Reprised, Revised, and Revived. Reviews in American History* 28. June, 2000: 245–50.

Bandur, Maggie. "On the Road Again: A Review of *Adventures in Autobumming* by Sinclair Lewis. Omo Press, 2017." *The Sinclair Lewis Society Newsletter*, 27 (Fall *2018*).

Beck, Warren. "How Good is Sinclair Lewis." *College English* 9 (January 1948): 173–80.

Becker, George J. "Sinclair Lewis: Apostle to the Philistines." In *Critical Essays on Sinclair Lewis*, edited by Martin Bucco, 104–11. Boston: G. K. Hall & Co., 1986.

Bender, Thomas. *Community and Social Change in America.* Baltimore: Johns Hopkins University Press, 1982.

Blake, Nelson Manfred. "How to Learn History from Sinclair Lewis and Other Uncommon Sources." In *American Character and Culture: Some Twentieth Century Perspectives*, edited by Johan A. Hague, 33–47. Deland, FL: Everett Edwards Press, 1964.

Bloom, Harold. Introduction to *Modern Critical Reviews: Sinclair Lewis.* New York: Chelsea Publishers, 1987, 1–4.

———, ed. *Modern Critical Reviews: Sinclair Lewis.* New York: Chelsea Publishers, 1987.

Bogue, Allan G. *Frederick Jackson Turner: Strange Roads Going Down.* Norman: University of Oklahoma Press, 1998.

Breen, T.H. "Will American Consumers Buy a Second American Revolution?" *Journal of American History* 93 (September 2006): 404–08.

"Briefer Mention." *Dial.* January, 1921. https://books.google.com.
Brinkley, Alan. *Culture and Politics in the Great Depression.* Waco: Markham Press Fund, 1999.
———. *The End of Reform: New Deal Liberalism in Recession and War.* New York: Vantage Books, 1996.
Broun, Heywood. "Books." *New York Tribune*, October 20, 1920. https://www.newspapers.com.
———. "Books." *New York Tribune*, October 22, 1920. https://www.newspapers.com.
Brown, Daniel R. "Lewis's Satire—A Negative Emphasis." In *Modern Critical Reviews: Sinclair Lewis*, edited by Harold Bloom, 51–62. New York: Chelsea House Publishers, 1987.
Bucco Martin, ed. *Critical Essays on Sinclair Lewis.* Boston: G. K. Hall & Co., 1986.
———. Introduction to *Critical Essays on Sinclair Lewis.* Boston: G. K. Hall & Co., 1986, 1–27.
———. "Introduction." In *Main Street: The Story of Carol Kennicott*, by Sinclair Lewis, vii–xxi. New York: Penguin Books, 1995.
Campbell, Ballard C., ed., *The Human Tradition in the Gilded Age and Progressive Era.* Wilmington, DE: Scholarly Resources, 2000.
Canby, Henry Seidel. "Vicious Ignorance." *Saturday Review of Literature.* March 12, 1927.
Cayton, Andrew R.L. and Susan E. Gray, eds. *The American Midwest: Essays on Regional History*, eds. Bloomington: Indiana University Press, 2001
Chambers, John Whiteclay II, *The Tyranny of Change: America in the Progressive Era, 1890–1920*, 2nd edition. New York: St. Martin's Press, 1992.
Chwast, Seymour. "Sketchbook: Heroes and Antiheros," *New York Times Book Review.* March 24, 2019.
Cmiel, Kenneth. "Destiny and Amnesia: The Vision of Modernity in Robert Wiebe's 'The Search for Order.'" In *American Retrospectives: Historians on Historians*, edited by Stanley I. Kutler. Baltimore: Johns Hopkins University Press, 1995: 294–310.
Cohen, Lizabeth. *A Consumers' Republic: The Politics of Mass Consumption in Postwar America.* New York: Alfred A. Knoph, 2003.
———. "Escaping Steigerwald's 'Plastic Cages': Consumers as Subjects and Objects in Modern Capitalism." *Journal of American History* 93 (September 2006): 409–13.
Conn, Peter. *The American 1930s: A Literary History.* Cambridge: Cambridge University Press, 2009.

Connaughton, Michael, comp. *Sinclair Lewis at 100: Papers Presented at a Centennial Conference.* St. Cloud, MN: St. Cloud State University, 1985.

Conroy, Stephen S. "Popular Artists and Elite Standards." In *Critical Essays on Sinclair Lewis*, edited by Martin Bucco, 197–203. Boston: G. K. Hall & Co., 1986.

———. "Sinclair Lewis's Sociological Imagination." In *Modern Critical Reviews: Sinclair Lewis*, edited by Harold Bloom. New York: Chelsea House Publishers, 1987, 71–82.

Cooper, John Milton, Jr. *Pivotal Decades: The United States, 1900–1920.* New York: W.W. Norton, 1990.

Croly, Herbert David. *The Promise of American Life.* Edited by Arthur M. Schlessinger, Jr. Cambridge: Harvard University Press: Belknap Press, 1965.

Crunden, Robert M. "Thick Description in the Progressive Era." *Reviews in American History* 19. December 1991: 463–67.

Daniels, Howell. "Sinclair Lewis and the Drama of Dissociation." In *Modern Critical Reviews: Sinclair Lewis*, edited by Harold Bloom, 83–102. New York: Chelsea House Publishers, 1987.

Darda, Joseph. "The Philosophy of Creative Writing." *Los Angeles Times Book Review*, February 25, 2019. https://lareviewofbooks.org/article/philosophy-creative-writing/.

Davis, Elmer. "Mr. Lewis Attacks the Clergy: In 'Elmer Gantry' He Deals a Blow Beneath the 'Bible-Belt.'" *New York Times Book Review.* March 13, 1927.

DeVoto, Bernard. "Sinclair Lewis." In *Critical Essays on Sinclair Lewis*, edited by Martin Bucco, 57–60. Boston: G. K. Hall & Co., 1986.

Dixon, Wheeler. "Cinematic Adaptations of the Works of Sinclair Lewis." In *Sinclair Lewis at 100: Papers Presented at a Centennial Conference*, compiled by Michael Connaughton, 191–200. St. Cloud, MN: St. Cloud State University, 1985.

Doctorow, E. L. "Afterword." In *Arrowsmith*, by Sinclair Lewis. New York: Signet Classic, 1998.

Donahue, Kathleen G. *Freedom from Want: American Liberalism and the Idea of the Consumer.* Baltimore: Johns Hopkins University Press, 2003.

Dooley, D.J. "Aspiration and Enslavement." In *Critical Essays on Sinclair Lewis*, edited by Martin Bucco, 136–50. Boston: G.K. Hall & Co., 1986.

Dumenil, Lynn. *The Modern Temper: American Culture and Society in the 1920s.* New York: Hill and Wang, 1995.

Etulain, Richard W, ed. *Does the Frontier Experience Make America Exceptional?* Boston: Bedford/St. Martin's, 1999.
F. A. [Francis Hackett]. "God's Country." *New Republic*. December 1, 1920. www.unz.com.
[Farrar, John]. "The Literary Spotlight." *Bookman*. September, 1922: 54–59. www.unz.com.
F. P. A. [Franklin P. Adams]. "The Conning Tower." *New York Tribune*, October 19, 1920. https://www.newspapers.com.
Flanagan, Maureen A. *America Reformed: Progressives and Progressivisms 1890s–1920s*. New York: Oxford University Press, 2007.
Fleming, Robert E. *Sinclair Lewis: A Reference Guide*. Boston: G. K. Hall, 1980.
Ford, Ford Maddox. "Dodsworth by Sinclair Lewis." *Bookman*, April, 1929.
Forster, E. M. "A Camera Man." *Life and Letters* 2: May 1929: 336–43.
———. "Our Photography: Sinclair Lewis." *New York Herald Tribune Books*. April 28, 1929.
Fox, Richard Wightman and T. J. Jackson Lears, eds. *The Culture of Consumption: Critical Essays in American History, 1880–1980*. New York: Pantheon Books, 1983.
Geismer, Maxwell. *The Last of the Provincials: The American Novel: 1915–1925*. Boston: Houghton Mifflin, 1949.
Gilmore, Glenda Elizabeth, ed. *Who Were the Progressives?* Boston: Bedford/St. Martin's, 2002.
Goldstein, Ralph. "Arrowsmith Endures in the Pandemic." *Sinclair Lewis Society Newsletter* 29 (Spring, 2021).
Goodwyn, Lawrence. *The Populist Moment: A Short History of the Agrarian Revolt in America*. Oxford: Oxford University Press, 1978.
Grebstein, Sheldon Norman. *Sinclair Lewis*. New Haven: Twayne Publishers, 1962.
———. *Sinclair Lewis's Unwritten Novel. Philological Quarterly* 37 (October, 1958): 400–09.
Hawley, Ellis W. *The Great War and the Search for a Modern Order: A History of the American People and Their Institutions 1917–1933*, 2nd ed. Prospect Heights IL: Waveland Press, 1997.
Hine, Robert V., John Mack Faragher, and Jon T. Coleman, eds. *The American West: A New Interpretive History*. 2nd ed. New Haven: Yale University Press, 2017.
Hoffman, Frederick J. *The Twenties: American Writing in the Postwar Decade*. New York: Viking Press, 1955.

Howe, Irving. "The World He Mimicked Was His Own," *New York Times Book Review* (October 1, 1961).

Hughes, Serge. "From Main Street to the World So Wide." *Commonweal*. April 6, 1951.

Hutchisson, James M. "Introduction." In *Babbitt* by Sinclair Lewis. New York: Penguin Books, 1996.

———. *The Rise of Sinclair Lewis, 1920–1930*. University Park: Pennsylvania State University Press, 1996.

Jacobs, Meg. *Pocketbook Politics: Economic Citizenship in Twentieth-Century America*. Princeton: Princeton University Press. 2005.

Johnson, Owen. "Sinclair Lewis as a Polemicist. *New York Herald Tribune*. September 17, 1922. http://chroniclingamerica.local.gov.

Johnston, Robert D. "Influential Works about the Gilded Age and Progressive Era. In *A Companion to the Gilded Age and Progressive Era*, edited by Christopher McKnight Nichols and Nancy C. Unger. Hoboken, NJ: John Wiley & Sons, 2017: 437–49.

———. "Re-Democratizing the Progressive Era: The Politics of Progressive Era Political Historiography." *Journal of the Gilded Age and Progressive Era* 1. January 2002: 68–92.

———. "The Possibilities of Politics: Democracy in America, 1877 to 1917." In *American History Now*, 3rd ed., edited by Eric Foner and Lisa McGirr. Philadelphia: Temple University Press, 2011: 96–124.

Johnston, Robert D. and Burton J. Bledstein, eds. *The Middling Sorts: Explorations in the History of the American Middle Class*. New York: Routledge, 2001.

Koblas, John J. *Sinclair Lewis: Home at Last*. Bloomington, MN: Voyeuger Press, 1981.

Kronenberger, Louis. "Sinclair Lewis Parts Company with Mr. Babbitt: His American Abroad in 'Dodsworth' Is a Bird of Rather Different Feather." *New York Times Book Review*, March 17, 1929.

Krutch, Joseph Wood. "Mr. Babbitt's Spiritual Guide." *Nation*. March 16, 1927.

Laird, Pamela Walker. *Advertising Progress: American Business and the Rise of Consumer Marketing*. Baltimore: The Johns Hopkins University Press, 1998.

Lauck, Jon K. *From Warm Center to Ragged Edge: The Erosion of Midwestern Literary and Historical Regionalism, 1920–1965*. Iowa City: University of Iowa Press, 2016.

———, Gleaves Whitney, and Joseph Hogan. eds. *Finding a New Midwestern History*. Lincoln: University of Nebraska Press, 2018.

Lea, James. "Sinclair Lewis and the Implied America." In *Critical Essays on Sinclair Lewis.*, edited by Martin Bucco, 184–96. Boston: G. K. Hall & Co., 1986.

Lears, Jackson. *Rebirth of a Nation: The Making of Modern America 1877–1920.* New York: Harper Collins, 2009.

Lears, T. J. Jackson. "The Concept of Cultural Hegemony: Problems and Possibilities." *American Historical Review* 90 (June 1985): 567–93.

———. *No Place of Grace: Antimodernism and the Transformation of American Culture, 1880–1920.* Chicago: University of Chicago, 1994.

Levine, Lawrence W. *The Unpredictable Past: Explorations in American Cultural History.* New York: Oxford University Press, 1993.

Lewis, Sinclair. *Ann Vickers.* Garden City: Doubleday, Doran, 1933.

———. *Arrowsmith.* New York: Signet Classic, 1998.

———. *Babbitt.* New York: Penguin Books, 1996.

———. *Cass Timberline.* New York: Random House, 1945.

———. *Dodsworth.* New York: Signet Classic, 1980.

———. *Elmer Gantry.* New York: Harcourt, Brace and Company, 1927.

———. *Free Air.* New York: Harcourt, Brace, and Howe, 1919.

———. *It Can't Happen Here.* New York: New American Library, 2005.

———. *The Job: An American Novel.* New York: Harper, 1917.

———. *Kingsblood Royal.* New York: Random House, 1947.

———. *Main Street: The Story of Carol Kennicott.* New York: Penguin Books, 1995.

———. *The Man Who Knew Coolidge: Being the Soul of Lowell Schmaltz, Constructive and Nordic Citizen.* New York: Harcourt, Brace and Company, 1928.

———. *Mantrap: A Story of the Northern Wilds.* New York: Harcourt, Brace & Company, 1926.

———. "The Passing of Capitalism." *Bookman*, December, 1914.

———. *The Trail of the Hawk: The Comedy of the Seriousness of Life.* New York: Harper & Brothers, 1915.

———. *World So Wide.* New York: Lion Library Editions, 1956.

L. L. [Ludwig Lewisohn]. "Babbitt." *Nation.* September 20, 1922.

[Lewisohn, Ludwig]. "The Epic of Dulness." *Nation.* November 10, 1920. https://books.google.com.

Light, Martin. "Dodsworth: The Quixotic Hero." In *Modern Critical Reviews: Sinclair Lewis*, edited by Harold Bloom, 119–26. New York: Chelsea House Publishers, 1987.

———. "The 'Poetry and the Tragedy' of the Car in Sinclair Lewis's Novels." *Kansas Quarterly* 21 (Fall 1989): 23–33.

———. *The Quixotic Vision of Sinclair Lewis*. West Lafayette: Purdue University Press, 1975.

Limerick, Patricia Nelson. "Turnerians All: The Dream of a Helpful History in an Intelligible World. *American Historical Review* 100 (June 1995): 697–716.

Lingeman, Richard. *Sinclair Lewis: Rebel from Main Street*. New York: Random House, 2002.

Link, Arthur S. and Richard L. McCormick, *Progressivism*. Arlington Heights: Harlan Davidson, 1983.

Littell, Robert. "Babbitt." *New Republic*. October 4, 1922. http://www.unz.org.

———. "The Preacher Fried in Oil." *New Republic*. March 16, 1927.

———. "The Storm Over 'Elmer Gantry.'" *Literary Digest*. April 16, 1927.

Livingston, James. *Why Is There Still Socialism in the United State? Reviews in American History* 22. December 1994: 577–83.

Lovett, Robert Morse. "An Interpreter of American Life." *Dial*. June, 1925.

Maglin, Nan Bauer, "Women in Three Sinclair Lewis Novels." In *Modern Critical Reviews: Sinclair Lewis*, edited by Harold Bloom. New York: Chelsea House Publishers, 1987, 103–18.

Marchand, Roland. *Advertising the American Dream: Making Way for Modernity, 1920–1940*. Berkeley: University of California Press, 1985.

McCoy, Thorunn Ruga. "Dodsworth's Revelation: Motoring Toward Self." *Midwest Quarterly* 1, Fall 1999: 21–32. web.a.ebscohost.com.

McElvaine, Robert S. *The Great Depression: America, 1929–1941*. Rev. ed. New York: Times Books, 1993.

McGovern, Charles F. *Sold American: Consumption and Citizenship, 1890–1945*. Chapel Hill: University of North Carolina Press, 2006.

McInnes, Paul-Vincent. "Surviving Modernity: Sinclair Lewis and the 1920s." eSharp 4, Spring 2005: 1–15. https://www.gla.ac.uk.

McLaughlin, Robert L. "'Only Kind Thing Is Silence': Ernest Hemingway vs. Sinclair Lewis," *Hemingway Review* 6 (1987): 46–53.

Menand, Louis. "Imitation of Life: John Updike's cultural project." *New Yorker*, April 28, 2014.

Mencken, H. L. "Consolation." *Smart Set*. January, 1921. https://books.google.com.

———. "Escape and Return." *American Mercury*. April, 1929.

———. "Portrait of an American Citizen." *Smart Set*. October, 1922. https://library.brown.edu.

Michels, Steven. *Sinclair Lewis and American Democracy*. Lanham, MD: Lexington Books, *2017*.

Milne, W. Gordon. "Lewis's Muted Influence as Artist and Social Commentator." In *Sinclair Lewis at 100: Papers Presented at a Centennial Conference*, compiled by Michael Connaughton, 87–93. St. Cloud, MN: St. Cloud State University, 1985.

Milner, Clyde A., II., ed. *A New Significance: Re-envisioning the History of the American West.* New York: Oxford University Press, 1996.

Morgan, Dennis, MD. "Dr. Arrowsmith Hangs Out His Shingle." *The Sinclair Lewis Society Newsletter* 29, Spring 2021.

Moscowitz, Marina. "Public Exposure: Middle-Class Material Culture at the Turn of the Twentieth Century." In *The Middling Sorts: Explorations in the History of the American Middle Class*, edited by Robert D. Johnston and Burton J. Bledstein. New York: Routledge, 2001, 170–84.

———. *Standard of Living: The Measure of the Middle Class in America.* Baltimore: Johns Hopkins University Press, 2004.

Nafisi, Azar. *The Republic of the Imagination: A Life in Books.* New York: Penguin, 2014.

Neary, Lynn. "Doctorow Wove Fact and Fiction to Imagine America as it Could Be." http://www.npr.org.

Overton, Grant. "The Salvation of Sinclair Lewis. *Bookman.* April, 1925. www.unz.com.

Painter, Nell Irvin. *Standing at Armageddon: The United States, 1877–1919.* New York: W. W. Norton, 2008.

Parnass, Larry. "Why Writer Sinclair Lewis Keeps Paying Dividends from Pittsfield, and Will Forever," *Sinclair Lewis Society Newsletter* 27 (Spring 2019): 11 and 18–20.

Parry, Sally E. "*Dodsworth* and *World So Wide*: Sinclair Lewis's European/American Dilemma." In *Sinclair Lewis at 100: Papers Presented at a Centennial Conference*, compiled by Michael Connaughton, 27–34. St. Cloud, MN: St. Cloud State University, 1985.

Peterkin, Julia. "Notes of a Rapid Reader." *Saturday Review of Literature.* April 16, 1927.

Pugh, David G. "Baedekers, Babbitry, and Baudelaire." In *Critical Essays on Sinclair Lewis*, edited by Martin Bucco, 204–13. Boston: G. K. Hall & Co., 1986.

Rascoe, Burton. "A Mirror of Mediocrity." *New York Tribune.* September 17, 1922. https://chroniclingamerica.local.gov.

Reagan, Patrick D. *Designing a New America: The Origins of New Deal Planning, 1890–1943.* Amherst: University of Massachusetts Press, 2006.

Robertson, James Oliver. *American Myth, American Reality*. New York: Hill & Wang, 1980.

Rodgers, Daniel T. *Contested Truths: Keywords in American Politics Since Independence*. New York: Basic Books, 1987.

———. "In Search of Progressivism." *Reviews in American History* 10 (December 1982): 113–32.

———. *The Work Ethic in Industrial America: 1850–1920*. Chicago: University of Chicago Press, 1979.

Rosenberg, Charles E. "Martin Arrowsmith: The Scientist as Hero." In *Modern Critical Reviews: Sinclair Lewis*, edited by Harold Bloom. New York: Chelsea House Publishers, 1987, 41–50.

Rubin, Joan Shelley. *The Making of Middlebrow Culture*. Chapel Hill: University of North Carolina Press, 1992.

Scharnhorst, Gary and Matthew Hofer, eds. *Sinclair Lewis Remembered*. Tuscaloosa: University of Alabama Press, 2012.

Schorer, Mark. *Sinclair Lewis: An American Life*. New York: McGraw-Hill Book Company, 1961.

———, ed. *Sinclair Lewis: A Collection of Critical Essays*. Englewood Cliffs: Prentice Hall, 1962.

Shi, David E. *Facing Facts: Realism in American Thought and Culture 1850–1920*. New York: Oxford University Press, 1995.

———. *The Simple Life: Plain Living and High Thinking in American Culture, 1850–1920*. New York: Oxford University Press, 1985.

Simon, Bryant. "One Side of Main Street." *Reviews in American History* 22. September 1994: 461–67.

Simpkins, David Allen. *Becoming Sinclair Lewis*. Independent Publishing, 2017.

Sinclair Lewis Society. https://english.illinoisstate.edu/sinclairlewis.

Sinclair, May. "The Man From Main Street." *New York Times Book Review and Magazine*. September 24, 1922. https://timesmachine.nytimes.com.

Slotkin, Richard. *The Fatal Environment: The Myth of the Frontier in the Age of Industrialism, 1800–1890*. New York: Harper Perennial, 1994.

Steigerwald, David. "All Hail the Republic of Choice: Consumer History as Contemporary Thought." *Journal of American History* 93 (September 2006): 385–403.

Susman, Warren I. *Culture as History: The Transformation of American Society in the Twentieth Century*. New York: Pantheon Books, 1984.

Takayoshi, Ichiro, ed.. *American Literature in Transition, 1920–1930*. Cambridge: Cambridge University Press, 2017.

Taylor, Rachel Annand. "Dodsworth." *Spectator [Literary Supplement]*. March 23, 1929.
Thelen, David. "Memory and American History." *Journal of American History* 75 (March 1989): 1117–1221.
Tong, Scot. "100 Years of Sinclair Lewis' Babbitt. https://www.bur.org. December 27, 2022.
Tyrell, Ian. "Robert Wiebe's *The Search for Order*, Fifty Years On." *Journal of the Gilded Age and Progressive Era* 17 (April 2018): 397–411.
Turner, Frederick Jackson. "The Significance of the Frontier in American History." In *The Frontier in American History*, edited by Frederick Jackson Turner. New York: Henry Holt and Company, 1921, 1–38.
Updike, John, "Exile on Main Street." *New Yorker*. May 17, 1993. http:/archives.newyorker.com.
———. "No Brakes: A New Biography of Sinclair Lewis." *New Yorker*. February 4, 2002. http://archives.newyorker.com.
Van Doren, Carl. *Sinclair Lewis: A Biographical Sketch*. Garden City NJ: Doubleday, Doran, 1933.
———. "St. George and the Parson." *Saturday Review of Literature*. March 12, 1927.
———. "Zenith Meets Europe." *Nation*. April 3, 1929.
Van Doren, Mark. "First Glance at the Season's Books." *Nation*. April 20, 1927.
Vidal, Gore. "The Romance of Sinclair Lewis." *New York Review of Books*, October 8, 1992. http://www.nybooks.com.
Wallace, Ben. *Ben-Hur: A Tale of the Christ*. New York: Harper & Brothers, 1880.
Wallace, Mike. *Mickey Mouse History and Other Essays on American Memory* (Philadelphia: Temple University Press, 1996).
West, Rebecca. "Notes on Novels." *New Statesman* (October 21, 1922).
———. "Sinclair Lewis Introduces Elmer Gantry." *New York Herald Tribune Books*. March 13, 1927.
Whipple, T. K. "Arrowsmith by Sinclair Lewis." *New Republic*, April 15, 1925, 3–4.
———. "Glass Flowers, Waxworks, and the Barnyard Symphonies of Sinclair Lewis." In *Modern Critical Reviews: Sinclair Lewis*, edited by Harold Bloom, 9–22. New York: Chelsea House Publishers, 1987.
———. *Sinclair Lewis*. In *Critical Essays on Sinclair Lewis*, edited by Martin Bucco, 40–46. Boston: G. K. Hall & Co., 1986.
Wiebe, Robert H. *The Search for Order, 1877–1920*. New York: Hill and Wang, 1967.

Wilson, Edmund. "Salute to an Old Landmark." In *Critical Essays on Sinclair Lewis*, edited by Martin Bucco, 71–74. Boston: G. K. Hall & Co., 1986.

Woolner, David B. and John M. Thompson, eds. *Progressivism in America: Past, Present, and Future.* Oxford: Oxford University Press, 2015.

Young, Stephen A. "The Mencken-Lewis Connection." *Menckeniana* 94 (Summer, 1985). https://www.jstor.org/stable/26483767#metadata_info_tab_contents.

INDEX